HOLLYWOOD'S AMERICA

HOLLYWOOD'S AMERICA

Social and Political Themes in Motion Pictures

BY

Stephen Powers

David J. Rothman

Stanley Rothman

WestviewPress

A Division of HarperCollinsPublishers

Copyright © 1996 by Westview Press, A Division of HarperCollins Publishers, Inc.

Published in 1996 in the United States of America by Westview Press, 5500 Central Avenue, Boulder, Colorado 80301-2877, and in the United Kingdom by Westview Press, 12 Hid's Copse Road, Cumnor Hill, Oxford OX2 9JJ

A CIP catalog record for this book is available from the Library of Congress.
ISBN 0-8133-2932-9 (hc) — ISBN 0-8133-2933-7 (pb)

The paper used in this publication meets the requirements of the American National Standard for Permanence of Paper for Printed Library Materials Z39.48-1984.

10   9   8   7   6   5   4   3   2   1

Dedications

Stephen Powers:
To my parents and my children
for their love and inspiration.

David J. Rothman:
For Emily, who has done much more
than she realizes.

Stanley Rothman:
To Larry, Barbara, Stacey, and Lana,
with deep affection.

Contents

List of Tables   xi
Preface   xv

1 Studying Hollywood   1

   Assumptions   1
   The Study   5

2 Hollywood's History and the Politics of Motion Pictures   14

   The Studio Era   14
   The Transition   19
   The New Hollywood   23
   Hollywood in the 1980s   30
   Conclusion   36

3 The New Hollywood Elite: A Profile   40

   Creative Control and the New Hollywood Elite   43
   Self and Society   46
   The Evidence of Systematic Surveys   52
   Power and Personality: The Thematic Apperception Test   67
   Conclusion   75

4 Hollywood Views the Military   81

   The Study   82
   Motion Pictures, Public Opinion, and the Military   97

5 Crime, Violence, and the Police   101

   The Rising Tide of Crime and Violence   104
   Conclusion   116

6 Religious Decline?   120

   Biblical Tales and Other Movies from 1946 Through 1965   124
   A Content Analysis   127

The Eclipse of God, 1966–1990   131
Conclusion   136

7   Hollywood's Class Act   138

Changing Representations of the Rich in Hollywood Movies   139
Conclusion   151

8   The Politics of Gender   153

Men and Women Characters from 1946 to 1965:
  In the Tradition   153
Men and Women Characters from 1966 to 1990:
  After the Revolution   159
The Hollywood Elite and Feminism   168
Conclusion   169

9   A New Deal for Minorities?   172

Early Minority Representations: 1946–1965   173
Whites and Minorities Compared   175
New Patterns of Minority Representation: 1966–1990   182
Conclusion   186

10 Box Office Hits: 1990–1994   188

Supercops and Psycho-Robbers   188
Mad Dogs in the Military   190
Wealth and Power   190
Supernatural and Science Fiction Stories   191
Gender Wars   192
Minority Roles   193
Conclusion   193

11 Hollywood and the Moviemakers   195

The Larger Context   195
Television, Motion Pictures, and the New Sensibility   205
The Transformation of the American Civic Culture   208

Appendixes:

A. The Poverty of Film Theory   217
     *Film Theory, the Formalist Legacy, and
       the Idea of the World as Discourse*   217
     Contemporary Film Theory: Readings   226

     Politics, Film Theory, and the Ghost of Walter Benjamin   242
     Conclusion and Prospectus   245

B. The Interview Sample   251
     Sample   251
     Questions Asked of Elite Groups   254
     Questions Loading on Each Factor   255

C. The Movie Sample and Content Analysis   257

References   272
About the Book and Authors   287
Index   289

Tables

3.1	Backgrounds of Elite Groups—Percent in Each Category	53
3.2	Political Liberalism Factor Analyses—Mean Score	55
3.2A	Collectivist Liberalism Factor	58
3.2B	Expressive Individualism Factor	59
3.2C	Alienation Factor	60
3.3	Social Attitudes—Percent of Respondents Who Agree with Statements	62
3.4	Social Attitudes About Moral Issues—Percent of Respondents Who Agree with Statements	63
3.5	System Alienation—Percent of Respondents Who Agree with Statements	65
3.6	Perceived Influence of Key Groups vs. Preferred Influence by Movie Elite	66
3.7	Psychological Traits: Comparison of Means—Movies vs. Business	70
3.8	Elite Groups by Percent of Authoritarian Types	73
3.9	General Social Survey Questions: 1972–1982, 1990, and 1993	74
4.1	Sample Films with U.S. Military Characters	83
4.2	Images of the Military and the U.S. Government in Military Movies	84
4.3	Military Character Ratings	85
4.4	Percent of Military Characters with Patriotic Goals	88
4.5	Percent of Characters Using Authority and Discipline as Methods	88
4.6	Percent of Characters Using Violence as a Method	89
4.7	Percent of Characters Using Deceit and Trickery as Methods	90
5.1	Comparison of Crime, Violence, and Victimization in the Movies with Actual Crime	105
5.2	Character Rating of Law Enforcement Personnel	107
5.3	Law Enforcement Characters' Moral Goals and Violent Methods	108
5.4	Percent of Law Enforcement Characters Victimized	108
5.5	Percent of Law Enforcement Characters Committing Crimes	109
6.1	Percent of Characters of Known Religious Identity	128
6.2	Percent of Religious vs. Nonreligious Character Ratings	128

6.3   Percent of Religious vs. Nonreligious Characters Identified Who
        Fail to Achieve Goals   129
6.4   Percent of Religious Workers, Nuns, and Missionaries' Character
        Ratings   129
6.5   Percent of Religious Workers, Nuns, and Missionaries Who Are
        Successful/Unsuccessful   130
6.6   Percent of Movies in Which Supernatural Events Are Present   131
6.7   Percent of Sources of Supernatural Events   132

7.1   Portrayal of Business in Sample Movies   144
7.2   Character Ratings of Wealthy Characters vs. Nonwealthy
        Characters   145
7.3   Selected Goals of Wealthy Characters vs. Nonwealthy Characters   147
7.4   Selected Methods of Wealthy Characters vs. Nonwealthy
        Characters   149

8.1   Percent of Women and Men Characters in Sample Movies   154
8.2   Percent for Romance, Self-Interest, and Protecting Others as
        Goals for Women and Men Characters   155
8.3   Percent of Women and Men Characters Who Marry, Are Married,
        or Are Widowed   156
8.4   Percent of Women Characters in Traditional and Nontraditional
        Occupations (All Women and Star/Supporting Women)   157
8.5A   Percent of Women Characters in Traditional vs. Nontraditional
        Occupations Married at Film's Opening   157
8.5B   Percent of Women Characters in Traditional vs. Nontraditional
        Occupations with Romance as a Goal   157
8.6   Percent of Movies Featuring Nonmarital Sex and Consequences   158
8.7   Percent of Positive and Negative Character Ratings for Women
        and Men Characters   164
8.8   Percent of Women and Men Characters in Business and Their
        Character Ratings   165
8.9   Percent of Women Characters in Traditional vs. Nontraditional
        Occupations Using Authority or Discipline as a Method   166
8.10   Percent of Women Characters in Traditional vs. Nontraditional
        Occupations Showing Greed or Malevolence   167
8.11A   Percent of Women and Men Characters Who Use Violence
        as a Method   167
8.11B   Percent of Women Characters in Traditional vs. Nontraditional
        Occupations Who Use Violence as a Method   167
8.12   Percent of Negative and Positive Ratings for Women in
        Nontraditional Occupations and Men in the Same
        Occupational Categories   168

9.1	Percent of Characters According to Race	175
9.2	Character Ratings of Minorities vs. Whites	176
9.3	Character Rating Breakdown of Minority Characters	177
9.4	Percent of Minority and White Characters with Moral and Political Goals	178
9.5	Percent of Minority and White Characters Using Charm/ Rational Persuasion as Methods	179
9.6	Percent of Minority and White Characters Using Authority/ Discipline as Methods	179
9.7	Percent of Characters Resorting to Violence by Race	180
9.8	Percentages of All Black and White Characters Committing Crimes	181
9.9	Racial Composition of Characters Committing Crimes	181
9.10	Percent of Major Black and White Characters Committing Crimes	181
9.11	Percent of Black and White Characters Committing Crimes— Rated Positive, Negative, Mixed	182
9.12	Percent of Nonneutral Characters in Military and Law Enforcement Occupations	184
C1	Number of Films by Decade, Population, Sample, and Availability	258
C2	First and Second Movie Sample Breakdown	260

Preface

This book is unique. It combines the most extensive systematic content analysis ever completed of social and political themes in motion pictures from 1946 to the present, with the most detailed study ever conducted of the political views and personalities of a random sample of leaders in the motion picture industry. The two studies are integrated with a broad historical discussion of changes in American life, as part of an effort to understand the impact of the American motion picture industry on America and the impact of trends and events in America on American motion pictures. We are thus engaged in a sociological study of the motion picture industry, a task that has been undertaken by few others, except for Marxist and neo-Marxist scholars.

The book, part of a larger study of leadership and social change in the United States directed by Stanley Rothman, is one of a series that includes volumes on television, the press, and high school history textbooks, among other subjects.

The inspiration for the studies comes in large part from political scientist Harold Lasswell and sociologist Daniel Bell. As early as in the 1950s, Lasswell maintained that the key strategic elites (leadership groups) of the twentieth century would increasingly be those concerned with the creation and distribution of symbols for either knowledge or entertainment (Lasswell and Lerner, 1952). Bell made a similar point and also sketched the impact of such elites upon American society (Bell, 1973, 1976). His argument, which we accept, is that certain key changes in American society have produced a cultural elite (broadly defined) that has become critical of bourgeois society and is contributing in important ways to transforming its social values and replacing them with new ones.

It is only recently that social scientists have begun to study these newly powerful strategic elites, at least in part because their role did not become substantially significant until the 1960s, though there were antecedents, for example, in journalism and academia. As political scientists and sociologists have begun to relate the study of various cultural elites to other elements of the political system, they have encountered other analysts from university language and literature departments with their own approach to what has come to be called "cultural studies." The cultural studies approach tends to be antithetical to that of contemporary social science, though it is beginning to influence social science as well. As of now, cultural studies dominates academic film criticism.

Social scientists assume that the interaction between ideology and social structure can be studied empirically and with reasonable objectivity. Non-Marxists
also assume that such interaction is possible. They believe, as did Max Weber, that
sometimes one and sometimes the other factor plays the more important causal
role.

Many scholars who specialize in cultural studies seem to argue that it is impossible to understand anything but cultural representations. From their perspective, such representations are the only analytically accessible manifestations
of society and should be analyzed in the same manner as literary texts. The approach of these scholars is both analytic and anecdotal. They feel little need to
study a well-chosen sample of films because if American culture is dominated by
a particular group, all films represent the same social reality. Of course, the more
radical of these academics deny that one can uncover enduring meanings by
closely examining texts.

Our book is clearly a work of social science. The major instruments used in the
study, aside from standard historical and political analyses, are: (1) a massive survey of twelve leading elite groups administered by means of a complex survey instrument that tapped the social backgrounds, social and political attitudes, and
key personality dynamics of various leadership groups in the United States, including the makers of motion pictures. All in all, over 1,750 respondents were interviewed; (2) a series of systematic content analyses of a random sample of top-
grossing motion pictures from 1946 to the present. The data we have collected is
being deposited at the Roper Public Opinion Center at the University of
Connecticut for use by other scholars. Making the data available contributes to
public scholarly dialogue and thus to understanding.[1]

The book begins with a detailed discussion and justification of our methodology. We explain the methods involved in completing a systematic, long-term content analysis of a representative sample of films. We then examine both the
strengths and weaknesses of the approach and discuss our survey of the motion
pictures' creative elite. We briefly contrast our approach with the poststructuralist film theory that dominates academic film criticism today. At the end of the
book, in Appendix A, "The Poverty of Film Theory," we develop a much more detailed critique of the dominant cultural studies approach to contemporary academic film theory. We maintain that a broad sociological and empirical approach
to the study of social messages in motion pictures is more likely to provide us
with useful insights than a subjective, symbolic analysis that assumes that the
hegemony of certain ideas is embedded in symbolic representations that are to be
analyzed as literary texts.

Since we are persuaded that some of the changes that have taken place in the
content of motion pictures in recent years are a function both of historical structural changes in the motion picture industry and of the attitudes of moviemakers, Chapters 2 and 3 examine these factors. Although some of the results of our
survey of the creative Hollywood elite have been presented before, this is the first

time that they have been examined in depth and compared with those from studies of other leadership groups. We have found that the Hollywood elite is generally more liberal than many other elites. In this book, we demonstrate that Hollywood liberalism is not necessarily the same as that of other comparable liberal groups. For the first time, too, we present the results of the Thematic Apperception Tests administered to all the groups we studied and our discovery that (not surprisingly) ideological differences among the various elite groups we studied are associated with personality differences.

Chapters 4 through 10 describe the results of a systematic standardized content analysis of a random sample of the ten top-grossing films for each year from 1946 through 1990. The analysis of social and political themes, performed on a total of 159 films, was completed by scorers who knew nothing about the purposes of the study. In these chapters, we describe shifts in motion picture treatment of the military, government, business, religion, social minorities, and crime, violence, and the police. A short afterword updates the sample to 1995. Although the analysis of the past five years is anecdotal and discursive rather than systematic, it is based on the coding scheme we used for the earlier material. Our evidence indicates that the patterns we discuss in Chapters 4 through 9 have not changed.

We conclude by examining the role and nature of the motion picture industry in the broader perspective of changes in American society, especially in recent decades. In Chapter 11, we place the motion picture industry in its societal context, capping our analysis of the interaction between audience and industry. It is our argument that influence runs both ways. The industry contributes to change in the society even as it is influenced by societal economic, social, and political changes.

We should add a statistical note. We have not reported tests of significance for the results of our content analysis. In most cases the sample is so large that, although the results are statistically significant, it is not necessary to report this every time. In the few instances in which the samples are quite small, we have included tables showing very large shifts of values and clear directionality, even though the results are not statistically significant.

Stanley Rothman conceived the study, provided the theoretical framework, wrote the preface and concluding chapters, extensively edited other chapters, and rewrote most of Chapter 3. Stephen Powers supervised, and wrote up the results of, the content analysis (Chapters 4 through 10). He is also primarily responsible for Chapter 2 on the history of Hollywood and worked with Stanley Rothman on Chapter 3. David Rothman is entirely responsible for the theoretical Appendix A, "The Poverty of Film Theory." He also used his considerable skills to heavily edit many of the other chapters in the book. Indeed, the sections of the book that sing are those he extensively revised.

The study was primarily supported by grants from the Sarah Scaife Foundation, the Earhart Foundation, and the Olin Foundation. And, of course, our usual thanks goes to Jinny Mason, who despite some political disagreements with her boss, and the difficulty of working with so obsessive a character, played an indispensable role in the successful completion of this work and kept us all honest.

Stephen Powers
David J. Rothman
Stanley Rothman

NOTES

1. A brief discussion of our methodology will be found in Chapter 1. A more detailed discussion will be found in Appendices B and C.

HOLLYWOOD'S AMERICA

1

Studying Hollywood

Assumptions

Any successful moviemaker in America wields a power unmatched by that of other contemporary artists: immediate contact with incredibly large and diverse audiences. Only a small handful of painters, writers, or even pop musicians can hope to reach such immense numbers of people so quickly. The only industry that can compete with Hollywood moviemaking in this respect is television, which is closely allied with the motion picture industry. In fact, the movie industry has been entwined in the development of television since the mid-1950s.

Given this mass audience, Hollywood movies present a particularly rewarding subject for scholars and critics interested in aesthetic objects because of what they reveal about the society that produces them. Such an investigation of the relationship between movies and society is the purpose of this book. We will describe documentable developments in Hollywood film content and style over the past fifty years, the evolution of Hollywood as an industry and social institution, and the way these developments fit into larger patterns of social change. In this chapter, we discuss the premises and the approach we take and briefly contrast our approach with a large body of contemporary film theory that also addresses the relation between film and American society and politics, albeit in very different terms.

Because of our interest in movie content and its relation to social change, we focus our attention on the people who make the movies. Although most movies, particularly those that Hollywood produces, have always been group efforts, the number of creative workers is relatively small. As a result, we argue that they form a definable and relatively cohesive social leadership cadre in America, an elite group that has come to wield increased influence in American society since World War II. We therefore examine the correlations between the backgrounds, attitudes, and beliefs of this Hollywood elite and the style and content of the movies that they make.

In discussing the Hollywood filmmakers as an elite leadership group, we rely upon a strand of social theory that can be traced back to Vilfredo Pareto

(1848–1923) and Gaetano Mosca (1858–1941), as well as to so diverse a group of American social scientists as Harold Lasswell, C. Wright Mills, and Robert Dahl. Beginning in the 1930s, Lasswell and other political scientists and sociologists maintained that American politics involves competition among various elites for the support of the larger public.[1] Other scholars such as C. Wright Mills (1956) argued that a single, hegemonic group dominates American society and compromises democratic aspirations because it holds too much concentrated power. His arguments found support in the writings of such scholars as G. William Domhoff (1967, 1983) and Thomas R. Dye (1983), among many others.[2] Conversely, following Lasswell's lead, other scholars including Robert Dahl (1961, 1970, 1982, 1989), Dahl and Domhoff (1977), and Suzanne Keller (1963) have argued that American politics are characterized by pluralistic conflict among a variety of elites, none of which has ever fully dominated the social or political order. These theories of elite leadership are useful in that they help us to understand how different attitudes and beliefs in the society bear fruit in group action, whether that be politics, law, or the control of symbols and information.[3] The question of how information can be understood as a province of elite leadership deserves elaboration. Many elite theorists have come to think that it is not only economic power or the control of traditional institutions (such as the church) that determines the direction of political and social change. They argue that elites responsible for the creation and dissemination of new cultural symbols now play a more significant role in contemporary American society than at any time in the past.[4] Whereas traditional elites include such groups as leaders of the military, business, and various religious institutions, the newer information elites include national media journalists, leaders in the television industry, and Hollywood writers, producers, and directors. Most of these new groups derive their authority from the control of cultural symbols rather than from capital, instruments of violence, or long-standing social institutions.

In a society in which electronic communications technology has come to play roles that were unimaginable only fifty years ago, the new elites enjoy a power also, until recently, unimaginable in scope and size. It is not a power affiliated with state or religious authority, so it is more difficult to describe its workings, but it can best be characterized as cultural, in the broad sense. With a number of other elite theorists, we think that the postindustrial cultural elites are often in ideological conflict with the older leadership groups on a wide range of issues, and, like the members of any leadership group, the new cultural elites seek to put their ideas into practice. Battles over the content of Hollywood movies and other mass media thus run along a fault line in the society that represents a conflict among its elite groups. As elite groups have so much to do with the way any society develops, this conflict is of great import.

Accordingly, we take the position that Hollywood films are the product of a highly educated, affluent, and powerful leadership group that is vying for influence in America with other more traditional groups. The Hollywood elites do not seek power (for the most part) as an end in itself. Rather they seek to persuade Americans to create the kind of society that they regard as just and/or good. In short, they seek to propagate an ideology that they believe should be held by all decent people.[5]

As we discuss at length in Chapter 2, developments in the attitudes of the Hollywood elite and in their movies accompanied changes in the structure of the film industry in the 1950s and the 1960s, changes that allowed creative dissent to become established in Hollywood in a way that it could not have, for example, in the 1930s. Although the people who manage Hollywood have always been powerful, within the past fifty years the extent of their power, their notions about how they should use it, and the ideas that they would like to promulgate with it have changed substantially.

Our survey indicates that, far from being conservative or reactionary forces in the society as many academics insist is the case, elite directors, writers, and producers now usually espouse liberal or leftist perspectives that became prominent in the 1960s. Further, our systematic content analysis of a random sample of motion pictures since 1945 establishes that the movies of this creative elite articulate these new attitudes, which stand in marked contrast to those of the majority of the American public (and traditional elite groups) on a wide range of issues. This comes as no surprise. A very substantial majority of moviemakers explicitly affirm their belief that motion pictures should encourage social reform.[6]

Hollywood is not monolithic. Its creative elite contains persons who adhere to a variety of world views. Indeed, the best of the creative elite is often divided against itself as the requirements of the craft individuals practice clash with pragmatic concerns about money or deeply held social views.

Of course, it is not surprising that the social turmoil of the 1960s and 1970s left its mark on this group, although the seeds of change were planted earlier. As we will show, however, the extent of the transformation and its durability, are greater than most people imagine. Since 1980, movies may have relaxed their grasp of liberal ideas in a few instances, but there has been no significant ideological reversal. We do not find that members of the Hollywood elite have rushed to cater to the mass audience, although of course they do aim to entertain. If anything, the pace of change in movie content accelerated in the 1980s, and there has been no subsequent retrenchment since then, either.

Many film scholars believe that Hollywood movies reveal important truths about how America is changing. They tend to approach the study of films from a politically radical perspective (usually anecdotally) and we rarely find their descriptions of trends in representation convincing. Given the long-term changes that have transformed the industry, we believe it makes sense that recent movies are considerably more liberal in terms of character depiction and narrative line than older movies. That is one of the key hypotheses that we tested in our content analysis. Thus, we can provide a large body of evidence to counter arguments like Ryan and Kellner's in *Camera Politica:* ·

Our study focuses on the relationship between Hollywood film and American society from 1967 to the mid-eighties, a period characterized by a major swing in dominant social movements from Left to Right. . . . We noticed particularly that
Hollywood film, which seemed to us to be gaining in importance as a mobilizer of
public energies, was actively promoting the new conservative movements on several
fronts, from the family to the military to economic policy. (xi)

We find that this view of Hollywood leaders' conservative leanings does not accurately reflect the explicit attitudes of the Hollywood elite or the trends in
Hollywood movies throughout this period. Both of our sets of data—about the
filmmakers and about the movies themselves—support our conclusions.

A standard objection to arguments like ours is that while leaders in the television and motion picture industries may constitute an information elite, they are
first and foremost men and women of business, who must follow the market. A
number of social scientists who write about media thus find it difficult to imagine that big business, such as companies operating in Hollywood, might be led by
an elite group that feels alienated from traditional American institutions, including certain business institutions. As the sociologist Herbert Gans recently argued
in a short essay "Hollywood Entertainment: Commerce or Ideology": "Hollywood's products are made by commercial firms for whom profits are prior to ideology . . . entertainment caters to a set of specific and fickle audiences, and has to
be, virtually by definition, deviant, daring, and even oppositional to the values of
these audiences" (1993:151).[7]

But in a society in which communication technology plays an ever more important role, the control of images and stories is by definition a form of power.
As any casual observer of the political scene surely realizes, one need no longer be
a member of the traditional elite groups to affect even national policy. This has
been the case at least since Walter Cronkite broadcast his coverage of the Tet offensive to millions of homes.

Further, the parameters of acceptable storytelling are not as constricted as Gans
suggests. Economic arguments about the relation of film to society cannot account for the desire of elite groups to control images and stories without necessarily converting them into monetary advantage.[8] Indeed, as we show in subsequent chapters, many members of the Hollywood elite feel this desire quite
strongly and by their own account try to act on it in their work. This is not to
argue for a simple one-way direction of influence. We argue that over time and
subtly, Hollywood has transformed its audience, even creating the demand for
new products. As we shall note again, the bottom line is profitability. Filmmakers
who do not make successful films are not able, in the long run, to raise money.
All this means, however, is that filmmakers cannot move too far from their audiences' tastes and preferences. However, provided they create entertaining films
that are not too didactic, they can "do good" and make a profit at the same time.

Thus, in any given year, one can find popular films that affirm conservative or liberal conceptions of reality.

Just as important, the creators of mass entertainment are men and women who live in a social order that influences them. Their views of reality are affected by the culture of the society in which they live. However alienated they may be from that society, their work reflects it to some extent. Nevertheless, over time and gradually they contribute to the development of audiences that support new views of reality. At one time, for example, watching the presentation of certain kinds of sexual activity would have been avoided by at least some moviegoers who now accept such presentations as appropriate film fare in part because Hollywood's product has gradually changed their view of what is acceptable. The pattern of interaction among the creators of film, public preferences, and the society's culture, therefore, is a fairly complex one. We hope to contribute to a greater understanding of the interaction among these factors.[9]

Our characterization of the attitudes and beliefs which undergird the actions of the Hollywood elite has nothing to do with naive notions of "bias" or conspiracy. Bias only makes sense as an explanation if there is intentional distortion, and that is not our argument. Rather, as we have said, the Hollywood elite shares a set of political and cultural assumptions that it views as natural (as all of us view our own assumptions) and that it seeks, as do others, to put into action. These Hollywood leaders do not do this in a concerted or conspiratorial way; yet because there is general agreement on certain core issues (which we elaborate on in later chapters) the totality of their work suggests a more or less coherent ideology. That ideology is generally left-leaning and highly critical of traditional features of American society.

Our contribution is to study this particular elite group more closely and systematically than it ever has been examined in the past. We focus on the backgrounds, attitudes, and personalities of the Hollywood elite in comparison to other elites and on the types of information that Hollywood produces and disseminates. The purpose is to understand how Hollywood leaders tend to view America and in what directions the Hollywood elite would like to see the society develop.[10]

In the remainder of this chapter we describe how we put our own analyses together and justify our approaches in the context of broad theoretical debates about how to comprehend the relationship of mass art to social change.

The Study

To study the motion picture elite, we administered a lengthy questionnaire to a sample of leaders in the industry.[11] To examine changing social and political themes in motion pictures, we completed a quantitative content analysis of an extensive random sample of top box office films from the end of World War II to

1995. The purpose of the content analysis was to identify types of representation and to analyze how they have changed over time in order to broaden, but not replace, the interpretation of individual movies and groups of movies from carefully derived empirical data.

Such a systematic study of the social and political attitudes of the Hollywood elite, coupled with systematic content analysis of hundreds of major box office movies and thousands of film characters, has never been undertaken. The reason that no one previously attempted the task of developing meaningful, reliable categories for film content is that the daunting project is plagued with time-consuming methodological and epistemological problems.[12]

The purpose of the random sample was to insure that we discuss a representative sample of films. After all, anecdotal evidence, although compelling, is insufficient to back up claims about the larger industry as a whole and its relation to the rest of society. No matter how powerful the arguments, every anecdotal critic ends up discussing films that are chosen because they support his or her view. What we wanted to do, however, was to provide a different kind of evidence and on a much larger scale.

Obviously, empirical evidence of the kind that we use is valuable only in discussing particular kinds of questions—but in those cases it is quite powerful. It will not help in a lengthy analysis of *E. T.* or provide useful information about the directorial style of Frank Capra. However, if the question has to do with overall industry trends and their social or political significance—for example, whether Hollywood movies have, as a whole, become more conservative or liberal in the representation of feminist issues or whether they tend to depict the military in a different way than they used to—then the data we have collected become a highly useful tool.

We could have chosen to sample all films produced in Hollywood but opted to sample the ten highest-grossing films for each year. We did this partly for practical reasons. Such films are easier to locate and allowed us to finish within a reasonable time frame. But we also chose to limit our study on theoretical grounds, in order to target films that have reached wide audiences and therefore potentially have had greater impact on large numbers of people.[13] Each motion picture in our sample was coded by two individuals who, in double-blind tests, agreed with each other on the key variables used in this study a minimum of 70 percent of the time. The agreement happened despite the fact that they knew nothing about the purposes of the study or about the hypotheses guiding the authors' research. We discarded themes for which a 70 percent level of agreement could not be achieved. The categories of analysis are explicitly defined in a codebook (for a fuller discussion, see Appendix C).[14]

We are the first to concede that the data we collected do not provide indisputable evidence about anything; they need to be interpreted and judged before they make sense. Nevertheless, as we will show, the movie data strongly support the argument that systematically changing trends in representation have characterized most of the industry over the past fifty years. It also allows us to describe a number of these major trends with much greater specificity than has anyone else in the past. Further, the changes correlate with the transformed ideological tendencies of the Hollywood elite, whose attitudes on a wide range of issues now differ significantly from those of traditional elites and of the public at large. In short, if used with the appropriate caveats, the testing of a critical argument against these two bodies of empirical data makes for a powerful analysis.

The purpose of working this way and making our data publicly available is to permit replication of our findings and encourage systematic discussion. Content analysis is no substitute for the richness of more subjective readings of individual films in a critical context, but our study is unconcerned with the very real pleasure or pain that individual movies afford as art. In other words, we did not judge the quality of the films we describe and we did not choose them based on aesthetic criteria. Our study, therefore, avoids the various methods of aesthetic analysis. Our purpose is to describe and analyze society, which is not a province of aesthetics. This is not to say that our findings are objective in some absolute sense. They are, however, replicable using standard public methods. We should add that the method inevitably simplifies films, and that it can never fully capture the messages conveyed by individual films.[15]

The trick, of course, is to develop categories that are simple enough to allow for intersubjective agreement and that can be counted, yet tell us something interesting about those aspects of films with which we are concerned. For example, to examine the changing role of traditional religion in Hollywood films, we counted, among other things, the number of characters in films who are identified with religion and compared their moral ratings, as well as their success in achieving goals, with those of characters not identified as religious or identified as non-religious (see Chapter 6). We believe that the information thus gathered, in conjunction with other data, enables us to make reasonably sound generalizations about this question.

We have divided our statistical analysis into three ten-year periods and one fifteen-year period, for both practical and theoretical reasons. Practically, we do not have enough cases to statistically analyze periods of shorter length. Theoretically, it seems clear to us that, despite the manner in which the media analyze Hollywood, the production of a number of films dominated by one theme or genre for two or three years does not necessarily a trend make. Such shifts often turn out to be merely blips on the chart, revealing little or nothing about long-range patterns of representation.

We should add that we are quite aware that artistic decisions in the movie industry are not monolithic. Thus, a small number of pictures characterized by a given theme or approach does not necessarily mean very much. One can find cases to prove almost anything. For example, the finding that a small percentage of films during each ten-year period presents businessmen as fools probably means something quite different than the finding that *most* films represent them in that light. In the former case, such representations may merely be (among other possible interpretations) affectionate satires of strongly supported institutions or the work of a small minority. In the latter situation, a strong case can be made for the proposition that those who are responsible for creating the films do not generally hold favorable views as to the general intelligence of businessmen and women.

Developing categories is a complex procedure involving a good deal of effort. Again and again, one is forced to modify or drop categories that one had hoped would be successful. We initially drew much of our coding scheme from an earlier study of television originally organized by one of the authors. We discovered, however, that motion pictures are far more complex than television shows and that we could not achieve a sufficiently adequate level of coder agreement on many of the categories used for the earlier study. Our content analysis is supplemented by anecdotal discussions of various films. The purpose of this discussion is illustrative. It is not designed to prove anything. In keeping with the content analysis it is also quite straightforward. We make little effort to go beyond the obvious in describing the films so used.

Our perspective is sociological, based on the premise that human societies are inherently phenomenal, even when the object of investigation is the way in which they tell themselves stories or create symbols, as in the movies. Social phenomena are quite different and always more complex than any representation or agglomeration of representations of them, however complex those representations may be. To study society—even those institutions in society most concerned with creating representations—is a very different thing from studying only representation in and of itself.

Our work is not audience research, in which social scientists analyze the multiple subjectivities of response.[16] Instead, we describe the changing social and political content of motion pictures, to which there is obviously a wide variety of responses. In our view, the subjectivity of response, or reception, does not contradict the notion that there is an actual art-object provoking the response. For example, some critics have argued that *Invasion of the Body Snatchers* (1956) was a cold-war anticommunist motion picture, while others have maintained that it was an attack on McCarthyism. Similarly the film *High Noon* (1952) was praised as a defense against McCarthyist threats and also criticized as a fascistic attack on democratic values. *Blade Runner* (1982) has been praised as a critique of technology and criticized as an attack on both Asians and women. To focus on a particular critic, in *Backlash: The Undeclared War Against Women*, Susan Faludi cites both *Fatal Attraction* (1987) and *The Hand That Rocks the Cradle* (1992) as attacks on women. *Fatal Attraction*, she claims, attempts to demonstrate that women who choose professional careers are driven crazy. But certainly the film could be seen as warning men that philanderers have to pay the consequences of their actions. As for *The Hand That Rocks the Cradle*, the female characters are much stronger than the men. Indeed, when confronted with Faludi's analysis, Sherry Lansing, one of the producers of *Fatal Attraction*, claimed the film was intended to demonstrate that males who philander will incur costs (Andrews, 1993).[17] The point is that however divergent the interpretations, there has to be some understanding that there is in fact a work to which these interpretations refer—otherwise there could be no notion of subjectivity to begin with. That is the philosophical assumption that makes our work possible, keeping in mind that our statistics cannot be used to bolster individual readings.

To many readers, this may seem like a statement of the obvious, but as we will see, the question of what constitutes content lies at the heart of a number of highly contentious debates in contemporary film theory and cultural studies. At this point, it helps to remember that we need not define content in the abstract in order to acknowledge that it exists and that we can recognize it, judge it—and, if the appropriate methods are used—code it. Even the most radical forms of interpretive subjectivity require the hypothetical existence of the object (or concept) they purport to examine. Samuel Beckett, who understood this problem profoundly, plays with it in his usual paradoxical style when he has one of the characters in *Waiting for Godot* say of God, "The bastard! He doesn't exist!" In practice, it is not as difficult to describe art-objects and forms of representation as many recent theorists of the arts would have us believe. For the assumption of content is what allows any discussion, including the most skeptical, to go forward to begin with.

Thus the subjectivity of aesthetic judgment does not threaten empirical investigation into content as much as it might at first appear. At the same time, we recognize that the systematic content analysis is only meaningful insofar as we acknowledge the reductive quality of the data and its carefully defined social science context.

Our aim, as social scientists, is neither to praise nor censure the particular films that we discuss, nor the individuals who write, direct, and produce them. Our study is not about either individuals or individual art works but rather aggregate trends (however much we may personally like or dislike particular films). Our goal is to describe social change and to provide the best empirical evidence we can for our arguments about evolving social formations in America.

In Appendix A to this book, entitled "The Poverty of Film Theory," we take up complicated questions raised by our empirical approach to film in the context of the recent growth of film theory and cultural studies. The burden of our argument is to make the case for empirical social science when the questions to be answered are explicitly about political and social developments and their relation to movie representation. Our discussion of contemporary academic film theory will of necessity be somewhat abstruse, befitting the writings of those whom we critique. We assure those of our readers who wish to limit themselves to the rather more straightforward prose of empirical analysis that they may skip Appendix A without losing the thread of our argument.

One final word. In our last chapter, as well as in this introduction, we make a few general theoretical statements about the impact of film. They are just that. We have little or nothing to add to the scientific controversy over the effect of motion pictures. So many variables are changing at the same time in our society that, we would argue, it is impossible empirically to determine the influence of one variable compared to another. Despite the thousands of studies designed to uncover the impact of the presentation of violence in television and film, we know little more about the subject than we did forty years ago. Given the many variables that apply in conducting a study involving human subjects, we still lack solid scientific answers to questions of influence.[18] Nevertheless our study assumes that motion pictures affect the opinions of many of those who view them to at least some extent over the long haul. This entails the belief that audiences perceive such films, whether or not they can articulate this, much the same as our coders do. These are not uncontested assumptions even by those who are not postmodernists. (For discussions see Parker 1994 and Bryant and Zillmanan, eds. 1994.) However, both research and common sense suggest that such assumptions are warranted even if it is impossible to establish them unequivocally. While some films may be ambiguous in some areas, and some people may see everything in the light of their ideological assumptions, most members of most audiences will agree on the very basic items for which we code, even if they do not freely articulate such beliefs. They can, for example, determine if a woman character is a housewife or a professional, a criminal or a law abiding citizen, a person who relies on force to gain her ends or who uses persuasion. By and large they can even tell the good guys from the bad guys. Most people would agree, for example, who the bad guys and the good guys and gals are supposed to be in *Terminator II* (1991), *Sleeping with the Enemy* (1993), *Dick Tracy* (1990), and *You Only Live Twice* (1967). Ordinary people are probably more likely to agree than academic critics, many of whom adhere in fairly rigid ways to a particular ideological perspective.

As we note, the influence of motion pictures on audiences is extremely difficult to measure, given, among other factors, all the other stimuli to which such audiences are subject. There is little reason to believe that a single film or even group of films significantly influences audiences' views over the long haul. However, if large numbers of motion pictures portray businessmen or Jews as thieves, blacks as violent or stupid, women as weak or clinging, and the military as corrupt, as a matter of course, it is reasonable to believe that such presentations will affect audiences to a significant extent, especially if the other mass media tend to characterize such groups similarly.

NOTES

1. The history of elite theory in the social sciences is described more fully in Rothman, Lichter, and Lichter (forthcoming) and Lerner, Nagai, and Rothman (1996).

See also Mosca (1939) and Pareto (1966). For the work of Harold Lasswell see Lasswell (1950, 1951, 1980) and Lasswell and Lerner (1952).

2. More recently the notion of class or power elite (military, industry, government) domination of American society has been partly replaced by the argument that America is dominated by white males, and that the subject peoples are women and minorities. Thus, poor white males and rich male capitalists are part of the same hegemonic group. It remains to be seen how widespread and long-lasting this new approach will turn out to be.

3. This is not to say that we are "elite theorists" who argue, as did Mosca and Pareto, that the elite concept provides the basic tool for analyzing all societies. We believe that such a conception is too simple. Our framework is derived primarily from Max Weber's.

4. Bell made an important contribution to this discussion in two classic volumes, *The Cultural Contradictions of Capitalism* (1976) and *The Coming of Post-Industrial Society* (1973).

5. We largely accept Clifford Geertz's analysis of ideology (1973) as a cultural system that provides its adherents with guides as to how the social world works and how it should work. We are not suggesting that all ideologies are equally valid, but the basis for evaluating contested ideologies is not an issue we shall deal with in this volume.

6. For the conventional academic wisdom on this subject, see Lazere (ed.) (1987), Clover and Rogin (eds.) (1990), and the citations in Appendix A to the essays on contemporary academic film analysis, which we critique at that point.

7. Gans's essay is a reply to "Hollywood Liberalism" by David F. Prindle and James W. Endersby, a recent empirical study of the attitudes of the Hollywood elite that supports our own study.

Although far from dominant, Gans's position is characteristic of that now adopted by some on the left and represents a distinct shift from earlier radical views of Hollywood as monolithically supporting traditional values. As we have already suggested, we suspect that this shift in perspective has occurred at least partially because it is increasingly difficult to maintain the classic leftist perspective in the face of the evidence.

8. As Michael Medved argues at length in *Hollywood vs. America* (1992) and elsewhere (1989, 1993), many of the subjects and treatments in the mass media are in fact highly offensive to large segments of the American audience and, according to Medved, Hollywood pays a price in profits for pursuing these lines. Recent intense debates (which cross political lines) in state and national legislatures about television content also indicate that there is sharp disagreement in the public about the acceptable boundaries of representation. As Medved argues, this too has turned large segments of the paying public away from mass entertainment.

9. Recently some conservative critics have expressed agreement with the argument that the market is what drives Hollywood to the apparent left. In general, such analysts argue, the Hollywood elite is actually fairly conservative on cultural matters. However, Hollywood fears those special interest groups on the left that might generate a firestorm of protest (see, for example, Sajak, 1994). The argument, it seems to us, contains elements of truth but is ultimately not persuasive.

10. The data for this study of elite filmmakers was gathered in 1982, but other studies have brought the attitudinal findings up to date. We doubt that personality structure has changed sufficiently in the time period between then and now to compromise our sample. For more detailed discussions of our questionnaires and samples, see Chapter 3 and Appendices A and B.

11. Some of the results of the study of the contemporary Hollywood elite appeared in "What Are Moviemakers Made Of?" (Rothman and Lichter, 1984). Other results can be found in Powers, Rothman, and Rothman (1993). We contacted a random sample of 149 writers, producers, and directors of the fifty top-grossing films from 1965 through 1982. Our source was *Variety*. Sixty-four percent of those contacted (ninety-six people) completed a lengthy questionnaire that asked them to provide a wide range of demographic data and to describe their opinions and beliefs on many social and political issues. For a full discussion of our interview methodology, see Rothman, Rothman, and Powers (1993). For a general discussion of our elite samples and the questionnaire, see Rothman and Lichter (1987), Lerner, Nagai, and Rothman (1995), and Chapter 3 and Appendix B of this book.

12. To ensure that the movie study would provide information on the films that were most widely viewed by the public, we derived our sample from *Variety* magazine's annual lists of top-grossing movies and, in the four most recent years, from their list of "All-Time Film Rental Champs" (this list takes video rentals as well as theater receipts into account). We randomly selected 35 of the 100 top-grossing movies from each decade (sampling more from 1946 to 1955, for a total of 50, to compensate for the unavailability of films). In addition, we added a 20-movie random sample from the years 1986 through 1990 to update the study, and these films are included with the 1976–1985 decade. We added a few motion pictures to our sample for other reasons (see Appendix B). From this total sample of 175 films, we were able to obtain and code 146 films. We next devised a systematic content analysis for the sample, designing it to obtain two types of information: demographic and personality features of characters, and treatment of specific themes—that is, various political or social issues. We used standard statistical procedures to verify the intersubjective reliability of our coding categories and only used those for which reliabilities averaged above .70 on a scale of 0 to 1 (if coders could not reach this level of reliability, the question was scrapped). After verifying the codes, we were able to compile detailed profiles of more than 4,000 characters, along with information on themes of all 146 films. Coders scored all the significant characters in every film on a number of demographic variables, including age, race, sex, marital status, socioeconomic status, and so on. The thematic variables that they scored have to do with narrative development, such as character function (positive, negative, or mixed), characters' motivations in the plot (e.g., greed, revenge, or romance), methods for achieving their goals (e.g., money, violence, or deceit), and so on. Once the data was coded, we could perform a statistical analysis to highlight certain kinds of films (such as military movies), issues (such as divorce), characters (such as women), or any of the other variables. For a more extensive discussion of our methods in the movie study, see Appendix C.

13. As a result, our choice, if anything, probably understates the alienation of Hollywood moviemakers from American bourgeois society, as revealed in their creative work. As Michael Medved has pointed out on numerous occasions, the most successful films are PG-rated, nonideological escapist films. These are more likely to reach the top ten list in any given year than various ideological or didactic films. Our own sample confirms his findings (Medved 1989, 1992, 1993). Still another weakness in our approach, discovered too late to rectify, is our inability to analyze the unique American genre, the western. The number of westerns that have reached the top ten list in the past 20 years has been insignificant. That is doubly unfortunate, given the fact that the classic book in that field (Wright, 1975), while ingenious, is a procrustean effort to fit westerns into Habermasian notions about the development of capitalism.

14. As with our earlier studies, the questionnaires, tapes, and scoring sheets will be deposited at the Roper Center at the University of Connecticut for the use of other scholars.

15. There are those who would argue that all we do is substitute one kind of subjectivity for another. In some ultimate sense this may be true, but certainly not on a workaday level. After all, simply counting the number of white or black major characters (or men and women) over time in motion pictures can give one a good deal of information about trends—as can counting the changing pattern of positions held by women in various professions over time and determining whether characters (men or women) use force of persuasion to achieve their goals. Those in the field find that most coders can even tell the good guys from the bad guys or those who should receive mixed moral ratings—perhaps the most subjective material for which we code—without much difficulty (certainly audiences can). If critics disagree with our interpretation, they can use their own coders to replicate our work.

The limitations of our approach lie elsewhere. Our coding scheme is too simple and we must be wary. For example, an unregenerate petty thief and Adolf Hitler might both be scored negatively from a moral perspective. Unfortunately, our categories do not permit a more complex differentiation if we are to achieve reasonably high levels of agreement among coders. Thus, more complex distinctions have inevitably to be discussed anecdotally.

16. There is a tremendous literature in this area. Among other more sophisticated works, see David Morley's *The Nationwide Audience: Structure and Decoding* (1980)(this work is about television). Morley's concern is with the complexities of audience response to a popular British television show. In contrast, we are concerned with describing content, not response. Although audience research can provide useful information, it would have been impossible for us to cover the range of films we examined through content analysis. Aside from the prohibitive expense, what can the reactions of a contemporary audience tell one about the reactions of an audience that viewed a particular group of films 40 years ago? Further, we could not have systematically examined films for such things as the shifting pattern of jobs held by women to measure changes in the presentation of women on the screen.

17. It used to be that to some Marxists any film which did not take an explicit Marxist stand was ipso facto supporting the capitalist system. Today, some feminists believe that any films that do not portray American women as they believe women should be portrayed are by definition patriarchal. Naturally, the interpretation that became part of the conventional wisdom was the one most consonant with the subjective views of film critics and academics, most of whom were (and are) probably to the left of the moviemakers. This is one of the reasons that, in spite of a great deal of evidence, many critics still see Hollywood as relatively conservative. In any event, we believe that the scoring system we have adopted is more balanced and yields a more accurate picture of the messages conveyed by films than either of the above approaches will.

18. For a summary see McGuire (1982).

2

Hollywood's History and the Politics
of Motion Pictures

The Studio Era

In America, as in France and other European countries, intellectuals have come to regard film as an art form in its own right, however much its critical discourse may borrow from other enterprises. Nevertheless, university film studies departments are relatively recent developments. Long before many critics and intellectuals began systematically to judge Hollywood movies on their artistic merits, show business had become an immense commercial enterprise.[1] As Leo Rosten wrote, in his influential work of 1941, *Hollywood: The Movie Colony, the Movie Makers*, by 1937 the movie industry ranked fourteenth in business volume in America, at just over $400 million (Rosten, 1941:378–379). It had also been organized into a formidable monopoly. For all intents and purposes, the film industry was controlled by only eight companies—the Big Eight—from the late 1920s until about 1950.[2]

Rosten's study demonstrated that power flowed directly from a small number of movie executives in New York and Hollywood (Rosten, 1941:260–261). They were extraordinarily tenacious and driven businessmen, and a large number of them were rags-to-riches Jewish immigrants who had first succeeded in other enterprises (Adolph Zukor in the fur trade, William Fox in the clothing business, Lewis Selznick in the jewelry business) before buying theaters and moving into the movie business. Others (Louis Mayer, the Warner brothers, Carl Laemmle) started out in the movie exhibition business and worked their way up (Gabler, 1988). From the turn of the century until about 1920, these men built the studio system, consolidated their power, and stabilized the industry in such a way that very few outsiders could subsequently enter the business.

The Studio System

The studio system was organized by executives of the Big Eight to promote maximum possible industry control.[3] Among other things, they established their own distribution networks. All productions had to be sent through the distribution network in order to reach the theaters, with the result that 95 percent of film rentals were paid to the eight largest Hollywood firms. In effect, it thus became almost impossible for smaller, independent producers to enter the market and compete with such established organizations. The large studios had created a virtual cartel that was able to eliminate competition (Gomery, 1986a:11–12).

Exhibition facilities (the theaters) were also organized to maximize profits and discourage new players in the industry. The practice of block booking forced theaters to buy movies in packages, ensuring that all of a studio's films, regardless of quality or length, would make at least some of their money back. Of course, this contract practice with the theaters also served to deaden competition from other studios or producers (Balio, ed., 1976:259).

The run, clearance, and zoning system further helped to monopolize theater business through shrewd administrative tactics. Under this system, which was regulated by clearance and zoning boards in each particular area, the large studios were able to control when and where their pictures played, and to prevent nonaffiliated moviehouses from showing the film until a certain period of "clearance" had passed. This reduced the film's drawing power, because it could not open in a second-run theater until its novelty had already begun to wear off. What this meant was that the studio-owned moviehouses always received the major draws, doing everything in their power to manufacture hits. The results were impressive. First-run theaters, which were almost always in the big cities and almost always the property, in one way or another, of the big studios, generated half of the entire movie audience in America (Balio, ed., 1976:259).

By organizing the industry in this way the five largest studios were assured that nearly all business would be split up among them. The other three would get a small piece of the pie while contributing more to the larger studios in rental fees and exhibition revenues. Given the organization of the system, it is not surprising that big studios easily found financing for both film production and the expansion of distribution and theater facilities, as profits were virtually guaranteed.

In the early days of the movie industry the few businessmen who owned theaters often risked their own capital for economic expansion. But in the 1920s, the movie industry had begun to attract the attention of Wall Street financiers, who poured capital into Hollywood (Balio, ed., 1976:193). From this point on, the New York executives would maintain a tight financial reign over the Hollywood production facilities.

This control had long-range implications for the types of movies produced. Controversy, innovation, and experimentation were discouraged.

> Each year the New York office decided how much money would be allocated for production, and then it became the production executive's job to bring in popular fare within the dictated constraint. New York officers hoped to regularize returns from the corporation's theaters, and as a result they discouraged producers from experimentation. Their aim was to stabilize the product, and this led to the familiar genres, stars, narratives and other formulaic elements associated with the studio era. (Gomery, 1986a:193)

Given the enormous success and relative stability of the Big Eight through the 1920s, it is understandable that banks preferred to do business with them and provided only limited funding to independent producers. Finance for Hollywood movies proceeded on a grand scale, with banks often putting up the money for a whole year's worth of product in one fell swoop. Thus, for the banks, the mainstream movie industry offered a diversification of investment risk that independents could not hope to match. Bankers had practically no incentive to fund production on a picture-by-picture basis. That was hit or miss, and most financiers felt it was unnecessarily risky. Again, the effect was to marginalize independent production. Because of the authority that studio executives already wielded within their own organizations, the exclusion of independent production from secure finance effectively eliminated the single most likely source of innovative or controversial films.

Since they had effectively eliminated serious competition, the major problem that the studios faced came from another source—their own workers. Unlike most other labor disputes then and now, however, this one focused on highly visible and even wealthy workers; actors, particularly stars, are highly talented people, irreplaceable in film production.[4] From the beginning, of course, production companies had competed to enlist star actors and actresses, drawn at first from the theater, who would make films more commercially successful. It was not long before the creative talent in Hollywood took advantage of the star system, realizing the potential power it held over the movie moguls. In fact, in the early days, the star system led to the creation of United Artists, when major film draws such as Charlie Chaplin and Douglas K. Fairbanks Jr., who had become independently wealthy, began to produce films themselves, in conjunction with well-known directors (Balio, ed., 1976:116).

Later, during the depression, the unionization of Hollywood's labor force, stimulated by the National Recovery and Wagner Acts, strengthened its position relative to the moguls. Eventually the entire industry was unionized (Gomery, 1986a:10) and collective bargaining turned out to be particularly effective for Hollywood's mass of employees. Union power contributed to the demise of the studio system, as it encouraged the growth of free-lancing in the 1940s. This meant that more and more often, the studios had to bid to get the artists they wanted, which cut their profit margins substantially (Gomery, 1986a:10).

In spite of the unions, throughout most of the studio era the movie moguls kept labor problems to a minimum by employing actors, writers, directors, and producers under seven-year contracts that, until the mid-1940s, could, in some cases, even be extended by the studios without the consent of the employees (Norman, 1987:288). Under these agreements filmmakers were especially vulnerable to studio authority.

This relationship began to change in the 1950s, when competition from television, along with the fallout from the Paramount antitrust case (which we discuss later), forced production cutbacks and made the seven-year contract an excessive financial liability for studios. A core of Hollywood employees remained, but contracts were of shorter duration, often even picture by picture. Negotiations occurred more frequently, and with television providing alternative employment for actors, salaries rose accordingly. By the end of the 1950s, the studios had lost a substantial measure of the powerful control they had once held over their labor force.

Studio Politics, the House Un-American Activities Committee (HUAC), and Censorship

Despite the fact that it early became a gigantic industry, film, as we suggested above, was never regarded merely as an entertainment commodity, even by industry pioneers. From the beginning, it was considered to be, at least potentially, a medium for "high" art, and also a powerful teaching medium, capable of influencing millions of viewers. Thus, as a result of their obvious power as ideological and expressive tools, Hollywood movies quickly became objects of censorship. In the 1920s, an admixture of fact and fiction about the decadent lifestyles of show-business characters fueled the fears and suspicions of industry critics, who already regarded movies as a threat to society. This initiated a long tradition that made censorship the most important political issue in studio control of filmmakers before the 1960s. This censorship had a two-fold genesis: suspicion, both inside and outside Hollywood, of the political left and an attempt to control representations of sex, violence, and general mores.

The famous HUAC investigations of the Hollywood film industry repeatedly focused on the danger that Communists might pose if they were allowed to influence movie content. After much bad publicity surrounding hearings commencing in 1947 (ten Hollywood writers were held in contempt of Congress and eventually served prison sentences), hundreds of Hollywood employees were blacklisted by the studios and purged from the industry (Brownstein, 1990:113–117).

As the blacklisting of the 1950s indicated, pro-censorship forces outside of the industry were not met by great resistance within it—at least not at the executive level where it really mattered; in fact, there was less difference of opinion with external critics than one might imagine. In *Hollywood: The Movie Colony, the Movie Makers*, Leo Rosten (1941) writes the following about the irony of accusations of Hollywood interest in communism in the late 1930s:

> When Hollywood turned out full force, in rapid succession, for aid to Poland, Finland, the Netherlands, and Greece, the charge of wholesale Communism in the movie colony became patently inept. The final joke lies in the fact that Hollywood's leaders probably stand to the right of Mr. Dies and make even less distinction between a liberal and a Bolshevik. The representative from Texas has never denounced the New Deal with as much animus as some of the movie leaders have done in the presence of this writer. (150–151)

Indeed, the political conservatism of the movie moguls played a pivotal role in the history of censorship in Hollywood. Though the career paths of Hollywood executives were varied, two things they shared were strong patriotism and a generally conservative political orientation.

Most of the movie moguls of the 1930s and 1940s had a special reverence for America, stemming in part from their immigrant family backgrounds and no doubt from their own success stories. John Taylor speaks of their "determination to become 100 per cent American patriots" (Taylor, 1983:114), and Neal Gabler went so far as to suggest that their "embrace of America" was "ferocious, even pathological" (Gabler, 1988:4). One could argue that such extreme patriotism was only a cynical manifestation of the moguls' obvious economic interest in selling movies. Certainly some of them were more liberal than Louis Mayer or Adolph Zukor, but for the most part their beliefs seem to have been quite genuine. As a result, although they may not have supported censorship movements in principle, Hollywood's executives favored movies that would portray American society uncritically, and so they used their executive authority to make sure that the majority of films did not create political controversy.

Long before the HUAC investigations, the movie moguls, fearing adverse publicity and ultimately public censorship measures through legislation at municipal, state, or federal levels, designated the Hays office as an internal instrument of censorship. Whereas the Hays office did not have the power actually to censor, its work led to the Production Code that the industry adopted in 1930 as a form of self-regulation (Facey, 1974:16–17).[5]

The Code had less to do with politics per se than with mores. The introductory statement of the Code affirmed the artistic merit of film, but the rest was an explicit formula for what would and would not be tolerated on the screen. Among other things, the Code declared that "entertainment and art are important influences in the life of a nation . . . the motion picture within its own field of entertainment may be directly responsible for spiritual or moral progress, for higher types of social life, and for much correct thinking" (quoted in Leff and Simmons, 1990:284).

Crime could "not be presented in such a way as to throw sympathy with the crime." Profanity was, in a word, "forbidden." Sex was restricted by nine separate stipulations. Examples:

> Adultery . . . must not be explicitly treated, or justified, or presented attractively. . . . Scenes of passion . . . should not be introduced when not essential to the plot. . . . In general passion should so be treated that these scenes do not stimulate the lower and baser element. . . . Complete nudity is never permitted. (Leff and Simmons, 1990:284–285)

Rereading the code now gives us a sense of just how much things have changed.

One of the most prominent and well-organized of the Hollywood watchdogs was the Legion of Decency, an organization within the Catholic Church, convened for the purpose of exerting pressure on the movie industry to adhere to the letter and spirit of the Production Code. The Legion provided gradings for movies as they came out: an "A" was acceptable, "B" signified a partial objection to film content, and a "C" meant that the picture was condemned. Catholics were urged to boycott not only condemned movies, but also "B" classification movies, although for "B" movies the prohibitions were not as strongly worded (Facey, 1974:161–165). As Les and Barbara Keyser, authors of *Hollywood and the Catholic Church* (1984), point out, the strength of the group lay in its potential to turn audiences away from certain movies and their power over the industry was "awesome" (Keyser, 1984:58). [6]

In the early 1930s, under substantial pressure from the Catholic Church and its Legion of Decency, moviemakers began to enforce the Code rigorously. By the mid-1930s, studios that released movies that did not adhere to the Code were heavily fined ($25,000), and the Production Code Administration had the power to ban films from all Motion Picture Association theaters (Leff and Simmons, 1990:52–53). Under the direction of Joe Breen, this system succeeded in holding moviemakers to fairly uniform standards of representation and, for the most part, satisfied moral critics on the sidelines. Although increasingly criticized, the Production Code remained in force until 1966, and it was formally replaced only in 1968 by the familiar rating system that ranges from "G" to "X," with the recent addition of "NC-17" to differentiate Hollywood films that more explicitly represent sex from those produced by the pornography industry. The lifting of the self-imposed censorship restrictions was a sign of how new conditions had created a favorable environment for dramatic alteration of American film content. In the wake of the new code, practices changed much faster than anyone probably would have believed was possible. In retrospect, however, we can see that these changes not only involved standards of representation but had been a long time in the making in other sectors of the industry and the society as well.

The Transition

After World War II, legal, technological, and social developments converged on the Hollywood film industry, undermining the economic foundation of the studio system. Some of these developments were obvious, whereas the ultimate significance of others only becomes clear in retrospect. The developments often interacted with each other. As we mentioned above, the antitrust suit against Paramount in 1948, combined with the increasing strength of unions, encouraged the growing practice of free-lancing. Free-lancing was further encouraged by production cutbacks in the wake of the Paramount decision, and eventually there was television (Schatz, 1988:4). Of course, television produced widespread changes that could not have been foreseen. In the end, these developments swept the old studio system away and sowed the seeds of the new Hollywood, which would come into being in the 1960s and 1970s.

Antitrust Violations

In May 1948, the Supreme Court decided *United States v. Paramount Pictures, Inc.*, a case that would radically alter the structure of the Hollywood movie industry. In the decision, the largest studios, known as the Big Five and Little Three, were held in violation of sections of the Sherman Antitrust Act, and the Court affirmed the District Court determination that the defendants had engaged in conspiracy to restrain trade. According to the Court, the studios had done so in a number of ways, including the following: (1) they set minimum prices for movie exhibition (*United States v. Paramount Pictures Inc.*, 131:141–142); (2) they "impos[ed] unreasonable clearances," i.e., the length of time that second-run houses and others had to wait before opening newly released films, which constituted "a conspiracy to restrain trade" (146–147); (3) they also conspired through the block booking practice, which the court held promoted noncompetitive, monopolistic practices: "Where a high quality film greatly desired is licensed only if an inferior one is taken, the latter borrows quality from the former and strengthens its monopoly by drawing on the other. The practice tends to equalize rather than differentiate the reward for the individual copyrights"(158).

These particular findings spelled the eventual demise of the studio system as it had functioned for almost thirty years.

In upholding much of the District Court's prior ruling and remanding the case to that court, the Supreme Court denied that "competitive bidding" was a satisfactory solution (the District Court's initial remedy, requiring that the studios license movies to the highest-bidding theaters), implying that theater divestiture was the best available solution. The District Court subsequently required the studios to sell off their theater holdings.

One other aspect of the Paramount case, unrelated to the outcome of the antitrust decision, was important for the future of Hollywood, although it was not directly an economic issue. The majority opinion of the Court stated that "moving pictures, like newspapers and radio, are included in the press, whose freedom is guaranteed by the First Amendment" (166). This statement opened the way for formal judicial review of the constitutionality of movie censorship, and that review came four years later, in 1952, when the Supreme Court decided *Burstyn v. Wilson*, a case in which a film *(The Miracle)* had been censored by the Commissioner of Education of New York.

In the *Miracle* case, the Supreme Court unanimously declared that the censorship of the film in question was unconstitutional. The majority opinion stated that "under the First and Fourteenth Amendments a state may not ban a film on the basis of a censor's conclusion that it is 'sacrilegious'" (343 U.S. 506). It also addressed the issue of film's "greater capacity for evil, particularly among the youth of a community." The opinion suggested that in certain instances some form of censorship might be justified, but that the Board had overstepped itself in this case: "If there be capacity for evil it may be relevant in determining the permissible scope of community control, but it does not authorize substantially unbridled censorship such as we have here" (502).

The Miracle decision greatly weakened the power of the local boards to influence censorship decisions. Although the Production Code did not fall for fourteen more years, the studios' ability to regulate film content in conjunction with other organizations had been successfully challenged. For its part, the Paramount case, because it required studios to sell off their theaters, ended absolute studio control over theater programming (Leff and Simmons, 1990:187). Breen's administration lost much of its clout throughout the 1950s and early 1960s, as a direct result of these two decisions.

The Television Revolution

The arrival of television in the early 1950s took a big slice out of movie attendance figures.[7] In response, studio heads cut production dramatically, and even major producers grudgingly began to gear production efforts around television. This was inevitable, as more and more actors, and even directors and producers, were defying the studios and working in the new medium (MacCann, 1962:16–17).

The Hollywood moguls did not make the transition as easily as their former employees and missed a key opportunity to get into the new industry at its birth (Monaco, 1979:30). Initially, the moguls stubbornly resisted television, but within a few years their resistance crumbled, beginning with Howard Hughes's decision to sell RKO's films to TV (Gomery, 1986b:54). At this point, however, the studios were too late to take the lead in television production and instead followed RKO in selling off their film libraries.

The Coming of Independent Production and United Artists

The developments that led to cutbacks in production in the 1950s encouraged two important new trends. The studios were struggling to beat spiraling production costs and maximize their profits on a declining number of motion pictures. One solution was to film bigger and more spectacular movies, which would pull in larger audiences. Another was to rent out all of the available studio space that they themselves had been using in the past. This is what made the rise of the independent producers possible, leading to the changes in Hollywood we focus upon in subsequent chapters. It was the final act in the demise of the old studio system, which had been created expressly to minimize the influence of independents in the chain of movie production and distribution.

Eventually, following the lead of United Artists, most of the studios evolved from monopolistically integrated businesses into much less powerful companies that more often than not contracted for individual works. As independents could now rent studio space for themselves, and studio producers and directors envied that autonomy, the studios began to sweeten the deals they offered their own production crews by granting greater creative license to directors and producers who could show that their work made money (Balio, 1987:41). Indeed, under the management of Arthur Krim and Robert Benjamin, in the early 1950s, United Artists seized upon the idea of independent production as a means of turning a competitive disadvantage—no production facilities—into an asset that would increase the company's market share. United Artists retained the right to distribute the films it financed, but filmmakers got to make their own creative decisions, usually retaining "final cut" rights and receiving a percentage of the profits.

This division of responsibilities marked the beginning of the contemporary system. In effect, the studio had to negotiate with producers before the film went into production to make sure the studio executives were going to get basically what they wanted. After that, however, the production crew was on its own, within more or less broad contractual limits (Balio, 1987:42). In light of production cutbacks, following the Paramount decision and then the television invasion, the idea was well-timed, as a growing number of artists were eager to work under these more favorable conditions. Independent production created opportunities for television actors, artists who had lost their contracts with the studios, and anyone who had previously decided to become independent.

The Talent Agencies

The proliferation of independents in Hollywood led eventually to the rise in power of large talent agencies modeled after Music Corporation of America (MCA). MCA was the most notorious entertainment agency of the 1950s, acquiring enough clients to bring substantial pressure to bear on studios that were already in decline. In the late 1940s, MCA acquired a large client list when it took over the smaller Hayward-Deverich Agency, and in the early 1950s, MCA got involved in television production, before any other large agency (Balio, 1987:77).

MCA's success as a talent agency and as a television producer was unrivaled throughout the 1950s. In 1962, MCA, under investigation for antitrust violations, as Paramount had been little more than a decade earlier, was obliged to choose between talent and production, and bought Universal Pictures after it gave up its contracts as a talent agency (Balio, 1987:78). Competitors such as William Morris and CMA quickly filled the void, and the new talent agencies drew even more power away from the studios throughout the 1970s and 1980s, working tirelessly to increase the bargaining power of their clients. Filmmakers and actors substantially benefited from their work with agencies, having moved as a group from being paid employees to being free agents with tremendously increased power within the industry.

The most significant result for film style and content from all these changes was the decline—or breakup—of self-censorship, epitomized by the eventual replacement of the Production Code by the new rating system. By the time the Code changed, however, Hollywood was already a vastly different place than it had been when the Code was first put into practice in 1930. The new rating system reflected a sea change in the industry that had been slowly taking shape for several decades.

The New Hollywood

All of the market developments and social and political forces against which Hollywood management had to fight had a profound effect on the longstanding struggle between entrepreneur and artist. As independent filmmakers became more and more able to gain a purchase in Hollywood, whether to make movies or television shows, the center of power gradually shifted in favor of this new crop of producers and directors. They slowly gained the reputation and financial backing to create their own small-scale studio operations. The breakup of the institutional constraints that accompanied the studio system thus set the stage for a much more thoroughgoing artistic freedom for filmmakers and led to a transformation of Hollywood as an industry and as an institution in society.

The Rating System

Part of the explanation of why Hollywood movies changed so greatly in a relatively short time in the 1960s involves the sudden loosening of restrictions over what Hollywood moviemakers could and could not show the public. The new production code, adopted in 1968, officially recognized the necessity of artistic freedom and the "odious" nature of censorship. It stated the following two objectives:

1. To encourage artistic expression by expanding creative freedom.
2. To assure that the freedom which encourages the artist remains responsible and sensitive to the standards of the larger society. (Mast, 1982:704)

What is interesting here is that the understanding of what is "responsible" and "sensitive to the standards of the larger society" has undergone a fundamental shift. The new rating system codified industry management of problematic material in terms of responsible inclusion rather than censorship. The new aim was more to describe than to judge.

Under the new rating system, sexually explicit representations, strong language, and especially violence (acceptable in varying degrees in PG–13 and R- and X-rated movies), became part of the formula for box office success. In 1993, soaring murder rates led the Clinton administration and the Congress to question the amount of violence on television (especially children's television) and in videos. Indeed, the moviemakers themselves have expressed concerns about the social impact of their medium and have questioned, for instance, the extent of violence on television for at least the past fifteen years .[8] But, as Gerald Mast noted, in *The Movies in our Midst* (1982), the issue is not easily resolved:

> Because the movies have sold sex and violence from the beginning (what extremely popular and public art ever sold anything else?), and because they were created within and supported by a society that condoned neither the doing nor the display of sex and violence, the motion picture industry has been in the paradoxical position of trying to set limits on how much it would let itself sell. The primary principle for regulation seems to have been "all that the market will bear," and when the market gets angry and will bear no more, curtailing its expenditures at the box office, the film industry repeatedly catches a severe case of moral fever. (Mast, 1982:xix)

What does seem clear, despite Hollywood's receptivity to market pressures, is that in recent years the public has become more tolerant of sex and violence in movies.

The rating system has contributed to this trend because it is a much more liberal instrument of movie review, very well-suited to testing the limits of the market. Appointed and supervised by Jack Valenti, an independent panel of adult viewers evaluates movies according to the type and frequency of sexual display, language, and violence contained in them, then decides what movies are appropriate for certain age groups. Nearly all movies, no matter what the content, are able to reach the market with some rating. Movies have thus been virtually freed from industry censorship and are instead "classified" by a tribunal supposed to approximate current standards of public morality.[9] The system generally satisfies Hollywood's demand for freedom of expression, limiting only what minors can view, and leaves the rest up to the viewer's discretion. Writers, directors, and producers, therefore, have little more to satisfy than their own sense of morality, informed by sensitivity to "what the market will bear," in making a film. Clearly, from the perspective of the creative talent in Hollywood, a diminished threat of censorship means more power to express ideas, especially those that may be highly provocative and controversial.

The New Wave and the Social Turmoil of the 1960s

Another aspect of change that we have not yet discussed was the growing influence of European filmmaking after World War II on young, well-educated U.S. filmmakers. As the independents began to gain power in Hollywood, they were able to bring their own ideas about moviemaking to bear, and, for a number of reasons, many of the directors they admired were European, particularly French directors such as Godard, Truffaut, Malle, and Chabrol. If factory films of the studio era were the least sophisticated form of moviemaking in the eyes of new Hollywood artists, these French films were the ideal, an apotheosis of the director in the creative work of film. Younger filmmakers therefore strove to develop their own version of the New Wave within the constraints of the American market, and the rise of independent production was fertile ground for these influences. As a result, in the 1960s, the American version of French New Wave cinema was born.

Paul Monaco, author of *Ribbons in Time*, argues that the international success of the New Wave was one result of the economic developments we have outlined above that had rapidly transformed the movie industry and its audience in the 1950s. Indeed, changes in American film might have been less pronounced if not for the fact that the composition of the audience had changed. Among other things, adults were staying home and watching television. Adolescents and young adults without children became the bulk of the movie audience. Because it explicitly appealed to these groups, New Wave cinema was able to gain a foothold in the American market, where the audience was now younger, more affluent, and better educated. And as a result of the baby boom, there were more and more people in those young audiences.

The middle and late 1960s, as Hollywood struggled to please this difficult new audience, were also the years when more and more independent and therefore independent-minded directors began to succeed in the industry. In doing so, they inevitably broke away from old genres and experimented with new ideas (Monaco, 1987:53–54). Many of their films were characterized by the reflexive play, inventive camera work, and deceptively rambling compositional style of New Wave movies (Carroll, 1986:64).

It is also important to recall that the New Wave in America was not an entirely foreign-born artistic movement, as Hollywood already harbored its own share of mavericks. The French directors themselves, writes Monaco, respected—even idolized—a few of the older Hollywood directors, such as John Ford, John Huston, Michael Curtiz, Orson Welles, and Alfred Hitchcock. They found in the work of these directors the seeds of their own theories about directorial authorship, even though it had been produced within the studio system (Monaco, 1987: 37). The theory of the "auteur" thus combined with, or was able to take advantage of, the developments within the business of moviemaking itself, to forge the 1960s and 1970s into a period of unprecedented freedom in film production.

For the younger directors in the 1960s, who wanted to do innovative work following in the steps of their New Wave progenitors, the key to success seemed to lie in exploiting the widening cracks in industry control over moviemaking, while capturing a large enough young audience to make a film profitable. Thus the social turmoil of the 1960s and early 1970s provided important dramatic material for Hollywood artists to work with, as it was politically charged and would guarantee recognition at the box office.

In fact, many have argued that one reason that the films of the European New Wave directors were so attractive to younger Americans is that the Europeans were revolutionizing the medium with new techniques that resonated with counter-cultural imagery.[10] Again, it is important to emphasize that although there were explicit ideological attractions to this work among a number of young Hollywood filmmakers, clearly there were also other reasons that it crossed the Atlantic. Nevertheless, it is true that many film historians, critics, and theorists argue that what happened to Hollywood movies in the 1960s included a disillusionment with particular kinds of stories. This was the result of political and social developments that threw those old-fashioned stories, and the attitudes that informed them, into a kind of extreme doubt, if not exactly the dustbin of history. Michael Wood, in *America in the Movies* (1975), takes this approach:

> The sixties were a decade that made life hard for a lot of old stories, an age that was full of an awareness of ugly, unavoidable realities: racism, torture . . . assassination . . . and the war in Vietnam; drugs, muggings, and turbulent, unmanageable cities. It was not that popular films had suddenly become false, for they had always been false. Just that they had become too false, false enough to upset the old, careful truce between wishes and facts.(Wood, 1975:194–195).

Like Michael Wood, Axel Madsen suggests in his book *The New Hollywood: American Movies in the '70s*, that the new movies were an inevitable response to social and political developments:

> The post-Vietnam, post-Watergate seventies have produced a numbness to pain and corruption that has rubbed off on the screen.
>   The Vietnam war, the explosion of street crime and of government intrigue at the highest level, seem to mock middle-class gentility and to make despair and cynicism more than fashionable. More than ever modern heroic acts seem to be possible only as schemes of fools and lunatics. Makers of formula mine new veins of popular moods and come up with screen fare that accepts corruption and sentimentalizes defeat. (Madsen, 1975:143–145)

Indeed, the social and political upheavals of the 1960s greatly influenced movie content.

We argue, however, that the way that these changes came about is different from what the statements that we have quoted above suggest, that is, that changes in Hollywood movie content were a more or less objective response to changes throughout the society. First of all, the thoroughgoing transformations in content that we document in subsequent chapters were only possible because of the changing structure of the film industry at the time. Any discussion that does not take these changes in the industry into account cannot satisfactorily explain how the movies also changed over this period. Further, the changes in content have had at least as much do with the evolving social and political attitudes of elite filmmakers and other cultural elites as with the general public's actual perception of the political events. For the new Hollywood elite has generally come to hold different views about a wide range of issues than the public, and, as we show in the balance of this book, these ideas tend to characterize the representations that they have created.[11]

Over the past several decades, the effects of European influence, politics at home, and developments in the film industry have emerged in different ways. Some directors succeeded by emphasizing free expression and the primacy of the individual, while criticizing institutions of which they were skeptical or suspicious. A number of extraordinary actors, including Steve McQueen, Paul Newman, Marlon Brando, Dustin Hoffman, and Al Pacino, rose to these roles, taking parts as social outcasts or critical renegades in many of their movies. Women stars like Jane Fonda, Barbra Streisand, Vanessa Redgrave, and Shirley MacLaine also took on roles associated with new political agendas like feminism. Filmmakers gave a wide range of characters more complex psychological attributes and made them more independent-minded. As Jowett and Linton point out, these parts—and the public personalities of the actors who embraced them— "would have had a great deal of difficulty surviving the rigidities required by the old studio system" (Jowett and Linton, 1980:78).

Relying on the new, independently contracted star system to provide mass appeal, directors diverged from old formula pictures such as westerns, cops-and-robbers dramas, glamour romances, and war stories. If we look at the western, for example, we see that from 1965 to 1971, five westerns made it into the top-ten box office takes for each year: *Shenandoah* (1965); *Hombre* (1967); *Butch Cassidy and the Sundance Kid* (1969); *True Grit* (1969); *Little Big Man* (1971).[12] *Shenandoah*, *Hombre*, and *True Grit* are more or less conventional fare, although the protagonist in *Hombre*, played by Paul Newman, is not the typical hero of earlier westerns but a renegade antihero, an alienated half-Indian/half-white outcast who dies at the end of the film. The other two films, *Butch Cassidy and the Sundance Kid* and *Little Big Man*, clearly play New Wave kinds of turns on the Western, audaciously parodying and undercutting the genre. If we add *Midnight Cowboy* (1969) to this list, a film that places John Voigt's deluded cowboy-stud in the gritty reality of contemporary New York, we can see how radically things had changed.

Midnight Cowboy, of course, was highly controversial, initially earning an "X" rating when it was released. Further, it has often been viewed as an American "auteur" film, "authored" as much as directed by John Schlesinger. The point is that the new movies were quite clearly (and self-consciously) undercutting the old genres. It is also worth noting that these changes heralded the death of the Western as a genre; very few of them have made it into the top-ten box office takes of any year since 1971, and those that have—*Blazing Saddles* (1974), *The Electric Horseman* (1980)—have hardly been traditional westerns, which used to be one of Hollywood's mainstays. Even Clint Eastwood's apparently more conventional *Unforgiven* (1992) casts the law (the sheriff, played by Gene Hackman) as racist and sadistic, and the protagonist as an uncontrollably violent, albeit reluctant, hired killer.

Other filmmakers experimented with new screen talent in films addressing controversial issues that would not have been approached in the past. With the right people and often the lure of spicy sexual scenes, much more graphic violence (made possible not only by technology but also by the new rating system), along with much more accomplished special effects for science fiction and action films, these films could bring a substantial return at the box office.

Independent Filmmakers

Many of the new films would never have been made in the studios, perhaps not even after censorship pressure was relaxed, but in the late 1960s and 1970s independent producers were already numerous. The hard evidence for the new freedom in production is in the figures for independent filmmaking. The dam broke in the late 1960s and early 1970s; although there were only nineteen independently produced films in Hollywood in 1968, there were over 100 in 1972 (Jacobs, 1977:15).

The careers of the major new directors who were involved in this movement indicate the potential that developed for innovative, personal filmmaking in Hollywood during the late 1960s and 1970s. These directors came to enjoy a prestige and power over their product virtually unknown under the old system. After producing *M*A*S*H*, for example, Robert Altman started his own production company, Lion's Gate Films, which grew into a ministudio in the 1970s (Smith, 1983:24). Mel Brooks described his creation of *Blazing Saddles* as "a big psychoanalytic session. I just got everything out of me—all my furor, my frenzy, my insanity, my love of life, and my hatred of death" (quoted in Smith, 1983:43). These are terms that would probably never have occurred to earlier studio filmmakers—they simply didn't have as much control as Brooks. Alongside box office hits like *The Godfather* and *Apocalypse Now*, Francis Ford Coppola directed several other films at Zoetrope Studios, where "he planned to create an updated version of the studio system of the 1930s" (Smith, 1983:63). George Lucas, maker of the three *Star Wars* blockbusters and several others, founded Lucasfilm Limited. Even Steven Spielberg, the most commercially successful writer/director/producer ever, "refers to himself as an 'independent moviemaker working within the Hollywood establishment'" (Mott and Saunders, 1986:3). The careers of these minimoguls in and of themselves indicate just how much the movie industry had changed by the beginning of the 1980s.

In short, the substantive control exerted by industry executives had all but evaporated by the early 1960s. By that time, most of the old moguls had died or left the industry, and, one by one, the major studios were picked up by gigantic business conglomerates.[13] The studios were forced to share power with television, talent agents, a growing number of independent producers, directors, and even star actors. A new group of filmmakers, who came up with the right combinations of script, cast, and technique, were empowered in the process, and many of them were decidedly anti-Establishment.

Cineplexes, Megablockbusters, and the New Genres

Slowly, the numbers of people attending movies began to rise in the 1970s. Following the sprawling metropolitan populations surrounding large cities, theater complexes sprang up in suburbia, particularly in malls and shopping centers. These were multiple, "cineplex" theater facilities, varying in size, that could run many different movies simultaneously. If one film was not selling tickets, it could be moved to the smallest theater, and more popular films could play in the largest ones (Jowett and Linton, 1980:44).

With the help of such innovations, in spite of a faltering economy, the film industry seemed finally to be recovering from its post–World War II downturn. Axel Madsen's comments are indicative of the optimistic take on the industry that pertained in the 1970s:

> The vast majority who left the movies for their television sets years ago are beginning to drift back. "People are going to the movies again," says Columbia Pictures president David Begelman. "The opportunity has been given back to us."
>
> The chronicle of Hollywood in the seventies is a story of change and renewal, under pressure. Inflation and recession are not among the film industry's woes—on the contrary. The downbeat economic reality of the mid-1970s is having the same effect as the 1930s depression had; it is sending people to the movies in record numbers. (Madsen, 1975:1–2)

Madsen was not optimistic about America itself, only about Hollywood's ability to turn a profit entertaining it. In this optimism he was not far wrong. Although the cost of producing films had escalated throughout the 1960s and 1970s, the increased interest in the movies and relative convenience of the drive-in, and later the mall theaters, significantly increased the profits that could be realized from a popular movie.

Further, with the unprecedented success of the first "megablockbusters," *Jaws* (1975) and *Star Wars* (1977), patterns of release and distribution changed, as a large part of the industry sought to manufacture other similarly successful movies (Kilday, 1989:60). Megablockbusters were generally not films that received critical acclaim, but they were successful because they specifically targeted the vast child and adolescent audiences of the suburban middle class. If they were well-marketed and produced (and were lucky), they could earn tremendous returns by opening simultaneously in a great number of theaters. This became the pattern for a large segment of Hollywood production, because there was simply so much money to be made if it were done right.

As a result of all these developments, the motion picture industry arrived at a critical juncture in the late 1970s. One hit movie could mean the difference between a profit and a loss on the entire year, so studios were willing to risk large sums of money on production and advertising for a single movie, if they believed it could gross $50 million or more. Again, this trend toward big-budget pictures fostered the development of the elite group of independent filmmakers with proven track records, and they became the individuals who most often received studio financing. In a 1987 study, sociologists Robert Faulkner and Andy Anderson found that from 1965 to 1980, only a tiny fraction of all Hollywood film producers with credits (7 percent, or ninety-two producers) made 740 films, over a third of Hollywood's entire output (Faulkner and Anderson, 1987:894).

The most significant aspect of this finding for our purposes is the way it concretely demonstrates that the big commercial pictures of the 1970s were made by a very elite group, but one that had nevertheless broken free of the studio system and was no longer constrained by anywhere near as stringent a code of self-censorship. Whereas Hollywood had changed and in some ways become a much more heterogeneous place, it was still dominated by an elite group, albeit of a very different kind than in the studio days.

This group comprised two classes of filmmakers: (1) directors who had brought a touch of New Wave to Hollywood at a time when genre films were unpopular (Altman, Scorsese, Coppola); and (2) even younger directors who were tuned into the youth market (Spielberg, Lucas). As the pressure for big movies mounted, studios became more cautious in financing self-consciously artistic films, and the young directors tended to dominate the blockbuster market. The slightly older filmmakers had to make the most of the 18-to-34 audience in order to compete at the box office.

In the late 1970s, filmmakers therefore synthesized new genres that could generate more widespread appeal than antigenre films. Some of them explored difficult issues, such as war, crime, and corruption. In general, however, they were more commercial than the "youth films" of the 1960s. Many of the new films offered treatments less characterized by moral angst (Mott and Saunders, 1986:3) but which incorporated elements of new, more or less anti-Establishment views. Among these new genres we could include the "renegade cop" picture, for example, which became a distinct subgenre with the success of the Dirty Harry movies.

Also, by 1985 the video revolution had created ancillary markets that would revitalize the smaller film, and since then independent Hollywood producers have multiplied in this new poststudio system. No new restraints comparable to those that the studios placed on themselves in their heyday have arisen. Whether more intense criticisms may again become fashionable and marketable in the future, it does seem clear that the new, independently oriented Hollywood had itself become fully institutionalized by the early 1980s.

Hollywood in the 1980s

The Talent Agencies and Conglomerate Ownership

In the 1980s, the movie industry became even more dependent upon huge talent agencies than it had been in the past, as independent production companies bid more and more for talent. As we pointed out above, the rise of these companies had accompanied the decline of the studio system, and their power originated in the decreasing numbers of long-term contract arrangements among studios, filmmakers, and actors. In the absence of long-term contracts, studio bosses found they could no longer bully talent; the writer, the director, and the star had to be persuaded to do each picture, and salaries and benefits continued to rise accordingly. As the power of talent increased, so did the influence of the agents, particularly those who could wield the collective clout of many important clients, and eventually agents became the indispensable middlemen, controlling access to talent (Litwak, 1986:50–51). A few talent agencies began to provide services for large blocks of Hollywood's newly independent creative talent, and as the agencies grew, producers and studios were required to make more and more deals with them to get movie production off the ground.

There was another industry development that fed independent production even more and made the emergence of some new kind of studio system unlikely. Although the executives of the conglomerates that were buying up the studios in the early 1960s were more sophisticated businessmen than the moguls, they lacked experience in handling films, film production, and film talent. As a result the parent companies came to rely on the expertise of their executives in charge of film production. These second-level managers were usually under 40 years old, and many had previously worked as talent agents (Monaco, 1979:46).

In giving over direct creative control in this way, the conglomerates sacrificed a large measure of control in the hope of obtaining a larger number of money-making pictures. Decision-making became less autocratic. Unlike the studio era moguls, these new Hollywood executives had to make deals with independent artists on an ad hoc basis. Often a good deal of creative power wound up in the hands of the talent agencies, which put together client packages for individual movies.

Essentially, this system of production remains intact today, making talent agents a vital link in the motion picture business and further insulating filmmakers from the studios. In fact, the agencies have become so powerful that their clients can virtually write their own deals, fostering a situation in Hollywood almost the opposite of what pertained in the past (Litwak, 1986:48). Directors, and even producers, benefit from their involvement with talent agencies, because they have more bargaining power when the agencies represent them. The advantages for the producers are even great enough to induce many independents to work with the studios through contractual arrangements brokered by the agencies. The studios provide the funds, the agencies provide the talent, and the producers bring the whole thing together, except that it is once again the agencies sealing the various deals (*The Economist*, 1989b:14). Actors have also benefited from their association with talent agencies, frequently securing percentages of profits from movies in which they star.[14]

The increased leverage of filmmakers and stars has helped to send production costs even higher. According to *The Economist*, "between 1984 and 1988 the average cost of making a film soared from $14.5m to $20.7m" (1989b:15). This trend shows no signs of reversing. The 1989 blockbuster *Batman* reportedly cost over $75 million to make and may ultimately gross ten times that much (*The Economist*, 1989b:5). By contrast, *The Abyss* cost over $60 million and may never recoup its costs (*The Economist*, 1989a:73).

Videos and VCRs

In the early 1980s, another technological innovation—the videocassette recorder (VCR)—again transformed the entertainment business. As television had in the fifties, pay television and VCRs threatened to sack the motion picture industry in the 1980s (as the information superhighway may transform it again later in this decade). VCR sales went through the ceiling in the United States, quadrupling from about a half million in 1979 to over 2 million in 1982, and then doubling again by 1984 (*The Economist*, 1983:72). Hollywood began selling films on video-tapes, but they were expensive, which limited the market.

As most people are probably aware, the industry has managed to turn the de-velopment of the video market to its advantage. Video-rental shops, which sprang up in the mid-1980s, have continued to expand the video market. Over time, stu-dios began lowering prices for mass-marketing and were thereby able to generate more direct retail profits. And in 1986, annual video rental profits actually began to surpass those of the box office (Kilday, 1989:65).

The new video market does not change the fact that filmmakers must generate profitable commodities, but VCRs have lessened the financial risk associated with any one movie because video rental helps to elongate the period over which a film recoups its production costs. Some box office flops have even become successes after having been released on video, finding markets that they otherwise would have missed (Gomery, 1986b:56). This has lessened some of the pressure on film-makers to produce blockbusters, allowing less costly and spectacular films to play a role in the overall market. Filmmaker Oliver Stone has remarked that

> about 1985 . . . there was a whole bunch of new independent companies coming in and because of the ancillary markets they were able to do their own distribution. And that made for a wider variety of selections. I don't think that *Blue Velvet* would have been made before 1985 or, for that matter, *Platoon*. These were made because of in-dependent companies so maybe there's a shift in the wind back towards the 70s when there used to be a lot of this type of movie. (Quoted in Norman, 1987:334)

These developments have indeed allowed a number of new directors, like Stone, to gain notice making "small" films that, as he rightly points out, might not have even been produced a decade earlier.

At the same time, we should note that the video revolution does not seem to have disturbed the poststudio structure of Hollywood as an industry. Although there is no doubt that other technological and industry developments will con-tinue to change the movie business, including further increases in the number of channels available and new technologies creating interactive "virtual reality" and the ability to create and transmit holographs, it does seem unlikely that any com-bination of events will soon have effects as revolutionary as those factors that led to the end of the studio system.

During the past three decades, Hollywood has been profoundly transformed. What was a monopolistic enterprise with extraordinarily tight constraints on representation and individual creativity has become a more decentralized business, where individual producers, directors, writers, and actors all vie for a share of the limelight, the profits, and the creative power. At the same time, however, the numbers of people involved are still relatively small, and they tend to hold a number of social and political attitudes in common, attitudes that differ radically from those of earlier generations of the Hollywood elite and from those of the public in general. As we will show in subsequent chapters, these attitudes correlate with the stories that movies from the new Hollywood tell us.

Recent Developments

Many observers agree that the presidency of Ronald Reagan resulted in a significant setback for the liberal political agenda. Some conservatives were even optimistic that they had won back a large segment of the American electorate. But we think that in the 1980s, Hollywood moviemakers and the movies themselves were characterized less by artistic reaction than by the refinement and commercialization of the hybrid American New Wave of the preceding fifteen or twenty years, when independent filmmaking came to the fore.

A few populist right-wing films, most notably the Rambo and Dirty Harry films, are usually cited not only as evidence of Hollywood's answer to a more conservative audience but of a resurgent conservatism rooted in the movie industry itself.[15] As we discuss in other chapters, however, even these films tend to exhibit a basic mistrust for any and all authority that is uncharacteristic of movies made before the 1960s.

In the late 1970s, filmmakers succeeded in creating new genres by combining elements of the antigenre film with older formulas. The new genre films closely parallel the old (romance, military, science fiction), but in form only; substantively, they are altogether new. An instructive contrast here could be drawn, for example, between most war movies up to about 1968 and the subsequent war films, most of which deal with the Vietnam conflict. The anti-Establishment sentiment that peaked in movies of the early 1970s has been replaced by more subtle criticism, but Hollywood's liberal ideological orientation is no less apparent. This is the case, we would argue, even in films like *Rambo: First Blood Part II* (1985), in which the protagonist, far from being a loyal soldier participating in a just war, is a violent, superhuman renegade who feels his country has betrayed him.

Peter Biskind, in his contribution to *Seeing Through Movies* (Miller, ed., 1990), remarks that it is not by accident that *Star Wars* has a dual quality, at once hearkening back to the formulaic simplicity of the 1950s and, paradoxically, also to "countercultural values" (Miller, ed., 1990:113). According to Miller, Lucas himself has suggested that the film could be viewed as a kind of allegory in which the evil Empire represents the United States and the brave rebel heroes stand for the North Vietnamese (Miller, ed., 1990:113). As this kind of contradiction in the themes of *Star Wars* suggests, the new directors of the 1970s and early 1980s wished to break away, at least stylistically, from the antigenre films of the American New Wave, but they were deeply influenced by the cultural changes of the 1960s. As a result, even the most commercially successful films often reveal an internal conflict. Biskind goes on to say that

> in borrowing, combining, and recombining elements from both right and left . . . the Star Wars trilogy breathed new life into the ideological consensus of the center on which their conventions depended, and succeeded in doing in the realm of culture what the Carter Restoration had, with only partial success, attempted in the realm of politics. (Miller, ed., 1990:120)

Although this may be an accurate assessment of the content of the *Star Wars* movies, it is probably not applicable to most movies of the period. The Hollywood center, especially in attitudes, is situated well to the left of that of the American public. Even many of the most popular movies, subject to market constraints, reflect these liberal views. Symbolic of the change in the Hollywood structure of power and values is a change in criteria that serve as the basis for judging which directors, motion pictures, and so on, now receive academy awards. In the old days, such awards were rarely granted to films that flopped. Since the mid-1970s, this has changed. "Quality films, generally on the left, whether they succeed or fail are the only ones now judged worthy of such awards as are those who produce or act in such films" (Grenier, 1993).

The present status of Hollywood opinion notwithstanding, at least two developments in the 1980s raised the possibility that the studios may again come to monopolize the motion picture business. In *Copperweld Corp. v. Independence Tube Corp.* (1984), the Supreme Court redefined conditions for the restraint of trade under the Sherman Antitrust Act. The Court held that parent corporations and wholly owned subsidiaries were incapable of conspiring with one another—an interpretation that might have substantially altered, if not invalidated, the earlier Paramount decision. Subsequently, parent companies of the studios began to purchase moviehouses and by the end of the decade owned almost one out of every six, or 3,500 out of 22,000. In absolute numbers, these figures are nearly comparable to those prior to the Paramount decision of 1948; however the important qualitative differences in industry organization that we have outlined above mitigate against the same type of control over movie content (Kilday, 1989: 65).

The second, related development involves the ongoing conglomerization of the studios' parent corporations. For example, in 1989 Time Inc. merged with Warner Communications to form Time-Warner, the largest entertainment company in history. The Time-Warner giant has not yet proven that bigness is necessarily bad for the industry or good for the internal operations of the company. Possibilities exist for vertical and horizontal integration, but these practices have not proven to be "a miracle cure to the risks of the movie industry." Despite the loosening of federal restrictions companies have not jumped at the opportunity to integrate vertically by buying up all the theaters; it is not always advantageous to take on the financial burdens associated with mass theater ownership. Also, in many instances horizontal integration of various entertainments is not advantageous or even feasible. It may be possible to integrate music and video, but many other commodities are incompatible with one another (*The Economist*, 1989b:8).

By 1989, Hollywood was a $5 billion industry (Kilday, 1989:65). Although the huge conglomerates now heading the studios invite speculation that Hollywood will again become a tightly controlled assembly line of entertainment commodities, the institution seems to have specialized to the point at which that is unlikely. Specialization requires a deference to those who are closest to the actual business of making movies—to the young professionals who work at putting together movie packages with agents and independent filmmakers. The process is generally one of negotiation and compromise, not coercion. The studios, primarily concerned with which films are most marketable, will invariably set the agenda in movie production, but beyond that, the industry is still organized to give filmmakers relative autonomy—including making final cuts—in actually filming a motion picture.

In fact, the current trends in Hollywood are consistent with a general pattern of specialization within large conglomerates. Media researchers at MIT and Stanford have predicted a "democratization of technology" within these institutions: "In other words, conglomerates will continue to conglomerate but within their gigantic empires will be multitudinous small units with virtual autonomy" (Walker, 1989:31). Thus, the motion picture industry may very well continue on a course that was set as early as the 1950s. Artistic control over movie content will remain intact as long as entrepreneurs grant that filmmakers know more about making movies—meaning, of course, movies that make money—than they do. There is much truth in the statement that "the more institutional and businesslike the studios become the more powerful is talent—the 'soul' in the entertainment machines" (*The Economist*, 1989b:16).

This is not to say that conglomerates made it easy for filmmakers in the 1980s and early 1990s, but that independent producers have held onto their turf in the entertainment business. In fact, the video business promises to open up the market to less commercially oriented artists whose films may be more overtly critical of the American social and political order. On balance, it seems that filmmakers maintain considerable artistic freedom as the industry heads into the second half of the 1990s.

A lingering issue that is unlikely to be resolved soon is the self-censorship question. Although attitudes about censorship have changed dramatically in a liberal direction over the past twenty-five years and seem unlikely to reverse themselves, the debate—one of the perennial flowers of American politics—continues. What responsibility do filmmakers have in providing entertainment to largely adolescent audiences? What are the implications of the availability of all kinds of movies in the home, as a result of cable television, video, and VCR technologies? Recently, Ni Yang and Daniel Linz, who study the content of R-rated and X-rated movies, came to the rather obvious conclusion that "widespread availability of R-rated movies on videocassettes or cable television means that young viewers may be more likely than ever to encounter violence, particularly sexual violence, on the television screen at home" (Yang and Linz, 1990:41). Thus the greatest threat to the movie industry may resurface in the form of censorship from outside the industry. For as one writer has observed, Hollywood often appears to be in the business of "an endless exploration of the dreams, wishes, growing pains and masturbatory fantasies of teen-age children" (Norman, 1987:336). Assuming that movies remain largely under the protection of the First Amendment, which seems likely, and that no centralized, self-regulating studio system emerges to rein in provocative representation, which also seems likely—what then will the movies that emerge in the next ten years tell us about American institutions, society, and ourselves?

Conclusion

In the 1960s and 1970s, a number of historical developments in American society, and in the film industry within that society, made the emergence of a new class of filmmakers, and their films, feasible. A list of these developments would have to include: (1) the breakdown, under the influence of antitrust decisions, increasingly powerful unions, technological developments, and other factors, of the studio system that led to the rise of independent production; (2) the court-backed assault on the old film board's brand of self-censorship; (3) the changing demographics of the U.S. film audiences after the advent of TV; (4) the increasing awareness, among the more cosmopolitan generation of post–World War II filmmakers, of European movie making; (5) a particular set of events, including the Vietnam War and Watergate, that, for many members of certain elite groups in the society, signaled a cultural crisis in America during the 1960s and 1970s; and (6) partly as a result of the above but also as a contributing factor, the continued transformation of America's traditional bourgeois culture, a theme that we will discuss in more detail in the final chapter of the book.

The key phrase in the penultimate item is "for many members of certain elite groups." To say that society is always changing is a truism worth repeating, but in certain periods the cliché is truer than in others. The widespread alienation from the traditional attitudes of their own society that many elite groups, including Hollywood filmmakers, suddenly came to feel during the 1960s constituted a powerful break with the past. As we show in the following chapter, that alienation still characterizes the filmmakers' outlooks on key social and political issues. In large part freed from studio control and internal and external censorship, the industry evolved in such a way that writers, directors, and producers were able to make films that never would have been produced under the old studio system. It is this revolutionary change in attitudes among the Hollywood elite, within the context of their new ability to exercise increased control over the films they made, that we examine in detail in the next chapter.

A Note on the 1990s

In the early 1990s, Hollywood has continued along the somewhat volatile course charted throughout the 1980s. The industry slumped in 1991, but by 1993 Hollywood was enjoying a robust recovery. Video sales and rentals alone topped $17 billion in 1992 and ticket sales broke records the following year (Bates, 1993; Armstrong, 1994). Blockbuster films with big budgets tend to perpetuate the boom or bust cycle for the larger studios. Jack Valenti reported, in 1991, that the average studio film must now gross nearly $40 million for the studios to break even (*Wall Street Journal,* 1991).

Independent film producers, in part susceptible to the financial fortunes of their larger counterparts in the industry, also had their ups and downs in the early 1990s. Nevertheless, a number of low budget films continue to succeed, bolstered by small independent financiers, the video rental industry (which allows for a niche market), and a strong demand for these films in foreign markets (Mathews, 1994; Nichols, 1992; *Los Angeles Times,* 1993). In 1991, for example, an off year for Hollywood, six of the summer's top ten films were low budget productions (Citron, 1991). The merger promoted by Spielberg, Katzenberg, and Geffen in the fall of 1994 seems unlikely to change the patterns that we have described (*New York Times,* October 13, 1994).

NOTES

1. Among others, John Taylor's account of Hollywood in the 1920s and 1930s, *Strangers in Paradise* (1983), emphasizes the movie moguls' lack of concern for promoting film as art. Exploiting the "commercial potential of culture" (19) was, in general, the first order of business.

2. According to Douglas Gomery: "Five firms dominated: Paramount, Loew's, Warner Bros., Fox, and RKO. Each of the Big Five owned substantial production facilities in Southern California, a worldwide distribution network and a sizable theater chain. The Little Three (Universal, Columbia and United Artists) maintained only production and distribution units" (Gomery, 1986:6).

3. A few bankers did fund independents but at a much higher cost to the producer. Tino Balio gives a sense of just how difficult it was for an independent to raise money to make movies: "During the thirties, an established independent obtained financing in the form of a residual loan from a bank, for example, the Bank of America. As a condition for the loan, the producer had to have a distribution contract and successful pictures in release. To provide security for his new project, he had to mortgage a number of his completed

pictures as well as the proposed one and to pledge the residual profits from his films in current distribution" (Balio, 1985:414).

4. *The Politics of Glamour*, David Prindle's study of the Screen Actors Guild, underscores the power that Hollywood labor, once organized, has always wielded, even when one doesn't include the big stars (Prindle, 1988:13–14).

5. The Production Code itself was authored in large part by two Catholics, Father Daniel Lord, a Saint Louis University professor, and Martin Quigley, publisher of the *Motion Picture Herald* of Chicago. As Facey points out: "Quigley brought [the] proposal to the attention of Will Hays, who arranged that Quigley have the opportunity of presenting it to the film producers. . . . The producers accepted the code substantially as it had been offered to them" (Facey, 1974:40).

6. The Legion of Decency changed its name to the National Catholic Office for Motion Pictures in 1965. The office was closed in 1980.

7. According to Balio, "Annual box office receipts declined from $1.692 billion in 1946 to $1.298 billion in 1956, or about 23 percent." Studio profits registered a tremendous decline, "from $121 million to $32 million, or 74 percent" (1976:401).

8. In our 1982 survey of the attitudes of the filmmaking elite, we found that 67 percent of those interviewed agreed or strongly agreed that "there is too much violence on television" (Rothman and Lichter, 1984:18).

9. Until the institution of the NC-17 rating, a great deal of pressure was placed on producers and directors to edit films that earned the X-rating. How the new rating will affect that practice remains to be seen. Janet Maslin suggests that it will allow even more freedom, eliminating the stigma of the catchall X-rating category for many movies with enough explicit material to surpass the R-rating (Maslin, 1990). Classification is the term used by Stephen Farber, author of *The Movie Rating Game*, to describe the new system. He was a member of the movie rating panel for a short time in 1970.

10. Neil Hurley, author of *The Reel Revolution*, wrote the following typical comment about Godard's work: "In a sense, he is always making the same film: western people impaled on the 'throwawayable' comforts of a synthetic civilization with an escalator standard of living, either socialist or capitalist" (1978:133).

11. There is, of course, a complicated relationship between the values and attitudes propagated by the "cultural elites" and the views of the average citizen. It is clear that over time but with increasing rapidity, the views of the former have a powerful impact on the views of the public. We shall discuss this matter in our last chapter and it is discussed more fully in Rothman, Lichter, and Lichter (forthcoming).

12. Of these films, our random sample turned up *Hombre* and *Butch Cassidy and the Sundance Kid* for coding.

13. "Universal fell to MCA in 1962; Paramount to Gulf and Western in 1966; United Artists to the Transamerica Corp. in 1967 and Warner Bros./Seven Arts to Stephen Ross' Kinney National Service in 1969" (Kilday, 1989:60).

14. Prindle (1993) ascribes more power to the contemporary studios and to television networks and rather less to independents than we would (Chapters 2 and 3). There is no question but that both of these do exert pressure on filmmakers to produce for mass markets rather than to "indulge" artistic integrity or to produce tendentious motion pictures that concentrate on social and cultural issues. However, Prindle fails to understand the symbiotic relation that exists between the studios and the independent filmmakers, which,

within broad limits, allows creative content to be determined by the filmmakers. The same holds for those directly employed by the studios.

15. There is a tremendous amount of literature like this, particularly in books and essays in the field of film theory. See, for example, the Special Forum edited by Carol J. Clover and Michael Rogin (1990:1–123),particularly the essays by Sobchack (24–49), James (78–98), and Rogin (99–123). All three essays are, in one way or another, polemically hostile to what they consider to be the reactionary filmmaking of America in the 1980s. They also connect this filmmaking to Reagan's politics.

3

The New Hollywood Elite: A Profile

The debate over how popular media interact with politics and society is not a new one and takes place in every venue from scholarly publications to talk shows. One tendentious set of arguments has to do with whether television and movies only mirror the society that they depict or play more of a role in shaping the attitudes of audiences. Critics, scholars, and media people have staked out a variety of positions on this question, although most parties agree that visual media, in particular, do play some role in affecting the attitudes and behavior of their audiences.[1]

Those who grant greater force to the movies and television in shaping attitudes divide into a number of groups. At one extreme are those who explore all social questions through the analysis of representations. The most systematic of these thinkers are the film theorists, whose work we examine in Appendix A. For many of them, social reality can only be studied insofar as it is already represented; therefore, the interrogation of movie images is a version of politically engaged sociological analysis, albeit a method based entirely on analyzing the semiotic codes of fictive representation. In other words, to study the movies is by definition to study what they represent. To study movies that represent the American military is to study the American military. We find this semiotic analysis to be an impoverished social science, insofar as it cannot integrate empiricism and fact into analysis.

Other scholars with a more traditional sociological bent, descending largely from Marshall McLuhan, focus on the idea that it is the nature of the medium itself that has played the most substantial role in the impact of visual media on American society. Usually emphasizing television, they describe social changes that they think have already resulted because of the shift from a print to a video culture. Such arguments have less to do with content than with how communications technology determines the way a medium operates in society (usually in a detrimental way, most argue).

Perhaps the best-known theorist in this group is Neil Postman. His thesis is that American television, by its very nature, is organized to transform everything

it touches—from education, to religion, to politics—into homogenized entertainment, with dire consequences.[2] In *Amusing Ourselves To Death*, Postman argues that:

> Twenty years ago, the question, Does television shape culture or merely reflect it?
> held considerable interest for many scholars and social critics. The question has
> largely disappeared as television has gradually *become* our culture. This means,
> among other things, that we rarely talk about television, only about what is *on* tele-
> vision—that is about its content. (Postman, 1985:79; emphasis in original)

Postman believes that the medium is the message and the message is always entertainment. His book is one of the most convincing discussions of the social implications of this development yet to appear.

Despite the force of his argument, however, we think that the particulars of entertainment still matter. This is not because television has become our culture, as
Postman argues—that would render the distinction between television and culture meaningless and assign to the medium even more power than it really enjoys. Rather the stories that television and the movies tell us embody what many
people erroneously believe our culture is. There is still a difference between representation and reality and we can study representations separately from their
subjects, the better to understand the relation between society and media. Indeed,
if Postman is right, we have an obligation to do so, to insist that electronic visual
media representations constitute only one part of the complex society that creates them. Those who believe that the attitudes of the people who make movies
(and television) find expression in content, and that these attitudes (whether conservative, liberal, radical, or other) still have a cumulative long-range impact on
the audience, shaping political and social change, thus constitute a third group of
scholars, and they have not been quite so silent as Postman argues.[3]

Our premise is that the ideology of elite leadership groups has a powerful impact on society, particularly if those elite groups draw their status from control
over what images and information are disseminated through the culture. In this
sense, our argument is more about broad social change in America than it is
about the movies and other media in and of themselves. We are interested in the
movies because of what they can tell us about how one elite group—a particularly alienated one, as it turns out—perceives American society and therefore describes it, a description that may have an impact on the public whether or not
those doing describing are consciously seeking to lead society or change it.

In other words, we think that the messages movies convey are of social significance. They tell us how the members of an elite group see both their subjects *and*
themselves, and provide evidence about their relation to other elite groups. Note
that this project is quite different from objective description of the society that
the movies represent. Our method draws on empirical claims, not objectivist
ones—we measure and contrast attitudes and perceptions, not necessarily the
facts to which they apply (although we inevitably discuss those facts as well). For

example, when we discuss movie representations of the military, we are less concerned with how the military has changed—a related, but separate subject—than with how perceptions about it have changed, particularly among the Hollywood elite when compared with other elite groups and with the society at large. These attitudes are themselves facts that constitute one basis for policy and politics—and political conflict—in the larger society, especially if they are advanced by an elite group within the society. On the one hand, this ramifies Postman's point that media representations have more and more become the stuff of social order; on the other, it shows how these representations are themselves always part of a more complex social matrix in which their meanings are interpreted and contested. We are most interested in that matrix.

It is important to emphasize that we are not searching for systematic "bias" in media representations. "Bias" is not a useful term in this discussion. It carries the connotation of intentional distortion of an objective truth, and we do not think that this is what is occurring when the Hollywood elite presents a different world view than other, more traditional elites, a world view that resonates with the views of other new strategic elites (such as journalists) and is also traceable in its films. Rather, we think that the social and political attitudes of various groups in the society differ because of deeply held beliefs that have a number of sources. In particular, various elite groups have come to epitomize different ideological orientations within American society. It is the differences among these orientations that form some of our most volatile political fault lines and may well describe the curve of future conflicts in the society.

Our aim is neither to praise nor to censure this development that we think has the force of fact. Our more modest goal is to observe what has come to fill the creative space opened up by the decline of the studios and describe it as an aspect of broad social change in America. The purpose of this chapter, in particular, is to examine closely some of the social and political attitudes of the new Hollywood elite. These attitudes constitute an ideology resonant with those of other new leadership groups in the society and they contrast sharply with the attitudes of older, more traditional leadership groups, such as business leaders. The attitudes held by Hollywood's elite resemble those of various other new or newly powerful elites such as journalists and those who create television entertainment. However, we do more than simply make observations. Because we are persuaded that there is a relationship between culture and personality (Rothman and Lichter, 1984a; Rothman, 1992; Rothman, Lichter, and Lichter, 1984b), we empirically test our hypotheses about that relationship.

Accordingly, the first part of the chapter, which looks closely at the background and attitudes of the new Hollywood elite and how the members of that elite see these attitudes as manifest in their work, focuses on the statements of a number of well-known artists. The second part of the chapter discusses our statistical study of attitudes among the Hollywood elite, explaining our methods and our results. The third portion of the study discusses our research results regarding key personality variables. In this discussion we compare the motion picture elite with other elites sampled as part of a major study of social change in the United States. For reasons of economy of presentation, we sometimes stress a comparison between motion picture leaders and a sample of leading businesspeople, a traditional and fairly conservative group, though not as conservative as one might imagine. (A discussion of our sample of various leadership groups will be found in Appendix B.) We conclude by drawing some conclusions from the data for our arguments.

Where our work differs from that of our scholarly predecessors is that we have tried to substantiate our arguments with empirical studies of both expressed social and political attitudes of those who make the movies and, in subsequent chapters, with a content analysis of those films. It is important to remember that these studies provide only data, not arguments—nevertheless, if used carefully, they are powerful tools.

Creative Control and the New Hollywood Elite

Among critics who seek to draw connections between Hollywood filmmakers and the movies they make, a number have argued that after a brief flirtation with avant-garde filmmaking in the 1960s, Hollywood began again to uphold mainstream American culture in its movies—a culture that many of these critics find exploitive and immoral. Conservative critics, however, have argued that Hollywood now represents a new cultural elite, possessed of liberal social and political views at odds with those of the public it entertains. The substance of the debate usually centers on the presentation of specific issues—from religious beliefs, race relations, sex, and violence, to AIDS, the environment, science, and patriotism. What is true is that whatever their attitudes, moviemakers are freer to express them—and generally more interested in doing so, both in and out of movies—than they were in the heyday of the studios.

In the studio era, Hollywood stars and moviemakers generally took little interest in politics: "The only 'ism' in which Hollywood believed, Dorothy Parker remarked, was plagiarism" (quoted in Rosten, 1941:133).[4] As Leo Rosten wrote about Hollywood in the 1930s, the industry's short attention span governed its politics:

> It was foolhardy to worry about genuine or dangerous revolutionists in Hollywood. The inhabitants of the movie colony are scarcely fit to accept the discipline and deprivations of a fanatical cause. The moviemakers cannot remain consistent for long, personally or politically; they need quick and dramatic rewards . . . actors become as bored with a political role as with a stage role if the rehearsals are prolonged and the big show is postponed.(Rosten, 1941:158)

Among the lower echelons of Hollywood employees—actors, writers, directors, and producers—those whose politics were liberal generally kept their ideas to themselves. The moguls didn't necessarily care what their labor pool privately believed, but as one screenwriter observed, "'When you took a public position they felt their investment was being endangered'" (quoted in Brownstein, 1990:52).[5] In short, the studio era was a time when a handful of production executives vied for their share of the entire industry's wealth and prestige, keeping a tight reign on their talented labor pool and the movies they generated. The system was organized well enough that director Frank Capra complained in 1939 that "there are only half a dozen directors in Hollywood who are allowed to shoot as they please and who have any supervision over their editing" (Rosten, 1941:302).

As the studios declined, the new business-minded executives ceded power to the entrepreneurial artists, since the executives themselves didn't know enough about movies to do otherwise. This shift began gradually but gathered momentum in the late 1960s, when the film industry, still suffering from the decline in theater attendance that began with the advent of television in the 1950s, continued its search for fresh material and talent to lure the younger audiences to the theaters. Newly discovered writers, directors, and producers, who borrowed from the New Wave in Europe and created new variations of the old genres, ushered in an era in which the moviemakers themselves used the Hollywood establishment to their advantage. Even though the system of mass-produced Hollywood films all but disappeared, in other respects the studios remained the base upon which contemporary artists drew for financing, for employment, and ultimately for power and prestige. The new generation of moviemakers still needed Hollywood, but Hollywood also was forced to cater to filmmakers. For as censorship pressures diminished and desperate studios began to encourage innovative and experimental filmmaking, the young artists making their debuts in the late 1960s and 1970s saved Hollywood from financial ruin. These moviemakers—members of a new elite and the heirs to a tremendous information and entertainment industry—suddenly were able to purvey their own vision of American society to a shrinking but more affluent young-adult and adolescent audience.[6]

In *The Power and the Glitter*, Ronald Brownstein points out an important institutional evolution that helped synchronize the ideas of moviemakers and executives, making it much easier for Hollywood artists to have their way in movie production:

> In the early 1970s, after the remarkable success of *Easy Rider*, the graying men running the studios rushed to install in corner offices young executives they expected to fashion more hits out of the alienation of their peers. Those "baby moguls" had since moved up the ladder in Hollywood, losing their own alienation, acquiring in its place influence and enormous wealth, enough to make some of them wonder if they had become the people they used to ridicule. Anxiety that strong could produce action. "There is a whole generation of people who were active in the '60s, have a political consciousness, have achieved a point in life where they are successful, where they don't have to spend all of their time worrying about their careers," said producer Paula Weinstein, one of the HWPC's founders, "and they are really ready now to put their money down." (Brownstein, 1990:305)

This provides a partial explanation for the predominantly liberal slant of movies throughout the 1970s and 1980s. Whereas Hollywood's creative elite had previously been controlled by a substantially more conservative executive hierarchy, the New Hollywood became a more homogeneous mixture of liberal executives and artists. Generational and social change, combined with the changing markets created by the advent of television and the baby boom, resulted in the loss of Hollywood's more conservative institutional check upon movie content and empowered two different tiers of the movie industry that became closely aligned in their often critical views of American society.

On the surface, it may appear that Hollywood moviemaking became a considerably more independent and accessible industry—open to a multitude of artistic visions. In reality, power and creative control have shifted into the hands of a larger, but still insular group of individuals who have inherited access to the money undergirding movies, along with corporate influence and creative control from the old regime. This expanded oligarchy now consists of talent agents, a new generation of studio executives, and a relatively small number of directors. Most of the best-known directors in this group, those who most epitomized the shift, are by now middle-aged or older—Allen, Altman, Coppola, Kubrick, Russell, Brooks. Others, such as Lucas, Spielberg, Scorsese, and Stone, are younger, having risen to prominence on the strength of box office hits of the 1970s and 1980s.

Just as the moguls' Americanism inevitably found its way into the movies of the studio era, so too do the myths of a new generation of artists—who are now often entrepreneurs in their own right in Hollywood. The critical difference is that the ideas flow more directly from the artist to the screen and tend to offer quite critical and alternative visions of American society. As Mark Rosenberg stated while at Warner Brothers in 1979: "We all came out of the sixties . . . so we share some of the same sensibilities" (Watters, 1979:34). The momentous changes in the structure of the Hollywood industry have shifted the locus of power in Hollywood and the new artistic elite has subsequently left its own mark on movies of the past twenty-five years. The bottom line is still tickets, and in fact, record-breaking box office returns were the hallmark of the cinema of the 1970s and 1980s. Nevertheless, more than ever before, Hollywood artists in this period became free to decide what kinds of social and political messages their films would bring to audiences, even as they continued to entertain them.

The following statement by George Lucas still sums up the current balance of power in the movie industry, even though it was made in the 1970s:

> We are the pigs. . . . We are the ones who sniff out the truffles. You can put us on a leash, keep us under control. But we are the guys who dig out the gold. The man in the executive tower cannot do that. The studios are corporations now, and the men who run them are bureaucrats. They know as much about making movies as a banker does. They know about making deals like a real estate agent. They obey corporate law; each man asks himself how any decision will affect his job. They go to parties and they hire people who know people. But the power lies with us—the ones who actually know how to make movies. (Pye and Myles, 1979:9)

These new entrepreneurs in Hollywood sometimes refer to themselves as mini-moguls. They are extremely powerful in terms of their ability to reach a mass audience and to make huge sums of money, although they operate on a much smaller scale than any of the studio moguls ever did. The question is what this newly structured elite has made of its new power within an older institution.

Self and Society

The pervasive changes in popular movies over the past several decades were unquestionably linked to the social upheavals of the 1960s, which were in turn brought on by growing opposition to the Vietnam war; the civil rights movement; the loosening of strictures on divorce, promiscuity, and recreational drug use; and later Watergate and the women's movement. As we have pointed out, these historical changes cast the old Hollywood story formulas into doubt for both the new filmmakers and much of the changing audience. In the late 1960s and early 1970s, the young middle-class audiences were better educated and more liberal, unmoved by, if not outrightly contemptuous of, the familiar genres of the 1940s and 1950s. They were much more receptive to irreverent content and genre parody, which satirized older films and aspects of traditional society, as well.

The new moviemakers met with success precisely because they were members of this 1960s generation, tapping into the marketplace of popular culture at a critical period in Hollywood's history. That is not the whole story, however, for the Hollywood elite does not simply mirror these attitudes and developments in the larger society. It is closer to the cutting edge, despite the fact that it is part of big business. The elite was and remains disproportionately anti-Establishment in its social and political views and, as our survey data indicate, remains so even as a large segment of the American public continues to be ambivalent, or opposed, to the new social paradigms, however willing they may be to be entertained by them. Although the new Hollywood elite caters to its audience, it also, by its own admission, seeks to lead it and holds liberal views in disproportionate numbers. Consequently, movies throughout the Reagan era seldom abandoned the quite liberal and cosmopolitan views of Hollywood artists. A few movies that stirred controversy for catering to right-wing sentiments—such as Sylvester Stallone's Rambo films—provoked considerable criticism, both in Hollywood and among the predominantly liberal-left community of film critics. At a substantive level, however, most of these films contain ideas that were seldom seen before the changing of the guard in the movie business. Our discussion of *Rambo II*, in the chapter on the military, provides an insight into this change. Consider, for example, the irony that although a vast majority of Americans still say that they believe in God, the number of sympathetic leading characters in recent Hollywood movies who overtly express such beliefs is small. Also in short supply are traditional religious themes. [7]

When we look at what recent filmmakers have said about their craft and about society, we find overwhelming support for our argument about a sense of elite leadership among them, in spite of some critics' insistence that artists are heavily constrained by cultural conventions as they work themselves out in the market. Consider the explicit recognition of the director's contribution in the following two statements, the first by Francis Ford Coppola, the second by Robert Altman:

> Making a film isn't just stringing all that obligatory stuff together; it's trying to take a little of your own way of seeing the world and putting it out so they can see that too. (Kearney, 1988:23)
>
> Artists are telling someone else to look at their viewpoint . . . That's arrogant. At an audition I think, "Am I manipulating these people? Am I using them?" You question your motives. But you can't get away from your need to show things the way they look to you. (Kroll, 1981:72)

What is interesting about this is not the notion that individual artists have particular views, but rather that directors believe that their own attitudes are such an important part of the creative process of moviemaking. These comments would have been virtually inconceivable as recently as the 1950s.

In discussing Robert Aldrich's decision to direct *The Dirty Dozen* (1967), biographers Arnold and Miller write:

> Aldrich was attracted both to the action-adventure elements inherent in the plot— he regarded himself as the best action-picture director in the business—and to its central irony: the "heroes" of this tale were unreconstructed criminals— murderers, rapists, psychopaths; the "villains" were those in authority—not only the German generals the Dozen are sent to destroy, but also, by strong implication, the Allied commanders who are willing to commit the Dozen to certain death in an almost aristocratic game of war. It was precisely the kind of subversive twist Aldrich delighted in. (Arnold and Miller, 1986:123)

Aldrich's interest in emphasizing the anti-authority aspect of the story reflects the growing opposition to the Vietnam War at the time the film was made. Despite its World War II setting, the film actually marks the beginning of a new treatment of the military genre, emphasizing the alienation of the soldier from his superiors and a profound ambivalence toward military authority. Again, Aldrich's attraction to the story reflects his own political beliefs as much as the desire to turn a profit.

Robert Altman successfully incorporated these same types of images in his best-known box office hit, *M*A*S*H* (1970), a classic anti-Establishment, anti-authority film of the American New Wave period. Altman was one of the directors who helped turn Hollywood toward the youth market in the 1960s and 1970s and his personal political beliefs remain quite cynical. He has said that "in order to attain power, every nation, group, large culture or what-have-you has to have a slave class. And the slave class of America is the middle-class" (*Sight and Sound*, 1981:185). Clearly, this is a view of American society not shared by the vast majority of its members. In a 1982 interview, he complained that Hollywood was too commercial for his tastes, that studios "are simply not interested in the creative aspect of a movie. They have certain themes, certain characters they want to deal with because they sell" (Wohlfert, 1982:165). Although this criticism of the influence of the bottom line in Hollywood is probably accurate, the types of movies that the industry endorses are nevertheless different than those prior to the mid-1960s, as Altman's own more successful films demonstrate.

Martin Scorsese, whose films include *Raging Bull* (1980), *The Color of Money* (1986), and *The Last Temptation of Christ* (1989), is another influential and controversial moviemaker who came to prominence in the 1970s. In a *Playboy* interview with Scorsese, the interviewer comments that "the women in your other films are also allowed to be strong. *Taxi Driver*, for instance. Do you agree?" Scorsese responds:

> Oh, totally. Others have missed it, though I've really tried to make it clear. Even in *Alice Doesn't Live Here Anymore*, I was trying to do something radical in terms of women. But ultimately, we all came to the conclusion that it was OK if she wanted to live with somebody. I felt bad about it and thought maybe it wasn't a radical enough statement for that time of feminism.
>
> But I like women. A lot of the people who've worked with me for years are women. . . . I was the first instructor at New York University to allow women to direct. They didn't have any women directors. (*Playboy*, 1991:70)

Scorsese's intention of conveying certain messages in his films, in this case women's independence, is characteristic of the modern film director. Hollywood artists now frequently express this kind of personal concern about their films' messages, and to the extent that the market will bear it, they talk again and again about a desire to challenge traditional norms and values.

Significantly, most of this critique avoids economics. As entrepreneurs themselves, and consistently with their own beliefs, moviemakers tend not to criticize the basic tenets of capitalism, such as free enterprise or differential pay scales. Francis Coppola, for example, may be critical of the military in *Apocalypse Now* or of corruption in American society as depicted in the Godfather movies, but he appears to be supportive of capitalism and the idea of a traditional family. At the same time, his ideas for the future are radical and visionary:

> My dream is that the artist class—people who have proven through their work that they are humanists and wish to push for what Aldous Huxley called the desirable human potentialities of intelligence, creativity and friendliness—will seize the instrument of technology and try to take humanity into a period of history in which we can reach for a utopia. Of course, it is possible for the technology to be misused—we could end up with a Big Brother—but we could also have a balanced society, with an artist class leading the culture toward something approximating a happy family or tribe. (*U.S. News and World Report*, 1982:68)

Presumably, artists of Coppola's stature, who have significant financial control over what movies they will make, seek to embody such ideas in their work.

The further one looks, the more it seems that many major mainstream directors now believe that their movies embody a much-needed critique of modern America. Richard Lester, creator of *Superman II* and *Superman III*, "gently satirizes the Americana that was seen so lovingly in *Superman: The Movie*." Appropriately for this anti-Establishment director, an important theme in the movies is that "in a push-button society, the individual—even the superman— becomes increasingly insignificant" (Sinyard, 1985:160–161). Woody Allen echoes a similar theme. In 1987, Nancy Pogel described him as:

> disheartened at least as much as the early little man humorists were by civilization's "junk," by depersonalization and inauthenticity in modern life. "There's such a widespread religious disappointment," he has said, "a general realization about the emptiness of everything that's very hard for the society to bear."
>
> At the same time, he is more pragmatic than radical in his liberalism. Allen worked for George McGovern's 1972 campaign, although he preferred the more radical platform of Benjamin Spock. He also supported Eugene McCarthy and John Lindsay— all liberal, progressive candidates—for public office. He was disappointed with Ronald Reagan's election in 1980, because he felt that Reagan's domestic programs denied the poor and because he disliked Reagan's stance on nuclear weapons and the environment. (Pogel, 1987:23–24)

Allen's attitude toward creative freedom in filmmaking is unequivocal. "I don't think there has to be friction at all. I think it's a debilitating factor. I think we'd have better films if directors controlled them completely" (Shales, 1987:93).

Other filmmakers are more aggressive politically. Oliver Stone, director of such films as *Platoon* (1986), *Wall Street* (1987), *Born on the Fourth of July* (1990), and *JFK* (1992), describes himself as a left-wing moviemaker who soured on the American political system after he returned from Vietnam, particularly after Watergate. Stone comments:

> I was emotionally disgusted. I thought the cops were pigs. I was with Jimmy Morrison on that one. I was into more radical violence. When they took over NYU, and all the kids trashed the place, when Cambodia was invaded, I thought they were nuts. I said, if you want to protest, let's get a sniper scope and do Nixon. . . . Watergate was a key turning point. . . . I started to learn. Politically, I was relatively uneducated because I had hewed to my father's line [described as right-wing]. Watergate really sort of hammered the point home that the government was a lie. The government lied to us about Ho Chi Minh and it lied to us about the Vietnam War. I wrote *Platoon* then—in '76. (McGilligan, 1987:17–18)

Yet, despite the criticisms directed against him for *JFK*, Stone is hardly an outcast—indeed, his work has made him rich. We should emphasize that we think that there is no reason Stone's attitudes, embodied in well-made films, should not have found a large enough public to succeed. What is interesting is the relatively small number of other directors and movies that articulate different views. In general, American mainstream cinema is by no means radical—especially not as radical as Stone—but neither does it portray society in the sympathetic way that it once did. This is not exactly news and the point is not to deplore or praise this change as a social development, but instead, to try to measure it with some reliability and discover its meaning in the larger social context.

Actor-director Robert Redford has for many years been at the fore of the environmental movement. In the 1970s, Redford worked as a lobbyist "mostly with three organizations—the N.R.D.C. [Natural Resources Defense Council], the Environmental Defense Fund, and an energy task force of the Scientists' Institute for Public Information" (Singer, 1975:39). More recently his political approach has become more direct. Redford remarks, "The environment is no longer a dirty word. . . . Everybody is recognizing the fact that we have to start working together. So it is now a time of action" (Brownstein, 1990:271). Although environmental issues have been less prominent in movies of the 1970s and 1980s, Redford's comments reflect an activist outlook shared by much of Hollywood's elite and it is very likely that environmental issues will be more prominent in future films. Given Hollywood's mistrust of various established institutions, it is also very likely that these traditional institutions in the society—which are led by older and more traditional elite groups—will be represented as the perpetrators of environmental degradation, standing in the way of progress.

There are other perspectives, of course. Among the youngest of the established Hollywood elite are George Lucas and Steven Spielberg, widely known for their blockbuster movies of the late 1970s and 1980s. In spite of his obvious contempt for the Hollywood establishment, Lucas is not the most radical of the new American filmmakers by any means. Although he feels he was influenced by the events of the 1960s, Lucas has tried to move beyond nostalgia, admitting even in the early 1970s that he believes a bit in "that hokey stuff about being a good neighbor, and the American spirit" (Farber, 1974:8). Some commentators have pointed out that into the 1980s, his *Star Wars* movies continued to reflect this duality of views—at once "permeated by counter-cultural values" and "regressive values as well" (Miller, 1990:1150), in the way they represent the Empire and those who fight against it.

In a similar vein, Spielberg has said that he is "liberal about a lot of things but . . . bullish about America and the strength we have to maintain in a world that is growing stronger and stronger." Yet his views on a wide array of cultural issues are staunchly liberal. In an interview in 1985, he expressed a sensitivity to racial minorities that is characteristic of the modern moviemaker. "I think before *The Color Purple* comes out, my greatest minority story is *E.T.* That is a minority story that stands for every minority in this country. . . . E.T. wasn't like everyone else, he was picked apart and made very sick and almost died. I always felt *E.T.* was a minority story" (Breskin, 1985:70). Prompted to comment on the "spiritual" side of his movies, Spielberg's response was a mixture of mysticism and Carl Sagan:

> I've always believed there is a center to the universe, and everything sort of blasts off from the center in all directions. I've never felt that man was alone in the universe or that any of us were alone within ourselves. I believe that everyone has helpers. We are all tied together by the belief that there is something greater than us . . . I go outside and look up at the stars and I know we are not alone. It's almost mathematically impossible. And that's why I was always interested in films and ideas about alien life forms, life off the planet. (Breskin, 1985:77)

In general, his movies reflect an outlook that derives from his experience of social and political change in the 1960s and 1970s, fused with an underlying belief in America. It is this combination that seems to make his and Lucas's films successful at the box office.

The politics of John Milius, whose films include *Red Dawn* (1984) and *Conan the Barbarian* (1981), are even more atypical in Hollywood, despite these films' success at the box office. Asked in an interview: "What's your reply to the critics that branded *Dirty Harry* a 'fascist' movie?" Milius responded:

> They're coming from a very Eastern, liberal Establishment point of view. That sort of thing upsets them. They call it "fascist" the same way people in the Fifties called something "communist." It's an hysteria. Anything that is really indigenous to the West Coast, slightly out of control with a lot of energy, is dangerous to critics unless they can get a handle on it. Regardless of what movies I make, I think I will always be disliked by the Eastern critical Establishment, because the type of things I do are indigenously Western. (Gallagher, 1989:173–174)

Although Milius—and his movies—do not articulate progressive ideas in the same way that other directors we have discussed do, his views could hardly be characterized as conservative, in a broader sense. In fact, as we will see in subsequent chapters, his representations often partake of developments similar to those that characterize films that have apparently a very different message. To make the point anecdotally, we point out that Dirty Harry is not exactly a "good" cop of the old school; in fact, to ensure that justice is done, he has to act as a renegade, defying authority, which is represented as corrupt and inept.

The last three minimoguls we have discussed are comparatively moderate, branded as more than a bit conservative in Hollywood in their views of American society. If anything, their divergent attitudes demonstrate that Hollywood's elite is not necessarily bound by market constraints in choosing a liberal or conservative political perspective in filmmaking or that all filmmakers share the same views. What is interesting is that these filmmakers are generally considered to be the conservatives within the industry. As our survey indicates, the majority of today's movie moguls are quite liberal and cosmopolitan, apt to criticize traditional institutions such as religion, the police, the military, and the government, and they endorse a new sexual morality, all of which remains at odds with the way a majority of the public perceives the same issues.

Comparable attitudes are found among the television elite who, like their movie counterparts with whom they overlap, tend to judge what the public will like on the basis of what they like. They appear to be quite aware that provided they are subtle about it, liberal sermons will not necessarily drive away their audiences.

As cop show specialist Quinn Martin notes: "you must have a point of view, first entertain, then make them think underneath. . . . It doesn't have to be heavy, but I do think you can have a little substance in what you're doing as long as you entertain them along the way." (Quoted in Newcomb and Alley, 1983:72.)[8]

Barney Rosenzweig, producer of the 1960s show "Daniel Boone," is described by Todd Gitlin, who interviewed him:

> He instructed writers to portray the Revolutionary War by "making it Vietnam with the colonials as the Vietcong and the English as the Americans. Boone defended civil disobedience. Rosenzweig transposed the black studies controversy then raging across American campuses, into a story about Red Indian studies in which Boone's son supports a Cherokee chief's son living in Boonsboro who wants to learn about Indian culture." (Gitlin, 1983:269)

Liberal perspectives have become more pronounced on television and the movies in the 1990s and are increasingly acknowledged. At least some critics and directors consider this a shift from the conservative 1980s. However, as our content analysis demonstrates, 1980s films did not move to the right. Indeed, they more or less continued earlier trends (Dowd, 1993; Faludi, 1991; Ressner, 1988; Sharkey, 1989).[9]

The Evidence of Systematic Surveys

It seems, from what the moviemakers say, that they, like most other people, view the world through a particular set of lenses and that their ideology affects the manner in which they describe the world in films, subject to market limitations. Our statistical study supports this hypothesis. The motion picture elite, like the other cultural elites we studied (the television entertainment elite and the journalistic elite), is more liberal than traditional elites, such as those in business and the military, on economic issues. The most decisive split, however, is on cultural issues. Comparable data available from the General Social Survey (GSS), conducted periodically by the National Opinion Research Center (NORC) at the University of Chicago, suggest that Hollywood is also considerably more liberal than the American public, although the public and (we suspect) various elite groups are moving in the direction cultural elites have pioneered. At the time of our studies, movie and other new strategic elite groups also differed from more traditional elites such as business respondents in background characteristics other than race and gender. (Although this is changing, most elite groups we studied in the early 1980s were overwhelmingly white and male.)(See Table 3.1.)

TABLE 3.1 Backgrounds of Elite Groups (percent in each category)

Factors	Bureaucrats	Business	Congres. Aides	Judges	Labor Unions	Lawyers	News Media	Military	Movies	Pub. Intr.	Religious	TV-Hollywood
White	93.5	96.8	94.0	89.5	93.7	99.3	92.9	95.4	98.9	96.8	86.5	99.0
Male	93.0	93.2	72.4	94.7	96.8	98.6	79.0	99.3	98.9	69.4	84.8	92.3
From large cities	31.5	44.1	19.4	52.6	55.8	48.6	35.3	20.4	70.3	36.3	36.5	53.8
College graduate	97.5	86.4	94.8	99.1	38.9	100.0	93.3	100.0	62.6	100.0	97.8	75.0
Father service worker	5.5	23.5	3.7	1.8	9.9	6.0	10.1	6.6	8.3	1.3	5.7	1.0
No religion	6.5	12.3	24.6	14.0	4.2	26.4	50.0	7.9	54.9	41.4	0.6	39.4
Attends services at least once a month	36.6	53.4	34.4	37.2	49.4	30.4	14.4	67.2	5.5	16.7	97.7	6.7
Never attends services	30.1	12.0	20.9	11.5	10.5	23.6	48.7	7.9	62.6	37.2	0.0	44.2
Politically liberal	55.5	12.7	51.5	53.5	72.6	46.6	53.4	9.2	65.9	87.3	57.3	74.0

For example, the moviemakers are much more likely to have been raised in an urban environment than are business or military leaders. Seventy percent of the movie elite grew up in large cities compared to only 44 percent of the business elite and 20 percent of the military elite.

Filmmakers are also less likely to come from blue-collar backgrounds than are businesspeople, although about the same proportion of moviemakers come from such a background as do military leaders or lawyers. Thus 8.3 percent of the moviemakers identify their fathers as having been service workers as compared to almost 24 percent of businesspeople.

Moviemakers are, however, less likely to have graduated from college than most other leadership groups, traditional or newly powerful. Thus, only 63 percent of the moviemakers have obtained a BA as compared to 86 percent of businesspeople and 100 percent of the military elite.

Only 12 percent of businesspeople asked about their religious affiliation listed none, compared to 8 percent of the military, 55 percent of the movie elite, half the journalists, and 41 percent of public interest group leaders. The General Social Survey found that between 1972 and 1982, only 7 percent of the general public did not identify with some religion. By 1990, the number expressing no religious affiliation had risen but only to 8 percent. It rose to 9 percent by 1993. (See Table 3.9 for General Social Survey information on the general public.) In short, the public continues to identify with religion in far greater numbers than does the movie elite and traditional elites reflect public preferences much more closely than the newer strategic elites.

Even those movie industry leaders who do express a religious preference rarely grant organized religion an important role in their lives. Only 5.5 percent of the moviemakers report attending church as much as once a month compared to over 53 percent of businesspeople, 67 percent of military personnel, and 30 percent of lawyers. The figure for the general public during the 1980s was just over 50 percent. Only 12 percent of the general public said that they never attended church in the 1980s (rising to 16.5 percent by 1993) as compared to more than six out of ten of the motion picture elite, which is the least observant of all the leadership groups we studied.[10]

Only 13 percent of business leaders consider themselves politically liberal compared to 66 percent of the moviemakers. The percentage for military leaders is 9 and for corporate lawyers 47. From 1972 to 1982, only 27 percent of the American public identified themselves as liberal, whereas 30 percent regarded themselves as slightly conservative, conservative, or extremely conservative. In 1990, 26 percent of survey respondents remained liberal, whereas somewhat larger numbers of individuals (35 percent) considered themselves politically conservative. The figures were roughly the same in 1993. The movie elite is also overwhelmingly Democratic. In 1980, they gave only 29 percent of their vote to Ronald Reagan, 11 percent more than voted for Nixon (18 percent) when he overwhelmed McGovern in 1972.

Self-estimates of liberalism and even voting can conceal as much as they reveal. We asked all of our groups seventeen political questions and a smaller number of them additional questions (see Table 3.2). We subjected responses to a statistical technique called factor analysis that clusters question responses that correlate highly with each other. We actually found four such clusters that are discussed in other studies (Nagai, Lerner, and Rothman, 1994; Lerner, Nagai, and Rothman, 1995) and that tie in with a general interpretation of recent changes in American society discussed in the last chapter of this book.[11]

Analyzing ideology as consisting of several independent clusters of attitudes (dimensions) allows us to accommodate the possibility that an individual can hold liberal opinions on some issues and conservative opinions on others. It also enables us to summarize the results of several questions simultaneously.

The dimensions are ideal-type abstractions meant to represent and partially explicate the underlying link between otherwise disparate issue positions. The questions loading on each dimension are listed in Appendix B. (We only discuss three dimensions in this book; for the fourth dimension, regime threat, see Lerner, Nagai, and Rothman, 1996.)

The first dimension places "rugged" laissez-faire individualism, derived from America's Calvinist heritage, on one end and collectivist liberalism on the other. Max Weber (1930, 1947 trans.), Louis Hartz (1955), and Seymour Martin Lipset (1967) all have observed that America's uniqueness lay in its religious-cultural ethos. The Protestant ethic gave rise to a previously unknown degree of personal autonomy and a remarkable discipline of the passions that enabled the individual to achieve the goals of this world. It also fostered the psychological autonomy and self-restraint that led to the development of a strong but disciplined sense of

TABLE 3.2   Political Liberalism Factor Analyses—Mean Score

Group	Collectivist Liberalism	Expressive Individualism	System Alienation
Bureaucrats	99.49	99.98	97.68
Business	92.60	97.49	97.94
Congressional aides	98.51	99.69	97.94
Judges	101.75	97.50	94.78
Labor unions	105.22	96.09	104.88
Lawyers	98.87	103.45	92.99
News media	101.21	105.77	101.06
Military	93.85	92.38	95.47
Movies	100.67	106.14	106.45
Public interest	108.85	106.21	107.45
Religious	103.92	90.86	102.72
TV-Hollywood	100.16	106.58	104.04

self, thereby providing the psychological foundation of modern American liberalism and capitalism.

Persons adhering to these traditional values favor hard work, diligence, self-discipline, frugality, willpower, and rational foresight over the environment as the correct way to relate to the world. They stress sobriety over playfulness, restraint over expression, and reason over emotion.

Collectivist (or welfare state) liberalism emerged from the Depression Era (see, for example, Shils, 1980), often seen as the major source of contemporary American ideology (see, for example, Verba and Orren, 1985; Feldman, 1983). This type of liberalism rests on the belief that the central government should ameliorate the economic inequalities of the capitalist system, as opposed to adhering to the traditional "rugged individualist" view that economic well-being stems from individual effort and personal achievement.[12]

Collectivist liberals support the expansion of the welfare state, favor more government-induced economic equality, support government regulation of business "in the public interest," and hold that those who are economically unsuccessful are not ultimately responsible for improving their own condition. Interestingly, although it is not usually thought of as one of its components, we found support for environmental regulation of business to be another indicator of collectivist liberalism (see, for example, Lerner, Nagai, and Rothman, 1989, 1990). From the mid-1930s until the late 1960s, liberalism and what we have called collectivist liberalism were considered to be more or less synonymous.

The second dimension pits the traditional Puritan ethic of self-restraint on the right against expressive individualism on the left. The term "expressive individualism," coined by Bellah *et al.* (1985), refers to the free expression and satisfaction of individual desires in the pursuit of the good life.

Expressive individualism has as its core the priority given to free, unfettered expression of impulses, assumed to be good in and of themselves, and is characterized by a shift in the concept of the individual from a "being" (part of a great chain of being) to a "self." Historically, it marks a shift from traditional Puritan restraint to the free expression of impulse and rejection of the traditional for the new and avant-garde.

The difference between representatives of these views can be seen by comparing the reasoning used by pro-choice activists and their pro-life counterparts. Luker (1984) finds that pro-abortion activists are believers in situation ethics, in part because they are moral relativists, secularists, and utilitarians. The right to choose has often been stated in precisely these terms: a woman, not society or her family, has a right to "control over her own body" and thus the right to decide whether or not to have an abortion.

In contrast, Luker's pro-life advocates are traditionally religious and committed to a transcendent view of human action that restricts the possibilities of human choice and emphasizes human frailty and capacity for error. Thus, they reflect the traditional Western view of human nature. In classical, Catholic, and traditional Calvinist thought, all human beings possess a common nature related to their humanity and their place in the cosmos. Their common nature ties them to, even as it separates them from, other species as part of a "great chain of being." This "natural law" view provides a strong set of moral guidelines and to flout them is to risk committing sin. (For more on the abortion issue and the related questions comprising the expressive individualism dimension, see Lerner, Nagai, and Rothman, 1990.)

The third dimension contrasts system support with system alienation, another strand of contemporary ideology that emerged during the 1960s. System alienation rests on the belief, expressed in its pure form by the New Left, that the social order of bourgeois liberal society is inherently dehumanizing and repressive and its structures of authority inherently suspect.

Feelings of system alienation are closely tied to a critique of American capitalism, although feelings of general alienation and beliefs about the welfare state are separate ideological dimensions. One can support the system, for example, and also believe in the welfare state, as did many New Deal liberals before the Vietnam War. The opposite of system alienation is simply traditional patriotism, the belief that America is a good or even great society.

We can compare the various elite groups on each of the dimensions mentioned with a summary score of all the questions that fall in each dimension. To make it easier to follow the argument, we have standardized the overall mean (average) for all groups at 100. After that, we shall discuss the results on some specific questions that will enable us to compare elite views with those of the general public as measured by the GSS.

As Table 3.2 demonstrates, the liberalism of the motion picture elite is not, *au fond*, economic. Hollywood liberals are certainly farther to the left than business and the military, with a standardized score of 100.7 as against the former's 92.6 and 93.8 respectively, yet they fall well below the public interest group's score of almost 108.8 and even the 103.9 of religious leaders (see also Table 3.2A).

The moviemakers come into their own on the expressive individualism scores (see Table 3.2B). We find all but a three-way tie among them, the TV elite, and public interest group leaders. On this issue, they part company with religious and trade union leaders, both of whom are more liberal than the moviemakers are on economic issues but much more conservative on expressive individualism issues.[13]

The movie elite almost tops the scales on our measure of alienation with a score just above 106 (see Table 3.2C). They are closely followed by labor union leaders, but their score is considerably higher than that of journalists. It seems clear that although the alienation of the trade union leaders has to do with economic issues, that of the motion picture industry has more to do with a bourgeois cultural style, an issue to which we will return at the conclusion of this book.

The movie elite's responses to economic questions are basically consistent with a liberal, not a radical political agenda. Very few agree that big corporations

TABLE 3.2A   Collectivist Liberalism Factor

Mean	Group	Business	Military	Congres. Aides	Lawyers	Bureau-crats	TV-Hollywood	Movies	News Media	Judges	Religious	Labor Unions
92.60	Business											
93.85	Military											
98.51	Congres. aides	*	*									
98.87	Lawyers	*	*									
99.49	Bureaucrats	*	*									
100.16	TV-Hollywood	*	*									
100.67	Movies	*	*									
101.21	News Media	*	*									
101.75	Judges	*	*									
103.92	Religious	*	*	*	*	*	*	*				
105.22	Labor unions	*	*	*	*	*	*	*	*	*		
108.85	Public interest	*	*	*	*	*	*	*	*	*	*	*

*Indicates a difference that is significant at $p < .05$.

TABLE 3.2B Expressive Individualism Factor

Mean	Group	Religious	Military	Labor Unions	Business	Judges	Congres. Aides	Bureaucrats	Lawyers
90.86	Religious								
92.38	Military								
96.09	Labor unions	*	*						
97.49	Business	*	*						
97.50	Judges	*	*						
99.69	Congres. aides	*	*	*					
99.98	Bureaucrats	*	*	*	*				
103.45	Lawyers	*	*	*	*	*	*		
105.77	News media	*	*	*	*	*	*	*	
106.14	Movies	*	*	*	*	*	*	*	*
106.21	Public interest	*	*	*	*	*	*	*	*
106.58	TV-Hollywood	*	*	*	*	*	*	*	*

*Indicates a difference that is significant at $p < .05$.

TABLE 3.2C   Alienation Factor

Mean	Group	Lawyers	Judges	Military	Bureaucrats	Business	Congres. Aides	News Media	Religious	TV-Hollywood
92.99	Lawyers									
94.78	Judges									
95.47	Military									
97.68	Bureaucrats	*	*	*						
97.94	Business	*	*	*						
98.87	Congres. aides	*	*	*						
101.06	News Media	*	*	*	*	*	*			
102.72	Religious	*	*	*	*	*	*			
104.04	TV-Hollywood	*	*	*	*	*	*	*		
104.88	Labor unions	*	*	*	*	*	*	*		
106.45	Movies	*	*	*	*	*	*	*	*	
107.45	Public interest	*	*	*	*	*	*	*	*	*

*Indicates a difference that is significant at $p < .05$.

should be publicly owned (16 percent compared with 6 percent of businesspeople). They are somewhat more critical of American economic organization than are business elites. Thirty-eight percent maintain that the government should guarantee jobs to everyone, compared to 29 percent of business leaders, 23 percent of military leaders, and 80 percent of public interest group leaders. Sixty-seven percent of the moviemakers believe that private enterprise is fair to workers, whereas 89 percent of the business leaders but only 30 percent of public interest group leaders think so. Moviemakers are more supportive of government regulatory practices than are business elites. Only 50 percent agree that less regulation of business would be good compared with 86 percent of business elites and roughly 18 percent of public interest leaders (see Table 3.3).

Finally, they are substantially more likely than businesspeople to believe that environmental problems are quite serious (82 percent vs. 55 percent) and that government should strive to reduce the income gap between rich and poor (60 percent versus 29 percent). This does not mean that they are complete egalitarians. Ninety-four percent believe that the more able should earn more than the less able. Indeed, a majority of every elite group we studied believes that.

Expressive individualism represents a challenge to the traditional American emphasis on self-restraint, which largely derived from a Judeo-Christian religious heritage; expressive individualism posits experience as an ultimate good in and of itself, thereby encompassing notions of sexual liberation, all-embracing moral relativism, and a general disdain for religious institutions. In this context, we find that moviemakers' attitudes toward sex and marriage are far more permissive than those of business people (see Table 3.4). As of 1984, only 28 percent of the movie elite thought that homosexuality was wrong, whereas 60 percent of the business elite thought so, as did 66 percent of federal judges, 83 percent of military leaders, and 72 percent of religious leaders.[14] The public was more conservative than business leaders on homosexuality, though less so than the military and religious leaders: from 1972 to 1982, 67 percent responded that they believed homosexual relations were wrong and in 1990 this figure had risen to 72 percent. However it dropped to 62 percent in 1993. Only 13 percent of the moviemakers believed homosexuals should be prevented from teaching in public schools, compared to 51 percent of business elite. On this question, the public also remains far more conservative than Hollywood has been until recently. From 1972 to 1982, 44 percent of the public still agreed that homosexuals should not be allowed to teach, even in a more adult environment (colleges and universities). By 1990, the number of individuals indicating this preference had dropped somewhat, but still remained relatively high, at 32 percent. However it dropped to 27 percent in 1993. It is hard to avoid the conclusion that the mass media (newspapers, television, and movies) has had some impact.

Similar patterns are evident for adultery and abortion. Only 42 percent of moviemakers believe that adultery is wrong compared to 76 percent of business elites, 62 percent of lawyers, and nine out of ten religious leaders. Yet again, the

TABLE 3.3 Social Attitudes—Percent of Respondents Who Agree with the Following Statements

	Bureaucrats	Business	Congres. Aides	Judges	Labor Union	Lawyers	News Media	Military	Movies	Publ. Intr.	Relig-ious	TV-Hollywood
Big corps. should be nationalized and run in public interest	4	6.3	17.9	6.3	22.1	.7	12.7	3.3	15.9	37.6	19	21.3
It is not govt.'s role to insure everyone a job	66	71.3	63.4	51.8	34.8	57	52.1	77	62.2	19.9	44.6	55.8
American private enterprise system is fair to workers	82	89.1	68.7	77.7	42.1	83.8	70.4	94.1	66.7	30	63.6	69.3
Less govt. reg. of business would be good for the country	61.6	86.3	60.2	67.9	34.8	71.8	62.7	88.2	50	17.9	49.2	65.1
U.S. envir. problems not as serious as people led to believe	27.6	45.2	32.1	31.2	23.2	27.4	18.2	51.9	17.8	4.4	27.1	14.4
Under a fair system, people with more ability would earn more	90.5	90	78.3	91.1	84.9	89.9	86.4	93.4	94.4	71.4	83	94.2
The govt. should reduce the income gap	52	28.6	51.8	64.8	69.5	48.3	67.3	37.5	60	94.2	76.3	65

TABLE 3.4   Social Attitudes About Moral Issues—Percent of Respondents Who Agree with the Following Statements*

	Bureau-crats	Busi-ness	Congres. Aides	Judges	Labor Unions	Lawyers	News Media	Military	Movies	Pub. Intr.	Reli-gious	TV-Hollywood
Homosexual relations are wrong	47.5	60.3	53.5	66.3	61.1	39.9	23.9	82.8	28.4	11.5	71.6	22.6
Gays should not teach	3.3	51.2	30.1	38.1	39.8	18.8	14.6	70	13.3	8.3	36.8	14.5
Extramarital sex is wrong	67.4	75.9	68.2	66.1	72.8	61.8	46.5	82.3	41.8	54.8	89.2	49
A woman has the right to decide on abortion	81	79.8	80.6	80	87.4	89.9	90.3	73.5	97.7	94.9	37.8	97.1

*Data from 1984.

public is much more conservative than Hollywood: from 1972 to 1982, 70 percent of the GSS respondents indicated that extramarital sex is always wrong and in 1990, 77 percent felt this way, as did 76 percent in 1993. Finally, 98 percent of the movie elite believe a woman has a right to decide on abortion for whatever reason, as do 90 percent of journalists. These figures can be compared to 80 percent of the business elite, 74 percent of the military, and 38 percent of religious leaders. A similar question asked by the GSS was "Should it be possible for a woman to obtain a legal abortion if the woman wants it for any reason?" The public was much more conservative in its response to this question than either the movie or business elites probably would be. From 1972 to 1982, only 37 percent of the respondents agreed and although the figure rose to 41 percent by 1990, a majority of respondents (54 percent) still objected to unrestricted abortion. The absence of religious commitment is also an important indication of the movie elite's preference for expressive individualism over more restrictive codes of conduct.[15]

Five questions load on the system alienation factor and here again the motion picture elite scores high (see Table 3.5). For example, 75 percent of the movie elite believe that the goal of U.S. foreign policy is to protect U.S. business interests as compared to only 29 percent of businesspeople, 43 percent of bureaucrats, and 29 percent of lawyers who see foreign policy in those terms. Similarly, more than 60 percent of the moviemakers believe that the very structure of our society causes alienation compared to one quarter of the lawyers, about 30 percent of businesspeople, and 27 percent of bureaucrats.

Not surprisingly, we find that the movie elites' perception of the present distribution of power in America differs markedly from what they believe it ought to be (see Table 3.6). Moviemakers believe that leadership groups rank as follows, in descending order of influence: media, business, government agencies, labor unions, the military, religion, consumer groups, intellectuals, black leaders, and feminists. Their preferred order ranks thus: intellectuals, consumer groups, media, black leaders, business, feminists, labor unions, government agencies, religion, and the military. The fact that the three most traditionally authoritative institutions—government, religion, and the military—shift to the least influential positions in the moviemakers' ideal society, indicates a significant level of alienation. Only the creators of television's prime-time entertainment programs wanted to reduce the influence of religious leaders to the extent that the moviemakers did. We shall see that these attitudes are not without impact on the moviemakers' portrayal of these institutions since the mid-1960s.

We have no way of making a direct comparison of this statistic with institutional preferences among the public; however we can construct something similar from the GSS institutional confidence questions. Because this is an incomplete and inadequate set of indicators for comparison, it should be interpreted with caution; but it does *suggest* a relatively different set of priorities than among the movie elite. From 1972 to 1982, of those institutions in which respondents indi-

TABLE 3.5 System Alienation—Percent of Respondents Who Agree with the Following Statements

	Bureau-crats	Busi-ness	Congres. Aides	Judges	Labor Unions	Lawyers	News Media	Military	Movies	Pub. Intr.	Reli-gious	TV-Hollywood
Foreign policy does protect business	43	29	39.5	29.5	67.4	28.9	50.2	24.5	75.3	73.7	55.3	72.8
Social structure causes alienation	27.4	29.5	36.8	30.6	45.3	23.0	48.7	9.9	62.9	74.9	40.3	57.7
American legal system favors the wealthy	76.3	65	70.9	40.1	80.9	55.7	87.7	68.4	87.9	91.8	77.4	75.9
U.S. institutions need overhaul	20.5	32.4	24.7	18.9	48.9	8.8	27.3	19.9	52.3	48.1	41.5	46.5
U.S. morally obliged to defend Israel	61.3	61.8	65.9	78.3	76.9	60.2	72.2	61.6	79.8	82.8	69.3	75.5
CIA overthrows some-times necessary	60	75	63.4	48.1	55.3	61.8	54.8	85.5	44.5	25.7	35.8	38.5

TABLE 3.6   Perceived Influence of Key Groups vs. Preferred Influence by Movie Elite

Key Group	Perceived Influence	Key Group	Preferred Influence
News media	5.81	Intellectuals	5.01
Business	5.63	Consumer groups	4.56
Federal government agencies	4.95	News media	3.99
Labor unions	4.49	Black leaders	3.87
Military leaders	4.04	Business	3.76
Religious leaders	3.39	Feminists	3.74
Consumer groups	3.36	Labor unions	3.27
Intellectuals	2.93	Federal government agencies	3.08
Black leaders	2.75	Religious leaders	2.68
Feminists	2.64	Military leaders	2.01

cated a "great deal" of confidence, the military, religion, and banks ranked first at 34 percent each. Twenty-five percent of respondents indicated a great deal of confidence in major companies. Twenty-one percent expressed a great deal of confidence in the press, 18 percent in the executive branch of the federal government, 17 percent in television, and 14 percent in labor. By 1990, this set of preferences had shifted somewhat; the military retained its high rate of approval at 33 percent, major companies followed at 25 percent, organized religion had slid to 23 percent, the executive branch had risen to 23 percent, banks had declined dramatically to only 18 percent, the press had fallen to 15 percent, television dropped to 14 percent, and labor remained lowest at 11 percent. For the public, the military, religion, and major companies have remained the most highly regarded institutions, but two of these same institutions are the least preferred in Hollywood.

We tapped the movie elite's views on trends in their own medium of expression. Asked whether movies should be realistic, 71 percent agreed that they should. Sixty-seven percent agreed that movies should promote social reform, supporting the anecdotal evidence we presented earlier. Eighty-one percent *disagreed* that movies were too critical of traditional values, although 66 percent agreed that there was too much violence in the movies. Finally, 76 percent disagreed that there was too much sex in the movies—a statistic that shows just how differently this group views its art from the way in which the general public, which has consistently expressed concern over the issue, sees it.

Another recent survey of Hollywood elites confirms the results of our 1982 survey. Political scientists David F. Prindle and James W. Endersby surveyed 35 of Hollywood's moviemaking elite (actors, writers, directors, producers, and executives), asking them public opinion questions so as to compare their views more easily with those of the public. Their research indicates that Hollywood remains more liberal than the American public on a wide range of issues. Prindle and Endersby found that on economic issues, Hollywood elites are "more supportive of the idea of raising taxes, less admiring of American business, more favorably inclined toward government regulation of business, and less suspicious of labor unions than is the public in general." On social issues, they found a "general tolerance for unusual or deviant ideas and life-styles, and minority religions and ethnic groups." On foreign policy issues, Hollywood was "consistently supportive of negotiation over confrontation, and suspicious of the United States meddling beyond our borders." Finally, the new study found that even Hollywood executives, although somewhat less liberal than other respondents, were "still noticeably to the left of the general public." The authors also argued that it was virtually impossible to measure traditionally conservative attitudes among the Hollywood elite, as they could find few, if any, representatives of such attitudes (Prindle and Endersby, 1993:151–156).

Prindle and Endersby's results, like our own, suggest a general dissatisfaction with existing American institutions and values that has persisted in spite of a substantially more conservative orientation among both business elites and the public. To the extent that such attitudes are reflected in popular movies we must question the assumption that Hollywood merely caters to popular sentiments in entertaining America.

Power and Personality: The Thematic Apperception Test

Given what we know about the creative power and expressed attitudes of the new movie elite, what can we say about their underlying motivation? Are their reformist social and political attitudes undergirded by a genuine democratic personality structure or merely by a desire for power under the guise of idealism? Rothman and various colleagues have dealt with these issues in other publications (Rothman and Lichter 1982; Rothman 1992a; Lerner, Nagai, and Rothman, 1995; Rothman and Lichter, forthcoming, and in the last chapter of this book).

Using the Thematic Apperception Test (TAT) results from our survey of elites, we can provide an empirical measure of a theory derived from Daniel Bell's observation that while business elites are likely to be more achievement oriented, information elites are differently motivated. Bell argues that traditional American emphases upon achievement and instrumental rationality were derived from a Protestant religious inheritance. The erosion of this inheritance, along with rising affluence, has weakened these motivational patterns. The erosion is most pronounced among those groups at one remove from the central economic institutions of the society, such as artists, intellectuals, journalists, and other new "strategic elites." These new elites may not consciously wish to challenge important values and institutions undergirding traditional American society; they do so because, as a group, they tend to perceive psychosocial phenomena—in particular, power and achievement—differently than other groups.

If this hypothesis is true, moviemakers, one of three important components of the communications elite that Rothman has studied (journalists and television entertainment elites are the other two), should exhibit not only a lower need for achievement but also a greater need for power. They should also be characterized by a greater degree of general hostility, as well as a greater degree of narcissism. In the next few pages, we compare various personality traits exhibited by the sample of the movie elite with personality traits of the sample of businesspeople to determine if these moviemakers fit our psychodynamically oriented reworking of Bell's hypotheses.[16]

The TATs administered to these groups consisted of a set of five pictures of ambiguous social situations. Respondents wrote stories about the individuals depicted in the pictures, prompted by questions about what is occurring in the picture, what has led to the situation shown, what the people involved are thinking, and what the final outcome of the interactions is likely to be. We decided to rely on TATs because of what we consider to be a major flaw of cognitive multiple choice or sentence completion tests of personality, especially when used with sophisticated respondents. Such tests generally provide investigators with only a picture of the respondent's public self-image, not because respondents prevaricate but rather because relatively few people are capable of genuine self-reflection. The more sophisticated the respondent, the more complex his or her defenses. On most paper and pencil tests, sophisticated respondents often present an image of their ideal rather than a real self.[17]

The TAT stories are scored to assess the different motivations we have already mentioned. All of the scoring systems were developed in experimental situations, and a large body of empirical research, conducted over a period of forty years in some cases, indicates that they accurately tap a number of key personality traits (Atkinson, ed., 1958; Winter, 1973; McClelland, 1975; Winter and Stewart, 1978; Cole, 1979; Stewart, 1982; Zeldow et al., 1988). In the case of our study, the TAT results allow us to formulate correlations between patterns of personality and the social and attitudinal factors we have been discussing, such as separately gathered data on profession, background, and expressed political and social attitudes.

Our ideas stand as they are, but we think that the test provides extensive and consistently convincing evidence for them. Although in the final chapter of this book we will present an interpretation of our results that falls within the psychoanalytic tradition, broadly defined, the use of such measures of personality does not require a psychoanalytic orientation. Indeed, the scales themselves do not measure psychoanalytically defined variables, and the results could be incorporated into a variety of other frameworks. Relying on these empirically derived scoring systems requires only the belief that individuals are not always aware of their real motives and that such motives may be tapped effectively by presenting respondents with ambiguous stimuli. The empirical work of McClelland and others provides substantial support for that statement.

We should caution, as Lichter, Rothman, and Lichter have done elsewhere (1986), that these tests are designed only to measure differences between groups, as a matter of statistical probability. Nothing we say about statistical differences in group scores can be meaningfully applied to individual respondents.

Need for Achievement

David McClelland is perhaps best known for developing a scale with which to measure the strength of the desire to achieve. It was the first motive for which he developed an empirical scoring system and its validity has been systematically examined over a relatively long period of time. Achievement studies have shown that groups with high scores of need for achievement on the TATs are also inclined to moderate risk-taking and entrepreneurial or managerial success, even in noncapitalist societies. TAT themes are scored for *n* Achievement when stories express a concern about meeting a standard of excellence set for oneself (Atkinson, 1958; McClelland, 1961). Thus, we expected American business elites to average significantly higher in achievement need than the movie elite. The TAT results confirmed our expectations. Businesspeople score over 106 compared to the 99.14 of the Hollywood cultural elite.

Need for Power

The power motive is measured in terms of the need for power, fear of power, and need for power minus inhibition (Rothman and Lichter, 1982; Rothman and Lichter, 1984; Lichter, Rothman, and Lichter 1986). The methodology for the power analysis derives primarily from the work of McClelland and Winter (McClelland, 1961; McClelland, 1975; Winter, 1973; Winter and Stewart, 1978) who developed a set of criteria for scoring Thematic Apperception Tests (TATs) for power needs. Need for power (*n*-Power) is then evaluated by coders, trained to recognize certain linguistic expressions showing a concern for power.[18] For example, Winter's definition of "power imagery" within the stories involves three broad criteria. "Someone shows his power concerns through actions which in themselves express his power." "Someone does something that arouses strong positive or negative emotions in others." "Someone is described as having a concern for his reputation or position." There are a number of other indicators of power need such as "prestige of the actor," "stated need for power," "blocks in the world [obstacles]," "goal anticipation," and so on. These factors are all scored to yield a composite score that can then be used to compare groups of people that have been differentiated on other terms (for example, the movie elite versus the business elite).

The following account, by a movie elite respondent, is a good example of the type of story yielding a high need for power:

> The recruit is thinking that he will have to deal more subtly with the power that faces him. He will have to, perhaps, ingratiate himself with these cretins who wear stripes and bars. He is learning to adjust to the real world rather than to continue to fight it. He is going underground.

He will adjust, perhaps even excel at functioning in the world that he at first abhorred and tried to escape from. In time, he will take the place of the steel-eyed superior on the left and even find himself facing a sullen, cowering youth who is rebelling at *his* authority. He will survive, he will prevail, and he will propagate the system that he finds so repellent.

Personalities characterized by high *n*-Power scores tend to engage in competitive and contact sports, impulsive aggressive activity (such as public arguments), sexual aggressiveness, and unstable dating and marital relations. Power-oriented people are also attracted to symbols of prestige. With the effects of class differences taken into account, *n*-Power predicts ownership of sports cars and a large number of credit cards. High *n*-Power people also have a competitive or hostile stance toward those of higher status or power; they seek to dominate low-status individuals. Interestingly, as a group, respondents who write stories in which the characters seek power to help others, behave exactly the same as those who write stories about people seeking power for selfish ends. Persons with high-power scores can be effective leaders in the business community if impulse control is good (see below).

In general, we expected the moviemakers to exhibit a significantly higher need for power than businessmen, and this is more or less what we found. Standardizing the scores with a mean of 100, we found that moviemakers score just above 103. Businessmen, however, score just above 94 (see Table 3.7).

Inhibition, Sublimation

TAT researchers have formulated a scoring system that quantifies the degree to which the power motive is inhibited or sublimated. The number of "nots" a respondent uses in the stories he or she writes was found to correlate highly with evidence of inhibition. A high inhibition score indicates sublimation of power, while a low inhibition score is associated with evidence of a more direct expression of the power drive, including a tendency to anger easily and to engage in impulsive violence (McClelland, 1975). When the mean number of "nots" is sub-

TABLE 3.7   Psychological Traits: Comparison of Means—Movies vs. Business

Variable	Movie	Business
Power	103.10	94.25*
Fear of Power	103.04	99.10*
Power − "nots"	104.23	94.95*
Affiliation	99.08	95.70*
Achievement	99.14	106.52*
Narcissism	103.46	97.76*

*p < .05.

tracted from the *n*-Power score, it provides a measure of power that takes into account accompanying feelings of inhibition.

The higher the power minus "nots" score, the less power is sublimated. Our standardized scale finds a difference of 10 between the scores of the movie elite and the business elite.[19]

Fear of Power

This motive is scored when someone reacts to power with feelings of doubt, conflict, irony, or deception. It is also scored when characters seek power ostensibly to benefit others. In effect, it measures the ambivalence of being drawn to power and repelled by it.

Persons who score high on fear of power behave in ways that suggest that they are afraid of other people gaining power over them. Individuals strongly motivated by fear of power mistrust other people and institutional authority. They are very concerned with self and defending their personal autonomy and independence. Thus they find it difficult to cooperate with others in group activities or to compete with others or to take on responsibility in an institutional setting. Paranoid personalities tend to score very high on fear of power (McClelland, 1975; Winter, 1973).

The personality types that simultaneously score high on a need for power and a fear of power rationalize their power needs as required to protect themselves against others whom they think seek power over them. In other words, their very fear of power seems to generate a defensive need to feel powerful. The statistical profile of the personality types who score high on fear of power suggests that they tend to engage often in defensive projection and seek power indirectly—for instance, in a manner that avoids having to confront other power seekers directly.

The following TAT story by a journalist writing about a picture of men in uniform illustrates several facets of the fear of power. The reporter sets the story in World War II Germany. An army recruit, Franz, gets fed up with the Nazis and tries to escape. He is caught by soldiers who suspect he is an American spy. The reporter concludes his story: "The future for Franz looked bleak. Whatever he did—confess the reality or contrive to deny the accusation—would lead to the same end—execution."

The authorities are real brutes—Nazis. The outcome of the power relationship will be the protagonist's death. And a sense of irony contributes to the despairing tone. Either the truth or a lie, for different reasons, will produce equally dreadful consequences. The author could have had Franz escape or lie his way out of the dilemma. His future need not have been so bleak in a story less pervaded by a fear of power.

Again the moviemakers score significantly higher than businesspeople, 103 to 99.

Narcissism

Finally, we compared the two elites on the personality trait of narcissism. Healthy adult narcissism is a reservoir of self-esteem and is an adequate basis of positive self-feeling, while its negative side is responsible for its association with selfishness and egoism. People who lack confidence in themselves, who suffer from what psychologists call "narcissistic deficits," often rely on egocentric mechanisms to enhance self-esteem and maintain a sense of identity. This leads to behavior commonly termed narcissistic.

One way of enhancing self-esteem and maintaining one's identity is to adopt a wishful or grandiose self-image, whereby the narcissistic person denies the undesirable qualities that he perceives in himself and projects these traits onto others. This devaluation of others also protects the bearer against the feelings of deprivation caused by envy. In general, the narcissistic type uses others primarily to bolster self-esteem and thereby avoids seeing them as separate individuals with needs and identities different from those of the narcissist.

TAT stories characterized by a high degree of narcissism emphasize the gratification of exhibitionistic needs rather than interpersonal issues. These writers appear to be showing off, calling attention to themselves while ignoring any relationship that the story might invoke. Stories characterized by a high degree of narcissism also portray characters as exploitative, haughty, manipulative, grandiose, cold, ruthless, and/or hollow. This reflects the narcissist's tendency to project negative personality traits onto other people and to retain his or her self-esteem by denigrating others.

For example, writing a story about a picture of a man and a woman, a male TV news producer offers the classic portrait of an unfeeling seducer: "It has taken him six months to get Larry's wife into bed. Six months of cajoling, soft words, good wine, and, finally, words of love. Words unmeant but believed. Now it was all over. . . . And he wondered, how the hell he would get rid of her."[20] Again, the intuitive reading of this kind of story seems clear enough. However, the point is that as these stories accumulate and we correlate them with other divisions among the sample, patterns emerge that allow us to build reliable, statistical profiles.

Once again the motion picture elite scores very high on this personality dimension, a solid 103 compared to under 98 for business leaders.

Authoritarianism

Combining a number of these motive scores, McClelland and his coworkers developed a measure of authoritarianism, dividing those with authoritarian personalities into three types (McClelland, 1975). The first type, The Imperial Type, scores high on n-Power and inhibition and low on n-Affiliation. This type of person can subordinate his or her power needs to an organization and can, other things being equal, succeed as a certain kind of authoritarian businessperson or military leader. While unwilling to allow challenges to his or her own authority, this person governs reasonably fairly according to general rules.

> People with the imperial motivational pattern act in ways that build strong organizations. They like to be in them, to work for them. They like to work. They share with others out of a sense of obligation to the system. Their concern with justice inclines them to deal with people even-handedly. One should also recall that they also display the kinds of assertiveness (that) characterize men and women with high n-Power. (McClelland, 1975)

The Conquistador Personality

By contrast, a pattern of low inhibition levels in conjunction with high power and low affiliative needs defines a more impulsive power-oriented mentality. People with this motivational syndrome tend to reject institutional ties and to engage in overtly assertive or self-aggrandizing behavior. Such people seem willing to achieve heightened power goals by manipulating others, with little concern for others' wishes or interests. They may be rebels against authority, but their rebellion, however it is rationalized, ultimately serves the cause of self aggrandizement.

The Personal Enclave Type

Finally, McClelland delineates a power orientation that he calls the "personal enclave" type. Such people view the self rather than others as the locus of their efforts to gain feelings of power. They seek to feel powerful by incorporating strength through alliances with people, groups, or ideas they perceive as sources of power. Enclave types are characterized by high n-Power, low inhibitions, and high n-Affiliation.

Not surprisingly, given our previous findings, the Hollywood sample contains a significantly higher proportion of authoritarians (30 percent) than does the business sample (18 percent), though in neither case is a majority of the sample authoritarian (see Table 3.8).

TABLE 3.8   Elite Groups by Percent of Authoritarian Types

Groups	Total Authoritarian	Imperial	Conquistador	Enclave	Nonauthoritarian
Business	18.2%	5.4	10.7	2.1	81.8
Movies	30.2%	9.4	10.4	10.4	69.8

Significant at p < .05.

TABLE 3.9   General Social Survey Questions: 1972–1982, 1990, and 1993

	Percentage Response		
Question	1972–1982	1990	1993
GSS Q. 68A. A seven point scale on which the political views that people might hold are arranged from extremely liberal—point 1— to extremely conservative—point 7. Where would you place yourself on this scale?			
Extremely liberal, liberal, or slightly liberal	27	26	26
Moderate	38	35	36
Slightly conservative, conservative, or extremely conservative	30	35	35
Don't know or no answer	5	4	4
N=	10509	1372	1606
GSS Q.104. What is your religious preference?			
Protestant	64	63	64
Catholic	25	24	22
Jewish	2	2	2
None	7	8	9
Other	1	3	3
N=	13626	1371	1606
GSS Q.219. Sexual relations between two adults of the same sex—*always wrong?*			
Always wrong	67	72	62
N=	8991	917	1075
GSS Q.84B. Should known homosexuals be allowed to teach in a college or university—yes, no			
Yes	51	63	68
No	44	32	27
Don't know or no answer	5	5	4
N=	8991	917	1075
GSS Q.218. Opinion about a married person having sexual relations with someone other than the marriage partner—*always wrong*			
Always wrong	70	77	76
N=	8991	917	1075
GSS Q. 206G. Should it be possible for a pregnant woman to have an abortion for any reason— yes, no.			
Yes	37	41	43
No	59	54	51
Don't know or no answer	4	5	5
N=	6036	917	1075

(continues)

TABLE 3.9   *(Continued)*

Question		Percentage Response		
		1972–1982	*1990*	*1993*
GSS Q.153A. People running the country don't really care what happens to you—yes, no.				
Yes		51	–	–
No		44	–	–
Don't know or no answer		5	–	–
N=		1532	–	–

GSS Q.162A-M. As far as the people running these institutions, would you say you have a *great deal* of confidence?

Percentage responding a "great deal"

1972–1982	*%*	*1990*	*%*	*1993*	*%*
Military	34	Military	33	Military	42
Organized religion	34	Major companies	25	Organized religion	23
Banks	34	Organized religion	23	Major companies	21
Major companies	25	Executive branch	23	Banks	15
Press	21	Banks	18	Executive branch	12
Executive branch	18	Press	15	Television	12
Television	17	Television	14	Press	11
Labor	14	Labor	11	Labor	8

Question:	Percentage Response			
	1980	*1982*	*1990*	*1993*
GSS Q.105 How often do you attend religious services?				
Never	13.0	11.4	14.2	16.5
Less than once a year	7.1	7.5	9.0	8.7
Once a year	14.3	15.7	12.7	12.3
Several times a year	14.0	15.3	12.5	11.2
Once a month	7.1	6.7	8.9	7.1
Two–three times a month	9.7	8.1	10.2	8.7
Nearly every week	6.5	6.2	4.6	6.3
Every week	19.7	21.6	21.7	20.5
More than once a week	8.6	7.5	6.1	8.6
N=	1847	1461	830	1568

Conclusion

The American New Wave of the 1960s has been widely regarded as a renaissance in Hollywood—remembered not so much for the rise of independent production and innovative filmmaking as for its ground swell of fresh moral and political outlooks. Yet this increased freedom for the artist did not translate into a democratic system of doing business and it did not create a more pluralistic medium for expressing ideas. Since that artistic revolution took place, the industry has fragmented into numerous fiefdoms of independent production. The new positions of power no longer belong to a few studio executives, but to the talent agents of William Morris and MCA and to the executives of independent production companies such as Orion, Cannon, Tri-Star, and other, smaller firms. A handful of directors who frequently do their own writing and producing have also wrested considerable power from the Hollywood establishment.

Moviemakers still depend on Hollywood. Writers, directors, and producers must all submit, at least to some extent, to the "Industry Establishment" in order to get their start, secure agents, and gain the notoriety required to get financing for movies. But studios depend very heavily on this relatively small group of moviemakers to turn a profit. At the same time, censorship restrictions have diminished, independent production has diffused power, new financial arrangements yield huge sums to the moviemakers themselves, and like-minded studio executives grant actors, writers, directors, and producers unprecedented freedom to make movies with messages. These are some of the changes that have empowered the new creative elite in Hollywood.

These conditions have for some time favored the liberal and cosmopolitan ideas of a majority of Hollywood artists. Alternative views have surfaced in a modest number of popular films and a few are among our sample of top-grossing movies; but by and large modern films reflect liberal views. These, in turn, are sanctioned by an equally liberal community of film critics. For its part, the young viewing public enthusiastically patronizes Hollywood movies, perhaps unaware of the rather narrow range of beliefs that underlies and informs this type of mass entertainment. The extent and nature of the influence that these films will ultimately have on audiences is not well understood and is beyond the scope of this study. But any satisfactory explanation will have to account for the fact that for the past three decades, movies have cast a number of American values and institutions in a highly negative light.

Inevitably, any portrait we can render of the new Hollywood elite is impressionistic. It is the depiction of a group of influential people in motion. We cannot know how continued artistic success or failure, the further evolution of the movie industry, important historical events, or a myriad of other experiences might influence the attitudes of these artistic entrepreneurs and, in turn, the movies they make. Yet we can say that at this juncture the Hollywood elite is unquestionably to the left of the business elite and the public in a broad range of social and political views. As issues such as freedom in Eastern Europe, AIDS, race relations, the environment, and others arise, Hollywood retains both the ability and the will to influence large audiences with a relatively coherent set of liberal and cosmopolitan views. Moviemakers are much older and politically resolute than adolescent and young adult moviegoers, so one doubts that their basic inclinations will change much. It is more likely that they will move on to new issues, anti-institutional biases intact, and more or less in step with the contemporary liberalism prevalent among the media elite of the recent past.

Hollywood filmmakers are under no obligation to see the world in any way other than they choose. Further, as we discussed above, we emphatically do not think there is any "bias," let alone conspiracy, motivating the shifts in the social and political attitudes of the Hollywood elite and the content of the movies they make. But in contrast to many film historians, critics, and theorists, who often see Hollywood and its products as politically and socially conservative or reactionary, we find that liberal views have become more and more institutionalized in the movie business since the 1960s. In fact, according to the surveys, in many instances the outlook of the contemporary Hollywood elite is markedly different from the majority of the society, and quite critical of traditional American institutions such as business, organized religion, and the military. Further, fully 67 percent of those we interviewed in our sample explicitly state that they believe movies should contribute to social reform. Nothing suggests to us that this is likely to change any time soon.[21] While there are exceptions, the particular liberalism of the Hollywood community tends to be self-reinforcing. Indeed, like most people who associate only with their own kind, most of Hollywood's creative elite regards people with whom they disagree ideologically as hard-hearted ideologues. They see themselves not as persons who adhere to a particular perspective but rather as simply humane individuals who see the world as it is and as it should be.

Further, our data on the attitudes of the Hollywood elite suggest that elite moviemakers do not necessarily respond to shifting popular values and beliefs, as they might if their interests were purely commercial. Although there is, of course, a bottom line, many of the filmmakers see their work as a form of education, as well as entertainment, and use the freedom of the poststudio structure of the industry to try to convey strong political or social messages in one way or another, at the same time that they try to turn a profit. Even though recent films may not appear to be as openly critical of traditional American institutions as many of the films of the 1960s, they frequently resonate with the anti-Establishment attitudes of their post–New Wave creators. In subtle ways—by showing the assumption of bureaucratic heartlessness among the scientists in *E.T.* (1982); the incompetence and dishonesty of the military in *Rambo: First Blood, Part II* (1985); the sinister complicity of government, the police, and business with organized crime in *The Godfather* movies (1972, 1975, 1991), and so on—dissent has become characteristic of many of the top-grossing films of the new Hollywood, and it still predominates. When we turn to the films themselves, we will see that particular kinds of representation have evolved over time in ways that support these larger generalizations.

Finally, the moviemakers do seem to fit the orientation and personality style analyzed by Daniel Bell (1976) and Rothman (1992). Thus they seem to be characterized by the need for and fear of power as well as by a relatively high degree of narcissism. In short, they would seem to epitomize the personality type described by Lasch in *The Culture of Narcissism* (1978) and elsewhere (1977, 1985). If they represent what other writers have defined as postmodern or, in Lifton's terms, Protean man (Lifton, 1994), we face some problems as a nation. However, that is an issue that we must reserve for the final chapter of this book.

In that chapter, we shall also add additional elements to our equation. In our view the industry influences the public over time, even creating the demand for new products. However, its products are partially, too, a function of changes in the society over which it has little control and to which it can only react.

Two additional points should be made here. First, although we have, of necessity, written of Hollywood or the Hollywood elite, we are not asserting that Hollywood is monolithic. The creative elite in Hollywood is a diverse group. As our data has demonstrated, we are describing about general trends to which there are significant exceptions.

Second, as we shall see in our content analysis chapters, the creative product that emerges also varies widely in outlook, and the creative elite consists of individuals (whatever their perspectives) who differ in the extent to which social and political issues, as opposed to aesthetic concerns, are involved in their work. Again, we are referring to general patterns to which there are significant exceptions. Nevertheless, whatever their views, members of the creative elite, as do we, make assumptions about the way the world works. These assumptions inevitably color their creative efforts to some degree. Indeed, the less they are aware that these assumptions are just assumptions and mistake them for an ultimate truth, the more likely they are to incorporate them uncritically.

NOTES

1. For a brief recent review of the literature, see Graber (1993). Movies and television are not identical media, although since the video revolution they have become more closely intertwined, both economically and aesthetically, than in the past. Nevertheless, the debate over audience response usually involves both media.

2. In this group, we would also include Joshua Meyrowitz (1985, 1993) who is less pessimistic than Postman. We could also include Daniel Bell, insofar as his coining of the term "post-industrial society" depends on a recognition of the growing importance of all forms of communication to economic and other kinds of social interaction.

3. Journalistic coverage now takes it for granted that Hollywood movers and shakers are predominantly liberal and that this liberalism shapes their product. Journalists assume, however, that this phenomenon is of recent vintage (Dowd, 1993). Our evidence indicates that it goes back quite a way. The academic community and movie critics in general still assume that Hollywood leaders are conservative if not reactionary and that they serve the "white, heterosexual, male, privileged elite" and are part of that elite. For references, see the many sources cited in Chapter 1 as well as Gitlin (1974, 1983), and Lazere ed. (1987). For the smaller number who categorize Hollywood and its product as part of the adversary culture, see Grenier (1991), Stein (1979), and Medved (1989, 1992, 1993). Those who tend to see motion picture content as merely reflecting the desires of the public include Gans

(1993); Gomery (1986b); Litwak (1986); and Monaco (1979). Audiences do not necessarily categorize films as critical of dominant institutions when trained viewers would. This is why audience research cannot be used to establish the ideological content of motion pictures. The public can be influenced over the long run by images even if (perhaps especially if) the messages are conveyed subtly and packaged well.

Of course it is impossible to accurately measure the actual influence of the entertainment (as opposed to the news) media. For conflicting views, see, in addition to those already mentioned, Comstock (1980); Faludi (1991); and Yang and Linz (1990).

4. Ironically, Parker herself became one of the well-known victims of the studio blacklists in the 1950s.

5. Even Darryl Zanuck, described by biographer Leonard Mosley as a Republican with some liberal tendencies (he admired Roosevelt and despised the "Senate watchdogs" who kept an eye on Hollywood in the late 1940s and 1950s), feared that his relationship with New York financiers might be jeopardized by controversial films. Mosley remarks that after World War II, "the political skies over the United States were darkening and any attempt by Hollywood to tackle 'liberal' themes was being watched suspiciously by the McCarthyites in Washington, and nervously by the head offices of the movie companies in New York.... Even a registered Republican of Zanuck's standing had to watch what he was doing" (Mosley, 1984: 227–228).

6. In *The Movie Brats*, authors Michael Pye and Lynda Myles describe the relatively few dominant figures at the creative end of Hollywood business as "the men who, at the end of 1977, stood unchallenged ... within a new Hollywood. They inherited the power of the moguls to make film for a mass audience. And they [knew] the past of cinema like scholars; they grew with it and through it.... Knowledge and power and spectacular success all make them the true children of old Hollywood" (1979:7).

7. See the analysis later in this chapter, in Chapter 6, and in Medved (1989, 1992, 1993).

8. This, and the additional quotes about prime-time television, are to be found, with many other examples, in Lichter, Lichter, and Rothman (1994).

9. We are, in this and future chapters, emphasizing general trends. One can always find counterexamples. Hollywood is not and has never been monolithic.

10. Recent studies indicate that some Americans may be responding to this question by giving the answer that they think they should. However, there is no reason to believe that such behavior invalidates our comparison.

11. We are examining only the three major dimensions in this chapter. For a discussion of all four, see Lerner, Nagai, and Rothman (1996).

12. The phrase "collectivist liberalism" was originally coined by John Dewey (1930:104) and later used by Edward Shils, "Learning and Liberalism" (1980).

13. Sixty percent of those in the movie elite sample were of Jewish background, though only a small proportion of these were observant Jews. They tended to be somewhat to the left of their non-Jewish counterparts on all three factors. David Prindle (1993) argues that the liberalism of Hollywood can be traced to the liberal attitudes of Jews in the motion picture industry and to the general "riskiness" of the Hollywood business. Most Hollywood aspirants are always living on the edge and are often unemployed. Whatever the role played by those of Jewish background in Hollywood, his argument regarding the riskiness of the business is not persuasive for the following reasons: (1) artists have generally been on the left for most of this century; (2) big-name, successful stars and producers are on the left; (3) as we shall see, the radicalism of the Hollywood elite is far more a cultural and social

radicalism than it is an economic radicalism. Prindle also argues that the general atmosphere of Hollywood tends toward paranoia, at least partially because of the personalities of those who make up its population, many of whom are the products of dysfunctional families. He has a point, as we demonstrate later in this chapter.

14. We should not have to say this, but we will because we have been misunderstood in the past. Our discussion of homosexuality, abortion, and adultery in this book does not imply a moral judgment, whatever our personal beliefs. Critics are constantly making that assumption because we argue that support for the legitimacy of these behaviors is associated with a particular ideology rather than simply being part and parcel of the natural order of things. In this respect, they are a mirror image of their conservative counterparts.

15. There is considerable controversy regarding the wording of questions about this issue. Whereas most Americans, as late as 1993, rejected "abortion on demand," a majority, by that time, were willing to permit abortion for a wide variety of reasons including rape, danger to the health of the mother, and similar situations.

16. Here we are using the same procedures employed in a previous book by Rothman and Lichter (1982). We should stress that although we are interpreting (in the last chapter) some of these results in broadly defined psychodynamic terms, one need not do so. Neither the need for achievement nor the need for power, for example, are psychodynamic constructs. One can, after all, believe that some people like power without agreeing with Freud on the nature of the need for power.

17. For a more detailed discussion of these issues see Rothman and Lichter (1982: 52–79).

18. In our study, these coders scored the stories blindly, without knowledge of the other aspects of the work or the identities of the respondents.

19. The findings are a function of higher n-Power scores, unaccompanied by a rise in the number of "nots" in the stories scored.

20. The scoring system was developed by Dr. Jennifer Cole as part of her Ph.D. dissertation in psychology at the University of Michigan. Dr. Cole scored the protocols without being aware of either the nature of the sample or the purpose of the study. It has not been empirically tested, and must be used with caution.

21. There are conservatives in Hollywood but, on the whole, they are quiet about their political leanings. As one of the few conservatives willing to identify himself noted: "It's not socially acceptable" (*New York Times*, May 31, 1992:91ff).

4

Hollywood Views the Military

For at least two decades, public opinion surveys have shown declining support for a number of American institutions. Nevertheless, the U.S. military still enjoys one of the highest confidence ratings among institutions the public is periodically asked to rank.

During the 1980s, many film critics ascribed the continued relative popularity of the military to the Reagan administration, arguing that following the anti-Establishment films of the 1960s and early 1970s, which often criticized the military, movies from the late 1970s through the 1980s tended to portray the military more favorably. Terry Christensen, among others, laments Hollywood's susceptibility to the political winds of the Reagan era in his book *Reel Politics* (1987):

> Movies critical of American foreign policy were made throughout the Reagan years and some were popular successes, but the era will be remembered for a very different sort of film. Like President Reagan himself, these movies called up traditional values, emphasizing individualism, self-sufficiency, competition, courage, pride, and patriotism in a conveniently simplified world. . . . Nearly six years of self-congratulation culminated in the 1986 rededication of the Statue of Liberty, an orgy of patriotism produced in the lavish style of a Hollywood movie. And much of this patriotic frenzy is reflected in a group of films produced during Reagan's presidency. (Christensen, 1985:199–200)

Christensen, like many other critics, divides movies on foreign policy, which would include all military movies, into two camps: critical vs. affirmative representations. And Christensen, like many other critics, is decidedly hostile to what he sees as the reactionary treatments of the military in film—"an orgy of patriotism"—that accompanied the Reagan presidency. Although it is true that a few favorable portrayals of the military, in movies such as *Rambo II* and *Top Gun*, surfaced in the 1980s, this does not really represent a reaffirmation of traditional ideas about patriotism. Patriotism itself has never really been questioned in most of the movies about the military. What has been called into question is the institutional legitimacy of the armed forces. This trend began in the 1960s and was not reversed in the 1980s.

Our contention, then, is that any critical dichotomy between movies of "patriotic frenzy" and those that are "critical of American foreign policy" is of limited use in helping us to understand how military movies have changed over the past several decades. It does not help us to describe accurately broad shifts in the ways that military characters are represented. In particular, it does not trace with sufficient clarity changes in the various kinds of goals that the individual characters have and whether those goals are sympathetically or critically depicted. It also cannot accurately account for changes in the methods that military characters have used to achieve their goals and whether these methods are sympathetically or critically depicted.

Such changes in representation are not limited to the war movie genre. They could theoretically be traced in every film where military characters appear in any significant role. And based on our study, we would argue that regardless of the ideological split Christensen suggests, the military image in the majority of these films is now one in which the ends and means of war bear little resemblance to the traditional patriotism that used to characterize Hollywood movies. Further, this is the case whether or not the film appears to be patriotic. The changes subsume the ideological positions Christensen identifies, rendering them less relevant than they might at first appear.

The Study

Considering the number of films, characters, and categories involved, a comprehensive tracking of the multifarious and complex changes we have outlined is beyond the scope of individual impressions, however well-informed. So in order to gain a more thorough understanding of how the military image has changed, we have utilized our systematic content analyses of major motion pictures. Among the 146 films obtainable from our original sample, thirty-five contained military characters. Five additional films with military characters were added to the movies of the 1986 to 1990 period, bringing the total number to forty films. Finally four were added to update our analysis to 1994 and they are discussed in the afterword. A more detailed discussion of the military sampling procedure is found in Appendix C. Since within the population of 440 movies among the top-ten grossers from 1946 through 1990 only approximately fifty-five films somehow involve the U.S. military, we are confident that our movie sample is representative of the most popular films with major military characters since World War II.

For the character analysis, each character was coded for a number of demographic variables including race, sex, marital status, economic status, military rank, and so on. We also coded character ratings (positive, negative, or mixed), goals in the plot (for example patriotism, greed, or self-interest), and methods for achieving those goals (for example, authority, money, or violence). From our forty films, we thus generated profiles of 405 U.S. military characters; 165 of these were major characters. A listing of the forty sample movies is provided in Table 4.1).

Our thematic analysis provides data on representations of American institutions. Two variables from the thematic analysis are particularly relevant to this essay: presence of the U.S. military and representations of the U.S. government in which the military is present. The findings, based on these two thematic variables, and the more detailed character profiles of the military confirm our impression that there have been significant transformations in movies that represent the military during the past twenty-five years. These transformations appear to cut across conventional ideological categories to affect virtually all films in the sample and the changes are quite pronounced.

The Military and the State

The thematic analysis reveals that since the mid-1960s, the U.S. military is more likely to be portrayed negatively than positively. From 1946 to 1965, 40 percent of movies about the military portrayed the institution positively, in 40 percent the

TABLE 4.1   Sample Films with U.S. Military Characters (by decade)

1946–1955	*1956–1965*
Al Jolson Sings Again (1949)	Love Me Tender (1957)
Twelve O'Clock High (1949)	South Pacific (1958)
Snows of Kilimanjaro (1952)	No Time for Sergeants (1958)
From Here to Eternity (1953)	Sayonara (1958)
White Christmas (1954)	Anatomy of a Murder (1959)
Mister Roberts (1955)	On the Beach (1960)
Strategic Air Command (1955)	The Longest Day (1963)
	Goldfinger (1965)

1966–1975	*1976–1990*
The Russians are Coming (1966)	Close Encounters of the Third Kind (1977)
Casino Royale (1967)	Deer Hunter (1979)
Dirty Dozen (1967)	Muppet Movie (1979)
Hombre (1967)	Superman (1979)
You Only Live Twice (1967)	Private Benjamin (1980)
Patton (1969)	Stripes (1981)
M*A*S*H (1970)	War Games (1983)
Little Big Man (1970)	Cocoon (1985)
Catch-22 (1970)	Rambo: First Blood, Part II (1985)
Andromeda Strain (1971)	Platoon (1986)
Diamonds are Forever (1972)	Top Gun (1986)
	Good Morning Vietnam (1987)
	Predator (1987)
	Cocktail (1988)

military received mixed ratings, and in 20 percent the military was represented negatively. From 1966 to 1975, only 12 percent of the movies portrayed the military positively, in 62 percent of the movies images of the military were mixed, and in 25 percent portrayals of the military were negative. From 1976 to 1990, we find the most critical depictions of the military: 27 percent of the movies are positive, 40 percent are mixed, and 33 percent are negative. Secondly, in military movies, the U.S. government, where present as an institution, was portrayed negatively only 29 percent of the time prior to 1966. Whereas treatment of the government in movies featuring the military remained relatively stable in the few sample films we coded for the next decade (25 percent), it rose to 62 percent for the period 1976 to 1990. In other words, the government was treated negatively 50 percent of the time (in military movies) in the second two periods treated by the study. These findings from the thematic data, shown in Table 4.2, suggest that movies about the military have become significantly more critical of the U.S. armed forces and the government in the past twenty-five years. It is worth pointing out here that a film can appear to be patriotic and yet still represent the government in a negative light; *Rambo: First Blood Part II*, the film most commonly cited as the high-watermark of Reagan-era jingoism, does exactly this.

Officers and Gentlemen (1946–1965)

The character data provide detailed information on just how these increasingly critical films have changed the way military personnel are depicted over the 45-year period. For example, an important preliminary measure of the represented legitimacy of the military is the character rating of military personnel. For all characters in the study, this appears as positive, negative, or mixed. As Table 4.3

TABLE 4.2   Images of the Military and the U.S. Government in Military Movies (by decade*)

	1946–1955	*1956–1965*	*1966–1975*	*1976–1990*
Military				
% Positive		40	12	27
% Mixed		40	62	40
% Negative		20	25	33
N=38		15	8	15
U.S. Government When Military Present				
% Positive		29	25	12
% Mixed		43	50	25
% Negative		29	25	62
N=19		7	4	8

*In this and the following tables, the differences between the first and second decades are generally slight enough that we average them together in our analysis. The data for the 1986–1990 films are added to the data for the 1976–1985 decade.

TABLE 4.3   Military Character Ratings (by rank and decade)

	1946–1955 *1956–1965*	*1966–1975*	*1976–1990*
All military			
% Positive	53	47	46
% Negative	16	22	27
% Mixed	30	30	27
N=165	43	59	63
Senior officers			
% Positive	55	37	38
% Negative	14	23	38
% Mixed	31	40	24
N=93	29	35	29
Low-ranking officers			
% Positive	50	62	54
% Negative	21	21	18
% Mixed	29	17	27
N=72	14	24	34

indicates, the percentage of positive characters is 53 percent in the first two decades, dropping only slightly to 47 percent in the third decade, and remains there from 1976 to the present. The percentage of negative military characters does rise more markedly, from 16 percent negative in the first two decades to 22 percent negative in the third decade to 27 percent negative in the fourth period. At first glance, then, there appears to be only a marginal decline in the military image. When we control for rank, the results add a new dimension to this finding. In the first two decades, 55 percent of characters holding a rank above sergeant receive a positive depiction, but that rate falls to 37 percent in the third decade, and remains at 38 percent in the most recent period. At the same time, the number of senior officers receiving negative ratings rises substantially from only 14 percent negative in the first two decades to 23 percent negative in the third decade to 38 percent negative in the most recent period. Thus, senior-ranking officers, whose presence has also declined in proportion to that of soldiers of lower rank (from 67 percent in the first two decades to 59 percent in the third decade to 46 percent in the final period) are much more likely to be portrayed negatively. At the same time the image of the ordinary soldier, the grunt, has not suffered at all. Fifty percent are rated positively in the first two decades, 62 percent are positive in the third decade, and 54 percent are portrayed positively from 1976 to 1990. Negative portrayals have held at about 20 percent for the entire period of the study.

These figures suggest growing antagonism toward authority figures in recent films. When we look closer at the goals and methods of military personnel, we find strong evidence for this contention. Those military characters who are portrayed positively in the first two decades evince a strong moral commitment to military life. They exercise or obey an authority that is considered to be legitimate, even when it disrupts their personal lives or goes against their personal wishes. Those who act selfishly, instead of adapting to the institution, whether they are authorities or subordinates, usually end badly.

Of the movies in the 1946–1955 decade, *From Here to Eternity* (1953) provides the most diverse arrangement of character types, illuminating many of the broader trends. We can describe these trends through a critical summary of that film. The analysis is of course qualitative, but also informed by statistical profiles of military characters' ratings, goals, and methods.

The setting of *From Here to Eternity* is a military base in Hawaii just prior to the Pearl Harbor attack. The movie is filled with positive depictions of the rigor of Army life. Marching, giving and following orders, combat training, and rifle instruction are all integrated into the cinematography. Camaraderie and friendship are important aspects of the plot. The Army's authority is unquestioned and the virtues of a sense of duty and commitment to the Army are rewarded in the film. Characters with other motives or methods are punished.

From the opening scenes, it is obvious that Captain Holmes (Philip Ober) is disliked by his men and is an unsympathetic character. Near the beginning of the film, he tells Robert E. Lee Prewitt (Montgomery Clift), the bugler and ex-Army boxer, that "in the Army it's not the individual that counts," but Holmes is obviously a hypocrite. The precept is represented as true; Holmes fails by not observing it himself. His self-serving goal (the desire to make his company's boxing team the best in Hawaii) comes before his sense of duty and determines the negative use of his authority. These character faults are eventually exposed and the captain is disciplined by his own superiors for abusing authority.

Sergeant Milt Warden (Burt Lancaster) is the dutiful subordinate of Captain Holmes. He obeys and gives orders, looks after his men, and thrives on Army life. He is portrayed quite positively, although his romance with the Captain's wife sets up the inner conflict between duty and pleasure with which all the characters struggle. Ultimately, his sense of patriotism and love of the Army overcome his selfish desires, resolving the conflict. When criticizing Prewitt for refusing to box, he too emphasizes the central theme of the movie: "Maybe back in the days of the pioneers a man could go his own way, but today you've got to play ball."

The character of Angelo Maggio (Frank Sinatra) gives the audience a strong example of what to expect from selfish pursuits in the Army. Maggio is an undisciplined, hard-headed character who rarely submits to authority. His one saving grace, which accounts for his positive depiction, is his loyalty to his friend Prewitt. He disobeys orders one night, going AWOL from guard duty, gets drunk, hits an MP, and winds up in the stockade. There he is beaten up routinely by Sergeant Fatso Judson (Ernest Borgnine), who is getting even with him for a previous fight, and he eventually dies. Maggio's lack of a sense of duty and his unwillingness to follow orders are ultimately responsible for his death. Sergeant Judson himself, the least sympathetic character in the film, is immoral, self-interested, and violent. He also pays the price for his character flaws when Prewitt, avenging his friend Maggio's death, kills him in a knife fight.

Prewitt is also a positive figure. His obstinacy and romantic and vengeful pursuits ultimately bring about his death, but after all the trouble that his refusal to box brings him, Prewitt's love for the Army does not waver and it is precisely this quality that saves his character: "No I don't hate the Army ... I love the Army. ... A man loves a thing that doesn't mean it's gotta love him back. ... You love it then you gotta be grateful. ... I didn't belong no place 'til I entered the Army."

Although Prewitt is a sympathetic character, the dire consequences of disobeying orders become clear when he goes AWOL after being wounded in the knife fight with Sergeant Judson and is mistakenly shot dead while attempting to return to the base during the Japanese attack.

Looking at other movies from this decade, such as *Mister Roberts* (1955) and *Strategic Air Command* (1955), we find a similar pattern of character motivations and rewards. The second decade (1956–1965) also portrays the military in a manner similar to that of the first. Thus, in *The Longest Day* (1963), Colonel Benjamin Vandervoot (John Wayne), General Norman Cota (Robert Mitchum), and Brigadier General Theodore Roosevelt (Henry Fonda) are all portrayed positively. This corresponds with their sense of duty and patriotism, and appropriate use of authority and discipline, during the D day invasion. In the film *On the Beach* (1960), despite its thematic critique of the nuclear arms race, the one American portrayed, Commander Dwight Towers (Gregory Peck), is a positive figure whose adherence to Navy regulations (even though there is no Navy left) stems from the value he places on discipline. It is this quality that sustains him as the radioactive cloud, meaning imminent death, approaches.

The data base built up from these and other films of the first two decades supports the generalization of these closer readings. By far the most frequent goals and methods coded for military characters throughout this period are patriotism and authority and discipline. In the first two decades, 67 percent of the characters are coded as having patriotic goals (see Table 4.4). Sixty-seven percent of the military rely on authority and discipline as a method of achieving goals in the first two decades (see Table 4.5). The goals and methods alternatives are not mutually exclusive; characters could be coded for up to three goals or methods each. Still, there is no goal or method reported anywhere near as frequently as these two.

For the first two decades, our data back up the hypothesis that constraints on behavior are represented as taking precedence over the other goals and methods of military personnel. These characters are primarily motivated by a sense of duty and adherence to authority and discipline. Significantly, positive character ratings correlate very strongly with these goals and methods. Fifty-nine percent of the characters coded as patriotic had positive character ratings. Only 10 percent had negative ratings. These correlations are virtually the same regardless of the rank of the soldier (see Table 4.4). Forty-two percent of those characters who exercise

TABLE 4.4   Percent of Military Characters with Patriotic Goals (by decade, rank, and character rating)

	1946–1955	1956–1965	1966–1975	1976–1990
% All military	67		49	67
N=165	43		59	63
% Positive	59		49	51
% Negative	10		24	24
% Mixed	31		28	24
N=99	29		29	42
% Senior officers	76		57	72
N=93	29		35	29
% Positive	59		50	38
% Negative	9		20	38
% Mixed	32		30	24
N=63	22		20	21
% Low-ranking officers	50		37	62
N=72	14		24	34
% Positive	57		44	62
% Negative	14		33	10
% Mixed	28		22	28
N=37	7		9	21

TABLE 4.5   Percent of Characters Using Authority and Discipline as Methods (by decade, rank, and character rating)

	1946–1955	1956–1965	1966–1975	1976–1985
% All military	67		51	60
N=165	43		59	63
% Positive	42		43	36
% Negative	23		33	33
% Mixed	35		23	31
N=92	26		30	36
% Senior officers	72		60	72
N=93	29		35	29
% Positive	48		38	24
% Negative	19		33	48
% Mixed	33		29	29
N=63	21		21	21
% Low-ranking officers	36		38	47
N=72	14		24	34
% Positive	20		56	53
% Negative	40		33	13
% Mixed	40		11	33
N=29	5		9	15

authority and discipline are portrayed positively. Only about half as many, 23 percent, receive a negative character rating. Controlling for rank, we find that 48 percent of senior officers who exercise authority and discipline are positive figures. Only 19 percent are negative. For lower-rank officers, exercise of authority and discipline is more likely to correlate with a negative character rating. Only 20 percent of these characters are rated positively, whereas 40 percent receive negative ratings (see Table 4.5). Deceit and violence are practically nonexistent methods for military characters of this period, and none of the characters who resort to violent methods are portrayed positively (see Tables 4.6 and 4.7).

One film in the second decade, *Sayonara* (1958), does represent a departure from the status quo. The movie centers on the issue of American servicemen marrying Japanese women during the U.S. occupation of Japan after World War II. The character Major Lloyd Gruver (Marlon Brando) becomes disillusioned with the Air Force, which does not allow American-Japanese marriages, and he himself courts a Japanese performer. Gruver's friend, Airman Joe Kelly (Red Buttons), who is already married to a Japanese woman, is harassed by the Air Force and eventually given a stateside assignment that will separate him from his wife. Gruver attempts to intercede on Kelly's behalf, but to no avail. On the night before Kelly is to depart, after seeing a puppet show depicting two lovers who

TABLE 4.6   Percent of Characters Using Violence as a Method (by decade, rank, and character rating)

	1946–1955	*1956–1965*	*1966–1975*	*1976–1985*
% All military		7	29	38
N=165		43	59	63
% Positive		–	53	54
% Negative		67	29	17
% Mixed		33	18	29
N=44		3	17	24
% Senior officers		–	20	11
N=93		29	35	29
% Positive		–	71	33
% Negative		–	14	33
% Mixed		–	14	33
N=10		0	7	3
% Low-ranking officers		21	42	62
N=72		14	24	34
% Positive		–	40	57
% Negative		67	40	14
% Mixed		33	20	29
N=34		3	10	21

TABLE 4.7   Percent of Characters Using Deceit and Trickery as Methods (by decade, rank, and character rating)

	1946–1955	*1956–1965*	*1966–1975*	*1976–1985*
% All military		12	17	21
N=165		43	59	63
% Positive		60	40	23
% Negative		–	20	46
% Mixed		40	40	31
N=28		5	10	13
% Senior officers		10	20	18
N=93		29	35	29
% Positive		67	28	–
% Negative		–	14	100
% Mixed		33	56	–
N=15		3	7	5
% Low-ranking officers		14	12	24
N=72		14	24	34
% Positive		50	67	38
% Negative		–	33	12
% Mixed		50	–	50
N=13		2	3	8

choose to commit suicide rather than be separated, Kelly and his wife kill themselves. Gruver discovers them and subsequently decides to defy the Air Force rather than leave the woman he loves behind. In the closing scene, a reporter asks Gruver if he has anything to say to the "big brass" about his decision to marry a Japanese woman. He replies, "Yeah. Tell them we said *sayonara*."

Gruver and Kelly are portrayed positively, despite their refusal to accept and follow the Air Force's wishes. The villain of the film is their superior, Colonel Crawford (Douglas Watson), whose motivations are his dislike of the two upstarts and a blind adherence to authority and discipline where Air Force regulations are concerned. He gets Kelly and Gruver into trouble because of their involvement with Japanese women but is ultimately unsuccessful in his exercise of authority. General Webster (Kent Smith) is a positive character, yet he resembles the Colonel in that his attempts to use authority and discipline in upholding Air Force regulations are unsuccessful. Neither officer is able to control Major Gruver's actions, and his objections to military authority correlate with a positive character rating.

Officers and Gentlemen? (1966–1990)

Sayonara is a forerunner of the military films of the more recent two decades, in which critical or negative representation of military characters is clearly the dominant trend. These films often take overtly antiauthoritarian stands and elevate individuality over other, more traditional attitudes, such as the idea that loyalty to the military organization is the duty of a good citizen.

Even in the more patriotic films, contemporary producers tend to place military figures in extraordinarily isolated or fantastic contexts where the ends and means of war must be determined by the characters themselves. Thus, it seems quite natural for soldiers to be alienated, suspicious of authority, motivated by self-interested goals, and forced to utilize the most violent methods. Six of the twenty-five sample movies from the 1966–1990 period (*The Dirty Dozen, Patton, The Deer Hunter, Rambo: First Blood Part II, Top Gun,* and *Predator*) can be considered patriotic and all of these except *Patton* and *Top Gun* involve extraordinary circumstances. The remainder of the films have either too few military characters to establish a critical or affirmative image of the military itself or are entirely critical of the military establishment. Characters tend to be either anti-authority upstarts, corresponding with positive or at least mixed ratings, or they are hard-line, hypocritical types (usually high-ranking) who receive negative ratings.

The first patriotic movie from the 1966–1975 period, *The Dirty Dozen* (1967), presents an array of characters who typify the newer kind of military film. Major Reisman (Lee Marvin) is a heroic but undisciplined officer. Because of his checkered career, he is singled out by superiors to train a band of expendable convicts and lead them behind enemy lines to a German officers' retreat where they are to kill as many officers as possible. Reisman's superiors have the goals and methods that would previously have won them positive roles. General Denton (Robert Webber) and Colonel Everett Dasher-Breed (Robert Ryan) possess a sense of duty to the Army and use authority and discipline to get results, but coders find these characters to be portrayed negatively. General Worden (Ernest Borgnine), with similar goals and methods but sympathetic to Reisman's methods, still gets only a mixed character rating. Major Max Armbruster (George Kennedy), who functions as a liaison between Reisman and the commanding officers, is a positive figure but has no control over Reisman's men. In one scene the group is participating in war games and the men push him from a moving truck when they have no more use for him.

The men themselves are a band of mostly violent criminals, including one psychotic murderer, Archer Maggott (Telly Savalas). Although they do obey Reisman's orders, they have no allegiance to the military at all. Most have chosen to participate because they are awaiting execution and have nothing to lose anyway and because they will have their criminal records dismissed in the unlikely event that they survive the mission. Nevertheless, with the exception of Maggot, all the men achieve heroic status, as they are successful in killing a slew of German officers just prior to D day. In the meantime they do develop loyalties to each other.

The other patriotic movie from the 1966–1975 decade is *Patton* (1969). Although General Patton himself was a controversial figure and is portrayed as such in the film, *Patton* is a much more traditional war film. As we noted above, this film and *Top Gun* are the only overtly patriotic films that turned up in our sample in which the characters appear in situations that are not extraordinarily isolated or fantastic. The military appears in a relatively favorable light.

Of the three anti-military films of the third decade, *Catch 22* (1970) is the most outspoken. Yossarian and his fellow squadron members are forced to fly an interminable number of missions. One of the men, Orr, repeatedly crashes his fighter plane and later we discover that he does so to practice his plan for desertion—rowing a life raft to Sweden. The mess officer, Milo, starts a company (M & M Enterprises), symbolizing the capitalist system, that trades away such vital equipment as parachutes and first aid kits. Colonel Cathcard and Lieutenant Colonel Cord authorize and supervise a bombing raid on their own base in order to facilitate a deal between M & M Enterprises and the Nazis. General Dweezel is maniacal and inconsistent, ordering the execution of a Captain for groaning at a flight briefing and later taking no action against Yossarian when he shows up naked to receive a medal.

The military characters in this film, as well as those in *Little Big Man* (1970) and *M*A*S*H* (1970), who receive positive character-rating codes, are seldom patriotic and are more likely to take orders from their consciences rather than from their superiors. Those in positions of authority are immoral, deranged, tyrannical hypocrites and almost all receive negative ratings.

In the 1976–1990 period, except in *Top Gun* (1986), the same emphasis on fantastic situations and isolation prevails and the implicit or explicit critique of military authority is quite evident. Even an apparently noncritical movie like *Predator* (1987) creates a fantastic situation by introducing a sci-fi monster. Extreme isolation characterizes most of the other movies, even the patriotic films: *The Deer Hunter* (1979) and *Rambo, First Blood Part II* (1985).

In *The Deer Hunter*, Mike (Robert DeNiro), Nick (Christopher Walken), and Stevie (John Savage) are entirely isolated in the Vietnam scenes. There is no authority structure on which to rely. It is as if the war were being fought by isolated bands of individuals without anything in mind but survival. The first combat scene underlines the pointless brutality of war, as Mike executes, with a flame thrower, a Vietnamese soldier who has just tossed a grenade in a tunnel holding civilians. The event takes place without any military context—we don't even know if the soldier is North or South Vietnamese. After the three friends are captured by the enemy, they are forced to play Russian roulette. Mike tricks the Vietnamese soldiers into putting three bullets in the gun for the game and then shoots them all. The three friends make their escape and eventually reach safety, though not before Stevie loses his legs and Nick his sanity.

The strong friendships among them are not strengthened by the ordeal. Instead, the men are distanced from one another and from civilian life by the war. Stevie is afraid to leave the hospital and he and Mike have difficulty speaking to one another when Mike visits. When Nick, who has become a junkie, eventually kills himself in another Russian roulette game, Mike is with him, but is unable to prevent his death.

The three characters may be patriotic, but are more immediately motivated by self-interest. Moreover, Nick and Mike must resort to the most violent means to escape and survive. For all three soldiers, the outcome appears to depend upon chance and the strength of individual personality, not upon a coherent military organization. Even so, many critics pilloried *The Deer Hunter* as reactionary when it appeared, as the movie did not portray the war in a thoroughly negative light and evinced a good deal of sympathy for the plight of its middle- and working-class characters. This critical hostility toward *The Deer Hunter* has not abated with time; in an essay in *Representations*, the film scholar David E. James has characterized the film as "unapologetically imperialistic" (1990:87–88). Marlette Rebhorn, in *Screening America: Using Hollywood Films to Teach History*, praises the film, but does so because she feels that it does take a sufficiently critical stance toward American society: "*Deer Hunter* [sic] not only graphically depicts the brutality and degradation of Vietnam, but it also suggests that Russian roulette is merely an extension of an all-pervading violence typical of the society which produced both Michael and Nick" (1988:183).

Rebhorn distorts the plot of the film to score an ideological point. In fact, the first time we see the game of Russian roulette is when North Vietnamese guerrillas are using it as a way to toy with their American prisoners, gambling on their lives. Presumably, it is an extension of Vietnamese, not American society. We do not want either to praise or condemn the film here; we would nevertheless agree with Rebhorn's conclusion that the vision of America in *The Deer Hunter* is rather negative.

Rambo, First Blood Part II personifies the military in John Rambo (Sylvester Stallone); but he is a renegade, hardly a man who follows orders. He becomes a hero by distrusting and then defying authority. He is released from a hard labor prison, where he has served his sentence for beating up on dim-witted and malevolent police and military characters in the first Rambo picture, to search for MIAs in Vietnam. His orders are only to take pictures of prisoners, but he disobeys and frees some of the MIAs. The soldiers sent to pick him up, really mercenaries, are ordered by a U.S. government official to leave him behind. Rambo's commanding officer, Colonel Troutman (Richard Crenna), is powerless to help Rambo since he has no authority over the mercenaries. After being captured and tortured by Russian and Vietnamese soldiers, Rambo single-handedly escapes, massacres an endless stream of Russians and Vietnamese, steals a helicopter, and leads a band of MIAs to freedom. In the final scene, Rambo warns the government official that if he doesn't get the rest of the MIAs out he will come back for him personally and then riddles the command post with bullets. Although Rambo and Troutman are obviously patriotic figures, none of the characters in the movie that have any connection to the United States rely on authority and discipline. The whole outcome of the story hinges upon the violent actions of one superhuman, highly alienated warrior.

The anti-military films of the 1976–1990 period are even more critical of the military than the same class of films from the preceding decade. In *Private Benjamin* (1980), the female recruits are shown smoking pot on duty. The recruiting officer lies to Judi Benjamin (Goldie Hawn) to persuade her to join the Army. One female officer, Captain Lewis, is depicted as a paranoid martinet whose sexual preferences become a running gag. Colonel Thornbush attempts to rape Judi Benjamin in a plane. Another captain has sex with one of the recruits during a combat exercise.

In *Close Encounters of the Third Kind* (1977), the military lies to the public, staging a chemical spill and contamination in order to keep a UFO visit secret, though in the end the officials greet the extraterrestrial visitors warmly, even reverently, under the leadership of a French scientist. In *Wargames* (1983), though General Barringer (Barry Corbin) is not an entirely negative or impotent figure, another officer directly disobeys a missile launch order and is held at gunpoint by a subordinate. The alleged insubordination crisis precipitates installation of computer-controlled missile launching, setting up the film's premise of the possibility of an accidental nuclear war. Other military personnel in these movies are sometimes portrayed as silly, hypocritical, and/or psychotic.

Not surprisingly, the military character profiles of the past twenty-five years are substantially different from those of the first twenty years, bearing out the foregoing impressions. First of all, the continued salience of the goal of patriotism is clear as it pertains to 49 percent of the characters in the third period and 67 percent in the fourth period (see Table 4.4.). Similarly, the authority and discipline method is coded for 51 percent of the characters in the third decade and 60 percent in the fourth period (see Table 4.5).

There are, however, substantial declines in percentages of senior officers with patriotic goals who are portrayed positively and a corresponding increase in negative characterizations. For senior officers, positive patriotic characters drop from 59 percent in the first two decades to 50 percent in the third decade and decline to 38 percent in the most recent period. The number of negative patriotic depictions rises from only 9 percent in the first two decades to 20 percent in the third decade and then 38 percent from 1976 to 1990.

Similarly, a senior officer's exercise of authority and discipline is now more likely to correlate with a negative rather than a positive character rating. From 1966 to 1975, positive depictions of senior officers who adhere to methods of authority and discipline drop from 48 percent in the first two decades to 38 percent. From 1976 to 1990, they decline even further to only 24 percent. Conversely, in the first two decades, only 19 percent of senior officers exercising authority and discipline are rated negatively, but in the third decade this figure rises to 33 percent and in the fourth period to 48 percent. Among the low-ranking officers and recruits, authority and discipline becomes a more positive character trait. Only 20 percent of low-rank officers exercising authority and discipline are rated positively in the first two decades, but in the third decade the figure rises to 56 percent and remains at 53 percent from 1976 to 1990. Negative depictions decline from 40 percent negative before 1966 to 33 percent negative in the third decade and only 13 percent in the most recent period.

Alongside these declines in favorable representations of senior officers with patriotic goals and those exercising authority and discipline, there have been corresponding increases in the total number of violent or deceitful methods used; the majority of violent characters, most of them lower-rank officers, later earn positive ratings and the deceitful senior officers help propagate a negative image of the military.

Violent methods are up sharply both overall, from 7 percent in the first two decades to 29 percent in the third decade to 38 percent in the fourth period, and in the percentages of such methods that are portrayed positively, from 0 percent in the first two decades to 53 percent in the third decade and 54 percent in the last period. Interestingly, violence among positively depicted low-ranking officers rises from zero in the first two decades to 40 percent in the third decade to 57 percent in the latest period. Negative depictions decline from 67 percent to 40 percent in the third decade to 14 percent in the most recent period. Senior officers are much less likely to act violently and are regarded as villains for different reasons. Individual initiation of violence, then, has become an acceptable means for the ordinary soldier to employ, principally because the military's institutional legitimacy has all but vanished.

Deceit and trickery have also become more prevalent. Only 12 percent of characters rely on deceit and trickery to achieve their goals in the first two decades as compared to 17 percent in the third decade and 21 percent in the latest period. At the same time, the use of such methods is reevaluated by Hollywood. Pictured positively when used against World War II enemies or by enlisted men against authoritarian or bumbling officers, reliance on deceit and trickery is negatively portrayed from the late 1970s through the 1980s, because its use becomes overwhelmingly associated with "bad" characters who deceive their own men or the American public. Positive depictions of senior officers who use deceit and trickery declines from 67 percent to 28 percent in the third decade to 0 percent in the most recent period. In the most recent period, all of the senior officers coded for deceit and trickery receive negative ratings.

To a great degree, these changes in motives and methods result from the chaotic and isolated organizational setting that the characters are forced to cope with in recent movies. If the military can't take care of its own, then the soldier takes care of himself, by whatever means available.

The changes are particularly clear in Vietnam films like *Platoon* (1986) and *Good Morning Vietnam* (1987), not to mention the *Rambo* films. In these films and others like them, authority figures are often portrayed as incompetent, if not vile. The sense of community or fraternity, once a prominent feature of the military movie, barely survives, or if it does, becomes a source of sadism and evil. No better example can be found in our sample of the complete breakdown of loyalty and trust among soldiers than Barnes' (Tom Berenger) murder of Elias (Willem Dafoe) in *Platoon*.

In the new films, because soldiers are more likely to be motivated by survival than by a traditional notion of duty, violence becomes more predominant and tends to be depicted as a desirable method for soldiers to employ. Every man for himself. For one soldier in *Platoon*, Bunny (Kevin Dillon), who is earlier seen murdering a crippled peasant, Vietnam is reduced to a playground for carrying out sadistic acts of violence. He has only this to say about the war: "I like it here. The only worry you got is dying, and if that happens you won't know it anyhow."

In other recent films, characters face unrealistic, extremely isolated situations where lines of authority are minimal to nonexistent, or confused by meddling government agencies. A more recent example of this than the Rambo film is *Predator* (1987), in which the CIA draws Dutch (Arnold Schwarzenegger) and his men into a covert raid on a jungle terrorist base, by tricking them into thinking that they are on a hostage rescue mission.

In the newer films, there are fewer senior-ranking officers, and soldiers make more decisions on their own. When senior officers are present, they more often figure negatively and their motives and methods are suspect. Sergeant Major Dickerson (J. T. Walsh) from *Good Morning Vietnam*, is just such a character; he deliberately attempts to get Adrian (Robin Williams) killed by the North Vietnamese, because he doesn't like his politics and lack of respect for military authority. In these films, major characters are often alienated from their own military organizations, displaying a disregard for authority and discipline within the military chain of command. Adrian Crownauer (Robin Williams), the infamous DJ from *Good Morning Vietnam*, is an obvious example of this character type. Even in *Top Gun*, the most patriotic box office success since *Patton*, Maverick (Tom Cruise) gets into trouble with his superiors for breaking rules of dogfight engagement, buzzing a control tower, and generally doing things his way instead of following orders.

In short, if we examine their goals and motivations, we are left with the impression that most U.S. military personnel are selfish, irresponsible, often vicious, and rarely concerned with the interests of their country, much less the ordinary decencies. Plots in recent pictures frequently turn around the necessity of the hero's renegade status and willingness to break military rules, often purportedly to uphold a more humane ethical code that the military has compromised. The impact upon the public of such portrayals is just as significant when the depictions are part of a film's background, rather than part of an explicitly military film. Thus, the "soft" negative presentation of the military in films like *Close Encounters of the Third Kind* (a negative portrayal that has become commonplace) may not only have as great a long-range importance as that of a film like *Platoon*, it also provides more information about the underlying assumptions of the Hollywood elite.

Motion Pictures, Public Opinion, and the Military

In *Guts and Glory*, Lawrence Suid attributes the change in Hollywood military movies to "growing disenchantment with the Vietnam conflict." As a result of this, he writes, "Americans began to explore their longstanding love of the martial spirit and their previously unquestioned respect for the military establishment" (1978:3). In this kind of analysis, elite filmmakers share that questioning, tapping into this vein of dissent, responding to it as to a kind of cultural market.

Indeed, the substantial breakdown of authority in recent movies may represent a significant ideological shift among large segments of the population; however, as we pointed out initially, public opinion polls indicate that the public's faith in the military remains fairly strong. Moreover, this kind of argument presupposes a "free market" relationship between Hollywood and the film audience that is problematic. If anything, the developments we have been tracing follow historical and structural changes in the Hollywood film industry as well as changes within society as a whole. How else can we explain the simultaneous success of a patriotic film such as *Top Gun* and a much more critical film, *Platoon*?

The changes in the military image on film are the work of a new class of Hollywood filmmakers, whom we have found to be not only liberal and cosmopolitan in outlook, but also very critical of many American institutions— much more critical than the public at large. To recount one of our findings in Chapter 3, of various leadership groups, movie producers ranked the military fifth in perceived influence, but would have preferred that the military rank last in influence. Thus, we expected to find and did find, in films of the past twenty-five years, an image of the American military that is in step with the new Hollywood outlook. Indeed, as we have emphasized, our data indicate that even characters in so-called conservative military movies, such as the *Rambo* films, are portrayed much differently than they used to be.

In short, it would appear that the conflict between the individual and military authority has been resolved by the Hollywood elite, in favor of the individual. In the absence of commanding officers, individual choice is celebrated, independent action imperative. Those in authority are often suspect and have little real power over the story's course of events. In the midst of all the resulting narrative chaos, Hollywood soldiers now write their own orders and must resolve the moral problems of war for themselves. Consequently, there is no transference of responsibility and soldiers bear the full burden for their decisions and actions. That is why, for instance, the military characters in films about Vietnam appear to carry the moral weight of the whole war on their shoulders.

That was not the case in earlier films, when, by and large, soldiers simply followed the orders of those exercising legitimate authority in what was assumed to be a good cause. In many of the earlier movies, soldiers had difficulty sacrificing their personal lives for the good of the country. But although the conflict between the individual and authority was powerful, those who refused to bend lost out or were depicted as contemptuous. Those who willingly served their country were some of the most highly regarded characters on the screen. It would not be unreasonable to go further and suggest that this kind of relation to the military in America is still closer to reality—otherwise the military simply could not continue to exist as a legitimate institution, let alone engage in armed conflict. However one may feel about its particular aims, the Gulf War was in no way as chaotic as contemporary films make other military actions appear. In fact, it was quite the reverse. The soldiers participating assumed that they were led by competent and moral men and women whose authority they could readily accept.

The new military image, then, marks a retreat from historical authenticity and helps explain why the military movie as a quasi-documentary has fallen on hard times. That type of film provided audiences with a different kind of entertainment, in which there weren't so many moral dilemmas, so much irony, so much blood and naked violence. The audience was not as impressed by the personalities of the soldiers, because whatever individuality the soldier took with him into battle was far less important than what he did while he was there. But that was because the soldier was under orders and usually believed in their legitimacy (as did the audience), and it was easy enough for the audience to believe that his commanding officers knew what they were doing—that they cared about what they were fighting for and about their men's lives, or were, at the least, honest and competent.

We would not dispute the argument that a great many Americans have been disillusioned by their perceptions of historical events like the Vietnam War. We argue, however, that Hollywood producers, writers, and directors seem to have been disproportionately so disillusioned, and this helps to explain the high level of cynicism that emerges from Hollywood's more recent military images, even when they are packaged as patriotism. Consider the following lines of military characters from two different movies three decades apart:

> Colonel Robert (Dutch) Holland: I had to make a decision . . . I'm not getting out at all. I'm staying in the Air Force permanently. . . . Well, there are times when you're given certain responsibilities. You can't ignore them. . . . Sally, if there was a war on you wouldn't question any of this . . . But there is a kind of war. We've got to stay ready to fight without fighting. That's even tougher. That's why I made this decision. (*Strategic Air Command*, 1955)

> Co: What about orders?
> Rambo: No more orders Co. (*Rambo, First Blood Part II*, 1985)

The differences here typify the changes in films with military characters. Note that both of these films take a supposedly patriotic line, but Rambo's patriotism issues in a denial, not an affirmation, of military protocol.

In their harsh judgments of representations of the U.S. military, the majority of film critics and scholars seem to have been influenced by the developments of the 1960s and 1970s even more than the Hollywood elite. But given the data we have assembled, it makes little sense to argue that what we have been seeing since the 1980s is some kind of resurgent, old-fashioned patriotism. Patriotism has never really been a critical issue. The anti-military view continues to enjoy box office success in the popularity of films produced since the closing date of our study, such as *Born on the Fourth of July* (1990), which received a uniformly warm critical reception. Even recent films that do not appear to be critical of American foreign policy tend, on the whole, to present us with characters who have very different motivations and goals than did their patriotic predecessors. We expect that coding films such as Oliver Stone's second Vietnam story would only reinforce the statistical profile that emerges from our study.

Our study was completed before the collapse of the Soviet Communist regime began to affect Hollywood's depiction of the military. It is hard to know what direction it will take in the long run. One suspects that a bifurcation will occur in such treatment, as it has in movie and television depiction of many professionals (for example, doctors and lawyers). The good guys share the world outlook of the producers of those shows, whereas the bad guys are hidebound conservatives (Lichter, Lichter, and Rothman, 1991, 1994).

Some television shows, most notably an HBO exclusive, *By the Dawn's Early Light*, produced in the aftermath of *Glasnost*, were characterized by story lines in which some elements of the American and Soviet armed forces attempt to block the peaceful resolution of international conflicts. In the HBO film, which uses many of the conventions of the older, documentary-style military movies, a nuclear war between the Americans and Russians is triggered by internal Russian conflict (in this case, a group that wants to discredit the Russian leader). The Russian government apologizes after dropping a few bombs and the film's central conflict then shifts to infighting within the U.S. government. Predictably, the sympathetic characters are the officials who advocate accepting the Russian offer of peace, and, in a subplot, the bomber crewmembers who abandon their mission without authorization. These heroes are arrayed against fanatical hawks in the administration who want to bomb the Soviets into submission and have gained control of the presidency because the actual president (Martin Landau) is missing and feared dead.

On the bomber, the bad guys are those who wish to complete the mission. The film ends as the "good" officials, riding in a tactical military operations plane, ram Air Force One in order to kill the hawkish secretary of the interior (who has assumed the presidency after hearing that the president has been killed) and his advisors. In order to do this, the leader of the good officials (James Earl Jones) has to choose to disobey the acting president and follow Landau's character, who has not in fact been killed. A dovish president thus himself becomes a kind of dissident and this unquestionably patriotic film nevertheless represents all of its negative characters as high-level members of the U.S. government.

The question of whether recent military films take liberal or conservative stances towards American foreign policy makes little sense, because the ground has shifted—many of the films of the past twenty-five years question the legitimacy of any traditional military protocol whatsoever, even if the films appear to be jingoistic. Although this may change, the movies of the past twenty-five years make it look unlikely. It seems that Hollywood's new vision of military authority and the individual's relation to it has had a considerable and lasting impact on American popular culture and is not about to shift back to an older code. Indeed, our analysis of the evaluation of the military in films from 1990 through 1994 (Chapter 10) reveals a continued downward spiral in its portrayal.

5

Crime, Violence, and the Police

The widely publicized beating of Rodney King and the violence that erupted subsequent to the not-guilty verdict for the four Los Angeles police officers charged, underscores the increasingly difficult questions we now face about urban violence and public order. In doing their jobs, police officers confront dilemmas—walking a "tightrope" (to borrow a Clint Eastwood movie title) between excessive and insufficient use of force. Dubious images of law enforcement, prevalent in recent popular movies, may only reinforce the public's perception of the police and of the legal system as profoundly flawed institutions. They promote the idea that police are either heroic, violent renegade cops or corrupt, ineffective, and inept fools. Indeed, although most Hollywood cops haven't exactly become the bad guys, they now actually share many negative qualities previously associated only with villains.

These recent characterizations are probably less indicative of a conscious effort to malign the police than of a larger set of predispositions held by moviemakers that prompt them to cast the police as products and victims of their sordid working environment. In contemporary films, the police are only rarely shown as organization men—members of a well-ordered and competent institution protecting an essentially just system of law and decency. Instead, they are predominantly mavericks of one kind or another. They confront, and are themselves victims of, a corrupt society in which politicians, businessmen, the legal system, and sometimes even the police force, have either failed to protect citizens or have deliberately violated the social contract. Not surprisingly, crime, violence, and victimization escalate in this Hobbesian world, becoming more a part of police work, as cops are immersed in an environment where justice and order take a back seat to the laws of necessity and survival.

One can argue that these characterizations of police roles are only tailor-made to cater to a moviegoing public that judges a movie's value by its body count. But the public's acquired taste for bloody violence and crime seems to be only a contributory factor, in spite of the industry's insistence that it merely gives the people what they want. At least as important is the fact that Hollywood's projection of its own social and political views now makes it more likely that movie characters will act in extreme and sensational ways, whether they are in positions of authority or not. This is so because, on the one hand, movies tend to represent "the system" and its leaders as suspect, and on the other hand, because individual characters—subordinates and those outside of these institutions—must contend with or somehow circumvent this corrupt system's perverse influence. Thus, crime and violence are not only exaggerated, but increasingly become acceptable means of coping with a world "gone crazy."[1]

As we have already demonstrated, contemporary moviemakers sustain a comparatively high level of alienation and mistrust of authoritative institutions combined with a strong egalitarian bias, so they are more likely to portray certain types of characters as alienated from their respective institutions. In this case, the "outsiders" on the police force today more frequently ignore or criticize conformance with normal rules and procedures and take matters into their own hands than they used to. They have to, because the system rarely provides the necessary help. The pattern is similar to that which we have found among military characters, except that portrayals of higher-ranking police officers are not as consistently negative. Instead, politicians, the business community, and deranged military types are more likely to provide the villains in stories involving the police.

For the military, Hollywood hero imagery has had some very real and adverse effects, even dating back to the studio days. Training-officers in wars past, confronted with the spectacle of one of Hollywood's most popular warriors, John Wayne, in a variety of combat roles, warned recruits about the dangers of placing too much stock in do-or-die heroics. The officers rightly insisted that this was a sure way of ending up a casualty and might unnecessarily jeopardize other soldiers. According to Lawrence Suid in *Guts and Glory*, "Wayne's influence reached not only enlisted men, but also the decision-makers and officers in the field. One high-ranking officer who was in Vietnam during the build-up of American forces in the mid-1960s thought the escalation of American efforts to win the war was at least 'in a simplistic sense' the response of people 'racing around trying to be John Wayne, applying force to a problem which required something else'" (1978:106).

Similarly unrealistic, Hollywood's representation of police work looks more like organized vigilantism than the measured use of force in bringing criminals to justice. Justice is more often than not dispensed by the police themselves in recent movies, without any account of the legal process that is expressly designed to prevent this. In the wake of many widely publicized instances of brutality in American cities, it is tempting to speculate about whether Hollywood's image of the police may influence the way some officers employ force in maintaining law and order. More than a few police departments in Los Angeles, New York, and elsewhere have come under attack from the media and the public for excessive use of force. In spite of their heroic status in fighting against near impossible odds, do Clint Eastwood and Mel Gibson character types help the image of the police and the justice system? Or does the spectacle of a breed of loose cannons make us all feel more insecure and afraid—not only of the criminals, but of the very professionals whose job it is to thwart them? Most public officials concede only that there are a very small number of these types on any police force, but if maverick cops have become the predominant image in the movies, how realistic will the public's perception be of the nature of the police and the work they do?

As the Rodney King episode clearly demonstrated, the negative publicity associated with excessive violence and abuse of authority has diminished public support, perhaps not only for individuals and departments but for law enforcement officials generally. At the same time, the threat of injury or death to officers continues to escalate and that makes it harder for them to determine appropriate responses to crime and violence while in the line of duty. Often, circumstances may not allow time for clear judgments. Perhaps contributing to the problem, Hollywood's view of the police seems to convey the necessity of extreme action and a disregard for rules and procedures in maintaining order. Conversely, standard operating procedures are the subject of much comedy in recent movies; they usually fail miserably and those involved appear foolish and incompetent.

During the past two or three decades, Hollywood moviemakers have almost always portrayed the system of law enforcement as less than exemplary. Movies such as *Serpico* or *Dog Day Afternoon*, which criticize aspects of law enforcement by emphasizing brutality, injustice, and corruption or more recently, movies making a joke out of police work, such as *Naked Gun* or *Police Academy*, project an ambivalent image of those entrusted to keep law and order. Even the right-wing hero imagery of *Dirty Harry,* and later the *Lethal Weapon* films, suggests that real police officers are too constrained by their superiors and/or the legal system to function effectively. Only renegade cops, like renegade warriors such as Rambo, have the guts to buck the system and get the job done. These movies constitute an anomaly within an otherwise liberal Hollywood establishment, but, interestingly, they encourage the view that unrestrained violence is a legitimate way to deal with evil and that controlled attempts to maintain order will not be successful. Of course, unlike Dirty Harry movies, the heroes in the various Lethal Weapon repeats are often pursuing such bad guys as racist South Africans, so the violation of rules is for a good liberal cause.

In evaluating changes in the depictions of law and order, we focus on contemporary police forces as well as lawmen in westerns.[2] From our sample of 1946–1990 films, we were able to obtain demographic statistics for a total of 331 characters involved in law enforcement, with more detailed profiles available for ninety-eight of these characters. These characters are found not only in movies specifically about the police and crime, but also in films in which the police may play only minor roles. The advantage of this approach is that it provides us with a composite image of depictions of law enforcement and crime in film that extends beyond the crime genre to capture more subtle images of the police in movies of all types.

The Rising Tide of Crime and Violence

Before focusing on law enforcement officials, it is helpful to glimpse the context within which these characters operate. Surveying the extent of crime and violence in popular movies, we can confirm what seems obvious to many: The world according to Hollywood has become much more violent and dangerous over the past twenty-five years. This condition establishes a backdrop against which not only police, but also other characters, seek to accomplish their objectives. The surroundings are contrivances of Hollywood. They tend to exaggerate the extent and nature of crime, corruption, and institutional failure and such movies bear little resemblance to the statistical realities of American life, whether for the police or for the average citizen. Nevertheless, these dramatic settings serve to make the characters' predicaments more compelling. The extreme action taken by Hollywood's heroes, within the environment that the movies establish, thus appears warranted and justifiable. Characters' responses to their surroundings are more limited in recent movies—crime and violence are often presented as necessary evils—and the result is a gross exaggeration of these behaviors for all characters. In earlier movies, where systemic evils were less prevalent, characters could rely on more traditional sources for help or guidance—such as from a superior officer, a rich uncle, the legal system, or a religious leader. Today, characters frequently have to go it alone or rely on a few trusted friends or acquaintances.

Realism, then, defined as a concern for the presentation of fact or reality, is not quite what Hollywood is after. It never has been. More accurately, Hollywood has exchanged one set of myths for another. In movies of the 1940s and 1950s, in part due to the Production Code restrictions and a much more conservative influence on movie content from the studio executives themselves (at least by today's standards), the characters' dramatic environs were much more hospitable—often sickeningly sweet. With the rising tide of social unrest that grew out of the 1960s, came a revolt, of sorts, against this idealized version of American life. The social turmoil of the 1960s, structural changes within the movie industry, the decline of box office receipts, and the increasing proportion of audiences that consisted of young people dealt a mortal blow to the old movie genres. The newer popular films of the 1960s and 1970s were permeated with a cynicism and suspicion of authority even more prevalent among many of the movie elite than among the general public. Extensive crime and violence in contemporary movies is a legacy of this earlier transformation of both the American film market and those with creative control over the movie industry. This legacy is one of a number of striking features of Hollywood's new American mythos—a much more troubled fiction than that presented in the studio days.

In the past two decades of the studio era, from 1946 to 1965 (see Table 5.1), the total number of characters committing crimes was only 14 percent of the total number of coded characters. This figure rose considerably to 28 percent in the 1966 to 1975 decade. Since then, the total number of characters committing

TABLE 5.1 Comparison of Crime, Violence, and Victimization in the Movies with Actual Crime (by decade)

	1946–1965	*1966–1975*	*1976–1990*
% Crime all characters	14	28	17
N=	1,454	858	1,695
% Crime major characters	27	46	38
N=	426	260	443
% Violence major characters	19	38	34
N=	426	260	443
% Major characters victimized	34	39	50
N=	426	260	443
Actual crime*	–	13	11
Actual crime**	1.2	2.2	5.5

*Rate for 1973–1975—average: 126/1,000. Rate for 1976–1989—average: 110/1,000. Criminal Victimizations of Persons and Households (National Crime Survey).

**Rate for 1957–1965—average: 11.5/1,000. Rate for 1966–1970—average: 22/1,000. Rate for 1980–1990—average: 55/1,000 (offenses known to police).

crimes has declined substantially, down to 17 percent from 1976 to 1990. However, if we look at the number of *major* characters committing crimes (excluding all characters coded as neutral), we get a much different impression. In the first two decades, about 27 percent of major characters committed crimes; however, in the third decade, crimes were committed by nearly half of all major characters (46 percent). Crime among major characters still declined somewhat in the most recent period but remained considerably higher than in the studio days, holding at about 38 percent (see Table 5.1).

Both these findings indicate that crime reached unprecedented levels in Hollywood movies in the 1965 to 1975 decade. Whereas the overall incidence of crime tapered off in the 1980s, major characters were still much more likely to engage in crime than they were before the mid-1960s.

Even more striking is the increase in the number of characters who resort to violence and the number who are victimized in some way. From 1946 to 1965, only two out of ten major characters resorted to violence as a method for achieving their objectives. From 1966 to 1975, the figure doubled, declining only marginally after that. The number of characters who are victimized has also sharply risen in the past twenty-five years. We have defined victimization fairly broadly. To quote from the coding instructions, "victimization takes place when the character is by deliberate action, negligence, or circumstance injured, held back, persecuted, or in some way disadvantaged by the acts of another." Examples of the categories include acts by: superiors, equals, or subordinates in the workplace; family members; friends or lovers; strangers; the justice system; business contacts; and so forth.

Nevertheless, although only 34 percent of major characters were victimized during the first two decades, the figure rose to 39 percent in the third decade and to five out of ten from 1976 to 1990 (see Table 5.1). As we shall see, whereas the police tended not to commit violent acts and were not the victims of violence prior to the mid-1960s, in recent years they have been drawn into the game and actually *contribute disproportionately* to the larger trends (see Tables 5.1, 5.3, 5.4, 5.5).

Relying on the FBI's national crime survey, we can make a reasonably accurate estimate of the extent of crime in movies compared to estimates of actual crime in American society. In Table 5.1, we present data for crimes known to the police for the years 1957–1965, 1966–1970, and 1980–1990. These estimates are considerably lower than those provided by more recent victimization data and are not comparable to them. Using these figures, we can see that crime rates in Hollywood movies are anywhere from five to forty times greater than in society. The FBI's victimization data (available for 1973, 1975, and 1976–1989) give us a more accurate picture of crime in society. When we compare the FBI percentages to movie crime rates, we still find that movie crime outstrips real crime. From 1973 until 1990, crime rates have ranged from 110 to 130 crimes per thousand on average. Comparable rates for the two most recent decades in the movies are 280 and 170 per thousand for all characters and 460 and 380 per thousand among major characters. Thus, crime in Hollywood movies is anywhere from two to four times as prevalent as actual crime estimated by the FBI victimization data. It is understandable then that critics of the motion picture industry have charged Hollywood with exaggerating crime and violence in the movies. By either of these comparisons, movies appear to have done so over the entire period of the study. In the most recent decades, crime has reached unprecedented levels in films and does not present a realistic picture of its place in American society.

Crime Doesn't Pay: 1946–1965

From 1946 to 1965, Hollywood offered very few surprises when law and order were concerned. The Production Code rather straightforwardly prohibited sympathy with criminals, any allusions to the idea that crime was somehow legitimate or justifiable, or disparaging images of the legal system. The following guidelines were set forth in the Production Code of the 1930s and remained in effect until 1966:

> General Principles. . . . Law, natural or human, shall not be ridiculed, nor shall sympathy be created for its violation.
> Crimes Against the Law. . . . These shall never be presented in such a way as to throw sympathy with the crime as against law and justice or to inspire others with a desire for imitation. (Leff and Simmons, 1990:284)

This represents only one example of a number of stipulations set forth in the Production Code, the movie industry's instrument of self-censorship for thirty-five years. In the studio era, movies dealing with police and crime usually conformed to these codes. The police were, by and large, the good guys, impartially enforcing the laws. Criminals, for the most part, were bad guys and they, rather than society, were usually responsible for their behavior.

Our content analysis demonstrates the truth of this proposition. Though only a few major characters in our study in the first two decades are police officials, an analysis of several key variables for major and minor characters of the period indicates that they occupy the moral high ground in fighting crime. Not one of the ten major law enforcement characters receives a negative character rating. Seven (70 percent) are positive characters and only three receive mixed ratings (see Table 5.2).

Throughout the entire period, the majority of law enforcers do what they do for moral or ethical reasons. In the first two decades, nine out of ten law enforcers are coded as acting for these reasons. Police officials in the first two decades are also unlikely to use violence. Only one out of ten characters (10 percent) resorts to violence in the 20-year period (see Table 5.3). Only three (30 percent) are victimized in any way, suggesting a certain invulnerability. When law and order are concerned, "right makes might" (see Table 5.4).

Another obvious indication of the legitimacy of law enforcement is the incidence of crimes committed by police officers. Not surprisingly, we find that in the first two decades only seven of fifty-eight police officers (12 percent) commit any type of crime. As significantly, only two of the ten main characters (20 percent) commit any crime (see Table 5.5). These four dimensions of the law enforcement

TABLE 5.2 Character Rating of Law Enforcement Personnel (by decade and rank)

	1946–1965	*1966–1975*	*1976–1990*
All law enforcement			
% Positive	70	75	64
% Negative	0	21	19
% Mixed	30	4	16
N=96	10	24	62
Supervisors			
% Positive	50	25	50
% Negative	0	75	31
% Mixed	50	0	19
N=24	4	4	16
Rank and file			
% Positive	83	85	70
% Negative	0	10	15
% Mixed	17	4	16
N=72	6	20	46

TABLE 5.3   Law Enforcement Characters' Moral Goals and Violent Methods (by decade and rank)

	1946–1965	1966–1975	1976–1990
% Moral			
All	90	75	73
Supervisors	100	25	81
Rank and file	83	85	70
% Violent			
All	10	67	45
Supervisors	0	75	25
Rank and file	10	65	52
N=	10	24	62

image change quite dramatically after 1965. Some fairly typical films of the period flesh out the statistics.

In *The Greatest Show on Earth* (1952), Buttons the clown (Jimmy Stewart), a doctor on the run for the mercy killing of his dying wife, is arrested at the end of the film. There is no looking the other way for detective Gregory (Henry Wilcoxon), the officer who tracks down Buttons. Even though Buttons heroically saves Brad's (Charlton Heston) life, giving away the clown's true identity, Gregory is still obliged to take the fugitive doctor into custody. After providing medical care, Buttons surrenders quietly to the detective, recognizing that the officer has his job to do. The underlying assumption is that the officer represents an impartial system of law that, regardless of his personal feelings, does not allow him the discretion to let Buttons go free.

In *Rear Window* (1954), Jeff (Jimmy Stewart) tries to convince his friend, detective Tom Doyle (Wendell Corey), that a man living across the back alley from him has murdered his wife. Even though he is skeptical, Doyle does his job and investigates the alleged crime but finds no convincing evidence. Jeff and his girl-

TABLE 5.4   Law Enforcement Characters Victimized (by decade and rank)

	1946–1965	1966–1975	1976–1990
% All victimized	30	71	63
N=	10	24	62
% Supervisors victimized	25	50	50
N=	4	4	16
% Rank and file victimized	33	75	67
N=	6	20	46

TABLE 5.5   Percent of Law Enforcement Characters Committing Crimes (by decade and rank)

	1946–1965	*1966–1975*	*1976–1990*
% All law enforcement	12	35	20
% Supervisors	10	36	15
% Rank and file	13	35	21
N=	58	115	158
% Major characters law enforcement	20	33	47
% Supervisors	25	75	25
% Rank and file	17	25	54
N=	10	24	62

friend, Lisa (Grace Kelly), still suspect the worst and continue to snoop on their own. Lisa breaks into the murderer's apartment and finds the woman's wedding ring (more evidence of foul play), only to have the murderer discover her when he comes home. Jeff calls the police and they arrive just in time to save Lisa from the murderer. They arrest her for burglary and take her to the station. In the meantime, the murderer realizes who is spying on him and goes to Jeff's apartment to kill him. As he attempts to throw Jeff (who is confined to a wheelchair with a broken leg) from the window, the police return with Lisa and detective Doyle, who now apparently believes there is sufficient evidence to question the murderer. Again, police are just in time to save Jeff and arrest the villain. In this film, although the police are minor characters, they perform well, providing critical support to the characters, who would have come to a bad end without their assistance.

Comedies such as *Some Like It Hot* (1959) also portray the police in an essentially uncritical manner—as good guys chasing after bad guys. The film begins with a carload of police speeding after a gang of bootleggers. Led by a federal officer, they raid a speakeasy and arrest the patrons. In the closing scenes of the movie, the federal agent detains all the gang members after one of the head gangsters, Spats Columbo (George Raft), is assassinated by a rival boss. Similarly, in *Road to Rio*, the police arrest the villains at the end of the movie and lead them away to jail. In *Father's Little Dividend* (1951), Stanley Banks (Spencer Tracy) leaves his grandchild unattended in a park while he plays soccer with a group of young boys. When he returns the baby is gone and he searches frantically for him, finally going to the police. The police Sergeant (Richard Rober), a positive figure, lectures Banks about his negligence. The sergeant informs him that the baby was discovered by an officer on duty and taken to the station. When the Sergeant shows Banks in to get his grandson, a crowd of officers are playing with the infant. Once again, the police save the day. *House of Wax* (1953) presents two law enforcement characters from the same mold as the others from the 1946 to 1965 period. Lieutenant Brennan and officer Jim Shane are the officers who save Sue from being killed in the wax museum. One of the men resorts to violence in the line of duty, but only to save a life and bring the two surviving villains to justice.

In *A Place in the Sun* (1951), the police quickly apprehend George Eastman (Montgomery Clift) for the murder of Alice Trip (Shelly Winters). Although there is some ambiguity about the exact circumstances of Alice's death, he is found guilty. In the end, the priest who comes to hear George's last confession resolves the issue of whether George has been justly sentenced for murder. The priest tells him that if he hesitated to save Alice from drowning because he was thinking of Angela (Elizabeth Taylor), then he is morally responsible for her death. George admits that he is guilty and although this may not have been enough to convict him legally, the movie leaves no doubt that morally George's arrest and conviction are legitimate. There is no implication of the society as being to blame for George's end, despite the structure of the Dreiser novel on which it is based. He is responsible for his own fate.

In *Guys and Dolls* (1955), Lieutenant Brannigan (Robert Keith) represents a somewhat less credible police officer. He fails to catch the gamblers in the floating crap game at the mission. Later, he is tricked into believing that the gamblers are not gambling, but have all assembled at the coffeehouse for Nathan Detroit's (Frank Sinatra) surprise wedding announcement. When the gamblers attend a prayer meeting at the mission after losing the bet with Sky Masterson (Marlon Brando), Brannigan is duped again. Sarah (Jean Simmons) tells him that these are not the same gamblers present at the crap game, therefore he has no case against them. In spite of this more satiric view of both cops and crooks, the basic integrity of the police is unequivocal. If the mission provides the moral carrot, Brannigan is the stick. Like the mission workers, he represents a moral social influence upon the gamblers, doing his best to prevent them from going all bad. Inspector Clouseau, from *Return of the Pink Panther* (1964), is a similarly foolish type of character but he too somehow manages to foil the villains and restore law, if not order. These last two films end happily enough but provide early glimpses of the kind of chaos that becomes more prevalent in later representations of law enforcement.

Lawlessness and Disorder: 1966–1975

The restrictions imposed by the Production Code upon movies about the law and crime had disappeared by the mid-1960s, victims of the demise of the studios themselves and changing social and political attitudes toward censorship and artistic freedom. The newer rating system allows much more liberty to filmmakers; and new generations of writers, directors, and producers began to alter their product accordingly, not only to meet the demands of the changing market but also to reflect their own views of the world more closely. Since the mid-1960s, most films about law enforcement have fallen into one of two broad categories: they tend to be either populist vigilante versions of justice, of which the Clint Eastwood films are the most noteworthy, or they are movies that portray law enforcement officials in an unsympathetic way, such as *Serpico* (1974) or *Dog Day Afternoon* (1976). The majority of police characters from 1965 to 1975 can be characterized, at polar extremes, as either heroes or villains.

In the renegade police officer films, law and order is obstructed by bureaucratic regulation and a justice system that is too soft on criminals. Police officers are often inept and ineffective, or worse, corrupt and part of the problem. The star is usually a superhuman and practically bulletproof hero who single-handedly restores order to the streets. The plot similarities between these movies and that of *Rambo II*, in which Rambo returns to Vietnam to score a moral and political victory for the failed war effort, are remarkable. By ignoring orders and defying authority, Dirty Harry, like Rambo, gets the job done, while others look on enviously.

Systematic content analysis demonstrates the changes quite persuasively. Whereas in the previous decades we discovered no negative representations of law enforcers, such images are 21 percent of the total in the 1966 to 1975 period (see Table 5.2). It is true that 75 percent of the portrayals remain positive, but the shift to violent methods, extraordinarily high levels of victimization, and substantially higher crime rates among police officers indicate that law enforcers are now more likely to be playing by the same rules as the criminals. The city streets are portrayed in a near state of anarchy where the law of the jungle seems to be the only standard for action.

The number of characters resorting to violent methods rises from 10 percent in the first two decades to an astounding 67 percent in the third decade (see Table 5.3). Victimizations of police officers rise from 30 percent prior to 1966 to 71 percent in the following decade (see Table 5.4). Forty percent of these victimizations fall into the category of "other or multiple victimizations." The number of crimes committed by officers of the law also jumps from 12 percent prior to 1966 to 35 percent in the following decade (see Table 5.5).

These themes can be illustrated by more closely examining some fairly typical examples of the police-crime genre during the period. In the *Enforcer* (1977), Harry Callahan (Clint Eastwood) is at odds with his superiors, who accuse him of being too tough on criminals, giving the police department a public relations black eye. Still, Harry's violent methods get results, but the emphasis is on order rather than law—or at least law is reduced to "Harry's law of the jungle." It is important to recognize that these most cynical views of the police force didn't originate in the allegedly reactionary Hollywood of the 1980s, but began in the 1970s with films like *Dirty Harry* (1971), and *Magnum Force* (1974). These films may have gained some of their appeal from a public reaction against expanded procedural rights for criminals and the escalation of urban crime at the time, but importantly, they also fell into step with Hollywood's developing view of authoritative institutions as corrupt and ineffective. They emerged at the same time that many other films were casting a critical eye on not only the police force but also on other traditional authority structures. Paradoxically, despite their strong populist and right-wing hero imagery, these films share attributes with other anti-Establishment films, applauding individuals who defy authority in order to achieve their goals.

The protagonists are unlikely heroes, in other respects average guys who in one way or another are forced to challenge the system. For example, Dirty Harry is a middle-aged, working-class figure whose relationship to his department is ambivalent at best. He's marking time in a sense and in *The Gauntlet* mentions that he gave up on being a hero and just wants his pension, if he lives long enough. It is his alienation from a sick and corrupt society that drives him to a kind of small man's heroism. He has no personal stake in fame or glory, just in his own survival.

Serpico (1973) provides this type of critical view of power and authority in the police force as well. The movie is based on a true story of corruption in the New York police department and it exemplifies the broader trend toward critical representations of law enforcement. Frank Serpico (Al Pacino) is the hero, a "clean" cop who won't take bribes and who eventually blows the whistle on the department. The rest of the police, including higher-ranking officers, are exposed as willing participants in a sordid network of bribery and extortion. Even the mayor's office ignores the problem until Serpico is finally set up by fellow officers and shot in the face in a drug raid.

In some of the films in this category, the stories are told from the perspective of the criminals. In *Dog Day Afternoon* (1976), the bank robbers Sonny (Al Pacino) and Sal (John Cazale) are the protagonists. As the story unfolds, with detailed accounts of personal and psychological characteristics of the two criminals, the audience feels more and more sympathetic toward them. On the other hand, the police force is portrayed as inept and untrustworthy. There are scenes of a gathering crowd of protesters menacing the police and cheering for Sonny. The overwhelmingly white police force mistakenly assumes that an aging black security guard in the bank being released by Sonny is an accomplice to the robbery. They briefly place him under arrest until Detective Moretti (Charles Durning) realizes what is going on. In the end, the federal agents take control of the situation: they shoot Sal and arrest Sonny at the airport. At one point, although they are still in the bank, Sonny makes the following statement to the bank manager, "See what they [the cops] did at Attica? Huh. Forty-two people they killed. The innocent with the guilty." These are just a few of a number of obviously anti-Establishment messages in the film. Films like this are much different from earlier movies that evoked some degree of sympathy for criminals. Previously, the character flaws of the criminals were rarely blamed on social ills, but rather on personal tragedies such as a bad upbringing or a crime of passion. In more recent films, the larger society is very likely to be implicated as the cause of misconduct and the criminals are often perceived as tragic victims.

In *Butch Cassidy and the Sundance Kid* (1974), another story evoking sympathy for the criminals, the marshal can't even persuade the townspeople to form a posse to chase Butch (Paul Newman) and Sundance (Robert Redford). The marshal's lack of authority is clearly demonstrated when a bicycle salesman stands up next to him to sell to the crowd that has assembled and gets a better response. Later in the film, the two outlaws actually hide out for a few minutes at Sheriff Bledsoe's house. Bledsoe (Jeff Corey) is a lawman whom they had apparently previously bribed or befriended. He tells them that they are "two-bit outlaws" and that they'll wind up dying "bloody" but he makes no effort to arrest or detain them. He only asks that they tie him up and handcuff him, so that if they are found together he won't lose his job. Conveniently, the victims of the two outlaw's crimes are not really people. They never actually kill or even harm any honest citizens. It is banks and railroads, pretty unpopular manifestations of exploitive wealth and power, that keep the two in business.

Blazing Saddles (1974), an offbeat Western comedy, features the outlaw Waco Kid (Gene Wilder) as the sidekick of Sheriff Bart (Cleavon Little), an unlikely lawman in the old west. At various points in the film, Bart, who is black, commiserates with his prisoners, smokes marijuana, and visits a prostitute. In this film, the mayor, the governor, the sheriff, and the railroads are all implicated as corrupt and immoral.

John Boorman's *Deliverance* (1973) is one of the best examples of the complete breakdown of law and order. Four men take a weekend canoe trip in the mountains of Georgia and wind up fighting for their lives. Two of the men, Ed (John Voight) and Bobby (Ned Beatty), are assaulted by two homosexual mountain men, when the outsiders stop alongside the river. Lewis (Burt Reynolds) and Drew (Ronnie Cox), paddling behind the other boat, arrive on the scene and Lewis kills one man with a bow and arrow. Subsequently the four canoeists argue about whether to go to the authorities about the killing. When Drew argues in favor of following the law, Lewis rebukes him, saying that there is no law in their circumstance. He suggests that standing trial in the back country of Georgia would be as good as being lynched.

From this point on, the law of survival prevails and all of the men except Drew, who dies on the river, are converted to survivalists by their experience. In fact, mild-mannered Ed quickly assumes Lewis's role, after the latter breaks his leg and can no longer lead the others. Ed murders the second mountain man to ensure their safe passage down river. The local police, who investigate the incident, are unable to learn the truth because the bodies are hidden and no charges are brought against the survivors. Several statements made by the officer in charge imply that Lewis was essentially correct—the three men have narrowly escaped a hanging by outsmarting the "redneck" authorities. Law enforcement in the film is portrayed as merely a vicious extension of a sick and deranged rural community.

The War on Crime (1976–1990)

The characterizations of the police officer as some type of superman with a badge and a gun, an impotent pencil-pusher, or a corrupt villain survived into the late 1980s, though in many cases law enforcers were portrayed as comic rather than serious characters. Many of the more serious critiques of the police, like those of the military, now shifted to comedy. The image of the institution continued to stress disorganization and incompetence if not outright malevolence. Thus, Harry Callahan (Clint Eastwood) is replaced by a more witty but even more explosive renegade like Martin Riggs (Mel Gibson) in *Lethal Weapon* (1987). Axel Foley (Eddie Murphy) in *Beverly Hills Cop* (1984) or Mahoney (Steve Guttenberg) in *Police Academy* (1984) are even more comic figures. These characters fly by the seat of their pants and show little regard for authority. The underlying messages are virtually the same in these newer films, despite the shift to more comic treatment.

Nineteen percent of the police with character ratings are portrayed negatively in this period; however, more characters now receive mixed ratings than in the third decade, so the percentage of positive images has declined slightly, down from 75 percent in the third decade to 64 percent in the most recent period (see Table 5.2). Percentages of characters resorting to violence in the line of duty decline in the fourth period, but only to 45 percent, a figure that is still much higher than in the first two decades (10 percent—see Table 5.3). The number of victimizations of police officers in the most recent period remains extremely high at 63 percent. This time one in five of the victimizations occurs at the hands of the officers' own superiors, such as in *Police Academy*.

The incidence of crime among all officers actually drops in the fourth period, down from 35 percent in the previous decade to 20 percent; however, among the law enforcement characters who receive character ratings, nearly half (47 percent), commit crimes (see Table 5.5). Thus, the emphasis on crime has shifted from an aberration to a conspiracy to one that is represented as a major part of police work, often glorified by star characters such as Martin Riggs in *Lethal Weapon* or Axel Foley in *Beverly Hills Cop*.

In *Police Academy,* the training officers are out to get the recruits because they don't believe that women or blacks or short, fat, or faint-hearted characters belong on the force. Lieutenant Harris (G.W. Bailey) is the chief villain, defender of the familiar all-white, male police force exposed in *Dog Day Afternoon*, who does everything he can to get the cadets thrown out of the program. Among other things, he is portrayed as a hypocrite and a peeping Tom, and in the final scenes he has to be rescued by the recruits after he is taken hostage by a gunman in a riot. For all his tough talk and arrogance, he really turns out to be a fool.

Two other dim-witted officers, obviously racist sycophants from among the group of recruits, become Harris's henchmen. Throughout the film, they try unsuccessfully to sabotage the rest of the cadets. Commandant Lassard (George Gaynes) is another pencil-pusher—a naive and half-senile character who seems to care more about his pet goldfish than about the academy under his command. Among the cadets, the ringleader Mahoney (Steve Guttenberg), does all he can to get thrown out of the academy until he meets Thompson (Kim Cattrall), a "cute cadet." Tackleberry (David Graf) is the "Dirty Harry" of the bunch, carrying a side arm even more deadly than a 44 Magnum. We learn that in step with Hollywood's "born to kill" image of the military, he is an ex-member of a Special Forces team.

Police Academy II provides the same type of oddball entertainment as its predecessor. Six of the cadets, including Mahoney and Tackleberry, are assigned to the worst precinct in the city. Captain Lassard (Howard Hesseman), the Commandant's younger brother, is a well-meaning but vacillating police officer who loses his job to an unscrupulous subordinate, Lieutenant Mauser (Art Metrano). The cadets get his job back for him when they finally subdue a gang of hoodlums who are terrorizing the precinct. In the *Police Academy* movies, the police are not, on the whole, portrayed as evil; rather they are bunglers and victims of political posturing. The mayor has called for a crackdown on crime as a part of her reelection campaign and the police force turns out to be ill-equipped to live up to its obligations.

Officer Frank Drebin (Leslie Nielsen), the protagonist of *The Naked Gun* (1988), is a slapstick comic hero whose escapades include unintentionally injuring a fellow officer and numerous law abiding citizens, destroying his own squad car, and making a complete fool of himself trying to protect Queen Elizabeth from being assassinated at a baseball game. Drebin is a character who seems almost to close the gap between the alternate images of cops in recent movies as either heroes or fools. He uses many of the same heavy-handed approaches as a supercop, ignoring or botching whatever normal routines he undertakes and he's such an idiot that he ultimately succeeds only by accident. He is regarded as a dangerous incompetent by those around him until they must grudgingly acknowledge his unwitting heroism.

Axel Foley from *Beverly Hills Cop* is a savvy but insubordinate officer—always in trouble for breaking the rules. He's at odds with his boss in Detroit, Inspector Todd (Gilbert Hall) and with Lieutenant Bogamill (Ronny Cox) in California for his unorthodox police work. When he first arrives in Beverly Hills, he gets arrested and then is assaulted by Sergeant Taggart (John Ashton). In the course of investigating his friend's murder, he gets Taggart and Rosewood (Judge Reinhold) in trouble for going to a strip joint with him for drinks. The two officers help Foley rescue Jenny (Lisa Ellibacher) from Victor Maitland (Steven Berkoff) without a search warrant or, indeed, any authorization from Bogamill. The rescue is successful but turns into a violent confrontation during which most of the suspects are shot. So much for due process. The rest of the police force arrives, but in Keystone-cop fashion they all run into each other in Maitland's driveway. In the end, Bogamill lies to Chief Hubbard (Stephen Elliot), reporting the events as if Foley, Taggart, and Rosewood followed procedures exactly. The chief knows he's lying but isn't really interested in the truth, only in how the story will play in the press. Typically, the police still get the bad guys, but they use extreme violence in the line of duty and they violate the law. (Foley brags about stealing bathrobes from the hotel; Taggart assaults Foley.) They are victimized, not only by the criminals but also by each other. Once again, in this movie the integrity of the police force is compromised by its favoritism and subordination to the wealthy magnates of the community. It takes an irreverent cop to break down the facade and uphold a higher standard of justice.

In *Lethal Weapon,* negative images of the Vietnam War play a large role in the plot. The maniacal antihero Martin Riggs (Mel Gibson) and his somewhat mellower partner Roger Murtaugh (Danny Glover) are Vietnam veterans. They wind up hunting down villains General Peter McAllister (Mitchell Ryan) and Joshua (Gary Busey), who were once CIA-commissioned drug runners in the Vietnam war. The two war criminals now operate "Shadow Company" for profit, smuggling heroin into the United States. Clashes with automatic weapons, grenades, helicopters, martial arts, and torture create a war right in the streets of Los Angeles. Riggs, and eventually Murtaugh too, ride roughshod over the rule books of law enforcement "to get the job done." The scene where Riggs and Joshua fight hand to hand on Murtaugh's lawn—a crowd of officers looking on—would be a fitting end to a Bruce Lee movie, except that the hero is a cop. Before Joshua can be collared by two ordinary patrolmen, he manages to steal one of their sidearms and has to be gunned down by Riggs and Murtaugh. To the very end, the more routine system just doesn't work.

Conclusion

In Hollywood movies since the mid-1960s, the police have become increasingly like the criminals they face. There is no evidence of a reversal of this trend during the 1990s. Today's Hollywood moviemakers draw a much thinner line between the heroes and villains than they did in the studio days, when the Production Code and a relatively conservative and patriotic Hollywood elite enforced a wall of separation between these two classes of characters. Police are still more likely to be motivated by moral considerations and goals than are criminals. But when we take into account the actions the police now take in the line of duty, one wonders whether noble intentions are meaningful enough distinctions.

Public anxiety about increased crime and violence in the 1960s and 1970s perhaps created a new demand for movies about law enforcement. At the same time, social upheavals associated with the New Left—Vietnam and Watergate—had upset the status quo in American society and the upheavals were reflected in popular entertainment. Representations of law and order in the movies shifted dramatically in response to both of these historical developments. Older stories of law enforcement and crime didn't seem to fit anymore. Police stories were not that popular in the 1940s and 1950s because Hollywood was concerned with selling a rather idealized, tranquil vision of American society to the public. When police were featured, they generally succeeded in protecting the public with a minimum use of violence or other extraordinary means. Officers were for the most part moral and decent authority figures providing a basic service to the community. A few dabbled in espionage and intrigue, but more often than not cops walked a beat or chased after crooks on the back streets.

In the late 1960s and 1970s, movies became more naturalistic. Officers of the law became more complex characters—more human—as opposed to being just symbols of law and order itself. They became more individualistic, too, entangled in the sordid world in which they worked. Frequently, they responded to the extreme violence and crime surrounding them by becoming more violent, more unpredictable, and more dangerous themselves.

Rank and file police officers rarely use violence in the first two decades we analyzed—only one of ten officers resorts to violence. In the third decade, violence becomes a method for two-thirds of rank and file officers. In the most recent period, half of these officers resort to violence (see Table 5.3).

In addition, the police become more susceptible to crime and corruption. In the first two decades of our study, only one of six officers commits a crime. By the third decade, 25 percent commit crimes and in the most recent period, twenty-five of forty-six (54 percent) rank and file officers commit some type of crime. Whereas a number of movies focus on corruption within the upper ranks of law enforcement in the third decade, this has not been the case in the most recent period. Instead, movies now tend to focus more exclusively on the man or woman on the street and it is there that we find the most pronounced changes (see Table 5.5).

Police officers have also become victims, especially rank and file officers. In the first two decades, only one of four law enforcement supervisors is victimized. In the third decade, two out of four are victimized. From 1976 to 1990, eight out of sixteen supervisors are victimized. Among rank and file officers, the proportion of officers victimized increases even more over time. In the first two decades, only two out of six officers are victimized in some way. By the third decade, victimizations increase dramatically to fifteen out of twenty (75 percent). In the most recent period, victimizations for rank and file officers remains extremely high, with thirty-one out of forty-six (67 percent) victimized (Table 5.4).

The picture we have presented so far is incomplete, for the overall shifts we have described conceal some sharp differences. The fact is that the authority of supervisory police officials has fallen much more sharply than that of the ordinary cop on the beat during this period (see Table 5.2).

In the first two decades, no supervisory personnel are portrayed negatively, though two of four receive mixed ratings. In the third decade, negative portrayals of supervisors rises to 75 percent (three out of four characters). From 1976 to 1990, 50 percent or eight of sixteen supervisors are positive, but 31 percent receive negative ratings. Among rank and file members, positive character ratings tend to predominate and the proportion receiving negative character ratings is substantially lower. Eighty-three percent of rank and file officers are positive in the first two decades. Eighty-five percent are positive in the third decade. In the most recent period, positive ratings decline for rank and file officers but only down to 70 percent positive. No rank and file officers receive negative ratings in the first two decades. Only 10 percent are negative in the third decade and only 15 percent are negative characters in the most recent period (see Table 5.2). Although a substantial proportion of supervisors are still portrayed positively and there has been a marginal decline in the image of rank and file officers, supervisors have clearly become a much less respectable cohort within the law enforcement professions than their subordinates.

One could argue that all these changes reflect real trends in society and that contemporary films are, in fact, more realistic than were those of the 1950s. Yet the kind of world portrayed in these films is often far more violent and dangerous than the real one. Nor does the popular press treat the police as negatively as do the movies.

After all, even articles in popular magazines, headlining instances of police brutality, report that "most American police are decent men and women doing honorable service" (Lacayo, 1991:17). Another article notes that "experts on police psychology insist that most officers are attracted to police work by the opportunity to protect and serve" (Lacayo, 1991:21). This is hardly the image conveyed by recent popular movies. The extent of violence and crime among police officers is grossly exaggerated. Moreover, crime and corruption within police forces have been unearthed in the past and continue to be uncovered at present. Why, then, have these rather negative representations of law enforcement only recently become so prevalent in popular entertainment?

Like the events affecting the film industry, the shifts in movie content sneak up upon us, as it were, and are not always obvious. This problem is complicated by the fact that movies that break away from the formulaic simplicity of various genres, though they are relatively small in number, can be traced back to the earliest days of the studio era. There have always been exceptions to the general trends in movie content and certainly exceptions remain, but this diversity is often used opportunistically by some academic film critics to strengthen a particular line of argument. Focusing in this chapter on law enforcement films, we have found that general and consistent patterns emerge as we systematically examine developments over a significant time period. A new genre of law enforcement movies has emerged in the past two or three decades, with very different messages from those from preceding decades.

The mid-1960s represent a decisive period because conditions favoring artistic freedom in moviemaking reached an optimum level, resulting in an unprecedented, wholesale transformation of movie content. Filmmakers took full advantage of their creative independence, which grew out of the crumbling studio system, and forged a New Hollywood. In this Hollywood, police officers are less removed from the criminals with whom they deal than they once were. They, themselves, are more likely to engage in criminal activity and they are increasingly portrayed negatively. This is especially true of supervisory personnel.

In addition, in some popular movies, renegade police officers, treated as heroes, also express a disregard for procedure and a heavy reliance on violent behavior. These maverick officers also challenge more traditional images of discipline and self-restraint, which they consider foolish. Like renegade warriors, these officers give the impression that extraordinarily powerful individuals must do what institutions cannot. Such films about law enforcement tell us that the more ruthless criminals become, the more violent and unrestrained the good guys must be. Moreover, this is presented as a good thing; because, without these aggressive individuals, institutions would be powerless against a whole range of worldly evils.

Ironically, stories of this type also muddle the code of behavior among heroes and villains and may also encourage us to accept the notion that violent, criminal behavior is the only effective means of maintaining order. It is hard to believe that today's films inspire any public confidence in the ability of real police to control themselves as they seek to control crime.[3]

N O T E S

1. There is all the difference in the world between the violence of Schwarzenegger in *True Lies* (1994) and the violence in Oliver Stone's *Natural Born Killers* (1994). Almost everyone knows that *True Lies* is a cartoon and that nobody really dies. Its popularity has something to do with its simple fairy-tale triumph of the good guys over the bad guys. In that way, it reenforces the part of everyone that says "Keep the violent antisocial part of you under control or you will suffer," for in the end good, embodied in the forces of authority, triumphs. *True Lies* is, thus, a film that supports public order. In contrast, Oliver Stone's film, whatever the director may say, seeks to undermine public order by "realistically" portraying (and half legitimizing) promiscuous violence in the society by almost everyone. See the discussion of related themes in Chapter 6. The above analysis is based on psychoanalyst Bruno Bettelheim's *Uses of Enchantment* (1976).

2. The number of westerns in our sample is quite small and does not affect the overall statistics. This fact alone (the traditional western was basically a morality fairy tale) tells us volumes about the changes that have taken place in American life.

3. In an essay in the *New York Times*, December 24, 1995 (E3), motion picture critic Caryn James admits that in recent films, criminals have often been treated more positively than police: "Crime, however, seems such an inherent part of American life that a film like *Heat* casually suggests that there is no real difference between a cop (Al Pacino) and the master thief he's pursuing (Robert DeNiro). . . . Movie audiences have always responded to sympathetic crooks, of course, but rarely has a good cop carried so little moral authority." James lays this largely to Hollywood's catering to increased public cynicism. There is no recognition that the actions of producers and directors may have played some role in this trend.

6

Religious Decline?

In the early 1990s, at least two films were produced that treated the Christian religion and those who practice it with reasonable respect, though neither motion picture made the top ten for the year in which it was shown. *Black Robe* (1991), a film about Jesuit missionaries to the Indians in what is now Canada treats a Jesuit priest, one of the major characters in the film, as a person of sincere humility and deep belief. Nevertheless, the Hurons, the recipients of his mission, are all but destroyed as the result of his efforts to convert them.

Shadowlands (1993), a fictional biography film about C. S. Lewis, treats the British author and his Christian beliefs seriously, though he is portrayed as something of a maverick and the Christian message he delivers periodically to audiences of middle-aged women is presented as thin and contrived. Theoretically, it will be less so in the future (as the picture ends), because after a tragic loss he finally opens himself to life.

There have, of course, been other films that present religion or religious characters in a positive light. On the whole, however, religious themes have played rather poorly in Hollywood movies for the past thirty years. In their efforts to entertain large audiences, moviemakers, since 1965, have largely ignored traditional religious themes, dwelling more recently on demonic forces or manifestations of the supernatural that bear little or no relationship to traditional Jewish or Christian stories. The veritable parade of epic biblical films—such as those of Cecil B. DeMille—packing the theaters only a few years earlier has disappeared, never to return.

Given the overwhelmingly nonreligious orientations of Hollywood's contemporary artists, this is hardly surprising. Thus, in spite of the fact that traditional religion is still important to the vast majority of Americans, recent movies are no longer concerned with traditional religious topics and biblical storytelling.

Most of the few notable exceptions, for example *Monty Python's Life of Brian* (1979) and *The Last Temptation of Christ* (1988), have taken such satiric or radical directions that the Catholic church and other religious groups have sharply criticized them. Even when movies seem to present a favorable image of western religious beliefs, as in, for example, *Oh God* (1977), the deity is seen, at best, from a Unitarian perspective and representatives of older religious traditions, if not depicted as benighted, are given short shrift.

Michael Medved argues that whereas movies focusing on religious topics might still draw large audiences if they were more orthodox, filmmakers have concentrated on irreverent accounts of the life of Christ, which have usually "flopped resoundingly at the box office" (Medved, 1989:1–4). Medved is persuaded that the negative treatment of traditional religion that he documents is the result of the hostility of the Hollywood elite to religion.[1]

A majority of movies depicting the afterlife or any kind of supernatural force seems to reflect a Hollywood preoccupation with satanic evil, religious satire, conflict between individuals, and supernatural evil that lacks a religious referent and interaction with benevolent or evil extraterrestrials. These newer box office hits are aimed at today's youth market and their treatment of religion is obviously quite different from what Hollywood offered in the past.

A *Time* magazine writer, arguing that Hollywood was renewing interest in religion, following such hits as *Field of Dreams* and *Ghost*, suggests that

> the preoccupation with the afterlife reflects the obsession of Los Angeles, the crystal-and-channeling capital of the country, where people can mention their past lives with the same seriousness as getting the car engine tuned. No doubt Shirley MacLaine's philosophical musings and Richard Gere's cassette-tape readings from the *Tibetan Book of the Dead* have permeated the collective unconscious of fortysomething producers forced to face mortality through the death of their parents and the tragic toll of colleagues who have died of AIDS. (Smilgis, *Time*, June 3,1991:70)

Indeed, Hollywood's "collective unconscious" seems to exert a tremendous influence on the handling of religious subject matter in popular movies. However, we find little evidence indicating that the filmmakers of the past twenty-five years are planning to engage in a more traditional treatment of religion and related topics.[2]

Moviemakers have transformed customary religious storytelling in three important ways. First, they have reoriented religious movies toward the darker side of spiritual belief. Conventional religious beliefs are presented, but only to provide a recognizable background against which evil can be made more compelling and powerful. Beginning with Roman Polanski's *Rosemary's Baby* (1968), Hollywood's new generation of filmmakers abandoned conventional religious stories and began churning out movies exhibiting a fascination with evil. A slew of movies about the devil or other demonic forces at work on Earth sprang forth, bringing impressive returns from the new "cineplexes" operating in malls across the country. People sat in theaters, drive-ins, or more recently in their own living rooms, fascinated at the spectacle of demonic forces overtaking unfortunate victims for no apparent reason. The effect on audiences of movies like *The Exorcist* (1974) was clearly substantial. The imagery appealed and these types of movies made for a number of box office hits in the 1970s. Special effects improved as audiences refined their appetite for the nightmarish amusement-park rides that the new genre offered.

Second, in the early 1970s, a number of movies began to satirize the practices of organized religions as archaic and authoritarian if not merely silly. Satire is perhaps the least prevalent of the themes we identify and the criticisms of religious practices or characters portrayed as religious are often fairly subtle. Fairly typical examples are *Tommy* (1975) and *The Witches of Eastwick* (1987). The latter film comically sympathizes with the devil and those who are wise to the presence of evil in the small town come to a bad end.

Finally, and most often, using very sophisticated techniques, moviemakers have reformulated the natural and supernatural worlds, exploring different kinds of realities that include elements of religion, mysticism, horror, science fiction, and the occult. We detect in a number of these films increasing ambiguity in the portrayal of good and evil. Evil is not always defeated by story's end and this is not simply to leave an opening for sequels. The stories frequently make a point of demonstrating that evil is beyond control and that we can all become helpless victims. In some movies, Hollywood presents a mixture of natural and supernatural occurences in the same story without drawing any clear lines between the two realms. For example, in *The Golden Child* (1986), the forces of good and evil are at play in the natural world and a select few individuals are empowered by them, influencing events both natural and supernatural. In *Beetlejuice* (1988), the afterlife is merely a ghostly and grotesque extension of natural existence and the living and the dead are able to commingle. In the comedy *Ghostbusters* (1984), the line between the supernatural and the natural worlds is very thin, but the supernatural world has nothing to do with traditional religious beliefs.

The difficulty of finally defeating evil is illustrated by the *Nightmare on Elm Street* or the *Friday the 13th* series of movies of the 1980s, none of which, incidentally, made the top ten. Most of these films, although assuming the supernatural, have nothing to do with traditional western religious themes. And, starting with the first film of each series, evil is seen to triumph in the midst of what appears to be a defeat.

A distinct variant of the supernatural films has drawn from the science fiction genre, focusing on the existence of supernatural powers in outer space. *Star Wars* and *Close Encounters*, for example, conjure up supernatural forces from the ruins of the religious sentiments of a bygone era in Hollywood. In these films, moviemakers have replaced God with less omnipotent and therefore less authoritarian supreme beings. Nevertheless, the spectacle of brilliant alien technology, far more sophisticated than anything on Earth, does have some parallels to biblical accounts of celestial phenomena. As Pye and Myles observe in their discussion of *Close Encounters*,

> These wheels of light careening through the sky have their historic parallels: the visions of the prophet Ezekiel, the idea of the chariot of God, the mandals of Jung. The fiery clouds of biblical texts become the boiling clouds and blinding light of Spielberg's film. Intervention from above, bringing hope at last, is a constant theme

at times of social crisis and change. Some God must save us, because we cannot save ourselves. And if God is an alien, with lights and wonder and color and music, then God is prettier than we thought. (Pye and Myles, 1979: 246)

Contemporary science fiction films are important to a discussion of Hollywood's treatment of religion because they do more than confront us with the possibility of other life forms. If that were the only message conveyed, the films would be less uplifting and entertaining. Rather, although sidestepping the issue of whether traditional beliefs about God, heaven, and earth have validity, at least some of these films comfort us with the thought that benevolent beings from outer space watch over us. In a sense, they suggest that although western society, built around scientific and rational principles, must inevitably relinquish its hold on ancient biblical accounts of the meaning of life, we can still hope for salvation from above.

Conveniently, this hope does not require the moral virtue once expected of religious characters. It is "everyman's" salvation. *Cocoon* (1986), like *Star Wars* and *Close Encounters*, conveys exactly this type of message. Regardless of the kind of lives they have led, the old folks in *Cocoon* will be taken by the aliens to a place where they'll never get any older and they'll never die. For these lucky individuals, salvation is no longer contingent upon predestination, faith, or good works, although it might at least require being in the right place at the right time.

Stanley Kubrick alludes to the new trend among science fiction films in a discussion of *2001: A Space Odyssey* (1968). Kubrick says, "The God concept is at the heart of the film." David Bowman becomes "an enhanced human being, a star child, a superhuman . . . returning to earth prepared for the next leap forward of man's evolutionary destiny" (Phillips, 1990:134). Importantly, Kubrick's idiosyncratic view of religion only retains the scientific concepts of evolution and our experiences with space travel, not really anything divine or spiritual at all. As in the other classes of films we have specified, if religion is present at all, it is now much less likely to have a moral influence upon the characters.

Of course, at least some science fiction movies, including such films as *Alien* (1979), deal with powerful evil forces that cannot be finally vanquished. Thus, the science fiction genre wrestles with many of the same issues that used to be dealt with in films emphasizing traditional religious beliefs.

What is it, then, that makes Hollywood so averse to a more positive treatment of organized religion? Why, even in the face of what appears to be a strong market potential, have writers, directors, and producers avoided this particular mainstream of western beliefs? Do they hold a grudge against the institutions that have constrained their expression in the past? That is partly Michael Medved's (1992) argument. Constrained only by the demands of the marketplace, Hollywood producers, actors, and writers attack bourgeois American culture and religion because they hate both.

Perhaps, but we do not detect much open hostility to religion in popular Hollywood movies; only, at worst, a decline in the sanctity of religion to a level commensurate with the rest of the characters (a secularization). Although this secularization of movies indicates a disregard for religion as an important authoritative institution, lack of interest rather than deep hostility seems to be the rule. Because of their secular views, filmmakers may simply be so intrigued by other alternatives that they do not wish to return to earlier types of religious storytelling. In any case, religion has fallen even farther out of fashion than the western, which is currently enjoying a modest comeback. To understand these recent trends in popular entertainment, it is important first to document the changes that we have described.

Biblical Tales and Other Movies from 1946 Through 1965

As we noted in Chapter 2, the Catholic Church, through its Legion of Decency and other more spontaneously established watchdogs, had a substantial impact on movie content and contributed to the studio executives' decision to create and strictly enforce the Production Code, the moral code for American movies from the 1930s through the early 1960s (Leff and Simmons, 1990; Facey, 1974). The moviemakers of this period were obliged to follow the strict guidelines set out in the Code for the respectful treatment of religious subject-matter. The code stated simply:

1. No film or episode may throw ridicule on any religious faith.
2. Ministers of religion in their characters as ministers of religion should not be used as comic characters or as villains.
3. Ceremonies of any definite religion should be carefully and respectfully handled. (Leff and Simmons: Appendix)

Reflecting the dictates of the Production Code for the sensitive handling of religious subjects, the large number of conventional religious stories appearing in our sample of top box office hits also attests to their wide popular appeal in the 1940s, the 1950s, and the early 1960s.

The Bells of St. Mary's (1946) is a typical example of the favorable treatment of religious themes in the studio era. It is a lighthearted account of a tense working relationship between a new pastor, Father O'Malley (Bing Crosby) and Sister Benedict (Ingrid Bergman), sister superior of a group of nuns operating a run-down city school. A miserly old businessman builds a large office building next door to the school, on land once owned by the parish (the land was sold to help pay off mounting debts). The nuns have been praying for a miracle, hoping that by divine intervention the old man will be inspired to donate the building for a new school. With a little help from above, it seems, and from Father O'Malley, the nuns prayers are indeed answered. By story's end, the aging businessman has a change of heart and becomes a benevolent philanthropist. He then happily donates the building to the parish, resolving the problem. The religious workers in the film are all exemplary characters. They work cooperatively in educating the children, in spite of their differences of opinion and methods. They represent a positive moral influence on the children and each other and they ultimately even succeed in reforming the miserly businessman. Their success in convincing the man to donate the school suggests that even those things beyond our control can go our way if we "keep the faith" and lead a moral life.

Samson and Delilah (1950) is a recreation of the biblical tale of Delilah (Hedy Lamarr), who cuts Samson's (Victor Mature) hair (the supposed source of his strength) and betrays him, handing him over to the Philistines. At the end of the film, Samson recognizes the impropriety of his pursuit of Delilah, at which point God restores his strength. He destroys the Philistine temple, killing hundreds of his enemies. The moral implication is that without God, Samson is easily defeated. When he does submit to a higher calling, Samson prevails. Once again, divine "right" makes might.

Quo Vadis (1952) recounts the persecution of early Christians by Nero and the decline of the Roman empire. The moral message is clearly stated in the closing scene. Marcus (Robert Taylor) asks: "Babylon, Egypt, Greece, Rome . . . What follows? A more permanent world, I hope. Or a more permanent faith. One is not possible without the other." Christianity is upheld as one of the cornerstones of Western civilization and of a more just and peaceful world. The Christians in the film are all portrayed positively and their persecutors are, of course, the villains. The fate of individual characters is less important than the moral outcome, the triumph of Christianity over worldly evil.

The Robe (1953) is a story of a Roman officer, Marcellius Gallio (Richard Burton), who oversees Christ's crucifixion and then wins Christ's robe in a game of dice. His slave Demetrius (Victor Mature) throws the cloak over Marcellius's shoulders and through the Robe's divine connection he becomes aware of Christ's true identity. At first, he attempts to block the revelation and he discharges Demetrius, a Christian. Demetrius leaves with the Robe, but Marcellius is plagued by guilt. Marcellius then travels through the holy land in search of Demetrius and the Robe. There he meets with some of the Apostles and others who knew Christ. After confessing his participation in Christ's crucifixion to Peter, he becomes a Christian. Soon after, he is arrested and accused of treasonous acts. The movie ends as the emperor orders Marcellius and Diana's (Jean Simmons) execution. In this film, the moral influence of Christianity is unequivocal and irresistible, even for Marcellius, and although the protagonists are persecuted, their faith in God brings them inner peace and salvation. Accordingly, we see their image in the clouds as they rise to their heavenly reward.

The Ten Commandments (1957) is a dramatic recreation of the life of Moses, his adoption into the Pharaohs' family, his exile, his leading of the Israelites out of Egypt, and his subsequent role as their lawgiver. From the time God reveals himself to Moses on Mount Sinai, Moses obeys and acts as God's instrument. In return for his obedience and piety, God grants him divine powers. Moses warns the Pharaoh that God will plague Egypt until the Israelites are freed from slavery. He parts the Red Sea so that the Israelites can escape from Egypt. Later, God carves the Ten Commandments in stone tablets, providing a new moral code for the Israelites. Any evil in the film is brought about by man. The devil is unseen. God punishes the Egyptians and even the Israelites for going against His wishes, but these acts are presented as just punishment and God is merciful with those who follow His commandments. As in other biblical films, the story follows the actual biblical account reasonably closely. Clearly, piety and moral virtue are rewarded in the film, whereas those characters with other motives come to a bad end.

Fred Zinneman's *The Nun's Story* (1959) takes place in a modern setting, though still in line with the Production Code, depicting the trials and tribulations of a young woman, Gabriella (Audrey Hepburn), who becomes Sister Luke after successfully training in a convent. The film explores Gabriella's inner conflict, stemming from her wish to pursue a promising medical career and a simultaneous desire to uphold her religious commitments. Gabriella finally decides she must leave the order, not because she wishes to pursue her career, but because she cannot overcome her hatred for the Nazis, who kill her father.

The nuns in her religious order are portrayed positively, irrespective of Gabriella's decision to leave. Moreover, when she does leave, her problems are not entirely resolved. Instead, the movie suggests that there are sacrifices in either direction and portrays her attempt to remain a nun as truly noble, though obviously immensely difficult for her. Gabriella, like the other nuns in the story, is shown to be an exceptional and exemplary individual. She is confronted by many worldly evils but responds with compassion and makes the world a better place through her efforts. Again, the tremendous influence of religious belief on the characters is clear.

The Sandpiper (1965) is a transitional movie that features a struggling single mother and artist, Laura (Elizabeth Taylor), who meets and has an affair with Dr. Hewitt (Richard Burton), a married Episcopalian minister—head master of San Simeon Prep School. The affair is short-lived. Dr. Hewitt confesses his adultery and goes back to his wife. However, in this movie, the cloistered life does not save Hewitt from temptation. He falls victim to his earthly desires. Significantly, Dr. Hewitt is the only one of seventeen religious workers in our sample of movies from 1946 to 1965 who receives a less than positive character rating. The film's mixed portrayal of the minister forecasts a shift away from reverential treatment of religious characters toward a more "normal" status for characters with religious affiliations compared to the status of those without any explicit religious identity. The moral influence of religion upon the characters is no longer self-evident and this trend is magnified in later movies.

A Man For All Seasons (1967), another Fred Zinneman film, is a holdover from the earlier period. It is a rather straightforward account of the life of Thomas More (Richard Burton) and the events leading to his martyrdom. The story is more of a drama than a religious tale, but it does focus on the man's unshakable faith and commitment to the Church in the face of Henry the Eighth's self-serving reforms. Although evil does triumph in the sense that More is executed for his adherence to his beliefs, as in earlier movies such as *The Robe* and *Quo Vadis*, the more forceful message of the film is More's moral victory, which transcends his persecution. The popularity of this film, at a time when other movies had begun to focus on evil, attests to the continued appeal of more traditional religious themes in spite of Hollywood's shifting interests.

From 1946 to 1965, then, traditional religion received very favorable treatment in Hollywood and, in exchange, studio moguls were often rewarded with large box office returns. The disappearance of these more conventional stories in the late 1960s reflected the declining appeal of religious themes to the new generation of moviemakers. By that time, Hollywood had learned that younger audiences, many of whose parents were staying away from the theaters and watching television in record numbers, could be entertained in a number of new ways. This market shift provided lucrative alternatives for those in Hollywood who, for personal or professional reasons, frowned upon conventional religious storytelling. The 1960s were a time of considerable experimentation in Hollywood, as well as in American society at large, and the younger audiences were malleable enough to permit the new moviemakers to change direction at the very same time that the industry's control over creative production was sharply weakened. The movie elite thus succeeded in transforming old genres or substituting new genres in their place that still earned the requisite box office returns. Our content analysis results indicate the declining importance and stature of religion in contemporary movies and also its replacement by other genres. Although we find evidence of Medved's charge of hostility to traditional religion, the major issue seems less hostility than it does indifference.

A Content Analysis

Thus far we have presented only anecdotal evidence. However, the illustrations used are based on a rather straightforward systematic content analysis of motion pictures that deal with religious themes, to which we shall now turn. We shall also offer some rather more detailed descriptions of films representing various permutations of the new supernaturalism.

Looking at the religious affiliation of characters, we find that the number actually identified as belonging to one religion or another has declined dramatically since the 1940s (see Table 6.1). In the 1945 to 1956 decade, 19 percent of the characters are identified as Protestants, Catholics, Jews, or individuals belonging to some other religion. Eighty-one percent are unknown, atheist, or agnostic. In the second decade, the number of religious characters drops slightly lower to 15 percent. In the third decade, the figure drops to 9 percent and in the 1976 to 1990 period it declines even further to about 4 percent of characters whose religious orientations are depicted in the films. As we shall see, the proportion of films (see Table 6.7) in which God or God's agents play a role also drops very sharply.

TABLE 6.1   Percent of Characters of Known Religious Identity (by decade)

	1946–1955	1956–1965	1966–1975	1976–1990
% Protestant, Catholic, Jewish Other	19	15	9	4
% Atheist, agnostic, unknown	81	85	91	96
Total	789	795	981	1737

When we compare the small group of characters identified with the Protestant, Catholic, or Jewish faith to all other characters we find a consistent pattern. In the first two decades, the character ratings (positive, negative, mixed) of the major characters identified with these religions are somewhat more likely to be positive than those of persons not identified with any of the three religions. In the first decade, 81 percent of these characters are rated positively compared to only 63 percent of characters identified as nonreligious. In the second decade, positive ratings decline slightly to 74 percent, but are still higher for religious than for nonreligious characters, only 48 percent of whom are positive in the second decade. In the third decade, positive ratings among characters identified as religious decline to 67 percent, but again remain higher than for nonreligious characters in that decade, who receive 48 percent positive ratings. In the fourth decade, however, religious characters nearly reach parity with nonreligious characters slipping to 56 percent positive ratings, whereas such ratings for nonreligious characters rise slightly to 52 percent. As compared to the ratings from earlier decades, the declining number of religious characters are no more likely than nonreligious characters to be portrayed positively (see Table 6.2).

In the same vein, the percentages of characters identified as religious who fail to achieve their goals has risen during recent decades. This corresponds with the authors' impression of a declining power of religion in predetermining the intentions and actions of and outcomes for religious characters. In the first decade, only 15 percent of the characters with religious ties are unsuccessful compared to

TABLE 6.2   Percent of Religious (R) vs. Nonreligious (NR) Character Ratings

	1946–1955		1956–1965		1966–1975		1976–1990	
	R	NR	R	NR	R	NR	R	NR
% Positive	81	63	74	48	67	48	56	52
% Negative	7	21	11	22	26	28	10	28
% Mixed	11	16	15	30	8	24	33	20
Total*	54	175	46	169	39	246	39	421

*Neutral characteristics are excluded from the totals in this table.

31 percent of nonreligious characters. In the second decade, 26 percent fail to achieve their goals compared to 33 percent of nonreligious characters. In the third decade, 23 percent of the religious fail to achieve their objectives compared to 33 percent of nonreligious characters. The greatest change occurs in the most recent period. The number of religious characters who fail to achieve their goals rises to 36 percent compared to only 28 percent of nonreligious characters who are defeated. Religious affiliation today actually seems to increase the likelihood that a character will fail to achieve her or his objectives (see Table 6.3).

Evaluating an even more narrow group of religious characters—religious workers, nuns, and missionaries—we find further evidence of the declining prestige of religious institutions in Hollywood movies. Among these individuals, character ratings are, with only one exception, entirely positive in the first two decades, but they fall markedly in the last two. From 1946 to 1965, sixteen of seventeen religious workers are rated positively and the one exception (Dr. Hewitt, from *The Sandpiper*) receives a mixed rather than a negative rating. In the third decade, positive depiction declines to four out of seven or only 57 percent positive. The remaining three (43 percent) are presented as negative characters. In the most recent decade, only three of six religious workers (50 percent) are presented positively, two are represented as negative characters, and one receives a mixed rating (see Table 6.4).

TABLE 6.3   Percent of Religious (R) vs. Nonreligious (NR) Characters Who Fail to Achieve Goals

	1946–1955		1956–1965		1966–1975		1976–1990	
	R	NR	R	NR	R	NR	R	NR
% Success	59	50	48	50	54	51	54	57
% Defeat	15	31	26	33	23	33	36	28
% Mixed	26	19	26	17	23	16	10	15
Total*	54	175	46	169	39	246	39	421

*Neutral characters are excluded from the totals in this table.

TABLE 6.4   Percent of Religious Workers, Nuns, and Missionaries' Character Ratings (by decade)

	1946–1955	1956–1965	1966–1975	1976–1990
% Positive	100	86	57	50
% Negative	0	0	43	33
% Mixed	0	14	0	17
Total	10	7	7	6

We find the same pattern in the presentation of goal attainment. In the first decade, all the religious workers either succeed in achieving their objectives or some of the issues remain unresolved. In the second decade, 86 percent score similarly. Since this was the era of Biblical epochs, a disproportionate number of religious characters are persecuted. Mitigating against this lower success rate for religious characters trying to achieve their objectives is the image of Jews and Christians serving a higher purpose. We must also bear in mind that, in spite of their predicaments, these characters are still overwhelmingly presented in a positive fashion that corresponds with their moral virtue.

In the third decade, although portrayals of religious workers are substantially less positive, 85 percent are still either successful or the outcome of their efforts is ambiguous. It is not until the most recent period that we find a precipitous decline. From 1976 to 1990, only 17 percent of the few religious workers in our sample meet with success. Conversely, whereas none of the religious workers are defeated in the first decade and only 14 percent fail to achieve their objectives in the second and third decades, 50 percent fail in the most recent period. So, although somewhat more ambivalent character ratings emerge among religious workers in the third decade, they are still overwhelmingly successful in attaining their objectives. By the most recent period, with the character ratings of religious workers continuing to decline, failure to achieve goals increases dramatically (see Table 6.5).

Overall traditional religious figures in the movies have suffered a multiple decline. They were once presented very positively, consistent with the reverence for religious institutions mandated by the Production Code. Since the mid-1960s, their reputation has become less exalted. The larger story of what has happened to religion in popular movies must be understood in light of a sharply diminished presence of religious characters. However, the decline of traditional religion has been accompanied by the increasing presentation of alternate sources of supernatural events. It is to this and related changes that we now turn.

TABLE 6.5   Percent of Religious Workers, Nuns, and Missionaries Who Are Successful/Unsuccessful (by decade)

	1946–1955	1956–1965	1966–1975	1976–1990
% Successful	70	43	71	17
% Unsuccessful	0	14	14	50
% Unresolved	30	43	14	33
N=30	10	7	7	6

The Eclipse of God, 1966–1990

New Sources of Power

A thematic analysis, designed to measure broader trends in the movies, suggests the magnitude of the shift from traditional religious to alternative supernatural themes. Supernatural events occur in only a few movies from 1946 to 1975 (nine movies or 10 percent, on average). However, in the 1976 to 1990 period alone, 14 movies (26 percent of the total movies coded for that period) involve such events. Among such films, the trend is away from more traditional depictions of God and religion, as indicated by the sharp decline in films in which God is the source of supernatural events. God is present in five of seven movies with supernatural events in the first two decades, but is present in only two of sixteen in the period from 1966 to 1990 (see Table 6.6).

Conversely, the devil is not present in any of the seven movies from the first two decades but is present in three of sixteen films in the two more recent periods. Even more interesting is that extraterrestrials, absent from top-grossing movies over the thirty years from 1946 to 1976, are the source of supernatural events in five of the fourteen films (36 percent) in which such events occur from 1976 to 1990. Further, 43 percent of the films involve supernatural events of a magical, mystical, or demonic kind that permeate the world. Together these trends clearly demonstrate the decline of traditional depictions of God and religion and a growing interest in films that present supernatural events as demonic or extraterrestrial.[3]

Religion and Horror

Rosemary's Baby (1968) is the first movie in our sample marking the transformation of movies on religious topics. It is a horror story of the impregnation of Rosemary Woodhouse by the devil. An elderly couple, the Castavets, who worship Satan slip Rosemary and Guy Woodhouse an evil brew, mixed in with some chocolate mousse, on the night the young couple conceive their baby. Subsequently, Rosemary dreams that she is raped by the devil and at the end of the dream sequence she cries out "This is not a dream, this is really happening." When she wakes up the next morning, her husband tells her that he made love to

TABLE 6.6   Percent of Movies in Which Supernatural Events Are Present

	1946–1955	1956–1965	1966–1975	1976–1990
% Present	13	10	6	26
% Absent	87	90	94	74
N=146	30	29	33	54

TABLE 6.7   Percent of Sources of Supernatural Events

	1946–1955	1956–1965	1966–1975	1976–1990
% God or agents	75	67	0	14
% Devil or agents	0	0	50	21
% Extraterrestrials	0	0	0	36
% Magic, mystical, or demonic	25	33	50	43
N=23	4	3	2	14

her after she passed out. She shrugs off the nightmare but soon finds out that she is indeed pregnant. The Castavets are thrilled when they are told the news and they recommend a doctor who is also in league with the devil. He prescribes a special drink that Mrs. Castavet will make for Rosemary. The potion nurtures the demon fetus whose evil origin is still unknown to Rosemary. Eventually she suspects something is wrong. She begins to crave raw meat and feels drugged all the time, but it is too late to change her destiny. When the baby is born, rather than trying to destroy it she is persuaded to love and nurture the infant, even after she realizes what has happened. Evil seems to triumph over good in the movie and no religious figures come to Rosemary's aid. She is isolated and powerless in her confrontation with evil. In the late 1960s, many other popular movies also shifted to an emphasis on the dark side of religious belief and, following this trend, some new genres emerged involving supernatural and extraterrestrial phenomena. Traditional accounts of religion and religious practices as integral and beneficial aspects of character's lives are now seldom seen.

The Exorcist (1974) was another landmark box office hit focusing on the power of Satan. The film graphically depicts the demonic possession of a young girl and the desperate attempt of two priests to exorcise the evil spirit from within her. Both of the priests are sympathetic characters, but rather than triumphing over evil through the practice of exorcism, the older priest dies before finishing the ceremony. The young priest, from that point on alone in the confrontation, finally must allow the demon to possess him. He then commits suicide by jumping out the bedroom window. The power of the devil in this film is so overwhelming that even the priests are destroyed by it. The devil enters the world, but no divine force intercedes to counter him. The priests rely on ancient rituals of exorcism that clearly have some power but the devil proves too potent an adversary. In spite of the efforts of the Catholic priests, the story emphasizes, God fails to control evil.

Uncontrollable evil also appears in *The Amityville Horror* (1979), though the origin of the evil is not as clearly associated with traditional religious categories, despite the presence of a priest as part of the plot. In this film, a demonic presence in a house has previously caused a young man to murder his family of six. When the Lutz family moves into the house a year later, an evil force prevents a priest from blessing it, a nun is sickened upon entering the home and is forced out, the priest's car goes out of control on the way to warn the Lutz's about the house, and the priest eventually goes blind. In one scene, when the priest tries to convince his superiors of the danger, he is accused of being mentally ill. Ordinary religious figures are powerless against, or blind to, the evil presence. Meanwhile, ghastly sludge oozes up from the toilets and on the family's last night in the house "all hell breaks loose." George tries to kill his wife with an ax. Fortunately, before he does kill anyone, George miraculously comes to his senses. The family flees from the house never to return. The story provides no indication that the evil has been conquered. Further, individuals must confront it in relative isolation, without the support of religious intermediaries.

Satiric Views of Religion

A few highly successful movies since the 1960s have satirized religious beliefs and institutions. Ken Russell's version of Peter Townshend's rock opera *Tommy* (1975) mocks the rituals associated with organized religion. The movie's hero, Tommy (Roger Daltrey), is a deaf, dumb, and blind introvert who discovers that he has a talent for playing pinball. His family of misfits, criminals, and perverts exploit his talent to get rich. They establish a pinball camp that attracts people from all over the world. They all come to play pinball, but the catch is that they must submit to being deprived of the same senses of which Tommy was deprived as a boy. In the end, they revolt and destroy the pinball camp. Tommy himself is spared and freed from what has become a meaningless ritual. As the film closes, he runs off, "free" again, to live his life as he pleases.

Many of the scenes in the film warn the audience of the dangers of ritual and following the crowd. At the start of the film, Tommy's family attends a mass at which rock musicians play and the crowd pays homage to its current idol, Marilyn Monroe. A young girl who idolizes Tommy runs away from home to attend his concert, only to have her face gashed when she is thrown off the stage. When the crowd revolts against the pinball wizard, they chant the lyrics of one of The Who's hit songs: "We're not going to take it. Never did and never will. Don't want no religion, as far as we can tell." The film celebrates the individual's emancipation from the hypocritical and authoritarian control of organized religion.

The Witches of Eastwick (1987) also satirizes religious beliefs by evoking sympathy for the devil. The story involves the seduction of three modern women by a devil in disguise. The devil, Daryll Van Horn (Jack Nicholson), masquerades as a mysterious and wealthy bachelor who buys an old mansion in a quiet New England town. The women fall victim to his charms and one by one he impregnates them. By the end of the film, the women successfully employ voodoo to subdue the devil and since they can control him, decide to remain at the mansion, raising their "little devils" as they please. The only religious figure in the film, Felicia (Veronica Cartwright), is portrayed as a sanctimonious puritan, possessed and destroyed by the devil for trying to interfere with his plans. If anything, the devil is presented more sympathetically than is the religious crusader and the three starring women (Susan Sarandon, Michelle Pfeiffer, Cher) turn out to be more powerful (though this is somewhat ambiguous) than the devil himself.

The Individual Against Supernatural Evil

In a number of movies in our sample, the individual is pitted against unknown supernatural forces whose sources are unclear. *The Shining* (1980), Stanley Kubrick's rendition of a Stephen King novel about a writer (Jack Nicholson) who goes mad, is such a film. After taking his wife and young boy off to stay at a deserted, haunted resort in the middle of the winter, Jack goes crazy. He sees a number of apparitions, commingles with dead guests, and finally attempts to murder his wife and child. The boy, who is clairvoyant, becomes aware of the danger and through his experiences we learn that the evil is of supernatural origin. In fact, Jack is the reincarnation of an innkeeper who murdered his own family years before. The mother and child do their best to fend off Jack's attacks and eventually escape the resort through a kitchen window. The boy hides outside, in a hedge grown in the pattern of a maze. Jack follows him in and becomes hopelessly lost, eventually freezing to death. In this movie, all the characters are victimized by the intrusion of the spirit world into the natural. Jack is predestined to become a murderer, because he has been one in a prior life. The boy's own supernatural powers enable the two victims to escape death, but only Jack, himself a victim of the evil forces, is defeated. The supernatural forces remain in play.

The characters in *Poltergeist* (1982) also must confront supernatural evil. A greedy developer builds a neighborhood over an old cemetery and because he has removed the headstones and left the bodies underneath, the spirits of the deceased are stuck between heaven and hell, so to speak. The company's best real estate salesman and his family live in a house that is haunted by these spirits. Their daughter can somehow communicate with the spirits and a demonic presence trying to lead her and the others into hell draws her into the limbo world. The child is returned with the help of a psychic who can communicate with the dead. But, importantly, the psychic fails to defeat the demon and the next night it returns, even though the psychic has declared the house to be "cleansed" of the supernatural presence. Once again the demon tries to take the family's children. Coffins of all the lost souls from the graveyard pop up through the ground and as the family flees the house, the demon destroys it and then vanishes. Again, in spite of a successful outcome for the protagonists, evil is beyond control.

Similarly, in *The Golden Child* (1986) a young Tibetan woman, Kee Nang (Charlotte Lewis) engages Chandler Jarrell (Eddie Murphy) to find and rescue the golden child, a Tibetan boy who has the power to save the world from evil. The boy has been kidnapped by an evil sorcerer who derives his supernatural powers from an evil lord of the underworld. When Chandler finds the boy, they escape briefly, but they must fight a flying demon and kill it with a powerful dagger. Supernatural powers, both good and evil, emerge in the story, but there is no explanation of their origin. Although the golden child has some power to combat the evil, he needs the help of ordinary individuals to prevail. The other bewildered protagonists must contend with the forces of evil without any understanding of why they exist or why they are chosen to assist the boy. Conventional religion offers no support to the characters and they are forced to confront the evil on their own.

In *Beetlejuice* (1988), a young couple, Adam (Alec Baldwin) and Barbara (Geena Davis) Maitland discover that they've been killed in a car accident and that they must now reside as ghosts in their house. The problem is that the house is sold to a family that they can't bear to be near, even from the other side of the grave. Bewildered and frustrated, they meet with their "afterlife" case worker, who is supposed to explain things and smooth their transition to the netherworld. Ignoring her warning to avoid contact with a certain "bioexorcist," a ghoul named Beetlejuice (Michael Keaton), who rids haunted houses of unwanted living guests, the young "dead" couple solicits him for assistance. Beetlejuice is a troublemaker who really wants only to steal Adam's wife for himself. The film presents a completely bizarre view of the afterlife. There is no supreme being, only a waiting room of newly deceased people with ghastly wounds and so on. Monsters slither about in a kaleidoscopic, abstract landscape and in the final scenes, a huge serpent from the netherworld gets into the house and threatens both the living and the dead. Beetlejuice is finally forced into restoring things to "normal" and the ghostly couple works out a livable arrangement with the new occupants of the house.

Powerful Aliens

As a distinct but closely related extension of the supernatural movies, the extraterrestrial films such as *Close Encounters* and *Star Wars* really synthesize two old film genres: biblical accounts of a benevolent, omnipotent Creator and UFO stories, previously full of threatening creatures from outer space. The images originate in two often conflicting intellectual power structures—religion and science—and the films presume to reconcile our badly shaken religious sensibilities with our modern faith in science and technology (which avoids "religious" matters).

Luke Skywalker of the *Star Wars* (1977, 1980, 1983) trilogy relies on a naturalistic kind of power, derived from all living things in the universe, known simply as "The Force." We can discern that the power of The Force transcends our ordinary conception of natural death because Ben/Obi-Wan Kenobe continues to be seen as an apparition instructing Luke on how to use his power. However, the Force is not quite equivalent to a divine power either, as it originates in nature and therefore has a certain scientific plausibility. Ben explains, "It's an energy field created by all living things. It surrounds us, it penetrates us, it binds the galaxy together." In a similar sense, the extraterrestrials in *Close Encounters of the Third Kind* (1977) have both natural and supernatural attributes. Although they look and act as innocently as children, they are obviously far superior in intelligence and knowledge, having mastered space travel.

Conclusion

In the movies of the studio era, religion was granted an especially high status; it was an institution upon which both heroic and ordinary characters relied for support. Religion held a special power over the lives of the faithful that enabled them to accomplish or to endure things that others could not. Consequently, not only religious workers, but also other characters holding religious beliefs were portrayed favorably more often than the nonreligious. These individuals were also more successful in achieving their objectives by story's end. Although religion itself may not have been at issue in many of these movies, its moral influence on the characters was quite pronounced.

In biblical stories, the Judeo-Christian religious heritage is presented as the progress of humanity against barbarism and evil. God empowers various individuals to protect and lead the righteous. Those who oppose God's plan meet with disaster. The power of religion over characters in more modern settings was overwhelmingly positive in the studio days. Religion provides a source of strength to those who believe, and they make the world a better place. The Production Code and the Hollywood moguls' conservative control over the industry mandated this kind of religious representation but, importantly, these movies also resonated with American religious sensibilities and remained very popular.

The elimination of censorship and other changes within the movie industry and American society in the 1960s and 1970s resulted in the replacement of these films with much more ambiguous representations of a declining number of religious characters. Perhaps even more important, Hollywood movies now also express a much greater apprehension about the presence of evil in the world—satanic evil and other forms of supernatural evil, as well. Whereas the forces of evil have multiplied in recent years in popular movies, there has been less good in the world, either supernatural or human, to combat it. Characters seldom expect divine or supernatural intervention or rely on the power of religious institutions to deliver them from supernatural evil. As a result, in many movies, characters have much less control over their lives.

Hollywood's new mythos has freed individuals from much of the restraint imposed by religious customs, as it has freed them from other restraints on behavior, but this has left characters vulnerable to unknown and uncontrollable evil. The super-naturalism that has replaced the authoritative religious storytelling of the past seems to reflect Hollywood's own agnostic torment. The Hollywood elite's "collective unconscious," as expressed in contemporary movies, emphasizes the individual's existential plight, but having abandoned so much of religious tradition, Hollywood is unable to offer compelling and authoritative alternatives. The kinds of movies that have filled the void have not ignored religion altogether but rather have recreated it in such a way that it loses much of its previously affirmative value. Whether movies shape or merely reflect our collective hopes or fears about this life or the next, Hollywood has conjured up a predominantly nightmarish alternative (Freddy Krueger-style) to more traditional stories surrounding Western religion.

Part of this trend may be a matter of choice on the part of a secular motion picture establishment. And yet one suspects that there is something more, both in the choice of plots and in their popularity among mass audiences. In Chapter 5, we discussed the hypotheses advanced by Bruno Bettelheim in *The Uses of Enchantment: The Meaning and Importance of Fairy Tales* (1976). Bettelheim argues that the violence of fairy tales (and they are very violent) serves a useful function. Children need to be assured that if they act at the behest of powerful, violent antisocial impulses within them, they will be destroyed by the more powerful magical forces of good. In this way, they come to identify with such forces and to turn their violent proclivities to socially responsible tasks. Self-control (the development of a superego) is fostered and children can become more or less comfortable with their impulses.

Insofar as we never fully succeed in mastering our violent antisocial drives and insofar as the child continues to function within the adult, it can be argued that most human beings require some mythic structure if they are to function effectively as responsible adults. The myth of the inevitable triumph of good over evil may seem simpleminded to the sophisticated who believe that they do not need such myths. They are, in fact, little different from the audiences they serve. They cannot find a satisfactory substitute for religion, though they continue to try. Their failure is reflected in a plethora of films that document the triumph of evil, an evil that, as in *Alien*, often emerges from the bowels of the victim. One suspects that these themes are, at least partially, a metaphor for a feared loss of control of the "evil" impulses within the self. For most of them, after all, as well as for increasing numbers of their audience, God is dead or at least very ill and the cultural norms that divide good from evil and punish the latter have been seriously undermined. Thus, almost anything is possible, including very primitive attitudes toward the supernatural. We shall return to this theme in the last chapter of the book.

NOTES

1. See also his *Hollywood vs. America* (1992). More recently, he has argued that the advent of a new generation of directors, writers, and producers, some of whom are self-consciously religious, is leading to a change in direction. Our data does not yet demonstrate such a shift (though it may be too early to notice it) and we are not persuaded that any major change is likely in the foreseeable future.

2. In 1994, the same argument was made. We think it dubious. For developments from 1990 to 1994, see Chapter 10.

3. It is clear that the development of space travel in the real world, as well as the increasing ability of Hollywood's technicians to simulate events in outer space, has also played a role in the growth of this genre.

7

Hollywood's Class Act

Europe has built a larger and more spacious wing of its imaginative literature on the foundations of class conflict than has America. This makes sense, as Europeans have tended to be more tortured and therefore more fascinated by class than have Americans. It would be hard to argue, for example, that any American playwright, ever, has exploited class divisions for satire as productively as Alan Ayckbourn, one of England's most successful playwrights over the past twenty-five years. This may be the reason why his plays have had trouble crossing the Atlantic, despite their tremendous popularity at home; they are topically British in a particular way that does not appeal to most Americans. Much of the humor of a farce like *How the Other Half Loves* is lost in translation.

It is tempting to respond that many American novels and movies do deal directly with class, if less overtly. What is *The Great Gatsby* if not a meditation on class in America? But Gatsby, we recall, began life as James Gatz. It is exactly because class in America has always been so much more fluid than in Europe that we believe he is able to transform himself into the American equivalent of an aristocrat, which is a bank roll, and be more or less accepted by society, even if he has virtually no past. As Nick Carroway puts it, "The truth was that Jay Gatsby of West Egg, Long Island, sprang from his Platonic conception of himself" (96). *The Great Gatsby* is about this kind of typically American self-fashioning, which blithely crosses supposed class boundaries. As Nick muses in the famous closing lines of the novel, America is the place that brought "man . . . face to face for the last time in history with something commensurate to his capacity for wonder," (163) and that wonder, the novel suggests, is that an entire world could be so lacking in a past, so new and socially empty, that anything was possible—a condition that no longer pertained in the old world. In the end, Gatsby fails to win back Daisy from Tom Buchanan not because he is merely a "self-made man," but because his business deals have been shady, involving him in bootlegging and gambling. That is his tragedy—not his low origins but the fact of so much wonderful self-confidence gone to waste and corruption.

In contrast, it is hard to imagine Shaw's Eliza Doolittle, a character created only twelve years before Gatsby (in 1913), crossing on her own the boundaries that separate her from her "betters," under any circumstances. The walls are too high and solid; she can't even talk the lingo. The point of *Pygmalion* is to reveal that those boundaries, which appear so insurmountable, are not "natural" but the product of social conditioning. Yet, whereas Gatsby is his own creation and seems to have been able to grasp that for himself in typically American fashion, Eliza can only be transformed by Higgins.

Keeping in mind this fluidity of American social and economic status, it is still unquestionably true that class and its boundaries have always figured in American literature and movies, as they have in the society. If anything, the more fluid status of American class divisions has meant that class has always had a kind of mysterious quality, one that calls for definition and redefinition—hence the fascination with Gatsby's mysterious past in Fitzgerald's novel.

From a sociological perspective, movies are particularly instructive in the ways that they portray class, because, as Marx long ago noted, perceptions of class are just as important as the material conditions that make those perceptions possible. Of course, this is not uncharted territory and the critical debate over class representations in film heated up in the 1980s. Some critics noted a tendency in contemporary Hollywood movies to treat the rich, particularly wealthy businessmen, unsympathetically. Most others, however, argued that as in other areas (women, the military, and so on), the 1980s witnessed a thoroughgoing political reaction led by Ronald Reagan that partly manifested in a new wave of conservative social representations emanating from Hollywood.

How much truth is there to these arguments? Has the content of Hollywood movies been consistently supportive of or adversarial toward the wealthy classes since World War II or did the pattern change over time, becoming more liberal in the 1960s and 1970s then reactionary in the 1980s? If there were such changes, can we explain them in a systematic way for large numbers of films? And if we can, what do they tell us about Hollywood's evolving representations of, and place in, the class structure of American society?

In contrast to the claims of Christensen, Rogin, Mills, and many others, a systematic analysis demonstrates that the rich, particularly rich men, are now usually portrayed as villains, as they have been increasingly for the past twenty-five years or so, whereas before that they used to fill a wide variety of roles, many of them protagonistic. Although this trend shows some small signs of change, Hollywood representations of the wealthy and of business have hardly returned to anything like what they were before the 1960s.

Changing Representations of the Rich in Hollywood Movies

In the 1940s and 1950s, movie moguls such as Louis Mayer, Adolph Zukor, and the Warner brothers wooed moviegoers with an idealized and glamorous image of American society, making many films that portrayed the wealthy in a favorable light. One way of interpreting this is to argue that these filmmakers believed strongly in the American economic system, which had, after all, made their own extraordinary financial success possible. Neal Gabler has characterized their feelings as stemming from "an absolute devotion to their new country . . . a ferocious, even pathological, embrace of America" (Gabler, 1988:3).

If this is the case, positive portrayals of the rich in the 1940s and early 1950s were not only a market response to masses of moviegoers who wanted to see or fantasize about how the wealthy lived, but also the work of an industry that wished to convey a positive or at any rate generous image of wealth and power in society. To be sure, some Hollywood movies represented the wealthy as cruel or pretentious people who felt only disdain for the rest of society—the greedy, unscrupulous banker Potter in Frank Capra's *It's a Wonderful Life* comes to mind as do most of the wealthy characters in *Holiday* (although both of these movies come before the opening year of our study, 1946). But most rich characters in the studio era had an egalitarian streak and were decent to commoners. Many of them were, like some of the moguls, "rags to riches" figures, whose positive characterizations hinged on their humanity and attachment to the rest of society. Indeed, as the saying goes, the rich are different—but only because they have more money. It is not the rich but rather snobs and those who take an irresponsible attitude toward other people, because of their own infatuation with class (like George Eastman [Montgomery Clift] in *A Place in the Sun*), who are negatively portrayed.

High Society (1956), a musical version of Philip Barry's *The Philadelphia Story*, provides a typical example of a mostly generous, even lighthearted treatment of the rich. Throughout its farcical turns of plot, the movie emphasizes that, despite certain tensions, people from different classes have much in common, that rich people have problems of their own, and that the rich need not be contemptuous of the rest of society, just as the rest of society need not be contemptuous of them. Throughout the film, the rich mingle in a nonantagonistic way with other classes—servants, musicians, reporters, and so on. Moreover, these relationships are basically sincere; people treat each other decently and help one another out, if possible. In one scene, the evening before the society wedding that is at the center of the plot, newspaper reporters Liz Imbrie (Celeste Holm) and Mike Connor (Frank Sinatra) cover an exclusive prenuptial soiree, and Liz, observing the wealthy partygoers with envy, remarks sarcastically: "You know, one of the prettiest sights in this pretty world is the sight of the privileged class enjoying its privileges." Surprisingly, Mike does not go along with the remark but responds in defense of the rich, arguing that "They're really not a bad bunch, when you get to know them."

Indeed, this is the tenor of the entire film and it is typical of the period in the way that it presents social interaction across class boundaries as relatively benign. All of the characters in *High Society* basically enjoy each other's company and have a wonderful time at the wedding, which constitutes the closing scene. The one exception to the rule of this representation of the wealthy in the film is social bounder George Kittredge (John Lund), who is engaged to Tracy Lord (Grace

Kelly) but whom she eventually throws over to remarry her less pretentious first husband, C. K. Dexter-Haven (Bing Crosby). Yet George is not portrayed negatively because of his class, but because of his stuffy, snobbish pretense, his inability to wear his class status rather more lightly.

Many other films from the first twenty years of our study provide similarly favorable, or generous, representations of the wealthy and of society's ability to integrate various social classes more or less comfortably. *Auntie Mame* (1959) represents most of its rich characters as generous and decent eccentrics. The film's dramatic conceit is that a young boy's father dies suddenly and he is taken, pursuant to the will, to live with his wealthy but bohemian Auntie Mame Dennis (Rosalind Russell). The film's only critique of the wealthy, as such, occurs when Mame's nephew Patrick (John Handzlik—boy, Roger Smith—adult), who has become a young man, meets and decides to marry a blue-blooded girlfriend whose family (herself included) is portrayed as shallow, boring, and bigoted. To prevent her nephew from becoming an unbearable snob, Mame invites them all to her apartment, where she succeeds in shocking them by introducing them to her friends, whom they see as "undesirables." Mame thus sabotages Patrick's relationship, restoring his wits; he eventually marries Mame's middle-class decorator, with his aunt's approval. As in *High Society*, the negative portrayal of some of the rich characters stems not from their economic privilege but from the fact that they take it so seriously, placing social status above all human decency. Once again, the lower- and middle-class characters appearing throughout *Auntie Mame* both profit from and help provide successful outcomes for the wealthy characters.

Other anecdotal examples of this kind of generous representation are easy to come by among top box office films of the first fifteen to twenty years after World War II. *The Unsinkable Molly Brown* (1964) represents class boundaries as malleable conventions that can be overcome by open-mindedness and generosity of spirit. *A Place in the Sun* (1951), based on Dreiser's 1925 novel *An American Tragedy*, portrays the business elite as decent, moral, and forthright, although they are somewhat effete and are insensitive to the hard lives of their workers. As noted above, the main character, George Eastman, is represented as a criminal, not a victim of society, when he plots to kill his working-class girlfriend in order to be able to marry the socialite Angela Vickers (Elizabeth Taylor). All of these films show the wealthy as able to get along with those who stand lower on the social ladder; leading characters who are rich are rarely, if ever, evil as a result of their class status.

In less important roles from films of this period, the rich are also represented in critically generous, if at times comical, ways. It is the eccentric millionaire, Osgood Fielding III (Joe E. Brown), who saves Joe (Tony Curtis), Jerry (Jack Lemmon), and Sugar (Marilyn Monroe) from the gangsters in *Some Like it Hot* (1959). In *The World of Suzie Wong* (1961), Mr. O'Neil (Laurence Naismith), a Hong Kong banker, takes a stand against a dinner guest who makes racist remarks about the Chinese (although O'Neil's wife and daughter are represented much less sympathetically).

One film from the earlier period, Billy Wilder's *The Apartment* (1960), is more cynical about economic privilege. In this movie, the big-business workplace, with its endless rows of identical desks for the underlings and padded offices for the brass, represents a faceless and impersonal corporation in which individuals count for very little. That alienated representational stance seems to motivate the film's plot as well, in which the officers of a large corporation abuse their power over their employee C. C. Baxter (Jack Lemmon), forcing him to loan out his apartment for their adulterous trysts. The implication is that everyone in a position of power got there by manipulative, if not immoral, means. In the end of this film, Baxter and elevator girl Fran Kubelick (Shirley MacLaine), one of the exploited women, can only escape the corrupt world of business by dropping out of it completely.

The existence of *The Apartment* hardly weakens our thesis; rather, it was a portent of things to come in representations of the business elite and other wealthy characters. Despite holdover films like *The Unsinkable Molly Brown*, by the early 1950s, the rich had begun to appear more often as selfish, greedy, and malevolent figures and their interactions with characters from other classes degenerated accordingly. The increasingly negative image of business as an institution and the wealthy in general evolved over the next twenty years, until the majority of rich characters appearing in the most popular Hollywood movies today are not heroes, or even fools, but villains. This shows little sign of changing.

Of the most successful and influential movies about business and the wealthy from 1966 to 1985, *The Godfather* (1972) provides a startling example of a transition from the portrayal of the rich as decent, humane, and more or less lovable individuals to the new code of not only greedy but often violent and malevolent tyrants. Of course the film is a gangster movie and in that tradition tells a story about rivalries in organized crime. However, an essential point of the film is that business, the police, the legal system, and the government are predominantly willing participants in the game. Payoffs, threats and intimidation, protection, gambling, drug-trafficking, and murder are all sanctioned by protagonists in the story. These are the types of activities that define wealthy and powerful figures, whether they are senators, cops, or Mafiosi. Indeed, as the film unreels, we come to see that the main thrust of the plot is the way that the Godfather's son, Michael Corleone (Al Pacino), gradually assumes an even more ruthless role than his father before him, murdering a corrupt police chief and a rival crime boss, and eventually ordering the execution of a number of other characters, including his own brother, who get in his way.

In *Arthur* (1981), we see the new code firmly in place. The wealthy heads of the Bach and Johnson families are, by their own admission, ruthless and manipulative. Several conversations between Arthur and these characters establish their unscrupulous attitudes and behavior. When Arthur (Dudley Moore) goes to see his father, Stanford Bach (Thomas Barbour), to protest the marriage that has been arranged between himself and Susan Johnson (Jill Eikenberry), Stanford doesn't even bother to justify using Arthur's inheritance to coerce him. He is quite matter-of-fact about his methods:

Stanford: We want this marriage Arthur. I want it. Burt Johnson wants it.
Arthur: Burt Johnson? He's a criminal!
Stanford: Ahhh. We all are Arthur . . . and as you know, we usually get
   what we want.

Arthur then visits his grandmother, Martha Bach (Geraldine Fitzgerald), who is portrayed even more negatively. Her response to Arthur's plea is: "Arthur, make no mistakes. You are too old to be poor. You don't know how. We are ruthless people. Don't screw with us. Arthur, I love you, but if you don't marry Susan I'll cut you off without a cent."

Susan's father, Burt Johnson (Stephen Elliott), is perhaps the worst of the rich characters, not only manipulative but violent. In one scene, he explains how he made his fortune. "Arthur, you know, I didn't inherit money like you did. I started with nothing. And yet, I was a millionaire by the time I was eighteen. Anyone stood in my way, they got hurt." These characters do not wish to have anything to do with their inferiors; Arthur is threatened with disinheritance, not because he is an obnoxious, playboy drunk but because he jeopardizes the family dynasty by freely mingling and falling in love with a plebeian. Although the film is a comedy, it is only Arthur who survives as a more or less lovable eccentric (like Auntie Mame) and the movie gets many of its laughs by representing the other rich characters not as eccentrics, but as monsters.

Given the structure of its plot, *Arthur* bears comparison with a much earlier film, *Holiday*. Whereas both movies are highly critical of the rich, in the later film, unlike in *Holiday*, most of the characters are not even given half a chance to make their own decisions about how to behave. The ethical question has been decided in advance. Wealth is not potentially corrupting but inherently evil and the characters are determined by these circumstances. In the earlier film, whereas most of the wealthy characters wind up appearing unattractive, the drama lies in the choices that they make on the way to that outcome—their class does not absolutely determine their character.

Negative portrayals of business and the wealthy class in recent movies can also be found in films in which they play only relatively minor roles. Dr. Alex Favor (Fredric March), the "Indian agent" in *Hombre* (1967), has become rich by embezzling government money paid to feed Indians on the reservation where he works. In *Diamonds Are Forever* (1972), the villain Blofeld (Charles Gray) is a multimillionaire who sends a laser gun into orbit that enables him to hold the world superpowers hostage to his demands. The film director in *Hooper* (1978) is exploitive and unconcerned about the safety of his stunt men. Ira (Zack Norman) is a villainous third-world "businessman" in *Romancing the Stone* (1984). Corporate executives in *Mr. Mom* (1983) and *The Electric Horseman* (1980) are shown to be selfish and uncaring, more concerned with their public image than with anything else. The villain of *Superman III* (1983), Ross Webster (Robert Vaughn), is a super-wealthy corporate executive. In *Beverly Hills Cop* (1984), Victor Maitland (Steven Berkoff) is a wealthy art gallery owner whose real occupation is international drug smuggling. The list of these utterly negative portrayals seems to be endless.

The conclusion we reach is that over the past forty years, there has been a considerable shift in the ways that major box office movies tend to portray businesspeople and wealthy characters. If anything, wealth has become synonymous with crime and corruption in most Hollywood movies of the past twenty-five years, whereas it used to be that rich characters could be portrayed in a number of ways and were often decent enough people, even heroes.

Business Portrayal and Wealthy Character Ratings: 1946–1985

Considering the multiplicity of characters in American movies, it is reasonable to suppose that it would be difficult to develop meaningful categories for coding them by social and economic status. In practice, however, many if not all characters are readily identifiable in terms of class definitions that produce high levels of agreement in actual coding. Our coders were instructed to assign social and economic status to characters by paying attention to their possessions, living quarters, neighborhood, type of car, and lifestyle. To quote from the protocols, "Rich—may be indicated by luxurious mansions, fur coats, or servants, country club membership . . . Middle class—comfortable but not luxurious . . . Working class—possesses basic material requirements. Possessions appear worn or well used . . . Poor—may include welfare recipients or those who lack adequate food, clothing, or housing." We were able to code 822 significant characters according to these criteria. Relying on this data base, we can compare representations of wealthy characters with those of the rest of society and evaluate changes in their character profiles over the 45-year period.

In America, which lacks an aristocratic tradition like Europe's, representation of big business has been one of the most important indexes of attitudes about class. When we examine our data on how big business has been portrayed in movies since World War II, we immediately see rather startling figures (see Table 7.1). In the first two decades of the period covered by our study, coders found roughly half of the movies portrayed business favorably and that only 18 percent of the movies in the first decade (and 14 percent in the second decade) portrayed

TABLE 7.1   Portrayal of Business in Sample Movies (percentages)

	1946–1955	1956–1965	1966–1975	1976–1990
% Positive	45	57	30	5
% Negative	18	14	40	45
% Mixed	36	29	30	40
N=48	11	7	10	20

it negatively. The rest of the portrayals were mixed. In the two most recent decades, this pattern is essentially reversed; from 1966 to 1975, only 30 percent of business portrayals are positive whereas 40 percent are negative. The negative figure rises to 45 percent between 1976 and 1990 whereas positive portrayals drop to a mere 5 percent. In a number of films, these changes result from a shift from cooperative to confrontational relationships between a rich and powerful business elite and the rest of society. Other characters must now contend with a corrupt and devious elite class who have the system rigged in their favor.

We are even more interested in the portrayal of individual characters than in overall thematic categories, because the character categories are more precise. Given the liberal attitudes of contemporary Hollywood moviemakers, we suspected that positive images of wealthy American women in new movies might mask a general trend toward negative depictions of wealthy characters. Thus, we separated characters according to gender and analyzed them over the 45-year period. Organized in this way, the data reveal that wealthy characters, especially rich men, are portrayed much more negatively than in the studio era.

The positive character ratings for male wealthy characters decline dramatically over the four decades of our study (see Table 7.2). In the first decade, the majority

TABLE 7.2   Character Ratings of Wealthy Characters vs. Nonwealthy Characters (by sex and decade, in percentages)

	1946–1955	1956–1965	1966–1975	1976–1990
Wealthy American Men				
% Positive	71	35	42	16
% Negative	14	29	38	56
% Mixed	14	35	21	29
N=107	21	17	24	45
Nonwealthy American Men				
% Positive	63	43	54	53
% Negative	18	37	30	25
% Mixed	19	37	16	23
N=488	99	67	96	226
Wealthy American Women				
% Positive	73	36	60	47
% Negative	18	27	7	18
% Mixed	9	36	33	35
N=54	11	11	15	17
Nonwealthy American Women				
% Positive	89	67	59	67
% Negative	–	8	15	11
% Mixed	11	25	26	22
N=173	36	24	34	79

of wealthy men are portrayed positively—71 percent. In the second decade, the figure drops drastically to 35 percent. In the third decade, it remains at only 42 percent and in the fourth decade positive portrayals of wealthy American men nearly disappear—16 percent positive. Although the decline in positive images obviously begins in the 1956 to 1965 period, as we have shown in the above dis-. cussion of specific movies, we observe that this was more a period of ambivalence toward the wealthy than of wholesale criticism. Negative representations of wealthy men in this period remain at only 29 percent; however, by 1965, this proportion has risen to 38 percent and from 1976 to 1990, a majority of wealthy men (56 percent) are portrayed negatively.

When we compare these figures to those representing the rest of American men, we find an obvious difference. In the first decade, other men are actually less likely to be portrayed positively—63 percent. In the second decade, positive portrayals of men drop considerably (to 43 percent) as do positive depictions of rich men. In the third decade, positive portrayals of American men in general rise to 54 percent and remain at 53 percent in the fourth decade, instead of falling again to 42 percent and then 16 percent, as occurred among the rich. Taken together, these figures show that in contrast to the first decade of the study during which rich men were usually portrayed *more* positively than other men, rich men are later only rarely portrayed positively. Moreover, those positive portrayals that were taken away from rich men could have reappeared primarily as "mixed" types, but we find that rich men usually have gone bad, not ambiguous. Negative portrayals of rich men rise steadily over the 44-year period. In contrast to this fourfold increase in negative portrayals of rich men, the proportion of other negative characters remains almost constant, averaging out at around 26 percent. In the fourth decade, negative portrayals of men who are not wealthy remain at only 25 percent. Thus, in the most recent decade, rich men are more than twice as likely to be portrayed negatively than are all other men.

Character ratings of wealthy American women are varied but much more favorable than for wealthy men. Still, wealthy women are less likely to be portrayed positively than other women throughout the entire period of the study. In the first decade, we find that 73 percent of wealthy women are favorable characters but other women are even more likely to be positive characters (89 percent). In the second decade, we find the same decline in positive images as for men, only 36 percent positive for wealthy women compared to 67 percent positive for all other women, but only 27 percent of women are actually portrayed negatively. In the third decade, unlike the men, wealthy women seem to recover, with 60 percent receiving positive ratings and only 7 percent negative ratings. In the fourth decade, positive portrayals decline again to 47 percent, but only 18 percent are negative characters. Thus, the trend toward negative character portrayal among the wealthy is much less consistent for rich women than for rich men and they seem more likely to receive "mixed" rather than "negative" character ratings in recent films.

Our data on the goals and methods of rich characters help us to understand why these character ratings have deteriorated. We find that whereas in the earlier movies rich men tended to be motivated by more benign goals or interests, such as romance, in more recent movies they are predominantly motivated by self-interest and greed. The methods they employ have shifted accordingly. Whereas in the first two decades these characters most often relied upon charm and rational persuasion to get what they wanted, deceit and violence later become at least as important and establish the characters as villains.

Romance was a favorite pursuit of wealthy men in the movies of the studio era (see Table 7.3). Forty-eight percent and 53 percent of wealthy men are interested in romance in these first two decades of the study. By the third decade, however, romance has declined to only 25 percent and in the most recent period only 18 percent of rich men bother with romance at all. Material gain has become a more likely motivation as romance has declined in importance for these characters. The

TABLE 7.3   Selected Goals of Wealthy Characters vs. Nonwealthy Characters (by sex and decade, in percentages)

	1946–1955	1956–1965	1966–1975	1976–1990
Wealthy American Men				
% Romance	48	53	25	18
% Self-interest	48	6	33	60
% Protect others	48	–	17	29
% Greed	14	24	38	49
N=107	21	17	24	45
Nonwealthy American Men				
% Romance	15	28	12	19
% Self-interest	36	22	25	33
% Protect others	40	18	16	28
% Greed	10	16	24	6
N=488	99	67	96	226
Wealthy American Women				
% Romance	54	54	33	47
% Self-interest	46	46	20	35
% Protect others	54	27	13	41
% Greed	–	–	–	18
N=54	11	11	15	17
Nonwealthy American Women				
% Romance	47	46	44	46
% Self-interest	28	33	32	44
% Protect others	33	25	24	40
% Greed	3	4	9	8
N=173	36	24	34	79

proportion of rich men motivated by greed has risen dramatically over the 45-year period. Only 14 percent of the rich men in the first decade are greedy. In the second decade, 24 percent are greedy characters but in the third decade that proportion rises substantially to 38 percent. In the fourth period, wealthy characters motivated by greed increase still further to 49 percent. Self-interest, viewed in conjunction with the goal of protecting others, tells us more about the image of rich American men. In the first two decades, these two goals are closely linked; 48 percent of the characters in the first decade are both self-interested and involved in protecting others. In the second decade, both of these goals tend to disappear. In the third decade, when self-interest and protection of others reappear, 33 percent of the wealthy characters are motivated by self-interest although only 17 percent are interested in protecting others. In the fourth period, this gap widens considerably: 60 percent of the wealthy characters are now self-interested and only 29 percent are concerned with protecting others.

These trends suggest that although wealthy men might previously have been self-interested, they were also capable of transcending this more selfish world and associating with and helping others, for example in friendships and romance. More recently, Hollywood's image of the wealthy American man is that of a highly alienated, isolated individual, much less capable of participating in the world around him. As a result, with few exceptions, wealthy men are quite contemptuous in recent movies and their relationship to other characters, particularly those from lower classes, is highly antagonistic.

The methods rich characters employ to achieve their goals provide further evidence of the declining civility of the upper crust (see Table 7.4). In the first two decades, rich men were more likely to use charm and rational persuasion to achieve their goals. Sixty-seven percent employ this method in the first decade, 59 percent in the second; in the third decade, the figure drops to 38 percent and remains at only 42 percent in the latest period. At the same time that this method is declining in relative importance, after 1965, rich men are much more likely to resort to violence to achieve their goals. Only 14 percent and 18 percent of rich men resort to violence in the first two decades, whereas in the third decade, 54 percent do so. Of course, violence has become more prominent in recent movies generally, but a somewhat lesser proportion of the rest of men (40 percent) use violence in the third decade. In the most recent period, violence declines to 36 percent among wealthy men, much closer in line to the violent behavior of other men (31 percent), yet this is hardly the glamorous image of wealth that was once prevalent.

The goals and methods of rich women indicate that their more favorable image reflects a complexity no longer shared by most rich men. Rich men have simply become villains, but rich women, although they have begun to participate in the corrupt world of wealth and power, are less suspect. Wealthy women are more likely in recent movies to be greedy, less likely to rely on charm and rational persuasion, and more likely to use violence to get what they want. However, they still

TABLE 7.4   Selected Methods of Wealthy Characters vs. Nonwealthy Characters (by sex and decade, in percentages)

	1946–1955	*1956–1965*	*1966–1975*	*1976–1990*
Wealthy American Men				
% Violence	14	18	54	36
%Deceit/trickery	19	12	12	38
% Charm/rational persuasion	67	59	38	42
N=107	21	17	24	45
Nonwealthy American Men				
% Violence	30	13	40	31
% Deceit/trickery	20	24	21	26
% Charm/rational persuasion	50	42	30	35
N=488	99	67	96	226
Wealthy American Women				
% Violence	–	–	20	29
% Deceit/trickery	9	36	13	29
% Charm/rational persuasion	64	64	47	41
N=54	11	11	15	17
Nonwealthy American Women				
% Violence	6	–	9	24
% Deceit/trickery	19	12	24	22
% Charm/rational persuasion	67	62	41	52
N=173	36	24	34	79

remain more interested in romance than rich men and their need to protect others appears more evenly balanced against self-interest.

In the first two decades, 54 percent of wealthy American women are interested in romance (see Table 7.3). This goal declines to 33 percent in the third decade but rebounds to 47 percent in the latest period. Unlike men, these women have actually become less self-interested in recent movies: 46 percent show self-interest in the first two decades, but only 20 percent and 33 percent retain this goal in the third and fourth periods.

Moreover, although greed is entirely absent for rich women in the first three decades of the study, in the most recent period, 18 percent are motivated by greed (see Table 7.3). The use of charm and rational persuasion also declines from 64 percent in the first two decades to 47 percent in the third decade and 41 percent in the most recent period. Finally, rich women become more violent in the two most recent decades. Violence is entirely absent for rich women in the first two decades, but in the third decade 20 percent are coded as violent and from 1976 to 1990, 29 percent of rich women are violent (see Table 7.4). Once again, we find that although rich women's character ratings do not suffer as much as men's, they have also become somewhat more unscrupulous. Based on our more comprehensive analysis of gender differences in popular movies presented in Chapter 8, we suspect that this mixed pattern is largely explained by more favorable treatment of successful career women in contemporary movies, perhaps because of the influence of feminism.

Despite these caveats on the representation of women, the findings bolster the argument that Hollywood's portrayal of the rich and business elite has become increasingly critical since the postwar decade. The change is not explained by a rise in mixed character ratings for men (though for women there is some increase here), but rather by a substantial increase in the number of negative ratings among wealthy men, particularly from 1976 to 1990. Perhaps most importantly, the decline in protagonistic roles occurs only among wealthy characters and is not part of a general trend for other characters.

At the same time, in a number of contemporary movies, the downward spiral of *motivations* and *behavior* among the wealthy seems to have contributed to a similar decline for other characters. Whereas one might argue that in earlier movies Hollywood usually promoted cooperation and social cohesion, representing the interplay of the wealthy and the rest of society as legitimate and productive, one is impressed by the tendency of newer movies to reverse this relationship. Interclass contacts in more recent films are less likely to produce positive results and the emphasis is no longer on the discovery of bonds among all classes of people (as in movies like *High Society* or *The Unsinkable Molly Brown*). The interplay among classes has become destructive; in a world in which the rich are often unscrupulous villains, other characters are drawn into deceitful, violent, or greedy activities as the only methods for thwarting or circumventing a corrupt and exploitive wealthy class.

This development at least partially explains the rise of violence among characters other than the wealthy. Looking at recent movies in our sample, we see that middle- and working-class characters must often resort to violence as they confront increasingly immoral, wealthy villains (*Diamonds Are Forever, Mr. Mom, Beverly Hills Cop*) or the nonwealthy characters are eventually corrupted by the wealthy and emulate their behavior (*The Godfather, Superman III*). Increased violence, then, has not become more prevalent in movies only as a means for satisfying the audience's desire for sensational entertainment, although it undoubtedly has that effect as well. In many recent movies, violence is symptomatic of a corrupt and vicious society with which all types of characters must contend. This explains why, ironically, violence is so often presented as an appropriate, justified, and even heroic course of action for the diverse characters portrayed in movies of all types. The suggestion is that the system does not work, and only a renegade such as John Rambo or Dirty Harry can win and retain integrity.

In effect, since the mid-1960s, an increasing number of Hollywood movies have featured a variation on the class struggle, in which characters are increasingly alienated from each other—this, despite the fact that, as we noted in the beginning of this essay, American society is still characterized by less rigid class divisions than most. Other films have simply portrayed American enterprise as rotten from top to bottom, a system that decent individuals have to fight tooth and nail if they are to salvage any dignity (*The Electric Horseman, Arthur*). Fewer and fewer movies support the idea that wealth and power can be legitimately acquired or that businessmen or the wealthy in general serve a useful purpose in society.

Conclusion

The films that the old studio system produced reflected a consensus about the integrity of the society, including the integrity of its class norms. Whereas villains could come from any class, the socioeconomic system in which they lived was rarely indicted as the source of their behavior and, as a result, violence and manipulation were usually not condoned as legitimate ways to advance in life. Most protagonists succeeded in their goals by working hard and playing by the rules; the system worked and if there were problems they could almost always be fixed. Wealthy characters were decent, sometimes mercurial, or even foolish citizens in many movies, but they were rarely villains.

The attitudes that informed such films began to change in the 1960s, as many members of a new generation in Hollywood came to see America as a flawed, materialist society, one in which the social and economic fabric is to blame for many individual problems and ills. This change is part of a broad ideological shift among certain strategic elites in the society that places them in a more adversarial stance than they once occupied. Hollywood producers, directors, and writers now tend to see the world very differently from the way the American public, traditional elites, and their own predecessors saw it. And just as the ideologies of the studio heads influenced movie content in the 1940s and 1950s, so too do the liberal and cosmopolitan ideas of a new class of moviemakers in the 1960s, 1970s, and 1980s. In the case of attitudes about social and economic status, the Hollywood elite now seems to embrace, rather unambivalently, a view of American big business and wealth as inherently corrupted and corrupting.

Given all this, the findings of our study, in this and other areas, are at odds with the observations of critics and film theorists, who argue that the Reagan years were characterized by a staunchly conservative reaction in American popular culture. In fact, despite a moderate retreat in some aspects of negative depictions of the wealthy, the much-vaunted conservatism of the Reagan revolution did not succeed in rolling back the multifarious changes that have been taking place in the past several decades in Hollywood, where a liberal elite remains in control of all aspects of the industry. Indeed, our data show that on balance, movies of the 1976–1985 decade were the most critical of business and wealth, presenting them as so corrupt that it's hard to see in this a reactionary glorification of patriotism and capitalism.

The public ultimately decides on the success of a film, voting with their feet. But many members of the Hollywood elite continue to make films that represent a very different picture of the world than a statistical profile of the American public would suggest should be the case if Hollywood were merely catering to public tastes. In terms of the representation of the rich, this image of class antagonism in film has involved the creation of a class of utterly unscrupulous, wealthy men, characters whose goals and methods are at odds with those of the rest of society. When these characters interact with others, the result is often a vicious cycle of corruption and violence, spurring ordinarily decent individuals to extreme behavior. Whatever intrigue this sensationalism holds for the viewer, these new films are far out of step with the experience and attitudes of the vast majority of Americans. And yet, as far as we can tell, given the attitudes of the Hollywood elite, these representations are unlikely to change soon.

8

The Politics of Gender

In the summer of 1991, in the wake of movies such as *Terminator 2: Judgment Day*, *Thelma and Louise*, and *V. I. Warshawski*, all of which feature heroines who resort to violence, a spate of articles appeared in the popular press discussing how gender roles in mainstream movies have changed during the past few years. In "Give Him a Puppy. And Get the Lady a Gun," Janet Maslin argued that "the season's heroines, in a departure from the window-dressing bimbo roles of just a year ago, are less likely to be lending support and comfort and more likely to be spitting nails" (sec. 2:1). And in "Killer Women," Julie Baumgold wrote that the current crop of heroines "are the inheritors of movie women like Kate Hepburn and Roz Russell, who were always quick-talking and strong, but these women are killers" (26).[1] Understandably, both articles focused on the current scene, suggesting that recent trends are just the latest twist—a response to the previous year's absurdly macho male heroes (Maslin) or another contemporary version of male sexual fantasy, albeit one tempered with political rectitude (Baumgold). Maslin and Baumgold made no pretense of providing a picture of longer-term trends, but their essays did raise the questions of whether something more than a season's mood is at work and whether or not these changes reflect larger trends in the movie industry and in society.

As those who have followed the development of academic cinema studies are aware, many film scholars have been preoccupied with similar questions for some time, devoting themselves to the analysis of representations of gender, especially representations of women.[2] Most of these rely heavily upon the cultural approach that we described in Chapter 1 and that we consider problematic. Our findings differ considerably from those of most feminist writers, including such very popular writers as Susan Faludi (1991).

Men and Women Characters from 1946 to 1965: In the Tradition

The representation of women in Hollywood films is not an issue of inclusion or exclusion, as in the case of racial minorities. Women characters appear in nearly all of the 146 top grossing films in our 44-year sample. Still, we know from our character data that popular movies are male-dominated for the entire period (see Table 8.1). Leading female characters represent only about 25 percent of all characters in our movie sample. This seems to be a consistent and rigid proportioning for men and women in the movies.

Although women have always appeared alongside men in star and supporting roles in Hollywood movies, their interests and activities were quite distinct from those of men for many years. In movies of the 1920s and 1930s, women first began to appear in strong roles—Marlene Dietrich, Greta Garbo, Mae West and others. These were worldly characters, often fallen women who were punished in the end, as Andrew Bergman points out in *We're in the Money: Depression America and its Films*; but they had escaped the world of domesticity for a time. Of Mae West's roles, Bergman writes:

> She made the female the hunter, not the hunted, an active participant in sex, rather than a passive and ill-starred victim. By asserting her faith in diamonds and baubles, she created the crudest kind of economic independence, but a woman with a safe full of jewelry would have to walk no streets. She could not be manipulated, refused to be solemn about her body and made it clear that she liked her pleasures and liked her freedom. She seemed in complete control of herself and her world. (Bergman, 1971:56)

These female characters did not compete with men, but rather occupied an entirely different world from them—a fanciful world of song and dance and excitement that must have appealed to many women in the audience. Women were a substantial component of the audience in the Depression years and Hollywood did not neglect their need for escape in the theaters.

By the 1940s, where our content analysis begins, things had changed again. The Production Code had made a real impact on the content of movies by the late 1930s and the war had taken away many boyfriends and husbands. Many more American women had begun to work outside the home, as well. In response to this turmoil in American life, Hollywood's female leads became much more interested in romance and family life. These were more ordinary interests that the moguls perhaps had decided were threatened by the war or compromised by the demands of work. Movies may have more closely mirrored the societal consensus of the day.

Although many female leads were extraordinary individuals (the roles of Katherine Hepburn and Rosalind Russell were quite powerful, for example), typ-

TABLE 8.1   Percent of Women and Men Characters in Sample Movies

	1946–1955	1956–1965	1966–1975	1976–1990
% Women	25	26	26	28
% Men	75	74	74	72
N=	718	736	857	1673

ically, female characters of the 1940s and 1950s sought to divert male attention away from the pursuit of careers, adventure, wealth, or even war or a life of crime and to channel more of men's energy into domesticity. The majority of leading female characters are young, attractive, and motivated by romance. Indeed, for many of the heroines of a large number of the films in our sample for this period—*The Egg and I* (1947), *Father's Little Dividend* (1951), *Seven Brides for Seven Brothers* (1954), *High Society* (1956), *Love Me Tender* (1957), *The Music Man* (1962), and many others—life revolves around the question of finding a husband or of how to resolve romantic problems in favor of conjugal happiness. The women characters' goals usually involve getting the men they care about to behave the way a "good" father or husband should. Although there are a number of different possible outcomes to these kinds of plots, most of the time the men wind up making concessions to this domestic sphere. Hence, many of these films are lighthearted comedies following the classical injunction to end with a marriage (or in some cases, when the couple is already married, to end with a pregnancy or at least a smoothing out of marital problems). A substantial number of the male characters are of course interested in romance themselves, independently of women's designs, but movies with significant roles for women usually focus on their pursuit of men—not the reverse.

The content analysis supports these assertions about popular films (see Table 8.2). For example, among a number of possible motivations or goals for female characters (up to three could be recorded for each character), romance is by far the most frequently coded goal for three decades running, coded for 50 percent, 45 percent, and 41 percent of women in the first three decades. Romance remains at 44 percent from 1976 to 1990 but "self interest" and "protection of others" (previously between 15 and 20 percentage points behind romance), are coded almost as often at 40 and 39 percent, respectively. Men are much less frequently motivated

TABLE 8.2   Percent for Romance, Self-Interest, and Protecting Others as Goals for Women and Men Characters

	1946–1955	1956–1965	1966–1975	1976–1990
Women				
% Romance	50	45	41	44
% Self-interest	32	28	28	40
% Protect others	33	19	18	39
N=	66	67	79	112
Men				
% Romance	21	30	14	17
% Self-interest	33	23	28	34
% Protect others	36	16	16	29
N=	156	137	181	331

by romance over the entire period of the study: 21 percent are coded for romance in the first decade, 30 percent in the second decade, 14 percent in the third period, and 17 percent in movies from 1976 to 1990.

Women are also much more likely to be married than men in movies from the first half of the study. The number of women characters who either get married in the course of a movie, are married at a film's opening, or are widowed (there are no divorces in our sample from this period) is consistently higher than for men. As Table 8.3 shows, 29 percent of all women fall into this category in the first decade and 23 percent do so in the second decade. For men, the figures are less than half that at 12 percent and 10 percent for the two decades.

Although women often work in the earlier movies, the kind of work they do correlates in a statistically significant way with their roles vis-à-vis romance. Women who hold traditional kinds of jobs usually do so only to survive. The traditional category includes women who are unemployed or working as a housewife, elementary or secondary teacher, nurse, secretary, waitress, or holding some other job conventionally associated with women. When these kinds of characters become romantically involved and marry (the two usually go together), work rarely remains important or desirable to them.[3] For example, in *Auntie Mame* (1959) Mame Dennis (Rosalind Russell), who is independently wealthy, only needs to work when she loses her fortune in the 1929 crash. She takes a position as a clerk in a department store, where she proves incompetent, but where she meets oil tycoon Beauregard Burnside (Forest Tucker), who marries her and restores her to wealth. When he dies in a mountain-climbing accident, she is left with a fortune and can then spend all of her time arranging the domestic relations of her nephew and servants.

In contrast, there are actually a significant number of women who hold non-traditional jobs in this period, such as jobs that were much more likely to be held by men in the society at the time. These nontraditional roles include college teachers, doctors, lawyers, CEOs, sales managers, military personnel, and other kinds of high-paying or otherwise elite jobs. As Table 8.4 indicates, in the first decade, 42 percent of women appear in nontraditional occupations and in the second decade, the figure drops to 38 percent, although when we exclude minor characters we find higher rates, 49 percent and 43 percent respectively, of star and supporting women in nontraditional roles.

TABLE 8.3   Percent of Women and Men Characters Who Marry, Are Married, or Are Widowed

	1946–1955	1956–1965	1966–1975	1976–1990
% Women	29	23	24	17
N=	182	188	227	464
% Men	12	10	10	8
N=	536	548	630	1209

TABLE 8.4 Percent of Women Characters in Traditional and Nontraditional Occupations (All Women and Star/Supporting Women)

	1946–1955	1956–1965	1966–1975	1976–1990
All women				
% Traditional occupations	58	62	51	39
% Nontraditional occupations	42	38	49	61
N=	109	118	150	270
Star/Supporting Women				
% Traditional occupations	51	57	48	28
% Nontraditional occupations	49	43	52	72
N=	45	44	61	81

There is, however, an extraordinary catch, alluded to above: the women who hold elite jobs are much more unlikely to be married at a film's opening and much *more* interested in romance (see Tables 8.5A and 8.5B). Further, during the first two decades of the study, those women in lead roles and nontraditional occupations are fully twice as likely to be motivated by romance than other women: 64 percent and 68 percent of these elite women (in the first and second decades) are motivated by romance as opposed to 30 percent and 28 percent of women in traditional roles. In short, movies of the 1940s and 1950s either present women as already linked to men through marriage or as pursuing men while working in careers. Thus, even single, working women are overwhelmingly portrayed in the

TABLE 8.5A Percent of Women Characters in Traditional vs. Nontraditional Occupations Married at Film's Opening

	1946–1955	1956–1965	1966–1975	1976–1990
% Traditional occupations	40	33	49	27
N=	63	73	77	105
% Nontraditional occupations	24	11	10	8
N=	46	45	73	165

TABLE 8.5B Percent of Women Characters in Traditional vs. Nontraditional Occupations with Romance as a Goal

	1946–1955	1956–1965	1966–1975	1976–1990
% Traditional occupations	30	28	34	52
N=	23	25	29	23
% Nontraditional occupations	64	68	34	43
N=	22	19	32	58

earlier period as romantic hopefuls, even though they may not have married. As we will see, this distinction between women in nontraditional occupations versus those in traditional ones is a key variable in distinguishing among various film themes and character types throughout the course of the study, for in the later periods this correlation between elite occupations and romantic motivation substantially lessens.

Pillow Talk (1959) exemplifies the representation of career-oriented single women in the context of romance during the first two decades of the study. Jan Morrow (Doris Day) is unhappy, even though she has an unusual high-prestige job as an interior decorator. The implication is that she has put her career ahead of her personal desires for romance and is suffering the lonely consequences: "bedroom problems," as the male lead, Brad Allen (Rock Hudson) puts it. In the course of the movie, she manages to domesticate the womanizing Allen (with whom she feuds throughout most of the film), who originally only wanted to bed her. The film ends with a vision of connubial bliss: Jan achieves happiness in a realm other than work; Brad, in contrast, becomes convinced that matrimony may hold deeper pleasure than philandering.

Corresponding to this emphasis on marriage over work as the appropriate denouement of emotional happiness for women, in the earlier movies we also find that women characters usually want children and the responsibilities of running a household and they rarely express any doubt of their suitability to these roles. The social consensus that runs through the films is that men and women serve very different purposes in life. Even the headstrong Molly Brown (Debbie Reynolds), in *The Unsinkable Molly Brown* (1964), realizes in the end that despite her success, saving her marriage is more important to her than anything else.

Given all this, it makes sense that Hollywood movies before 1965 usually condemn sexual activity outside of marriage. From 1946 to 1955, nonmarital sex figures in only 23 percent of the sample films (see Table 8.6). From 1956 to 1965, the percentage begins to rise, climbing to 38 percent. In both decades, characters are almost always punished in some way for engaging in what is usually represented as a morally reprehensible activity. In movies we have already looked at,

TABLE 8.6   Percent of Movies Featuring Nonmarital Sex and Consequences

	1946–1955	*1956–1965*	*1966–1975*	*1976–1990*
% Movies with nonmarital sex	23	38	48	57
N=	30	29	33	54
% Negative consequences for some/all characters	71	91	50	26
% Negative consequences for no characters	29	9	50	74
N=	7	11	16	31

such as *Pillow Talk* (which is comic), and others, such as *A Place in the Sun* (1951), *From Here to Eternity* (1953), and *The Apartment* (1960) (in which the outcomes are tragic or nearly so), nonmarital sex is a disaster for some or all of the characters, leading only to deception, pain, and even crime. Looking at the entire sample, we see that the overwhelming majority of films take similar positions in the first two decades.

These results, when taken together, are probably not very surprising to most readers. There is little question that the movies of this period portrayed women in a traditional way, although it is interesting to note how many of these women characters do hold relatively elite jobs when they work.[4] We are less interested in passing judgment on this state of affairs than in understanding the massive changes that occurred in this aspect of Hollywood film content beginning in the mid-1960s.

Men and Women Characters from 1966 to 1990: After the Revolution

It would be difficult to overestimate the changes in Hollywood representations of gender roles and especially of women since the mid-1960s. Many, if not all, of the earlier kinds of representation of women characters were modified, or even reversed outright, albeit in complex, interdependent ways. Of course, the relaxation of movie industry self-censorship allowed the introduction of sexually explicit material and, by the early 1970s, many movies emphasized sexuality in romantic relationships. Yet the changes were also deeper and more subtle than a quantitative increase in explicit depictions of sex at first suggests. In fact, as is the case with respect to other groups and institutions, it is clear that the 1980s were not characterized by a reactionary trend in representations of women, though many critics argue that they were. If anything, a liberal set of attitudes on sexuality and social and political issues involving gender have come to dominate Hollywood in the past twenty-five years, and they are manifest in film content. These attitudes may be more conservative than those Mulvey, Gledhill, Smith, Frank, Sobchack, de Lauretis, Brunette and Wills, and other contemporary film theorists hold, but, as we have seen, they are much more liberal than those of traditional elites and of the general public.

Changes in the depiction of sex have been the most sensational, and therefore they are a good place to begin describing the changes in representations of men and women since 1965. Under the new rating system that went into effect in 1968, sexually explicit material became more and more acceptable in films for adults. Sex outside of marriage quickly became an acceptable activity and as representations of sexual conduct became more daring, women's roles gradually expanded from the predominantly romantic to more complex characterizations. As a result of this, some movies problematized not only previous judgments about nonmarital sex but also the romantic idealism that generally surrounded marriage and

family life—sex hardly had to lead to marriage or scandal now, but could function as one aspect of an open-ended entanglement (and a way to sell tickets).
Although it became all the more graphic, it also became, if anything, less narra-
tologically consequential—hence, the invention of the obligatory sex scene that
does little to advance the plot.

Indeed, nonmarital sex increasingly appears in these films as a carefree, harm-
less behavior and, as everyone is aware, it has become a mainstay of box office hits
of the past twenty years. As Table 8.6 shows, in the 1966–1975 decade, the percentage of movies in our sample that represent nonmarital sex rises to 48 percent
(up from 38 percent in the previous decade) and in the most recent period from
1976 to 1990 to 57 percent. More striking is the finding that the negative consequences for characters engaging in nonmarital sex have radically declined. In
newer movies, characters who engage in nonmarital sex are far less likely to be
punished for their transgressions. We have already noted that 71 percent and 91
percent of movies from the two earlier decades show negative consequences for
some or all individuals. For the most recent two decades, the pattern is nearly reversed. In the 1966–1975 decade, films showing nonmarital sex split evenly between negative consequences for some or all individuals and no negative consequences for anyone. In the 1976–1990 period, nonmarital sex has negative
outcomes for some or all individuals in only 26 percent of the films (in only 6
percent are consequences negative for all characters), and in the rest (74 percent),
no individuals suffer any negative consequences whatsoever. For better or worse,
Hollywood has endorsed a judgment-free approach to sex outside of marriage
and the most recent movies are the most permissive. However much the society
may have changed, it seems fair to say that this permissive outlook does not reflect the basically conservative attitudes to which many Americans still adhere.[5]

The change in the quality and quantity of visible sex is significant in its own
right, but the accompanying transformations in the representation of romance
are probably even more important. In earlier movies, as we have seen, women are
predominantly interested in falling in love, getting married, and raising a family.
Men know this and often try not to get involved, but many of them are drawn
into romantic relationships anyway, destined, in happy endings, for quiet family
life. One character who exemplifies this male reticence is Professor Hill (Robert
Preston) of *The Music Man* (1962); another is Brad Hill, the character Rock
Hudson plays in *Pillow Talk*.

In the mid-1960s, these scenarios changed rapidly, as Table 8.2 makes clear.
Note that in the fourth decade, romance remains high as a goal for all women
characters, at 44 percent, but now "self-interest" runs a close second, coded for 40
percent of the female characters. In the previous decades, "self-interest," the second most frequently coded motivation for women, occurs for only 28 percent of
the sample. In short, in the course of the second half of our study period, romance quickly loses its preeminent rank as a motivation for women, at the same
time that depictions of sex multiply.

The late 1970s and especially the 1980s witness a correspondingly significant shift in women's roles, as other concerns intrude into these fictional lives. Unprecedented numbers of women begin to appear in nontraditional occupations, asserting their independence from men in a number of ways that dovetail with reconceived notions of romance (see Table 8.4). In the third decade, nontraditional occupations for women increase from 38 percent in the first two decades to 49 percent and in the fourth decade, the figure rises again to 61 percent. Among stars and supporting women, we find an even greater increase in the number portrayed in nontraditional occupations, which rises in the fourth decade to an astonishing 72 percent.

This last statistic is of the kind that should give pause to those who see Hollywood as, on the one hand, a mirror of existing social conditions or, on the other hand, a bastion of reactionary mythmaking. For despite the tremendous influx of women into the work force, this composite image does not represent women's employment in a realistic way. At the same time, it is a sure sign that depictions of women have changed in a liberal direction.

This hypothesis becomes all the more convincing when we look at some of the many films that represent romance as a secondary concern for women or at any rate a less consuming concern than it once was for the myriad women now represented in elite professional positions. In *The Electric Horseman* (1980), Halle (Jane Fonda) is an aggressive investigative reporter who gets her story, despite the interferences of romance. Unlike in earlier movies, in which romance and career often merge into a romantic narrative, in this case the two preoccupations conflict. In *Mr. Mom* (1983), Caroline (Teri Garr), a frustrated housewife with a college degree, becomes a high-powered business executive while her husband stays home and takes care of the kids, again leading to conflict. In the three *Star Wars* movies (1977, 1980, 1983), Princess Leia (Carrie Fisher) is an important military leader who engages in combat, repairs spaceships, participates in war strategy meetings, and gives orders. Until the conclusion of the three-film sequence, her romance with Han Solo (Harrison Ford) is portrayed as an annoyance and an obstruction to her more important responsibilities. In *Private Benjamin* (1980), the female recruits are put through the same grueling basic training as men. Judy Benjamin (Goldie Hawn) starts out as a blonde bimbo but winds up a successful military officer who, in the final scene, punches out her chauvinist fiancé and walks off on her own.

Among these leading women in nontraditional occupations, the goal of romance declines substantially from well over 60 percent in the first half of the study down to 34 percent and 43 percent in the two most recent decades (see Table 8.5B). At first we found it surprising that for women in traditional occupations, romance actually increases in importance as a motivation in the plot from about 30 percent in the first two decades to 34 percent in the third decade and 52 percent in the fourth period. But it is important to remember that all of this is happening at the same time that the percentage of women in traditional occupations is falling off dramatically and the number of women in nontraditional positions is correspondingly rising. One hypothesis that might explain this statistic is that the women in traditional occupations, who also evince a greater interest in romance, are the kinds of characters who appear in more traditional films and thus may be more closely focused as a group on that goal, even as their numbers decrease.

Further, even in films in which romance figures prominently and women work in more traditional occupations, romance often causes conflicts unfamiliar in the vast majority of earlier films. In *The Goodbye Girl* (1978), Paula (Marsha Mason) is a dancer who's getting too old for her craft. She's divorced and trying to raise her daughter, while simultaneously working, after having been abandoned by her last "live-in lover." Her career never really takes off, but she does work to support herself and Lucy (Quinn Cummings). Her relationship with a struggling actor, Elliot (Richard Dreyfuss), begins in hostility and mistrust, as she's been hurt so often before. Although played for laughs, the romantic terrain represents kinds of anger, confusion, and pitfalls unimaginable in earlier decades. The amorous resolution, when it arrives, is not marriage, but a kind of noninstitutional commitment, in which, to paraphrase the closing song, good-bye doesn't have to be forever (Elliot is leaving town temporarily for an acting job). This is a rather tentative echo of the wedding bells that usually signal the successful resolution of romantic comedies in the earlier periods.

One earlier film that maps out the ambiguous romantic world that we find in *The Goodbye Girl* is *The Apartment* (1960), an exposé of destructive male duplicity in both work and love. Again, in that film, the romantic solution arrives only after very difficult—in this case, life-threatening—developments that are the result of male sexual villainy. In this case, however, unlike in *A Place in the Sun*, the law cannot intercede—the protagonists simply have to drop out in order to survive, to escape from a system that is inherently corrupt and loathsome. In the same moral universe as *The Apartment*, we find movies like *Who's Afraid of Virginia Woolf?* (1966), which offers a vision of married life as a folie-à-deux, an endless round of games, degrading insults, self-destruction, and deceptions. Of course, the characters in these films are in particular situations—no film makes this clearer than the last, in which there are only four major characters, all of whom are highly particularized. Yet these examples of romance do typify the larger trends—which are, after all, only built up from these myriad examples.

We could cite many other films as examples of how romance and sex were reconceived over the past several decades. *Bob and Carol and Ted and Alice* (1970) and *Carnal Knowledge* (1971), although very different kinds of movies, form a convenient critical pair. The first is a satire both on marriage and on the new sexual codes that proclaimed it to be an outmoded institution. After a good deal of philandering, the four major characters eventually realize that the new sexual code of open marriage that they had thought would free them only reveals their own delusions. In the end, they pull back at the last moment from swapping spouses, all in the same bed. In the latter movie, Jonathan (Jack Nicholson), a promiscuous playboy, contrasts with his life-long friend Sandy (Art Garfunkel), who eventually does manage to free himself from what is represented as a deluded and debasing code of traditional sexual behavior. On the one hand, we last see Sandy espousing an ethic of sensitivity and renouncing his repressed and repressive emotional past, while living, after his divorce, with a woman much younger than himself. Jonathan, on the other hand, ends up, in middle age, unable to develop any meaningful relationships and we last see him visiting a prostitute, Louise (Rita Moreno), who has to arouse him by acting out an entirely servile role.

Sally (Meg Ryan), in *When Harry Met Sally* (1989), is an independent, modern woman, a successful author, determined not to become sexually involved with her best friend, Harry (Billy Crystal). The two sleep together eventually, but this compromises the friendship and, until the end of the story, fails to bring about a more serious commitment. Both are unwilling to concede their feelings for each other. This last film provides an interesting view of the contemporary barriers to intimate communication, just as likely to be a problem for women as for men at that point. Although this film may provide a more realistic view of modern life, it is quite different from earlier films that portray women as more willing participants in romance. All of these characters must find their ways in bewildering landscapes that simply did not exist in earlier mainstream American films.

Along with changes in the representation of sex, romance, and women's occupations, come new goals and methods for women characters, particularly in the late 1970s and 1980s. Their goals and methods for achieving those goals in film plots are more closely aligned with those of their male counterparts on the screen. One important difference: despite increased reliance on antagonistic methods, including greed or malevolence, violence, and the exercise of authority, women in previously elite, male jobs are less likely to be villains than men in similar positions.

Indeed, women are treated more favorably than men over the entire period. In the study, all star and supporting characters received character ratings (positive, negative, mixed) based on their roles in the films. As Table 8.7 shows, among the women, positive ratings occur for 80 percent of the characters in the first decade and then drop off but hold steady at around 60 percent during the next three decades. For men, the figures for each period run considerably lower: 64 percent, 48 percent, 50 percent, and 47 percent respectively. Also, negative ratings for men rise significantly over the four periods from 20 percent to 25 percent and then up to 32 percent in the second half of the study. Women's negative ratings remain constant and are substantially lower at only 12 percent for each period. Taken all in all, the sample suggests that although men always represent a greater proportion of the heavies, they have nevertheless become still more malevolent than women over the course of the study.[6]

In fact, since the mid-1970s, sympathetic roles for women have begun to include even tough, sensational vocations as well as elite ones, and finally, as we saw

TABLE 8.7   Percent of Positive and Negative Character Ratings for Women and Men
Characters

	1946–1955	1956–1965	1966–1975	1976–1990
Women				
% Positive	80	63	57	60
% Negative	12	12	11	12
N=	66	67	79	112
Men				
% Positive	64	48	50	47
% Negative	20	25	32	32
N=	156	137	181	331

in the introduction, highly violent characters. *The Witches of Eastwick* (1989) provides a recent notable example of the new image of women. The three protagonists in the film, Alexandra (Cher), Jane (Susan Sarandon), and Sukie (Michelle Pfeiffer), are all working women who become romantically involved with the devilish Darryl Van Horn (Jack Nicholson). Sukie, mother of six, has been deserted by her husband but still manages to work as a newspaper writer. Jane is recently divorced and works as a schoolteacher. Alexandra is a widow raising one child and working as a sculptor. To rid themselves of their demonic lover, all three must resort to violence and deceit. In spite of being victimized by Darryl and other men along the way, the women manage to win out in the end—beating the devil at his own game. The only negative woman in the movie is Felicia (Veronica Cartwright), the newspaper editor's more traditional wife. She is portrayed as a bible-thumping prude and Darryl sends evil spirits to possess and destroy her.

Whether women play business moguls, military heroines, supercops, or con artists, they tend to improve the overall image of these professions, because as a rule women are more likely to be portrayed favorably than men. Indeed, all the violent women in the three movies we mentioned at the beginning of this chapter are highly sympathetic. Further, when we control for the fact that women often escape the scrutiny to which men are subjected in certain roles, we find that stronger criticisms of specific American institutions in movies of the past twenty-five years correlate with the rising status of women characters. In other words, the women characters associated with disfavored groups are much more rarely associated with the groups' shortcomings, which tend to be embodied in male characters. Although the three movies we cited in the first paragraph of this essay were not coded for the study, they confirm our findings.

The same exceptional roles for women are found in elite occupations. As the business elite inevitably forms a kind of leadership cadre in a capitalist society, elite business seems an important professional category to demonstrate the new trend (see Table 8.8). Our statistics show that in the most recent period, big busi-

TABLE 8.8   Percent of Women and Men Characters in Business and Their Character Ratings

	1946–1955	1956–1965	1966–1975	1976–1990
% Women	15	3	6	33
% Men	85	97	94	67
N=	20	31	18	88
% Women positive	–	–	–	73
% Women negative	–	–	–	9
N=	1	1	1	11
% Men positive	33	15	29	30
% Men negative	67	46	29	44
N=	6	13	7	27

ness has become a new category of employment for women. In all the earlier periods, women were essentially excluded from occupations such as CEOs, sales managers and sales representatives, proprietors, and supervisors. In the first decade, only three women (15 percent) appear in any of these categories as opposed to seventeen men (85 percent). In the second decade, the figures are one woman (3 percent) and thirty men (97 percent) and in the third decade, one woman appears (6 percent) against seventeen men (94 percent). From 1976 to 1990, the number of women appearing in business occupations rises impressively to twenty-nine (33 percent) compared to fifty-nine men (67 percent).

More importantly, those women characters who have moved into the ranks are rated much more positively than their male colleagues. Susan (Elizabeth Perkins) in the movie *Big* (1988) provides this type of positive image of the businesswoman. Molly (Kirstie Alley) in *Look Who's Talking* (1989) also exemplifies this character type. Molly is a CPA trying to pursue her career while raising an infant. The father, a philandering, wealthy businessman, won't take responsibility for the child. Similarly, in *Moonstruck,* Loretta Castorini (Cher), another CPA, breaks out of her more traditional family role and previous engagement to pursue her fiancé's brother. In the fourth period, positively portrayed businesswomen outnumber businessmen with positive ratings by a ratio of more than two to one. Seventy-three percent of women are rated positively in business whereas only 30 percent of the businessmen are positive characters. Correspondingly, businesswomen are also far less likely to be negative figures than men: only 9 percent of the women receive negative ratings in contrast to the majority of businessmen (44 percent—the remaining 26 percent receive mixed ratings). Although women characters appear in a larger percentage of sympathetic roles than do men throughout the period of the study, findings for the most recent period are nevertheless significant. They explain how women have come to represent a formidable and much more legitimate cohort within the business ranks, at the same time that business as a whole can appear seamier and more corrupt than in the past.

These statistics have other dimensions. One way to break them down is to examine the methods that women characters use to achieve goals in the plot and how these methods are portrayed. For example, corresponding to the substantial increase of women filling nontraditional jobs, there is a large rise in the use of authority or discipline as a means of achieving goals. Among women in traditional roles, this method is seldom recorded over the entire period of the study (see Table 8.9), but it more than doubles as a method for women in nontraditional occupations after 1976, rising to 33 percent. For this group, using authority or discipline also correlates with positive character ratings. Examples of this are plentiful. In *Stripes* (1981), the two female MPs are positive authority figures whereas Sergeant Hulka (Warren Oates) and Captain Stillman (John Larroquette) are portrayed as idiots. Even the apparently reactionary *Rambo: First Blood Part II* (1985) features Co (Julia Nickson) as a political dissident and guerrilla fighter who aids Rambo (Sylvester Stallone). Similarly, in *The Enforcer* (1977), Kate Moore (Tyne Daly) is Harry Callahan's (Clint Eastwood) unlucky partner. She is killed in the line of duty, but not before she saves Harry's life in a shootout with convicts at San Quentin. In both *Police Academy I* (1984) and *Police Academy II* (1985,) women appear as strong, capable law enforcement officials, even though many male officers are portrayed as silly, incompetent, or both. Many of the women characters we cited above in elite professional roles, such as Princess Leia in the *Star Wars* trilogy, also fit this description.

Another development in women characters' methods is that they are generally more likely to resort to problematic goals and methods in the past twenty-five years than they were before. Among women in nontraditional occupations, the percentage motivated by greed and malevolence rises from 4 percent to 16 percent to 25 percent and remains at 22 percent in the most recent period (see Table 8.10). Among women holding traditional jobs, the figures are 0 percent, 4 percent, then up to 17 percent, and back down to 4 percent in the most recent period. Thus, since the mid-1960s, women in nontraditional occupations are more likely to be motivated in this way than women who fill more traditional roles.

TABLE 8.9   Percent of Women Characters in Traditional vs. Nontraditional Occupations Using Authority or Discipline as a Method

	1946–1955	*1956–1965*	*1966–1975*	*1976–1990*
% Traditional occupations	13	4	7	4
N=	23	25	29	23
% Nontraditional occupations	4	16	16	33·
N=	22	19	32	58

TABLE 8.10   Percent of Women Characters in Traditional vs. Nontraditional
Occupations Showing Greed or Malevolence

	1946–1955	*1956–1965*	*1966–1975*	*1976–1990*
% Traditional occupations	0	4	17	4
N=	45	44	61	81
% Nontraditional occupations	4	16	25	22
N=	22	19	32	58

Women characters are also now more likely to be violent. As Table 8.11A
shows, in the first two decades a very low percentage of women resorted to violence (about 7 percent) regardless of role. For men, the percentages are much
higher at 26 percent and 22 percent respectively. In the third decade, the percentage of all women resorting to violence rises substantially, to 23 percent, and
for men the figure climbs to its highest level, 44 percent. In the fourth period, the
percentage of women resorting to violence continues to rise, to 27 percent,
whereas for men, violence declines to 36 percent. Although violence generally increases for women after 1966, we find that women in nontraditional occupations
are more responsible for the trend than those in traditional roles (see Table
8.11B): 25 percent and then 34 percent of the women holding nontraditional jobs
are violent in the two most recent periods whereas traditionally employed women
hold at 17 percent for both periods. The use of violence has thus become an important new method for all women and since the mid-1970s nontraditionally

TABLE 8.11A   Percent of Women and Men Characters Who Use Violence as a Method

	1946–1955	*1956–1965*	*1966–1975*	*1976–1990*
% Women	8	7	23	27
N=	66	67	79	112
% Men	26	22	44	36
N=	156	137	181	331

TABLE 8.11B   Percent of Women Characters in Traditional vs. Nontraditional
Occupations Who Use Violence as a Method

	1946–1955	*1956–1965*	*1966–1975*	*1976–1990*
% Traditional occupations	0	4	17	17
N=	23	25	29	23
% Nontraditional occupations	19	10	25	34
N=	22	19	32	58

employed women are just as likely to resort to violence as men. In this fact, we again see that the critical concerns with which we began this article do indeed connect to larger trends and are not merely the product of a local swing in cinematic style, however graphic or explicit the violence of the latest crop of heroines may be.

Based on the shifts in women characters' goals toward greed and malevolence, and toward violent and authoritative methods, we would expect to see a decline in the numbers of positive portrayals overall and an accompanying rise in the negative treatment of women in nontraditional jobs or roles. As we have already noted, this is not in fact the case, although this discussion of methods makes those high positive ratings all the more interesting. Even when we control for occupation, looking at both men and women who hold elite jobs, it is clear that women come out far ahead of men and that the gap widens over time (see Table 8.12). Indeed, women maintain their advantage over men in character ratings *despite* their reliance on negative strategies in recent films.

The Hollywood Elite and Feminism

Women's increased importance in the work force is a reality of American society; nevertheless, Hollywood is not a reportorial community. The Hollywood elite has not discarded old myths for truth but created new myths to replace outmoded ones. In the case of representing the sexes, the goals and methods that women characters employ in their new roles, although these goals and methods are increasingly negative, do not diminish women's positive character ratings; however, the same types of occupations, goals, and methods are more likely to result in negative character ratings for men.

How can we explain these changing trends in representation over such a long span of time? On the one hand, a number of them—such as an increased emphasis on sexuality or the appearance of greater numbers of working women—

TABLE 8.12   Percent of Negative and Positive Ratings for Women in Nontraditional Occupations and Men in the Same Occupational Categories

	1946–1955	1956–1965	1966–1975	1976–1990
Women in Nontraditional occupations				
% Positive	72	74	53	65
% Negative	14	5	22	16
N=	22	19	32	58
Men in Same Occupations				
% Positive	62	49	50	46
% Negative	21	24	35	33
N=	138	107	149	260

appear predictable, based on changes that have occurred in the society generally, though Hollywood's contribution to these changes should not be discounted. On the other hand, the broad shifts in representation we have described cannot be accounted for by social changes that Hollywood simply mirrors. That kind of approach confuses the quality of the changes with the amount of change in the representations. Movies are not made by the public, however much it determines their success and influences their content. The movies are a gigantic industry and a mass art, and they are made cooperatively by a relatively small, elite group of people who hold particular beliefs and attitudes.

Hollywood elites overwhelmingly endorse liberal positions on issues that involve gender roles. For example, our survey indicates that fewer than 20 percent of the elite directors, producers, and writers strongly condemn adultery and fully 96 percent of the Hollywood elite are pro-choice on the abortion issue. All of this is at odds with attitudes among the general public that have become more liberal, but hardly to the extent portrayed in films. Although abortion is not a common subject in the movies, extramarital sex is and as we have seen, Hollywood representations of the latter have become much more liberal over the years.

The Hollywood elite is basically sympathetic to many other causes associated with feminism and liberal politics, as well. Thirty-two percent of Hollywood leaders support very aggressive affirmative action for women, agreeing that "women should get preference in hiring," whereas only 9 percent agree that "women are better off at home." Responses to these kinds of questions suggest that new movies may increasingly portray women in role-model fashion, placing larger and larger percentages of sympathetic women characters in elite occupations.

Conclusion

The contemporary images of men and women and the relations between them in box office hits reflect not only changing realities in society at large, but also new attitudes on gender among moviemakers themselves. In particular, although women continue to be underrepresented (only one woman appearing in films for every three men on average), their activities and personal characteristics have changed significantly. Most significantly, many women characters in films from 1976 to 1990 have adopted behaviors and occupations once limited to men. Women characters, especially those played by stars, are now much more likely to work in elite kinds of occupations; for example, women are now present in large numbers in business occupations from which they were once excluded. In fact, they appear at a much higher rate in such professions than is actually true in the society. Also, because they maintain a marked advantage over men in character ratings, women characters have entered these new occupations and adopted some of the same negative qualities as men, without suffering the criticisms that have been directed at male characters since the mid-1960s.

Among female characters, we find that since the mid-1960s, the increasing numbers in nontraditional occupations have become the most like men. These women are much less likely to be motivated by romance than in the past or to be married and are more likely to be motivated by greed and malevolence than women in traditional roles. They resort to violence and exercise authority much more frequently than in earlier movies, yet still garner very high character ratings. Together, these trends suggest that women in nontraditional occupations are now seldom portrayed as romantic and do indeed function more independently of men, even as they have come to behave more like them. Just as in other ways men's roles have changed and often require heroes to be isolated renegades fighting a corrupt system, many sympathetic women characters no longer play traditionally defined roles, but, like Paula in *The Goodbye Girl*, must utterly recreate their own lives in a lonely and rather dangerous world.

The way this has happened, taken as a whole, is not only a reflection of the changing social realities that movies inevitably represent, but also of ideological changes in American social elites. Indeed, the fact that moviemakers have tended to create the modern woman in the image of the Hollywood man, although the women almost always lack the more negative characterizations of men, reminds us of Hollywood's limitations in reconstructing American social realities.[7] Popular films have not become more realistic in recent years, they have simply exchanged old myths for new. The point is not to suggest that the trouble with new movies is that they aren't realistic enough, although many people seem to think this realism would be a desirable quality. Rather, it is to note that Hollywood's new women (and new men) are reconstructions that correlate with a postindustrial sensibility shared by many of the new elites but are still alien to the older elites. This sensibility is oriented in part around a left-liberal ideology of expressive individualism in which traditional gender roles are more often than not represented as anachronistic.

Further, our content analysis suggests that, however liberating the postindustrial sensibility may appear to the filmmakers when they articulate their own opinions, their fictional stories tell a less optimistic tale. D. H. Lawrence once wrote "trust the tale, not the teller." The vision of romance in many newer movies emphasizes alienation from old structures but is weak on new ways of relating. Very often, the characters (both men and women) appear emotionally isolated, fearful, and Machiavellian, however sympathetic. Impressions aside, this is quite clear from our data on the depictions of goals and methods for both men and women over time. Trends for the representation of women suggest that the traditional myths surrounding them—their civility, maternal instinct, and devotion to family—have declined precipitously in influence and men characters have become even more vicious, greedy, and villainous, particularly when they are in positions of authority. In romantic situations, most of the attractive qualities of domestic life have been replaced by scenarios that make human existence seem that much more lonely, unpleasant, and dangerous, for men and women alike.

In short, although a number of developments in the society have indeed changed the gender roles that many Americans play, Hollywood does not so much reflect these as it exaggerates them. Far from institutionalizing "bourgeois patriarchy," many Hollywood films—and filmmakers—now embrace extraordinarily liberal (and, in the case of sexual relations) alienated visions of how men and women relate to each other. Their vision is, at any rate, very different from that of the American public, which they not only entertain but seek to influence.

NOTES

1. Both of these stories received top billing. Maslin's piece was the lead article in the *New York Times* "Arts and Leisure" section for Sunday, July 21, 1991. Baumgold's article was *New York Magazine*'s cover story for July 29, 1991.

2. There are a number of small, scholarly, feminist journals that focus exclusively on these issues in their numerous articles on film. They include *Genders*, *Women & Performance* and *Women's Studies*, among others. Larger cinema studies journals like *Screen* and *Film Quarterly* have also published many essays in this area. One smaller cinema studies journal that often focused on these questions was *Ciné-Tracts*, which was published in Montreal between 1976 and 1983. A number of essays from that journal have recently been reissued in Ron Burnett, ed., *Explorations in Film Theory*.

3. Carolyn Galerstein has observed in her exhaustive 1930 to 1975 filmography, *Working Women on the Hollywood Screen*, in films of the period "a woman is not defined by her career . . . work is either explicitly or implicitly a temporary and secondary involvement, with the major emphasis on romance" (Gallerstein, 1989:xvi).

4. Basinger (1993) argues that the 1930s and 1940s films in which women work successfully in nontraditional jobs actually encouraged women to feel liberated (and good about themselves) despite the fact that in the last five minutes of the motion picture they give it all up for love. Molly Haskell (1973, 1987) made the same point earlier, arguing, pace Faludi, that the 1960s and 1970s were a period of backlash, in which really intelligent roles for women declined. To her, the 1980s actually represented an advance over the 1960s and early 1970s.

5. Although we have not done a study of this, we expect that a systematic content analysis of country music song lyrics, for example, would yield a very different picture of the American popular imagination on this issue.

6. The characters that appear not to be accounted for receive "mixed" ratings.

7. Some feminists (including Faludi) agree that recent movies tend to give female heroes the same attributes as traditional male heroes. As a result these feminists are highly critical of some newer films in which heroines engage in violence. Women's films, they argue, are those in which women are represented as competent, and nurturing, but not violent. In this interpretation *Howard's End* (1993) is a film favorable to women. *Terminator II* (1991) is not. We are inclined to think that this is a valid point, though we suspect that Faludi and some other feminist critics would find patriarchy regnant no matter what changes were to take place in the representation of women in motion pictures and other media. For discussions see Andrews (1993) and Weinraub (1993).

9

A New Deal for Minorities?

In recent years, the Hollywood establishment has displayed a relatively unprecedented interest in the inclusion of blacks and other minorities in mainstream films. Since black moviegoers are now estimated at 25 percent of the audience (compared with about 14 percent of the public), many commentators explain the upsurge in minority representation strictly in terms of the bottom line. Although the marketplace does exert strong pressures on moviemakers, it is impossible for Hollywood to know in advance just what kind of movies black or white audiences will favor. With the success of certain types of films in which blacks appear in important roles, such as *Beverly Hills Cop* (1984) and *Coming to America* (1988), Hollywood began to tap into this market and struggles to maintain the black audience today.

In the past two or three years, regrettably after the statistical part of our content analysis ends, the motion picture industry has turned to a number of black directors (Spike Lee, John Singleton, and Morgan Freeman, to name a few) to make films that appeal to black audiences.[1] Although the recent focus on the experiences of inner-city blacks differs substantially from earlier representations, our content analysis indicates that violence and crime have been on the rise among black characters since the mid-1960s, when they began to appear in much larger numbers. The inclusion of greater numbers of minority characters in top-grossing movies is an obvious improvement over the studio era, when they were not at all well represented. This trend is less about "realism" than about a new version of intergroup relations in America, one that is itself just as far removed from the facts as was its predecessor.[2]

In *Watching America*, a content analysis of America's prime time television shows, Lichter, Lichter, and Rothman also found that much larger numbers of minority characters appeared in shows after the mid-1960s. This chapter seeks to measure these trends and to account for the changes in representations of minorities in popular movies. For minorities, as for other groups of characters, we contend that quantitative and qualitative changes are not merely the result of market pressures on the movie industry but are also based on a set of values held by moviemakers themselves. More specifically, Hollywood's world view has an impact upon the extent to which minorities are included in the movies, upon the dramatic environs of the characters portrayed, and upon portrayals of individual behavior. We do not seek to make value judgments about the apparent trends but rather wish to offer an explanation for them that makes sense in light of our historical and attitudinal study of the people who maintain creative control of movies.

Our content analysis data document a major shift in Hollywood's representations of minorities beginning in the 1960s. Qualitative changes that we can discern in top-grossing movies with minority characters are somewhat different than those for TV shows. The Lichter, Lichter, Rothman study found that "writers and producers have been sensitive to issues of stereotyping in casting black roles since the mid-1960s. Not only are black characters shown more positively than whites but they are considerably less likely to commit crimes" (Lichter, Lichter, and Rothman, 1991:249). One important difference in our findings for the movies is that although major black characters are somewhat less likely to commit crimes, blacks, overall, are proportionately as likely to commit crimes as are whites. However, among major characters who do commit crimes, blacks are much more likely than whites to be portrayed positively. A second difference is that we do not find that "early messages of assimilation have been replaced by paeans to pluralism and ethnic coexistence" (Lichter, Lichter, and Rothman, 1991:251) in the movies. As the TV study found, movies from the 1960s and 1970s are predominantly assimilationist but in the 1980s, racial assimilation films are accompanied by an increasing number of movies emphasizing racial conflict. With the new emphasis on inner-city life, this type of film has, if anything, become more prominent.

In general, Hollywood is more likely to present minorities as positive characters than to present whites in a positive light, even where they share questionable attributes and behaviors. Nevertheless, Hollywood's rather alienated view of authoritative institutions, in which minorities happen to appear frequently (specifically the military and law enforcement), and its sensationalized representation of crime has tended to confine minority representations to rather narrow dimensions.

Thus, in spite of highly favorable portrayals, movies do not tend to project an image of minorities that corresponds to their diverse experience in American society. For example, movies that convey a sense of the accomplishments of blacks and other minorities in assimilating in American society are less pronounced now than they were in the 1960s and 1970s, probably because they are not considered realistic by most Hollywood filmmakers. This is so, in spite of the fact that nearly half of the black population is either working class, middle class, or upper class. Today, moviemakers seem preoccupied with exposing and rectifying the evils of racism and are thus inclined to convey a quite pessimistic view of race relations.

Early Minority Representations: 1946–1965

In the movies of the studio era, the few roles available to minority actors tended to be demeaning and could certainly not be considered in any way "role model" representations. Blacks made only brief appearances on the screen and if the roles were meaningful at all, the characters were usually portrayed in lower class occupations, for example as domestic servants or poor native Africans, sometimes with silly ideas and backward cultures. In the first two decades, movies such as *The Nun's Story* (1959), *The Snows of Kilimanjaro* (1952), and *Hatari* (1962) portray blacks as servile characters with little relevance to the story. In *The Snows of Kilimanjaro*, based on the Hemingway story of the same title, Gregory Peck plays Henry Street, a famous writer on safari in Africa. Black servants look after Street and perform all the mundane tasks in the camp atop Kilimanjaro, where Street suffers from a life-threatening wound.

In *The Nun's Story,* black Africans are portrayed as childish and ignorant. When Sister Luke (Audrey Hepburn) is assigned to a hospital in the Congo, Mother Matilda introduces her to the villagers. She tells her that "only one generation ago [the villagers'] fathers were savages in the forest. . . . We couldn't run the hospital without them," she adds. She also mentions that not all the natives have converted to Catholicism yet, pointing out "the witch doctor's fetish around their necks." We then learn that the villagers are segregated from the white patients, who are treated at a separate hospital, and the black men who work at the white hospital are referred to by the nuns as "boys." A particularly brutal scene in the film occurs when a black man clubs a nun to death at the hospital; the witch doctor has apparently told him that if he kills a white woman he will be free of the ghost of his dead wife. In short, this film depicts black Africans as members of a primitive society in need of reform.

In the opening scene of *The Egg and I* (1947), a black porter enters a compartment on a train. He serves an egg to the woman at the table and accidentally knocks it on the floor. He apologizes, "No harm done ma'am. It's only an egg." [Woman] "Only an egg!" [Porter]"Yes ma'am. Just a little old egg, that's all." [We don't yet know that the woman (Claudette Colbert) has been running an egg farm with her husband and has a soft spot for unborn chickens. She begins to berate him for breaking the egg and the porter retreats] "No ma'am. . . . Yes ma'am. . . . Yes ma'am. . . . Yes ma'am. Yes, indeed ma'am." In 1947, this may have been a relatively noncontroversial scene but by today's standards it is quite demeaning.

In *A Date with Judy* (1948), a black housekeeper makes her entrance singing "Swing Low Sweet Chariot. . . ." Judy's father, who has a headache, complains to his wife, "Can't you teach her another song?" [Wife]: "She's a very good cook, Melvin." Black characters in *Hatari* (1962) function as servants for a group of white live game capturers. None of the Africans in the film are game hunters, even though the leading characters are capturing animals native to the areas in which these men have lived for their entire lives.

By contrast, *Imitation of Life* (1959) is one of only a few sophisticated treatments of race relations between blacks and whites in the entire study. The film features two single mothers, one black and one white, struggling to survive and raise their children. Lora Meredith (Lana Turner), who is white, becomes a successful actress and throughout her career employs her black friend Annie Johnson (Juanita Moore) as a housekeeper. Much of the story revolves around Annie's daughter Sarah Jane (Karin Dicker/Susan Kohner), who is lighter-skinned than her mother and tries to deny her racial identity as she grows up. At the end of the film, Annie dies and only then does Sarah Jane rejoin the Merediths, realizing how much pain she has caused Annie by trying to escape her identity. The film is exceptional in its substantive treatment of racial prejudice and its suggestion of the psychological burdens borne by some blacks but it also balances this against the lifelong friendship of Annie and Lora, which suggests that perseverance, strength of character, and trust among individuals can sustain meaningful interracial friendships. One should note that the film is a remake of one that appeared originally in 1934, indicating that even much earlier it was possible to conceive of and produce a film involving a relatively complex treatment of interracial themes.

Sayonara (1958) is another exceptional although less optimistic film from this period. The film is in many ways an interesting predecessor of the anti-Establishment military movies of the 1960s, the 1970s, and the 1980s, portraying Japanese women and their American companions as victims of racism. The villains of the story are American Air Force officers who enforce a policy prohibiting racial intermarriage. In later movies, we find that white authority figures are frequently portrayed as racists, contributing disproportionately to the spectacle of widespread interracial conflict.

Whites and Minorities Compared

Hollywood movies since the mid-1960s have begun to include minority characters in much larger proportions than in earlier films (see Table 9.1). In the first decade (1946–1955), the percentage of minority characters coded is about 5 percent. In the second decade (1956–1965), only 6 percent of the characters are minorities. In the third decade (1966–1975), this figure nearly doubles, jumping to 11 percent. Finally, in the most recent period (1976–1989), the proportion of minority characters rises again, to 14 percent.[3]

TABLE 9.1   Percent of Characters in Movies According to Race

	1946–1955	1956–1965	1966–1975	1976–1990
% Whites	95	94	89	86
% Minorities	5	6	11	14
% Blacks	1.7	2.6	4.3	9.7
% Asians	.1	2.8	3.6	2.4
% Amerindians	.6	.3	1.3	.1
% Hispanics	2.5	.4	1.6	1.7
N=	718	736	857	1673

The representation of blacks in films has progressed more than that of other minorities. Blacks comprise 1.7 percent of the codable characters in the first decade, 2.6 percent in the second decade, 4.3 percent in the third decade, and 9.7 percent in the fourth period. Asians represent only .1 percent, 2.8 percent, 3.6 percent, and 2.4 percent in the four periods of the study. Amerindian characters appear in only a few of the sample movies, accounting for .6 percent, .3 percent, 1.3 percent, and .1 percent of all characters over the four decades. Hispanics are also very seldom seen in Hollywood movies, representing only 2.5 percent, .4 percent, 1.6 percent, and 1.7 percent of all characters over four decades. Whereas blacks have nearly attained levels of representation comparable to their numbers in society (12 percent in society), Hispanics still fall far short of this level (8 percent in society). Thus, if our sample is representative of the racial composition of minorities in top-grossing Hollywood movies, blacks and Asians have made considerable progress toward inclusion, especially in the past twenty-five years. Amerindians and Hispanics have not done as well.

So few minority characters appeared in top-grossing films in the first two decades that we have been forced to combine their numbers to obtain a slightly more reliable indication of how minorities and whites compare on character ratings (see Table 9.2). In these earlier decades, 60 percent of minority characters receive positive ratings compared to 62 percent of white characters. These figures would seem to run counter to our examples, but the finding is easily explained—members of minority groups in minor roles are portrayed negatively.

From 1966 to 1975, minorities are much more likely to be rated positively than are whites. Seventy-eight percent of minorities are so rated compared to 48 percent of whites. Only 15 percent of minority characters receive negative ratings compared to 27 percent of white characters. Seven percent of minorities and 25 percent of whites receive mixed ratings. In the most recent period, from 1976 to

TABLE 9.2   Character Ratings of Minorities vs. Whites

| | 1946–1955   1956–1965 | | |
	(Averaged)	1966–1975	1976–1990
Minority ratings			
% Positive	60	78	57
% Negative	20	15	18
% Mixed	20	7	25
N=	15	27	56
Whites ratings			
% Positive	62	48	49
% Negative	19	27	29
% Mixed	19	25	22
N=	396	231	373

1990, only 57 percent of minorities receive positive ratings; however, white characters remain at only 49 percent positive. Only 18 percent of minority characters are portrayed negatively whereas 29 percent of whites are rated negatively. Although there is some leveling off in the most recent period, in the past twenty-five years, minorities are substantially more likely to be rated positively and less likely to receive negative character ratings than whites in popular movies. Whites have clearly lost favorable ratings over time and a significantly larger proportion of whites in the later period receive negative character ratings.

In all the movies in the first decade of the study, only four Hispanics (all appearing in *Road to Rio*, 1948) are significant enough to the narrative to be coded with nonneutral character ratings (positive, negative, mixed). (See Table 9.3). All (100 percent) are coded positively.[4] In the second decade, two blacks are coded: one positively (50 percent) and one receives a mixed rating (50 percent). In that same period, eight Asians are coded. Three are coded positively, three receive negative ratings, and two receive mixed ratings. The one Amerindian rated from this decade is rated positively (100 percent). No Hispanics receive ratings (0 percent). These results confirm our initial impression that minorities were very seldom portrayed in Hollywood movies before the mid-1960s. Only fifteen out of 411 ratable characters during these two decades are members of some minority group.

TABLE 9.3   Character Rating Breakdown of Minority Characters

	1946–1955	*1956–1965*	*1966–1975*	*1976–1990*
Blacks				
% Positive	–	50	78	57
% Negative	–	–	11	14
% Mixed	–	50	11	29
Total	–	2	9	42
Asians				
% Positive	–	37	75	67
% Negative	–	37	25	25
% Mixed	–	25	–	8
Total	–	8	4	12
Amerindians				
% Positive	–	100	80	–
% Negative	–	–	10	–
% Mixed	–	–	10	–
Total	–	1	10	–
Hispanics				
% Positive	100	–	75	–
% Negative	–	–	25	50
% Mixed	–	–	–	50
Total	4	–	4	2

In the third decade, the pattern dramatically changes. We find 27 full character portrayals of minorities (10 percent) out of a total of 258 nonneutral characters. Seven out of nine blacks (78 percent) receive positive ratings with one negative rating (11 percent) and one mixed rating (11 percent). Three of four Asians (75 percent) are rated positively. In this decade, ten American Indians are rated: eight positively (80 percent), one negatively (10 percent), and one received a mixed rating (10 percent). Three of the four Hispanics portrayed (75 percent) receive positive ratings. In the most recent period, the total number of minority characters with nonneutral ratings rises to fifty-six out of 429 (13 percent). The number of blacks receiving character ratings increases six-fold: Of forty-two black characters rated, twenty-four (57 percent) are rated positively, six (14 percent) are portrayed negatively, and twelve (29 percent) receive mixed ratings. Of twelve rated Asians, eight are portrayed positively, three are portrayed negatively, and one receives a mixed rating. No major Amerindian characters appear in sample movies between 1976 and 1990. Two Hispanics appear: one portrayed negatively and the other rated mixed. Whites are portrayed much more negatively than minorities in the period from 1966 to 1990.

We find the same pattern when we examine the goals sought by the major characters and the means used to achieve these goals (see Table 9.4). Minority characters are more likely than whites to be motivated to some extent by moral or political goals, though the proportion motivated by such concerns changes with each decade. In the first decade, none of the four minority characters are motivated by this kind of goal. In general, the proportion rises in the following decades to 36 percent for the second decade, 33 percent for the third decade, and 50 percent for the final period. The incidence of moral or political goals does not increase for white characters.

The percentage of minority characters who employ charm or rational persuasion to attain their goals, including political or moral goals, increases, rising above that of whites in recent movies. Twenty-five percent of minorities use charm or rational persuasion to get what they want in the first decade compared with 36 percent for whites. Minority reliance on these means to attain goals improves in the second decade, rising to 36 percent at the same time that only 18 percent of whites are coded for these methods. The percentage dips for both groups in the third decade but remains substantially higher for minorities, at 30 percent, com-

TABLE 9.4   Percent of Minority and White Characters with Moral and Political Goals

	1946–1955	1956–1965	1966–1975	1976–1990
% Minorities	–	36	33	50
N=	4	11	27	56
% Whites	32	22	23	33
N=	215	181	231	373

pared to only 14 percent among whites. In the most recent period, the percentage rises considerably for minorities, up to 43 percent, but whites still trail behind at only 31 percent (see Table 9.5).

The percentage of minority characters coded as utilizing rational authority and discipline as a method of achieving their goals also increases as it declines for whites (see Table 9.6). No minority characters exercise authority and discipline in the first decade and only 18 percent do so in the second decade. In the third decade, 22 percent exercise some kind of authority. In the fourth period, this figure rises substantially for minorities, up to 32 percent. Among whites, authority/discipline actually declines over time—from 25 percent to 18 percent to 15 percent in the third decade. It then rises somewhat, to 22 percent in the most recent period, but it is now coded one-third less often than for minorities.

These categorizations of goals and methods must be interpreted cautiously, of course, but together they do seem to suggest a trend toward increased independence and responsibility —qualities that minority characters lack in many of the sample movies of the first two decades.

The proportion of blacks who resort to violence also rises substantially over the four periods of the study (see Table 9.7). No blacks are coded for violence in the first two decades (not surprising given that only one character is significant enough to be rated and coded for goals and methods). In the third decade, the percentage of blacks resorting to violence is only 11 percent. This is somewhat surprising given that whites are nearly four times as likely to resort to violence in the same period. By the fourth period, however, 31 percent of blacks resort to

TABLE 9.5   Percent of Minority and White Characters Using Charm/Rational Persuasion as Methods

	1946–1955	1956–1965	1966–1975	1976–1990
% Minorities	25	36	30	43
N=	4	11	27	56
% Whites	36	18	14	31
N=	215	181	231	373

TABLE 9.6   Percent of Minority and White Characters Using Authority/Discipline as Methods

	1946–1955	1956–1965	1966–1975	1976–1990
% Minorities	–	18	22	32
N=	4	11	27	56
% Whites	25	18	15	22
N=	215	181	231	373

TABLE 9.7 Percent of Characters Resorting to Violence by Race

	1946–1955	1956–1965	1966–1975	1976–1990
Whites	20	17	39	33
% Positive	45	50	34*	
% Negative	41	20	47	
% Mixed	14	30	19	
	(44)**	(30)	(214)	
N=1,000	215	181	231	373
Blacks	–	–	11	31
% Positive	–	–	64	
% Negative	–	–	14	
% Mixed	–	–	22	
			(14)	
N=53	0	2	9	42
Asians, Amerindians, Hispanics	–	33	39	43
% Positive	–	–	46	
% Negative	–	100	38	
% Mixed	–	–	16	
		(3)	(13)	
N=	4	9	18	14

*Data on character ratings are averaged for the third and fourth periods because only one black character (receiving a positive rating) resorts to violence in the third decade.

**Numbers in parentheses are total numbers of white, black, and other minority characters (Asians, Amerindians, and Hispanics) who resort to violence.

violence to achieve their goals. This figure is comparable to levels of violence among whites yet blacks are significantly more likely to be rated positively than whites. Of all major characters resorting to violence in the third and fourth decades, only 34 percent of whites are portrayed positively, 47 percent are rated negatively, and 19 percent receive mixed ratings. Conversely, 64 percent of blacks who resort to violence are coded positively, only 14 percent are rated negatively, and 22 percent receive mixed ratings. For Asians, Amerindians, and Hispanics who commit crimes, character ratings are much closer to those of whites: only 46 percent positive, 38 percent negative, and 16 percent mixed.

The same pattern that we detect for blacks resorting to violence seems to hold for those blacks who commit crimes (see Table 9.8). Over time, the percentage of blacks committing crimes in top-grossing movies has fluctuated at about the same rate as for whites. The percentage of blacks who commit crimes over the four periods of the study are 0 percent, 11 percent, 30 percent, and 15 percent, respectively. For whites, the percentage of characters committing crimes is 12 percent, 14 percent, 29 percent, and 17 percent, respectively.

These crime rates are much higher than those reported in American society. From 1976 to 1990, movie crime rates of whites are about five times greater than those reported in the FBI's national crime survey victimization tables. For black

TABLE 9.8   Percent of All Black and White Characters Committing Crimes

	1946–1955	1956–1965	1966–1975	1976–1990
% Blacks	–	11	30	15
N=	12	18	37	162
% Whites	12	14	29	17
N=	675	662	754	1374

characters, crimes are also exaggerated but only at about twice the rate of actual crime figures (Statistical Abstracts, 1992:185).

Looking at the racial composition of all characters who commit crimes, we find that whites are by far the largest subpopulation of criminals in the movies (see Table 9.9). Although the proportion of blacks who commit crimes rises from 0 percent to 2 percent to 4.5 percent to 8 percent over the four periods, 98 percent of characters committing crimes are whites in the first decade, 82 percent are whites in the second decade, 89 percent are whites in the third decade, and in the fourth period 80 percent are whites (see Table 9.9).

Among major characters with significant enough roles to receive positive, negative, or mixed ratings, we find that whites are more likely than blacks to commit crimes (see Table 9.10). No major black characters commit crimes in the first and second decades, 33 percent commit crimes in the third and fourth periods. In contrast, 27 percent of whites commit crimes in the first decade and 22 percent in the second decade. The percentages for the third and fourth periods are 50 percent and 40 percent for whites, respectively.

TABLE 9.9   Racial Composition of Characters Committing Crimes

	1946–1955	1956–1965	1966–1975	1976–1990
% Whites	98	82	89	80
% Blacks	0	2	4.5	8
% Asians, Hispanics, Amerindians	2	16	6.5	12
N=732	86	111	243	292

TABLE 9.10   Percent of Major Black and White Characters Committing Crimes

	1946–1955	1956–1965	1966–1975	1976–1990
% Whites	27	22	50	40
N=1,000	215	181	231	373
% Blacks	–	–	33	33
N=53		2	9	42

TABLE 9.11   Percent of Black and White Characters Committing Crimes—Rated
Positive, Negative, Mixed

	1946–1955	1956–1965	1966–1975		1976–1990
				Average	
Blacks					
% Positive	–	–	67	60	57
% Negative	–	–	33	20	14
% Mixed	–	–	–		29
N=17	0	0	3		14
Whites					
% Positive	48	38	36	37	38
% Negative	34	22	37	40	42
% Mixed	17	40	27		20
N=360	58	40	115		147

A breakdown of major characters who commit crimes, controlling for race and character rating, provides further evidence that moviemakers have portrayed blacks relatively more favorably than whites in recent decades (see Table 9.11 When we compare the character ratings of blacks and whites who commit crimes, we find that blacks are almost twice as likely to be portrayed favorably (67 percent blacks—36 percent whites). Positive characterizations of blacks outnumber negative characterizations about three to one over the past twenty-five years (approximately 60 percent favorable—20 percent unfavorable, on average). For whites, the ratio is about one to one (37 percent favorable—40 percent unfavorable) as shown in Table 9.11.

It is difficult to explain exactly why the relationship between violence, crime, and favorable character ratings holds so strongly for blacks and not for whites. But when we actually look at sample movies in which blacks and whites interact we can offer a plausible interpretation.

New Patterns of Minority Representation: 1966–1990

Among the more recent movies with minority characters in our sample we detect two major themes. First, many movies have simply shifted away from previously offensive portrayals in favor of an assimilationist pattern—that is, race is no longer a dramatic issue when minorities appear. When it is, minorities and whites try to resolve racial tensions or misunderstandings in the course of the story. The second type of movie, in which a large proportion of minorities is represented, involves the depiction of racial conflict within the military and law enforcement professions. In spite of the substantial increase in the numbers of minority characters portrayed, many films of the 1970s and the 1980s either focus on conflicts between blacks and white authority figures or cast blacks in comic, antihero roles that in other ways indict a corrupt establishment. Representations of Amerindians have resembled those of blacks although the latter appear much less frequently than do blacks.

Portraits of Assimilation

Before turning to those films in which race relations are represented as a serious problem, it is important to comment on the substantial number of films in which racial prejudice is now a less troublesome issue. In movies such as *To Sir with Love* (1967), *Andromeda Strain* (1971), and *Rocky III* (1982), minorities are integrated more fully into society than in previous decades: they are talented, function independently, and hold responsible positions. Certain allusions to race or comments about race may be made but are not particularly relevant to the story itself, or at least are resolved in the film.

In *To Sir with Love* (1967), Mark Thackery (Sidney Poitier) plays an out-of-work engineer who takes a teaching job at an English secondary school. The students are difficult for him to control at first but he manages to win them over by changing the curriculum for his class and trying to teach them some basic skills for becoming responsible adults. Several exchanges in the film indicate racial prejudices among the students: one boy jokes about the color of Mark's blood when he gets a cut in the schoolyard; at one point, another student refers to the teacher as "chimney sweep." Even though the students express these indiscretions, they soon begin to respect Mr. Thackery's unique contribution to their education and come to admire him. The fact that he is black actually has almost nothing to do with the story. Thackery is presented as an exemplary "individual" with a rare talent for teaching.

Another assimilationist story, *Guess Who's Coming to Dinner* (1968), explores the problem of interracial marriage between John Prentice (Sidney Poitier) and Joey Drayton (Katherine Houghton). John is black, Joey is white, and neither person's parents know of their plans to marry until the two arrive at the Draytons' for dinner one night. Joey's parents are stunned to find that John is black. John states that he won't marry Joey if her parents don't approve. In the course of their visit, Joey invites John's parents to join them for dinner. The parents meet and discuss the proposed marriage. Both mothers decide they favor the marriage but the fathers have doubts. Each of them fears that an interracial marriage will cause problems for the couple, especially for any children they raise. In the end, Mr. Drayton decides that the most important thing is for them to love each other and that as long as they are committed to the marriage they will be able to overcome any adversity.

Other movies present minority characters in similarly exemplary roles. In *Andromeda Strain*, an Asian woman works as a scientific researcher, black and Asian scientists attend a symposium, and a black woman works as a sophisticated medical technician and nurse. In *The Karate Kid* (1984), Mr. Miyagi's Asian heritage is never discussed and race really doesn't enter the story as any kind of problem. Miyagi is portrayed as a man who has been able to preserve much of his cultural heritage in America without any great difficulty. In *Lethal Weapon* (1987), Roger Murtaugh (Danny Glover) is the unlucky officer who draws super-cop Martin Riggs (Mel Gibson) as a partner. Murtaugh is a well-respected veteran of the police force and a number of other black officers (neutral characters), including his supervisor, appear throughout the film.

In *Coming to America* (1988), Akeem (Eddie Murphy) plays an African prince who comes to New York to find a bride. He doesn't want a woman to marry him for his money so he masquerades as a poor black man in Queens. He obtains a job at a hamburger joint and falls in love with the owner's daughter. The woman's father doesn't want her to associate with Akeem because he thinks he's poor. Instead, he tries to arrange for his daughter to marry an obnoxious but wealthy businessman. Blacks in this movie are seen in widely varying roles: African royalty, freewheeling playboys, responsible and hardworking people, and common street criminals. Once again, although the movie deals with some aspects of the inner city in a satiric way, blacks are not subject to any explicit racism and it does provide a wide range of roles for black characters.

Minorities and Institutional Criticism

Prior to 1966, no major minority characters (those rated nonneutrally) are employed in law enforcement or military occupations. In the third decade of our study (1966–1975), 37 percent of nonneutral minority characters are law enforcement or military personnel. From 1976 to 1990, the figure rises to 41 percent. The proportion of whites who hold such positions is considerably lower: 14 percent and 22 percent in the first two decades, in the third decade only 16 percent, and in the fourth decade 26 percent (see Table 9.12).

Although many of the new roles for blacks suggest a pattern of assimilation, some portrayals project another type of image altogether. Since the mid-1960s, Hollywood moviemakers have often shown black characters in somewhat adversarial relationships with white authorities within the military and law enforcement professions. Newer movies will often portray the characters within these in-

TABLE 9.12   Percent of Nonneutral Characters* in Military and Law Enforcement Occupations

	1946–1955	1956–1965	1966–1975	1976–1990
% Minorities	–	–	37	41
N=	–	–	10	23
Total	4	11	27	56
% Whites	14	22	16	26
N=	30	40	38	96
Total	215	181	231	373

*Major characters coded positive, negative, or mixed. "Neutral" characters were coded as neutral.

stitutions as villains—by, among other means, exposing their racist prejudices. In such stories, blacks and other minorities face injustice and adversity, if not outright persecution, and must either put up with shabby treatment or fight to overcome it. Since the structure of authority or the establishment is stacked against blacks and minorities in these films, it is not surprising that they are portrayed positively even when they engage in acts of violence.

Poking fun at racism and racial prejudice is a central theme in Mel Brooks's satire, *Blazing Saddles* (1974). Racism is used in the film to emphasize the corruption of the American West in the nineteenth century. In one scene a railroad workparty boss taunts a group of blacks: "Now come on boys where's your spirit? I don't hear no singing. When you was slaves you sang like birds. Come on, how about a good old nigger work song?" Racial prejudice against Amerindians and Asians is also satirized at various points in this comic farce. The star black character, Sheriff Bart (Cleavon Little), is a positive figure who, along with the Waco Kid (Gene Wilder), defeats the racist villains. Besides simply creating a crazy, funny parody of the Western, the film makes a point of criticizing business (in this case, the railroads), the government, law enforcement, and the white majority, partly by exposing their racist views.

As noted in Chapter 5, the overwhelmingly white police force in *Dog Day Afternoon* (1976) mistakenly assumes that a black security guard (also coded for law enforcement) being released by the bank robber Sonny (Al Pacino), because the guard is having trouble breathing, is an accomplice to the robbery. The police briefly place him under arrest until Detective Moretti (Charles Durning) realizes what is happening.

Axel Foley (Eddie Murphy), from *Beverly Hills Cop* (1984), is a savvy but insubordinate officer—always in trouble for breaking the rules. He's at odds with his boss in Detroit, Inspector Todd (Gilbert Hall)—who is also black—and with Lieutenant Bogamill (Ronny Cox) in California. When he first arrives in Beverly Hills, he is arrested by two white patrolmen after he is thrown out of a window onto the street. He is then assaulted by Sergeant Taggart (John Ashton). Throughout the film, he has to work around the Beverly Hills police force, which goes out of its way to cater to the wealthy and is thus unaware that a prosperous businessman from their own town is really an international drug smuggler.

In *Police Academy* (1984), the training officers are out to undermine the recruits, in part because they don't believe that blacks should be allowed on the force.[5] Lieutenant Harris (G. W. Bailey) is the chief villain, defender of the familiar all-white, male police force exposed in *Dog Day Afternoon*, who does everything he can to get the cadets thrown out of the program. Among other things, he is portrayed as a hypocrite and a peeping Tom and in the final scenes he has to be rescued by the recruits after he is taken hostage by a gunman in a riot. Two other dim-witted white males, obviously racist sycophants from among the group of recruits, become Harris's henchmen. Throughout the film, they try unsuccessfully to undermine the other cadets.

The lowly status of the black enlisted men of Oliver Stone's *Platoon* (1986) conveys the extent to which racism has condemned the black man to a life on the front line in Vietnam. At one point Junior (Reggie Johnson) replies to a white soldier's harassment by saying "Goddamn man. You break your ass for the white man. There's no justice around here." The soldiers' treatment of civilians, including women and children, emphasizes not only the brutality of the war but also the ease with which the Americans direct their fear and hatred at the Vietnamese people. A similar type of message is implicit in *Good Morning Vietnam* (1986). *Little Big Man* (1971) shows the senseless slaughter of Amerindians by the U.S. cavalry. The Indians are portrayed favorably, whereas the military is shown to be malevolent and treacherous.

Conclusion

As the civil rights movement progressed and as the New Hollywood emerged from the ruins of the studio era, the number of minorities, particularly blacks, appearing in films dramatically increased. Hollywood's new sensitivity to minorities illustrates some broader changes in the movie industry as well as in American society. In addition to the obvious changes in representation since the 1940s and 1950s, when minorities were all but excluded from movies, minorities are now portrayed more favorably than whites. Blacks have just about achieved proportional representation in the movies compared to the percentage of the population they represent and Hollywood portrays black characters more favorably than whites, even when they use violence and commit crimes.

Minorities, predominantly blacks, are also assigned in disproportionate numbers to the roles of police officer and soldier. One might expect moviemakers to depict these institutions as providing opportunities for blacks and other minorities to advance (certainly this has been the case in reality); however, minority characters in military and law enforcement roles are likely to encounter racism in these organizations. We have no direct quantitative measure, but favorable images of a larger percentage of blacks than whites who resort to violence and commit crimes may be partially explained by the racism they confront. This trend shows signs of vitality not only for blacks but for Amerindians in some current box-office hits. Undeniably, the Amerindian is portrayed very favorably in Kevin Costner's *Dances with Wolves* (1991). As in *Little Big Man* (1984), Indian culture is juxtaposed against the wasteful, greedy, and treacherous cavalry (again the military) that safeguards the white man's exploitive way of life by systematically annihilating the Indian.

Quite obviously, the picture of minorities has changed in movies since the mid-1960s. Hollywood is now more prone to filter its liberal attitudes toward minorities through a lens that is predisposed to focus on injustice, greed, corruption, and abuses of state power. Moviemakers are supposedly after more realistic portrayals of blacks. They are unlikely to achieve that goal when such large numbers of black characters fall into just two occupational categories, those of police officer and soldier. When whites and blacks are presented in conflict, it is far more often the white rather than the black whose fault it is, and the white is the person against whom it is often legitimate to resort to violence. In reality, the experience of blacks and other minorities in America is considerably more varied than that.[6]

NOTES

1. The number of black directors making pictures with relatively major budgets has gradually increased over recent years. In addition to those mentioned, Sidney Poitier, Eddie Murphy, Reginald Hudlin, Robert Townsend, and Michael Schultz have produced reasonably successful films. Overall, black directors have been producing some 10 to 15 mainstream films per years since 1990 (Cohn, 1994:41).

2. The number of films in the movies and on television in which interracial love affairs are presented has also increased, though none of these made it into our sample of top-grossing films (Buckley, 1991).

3. The relatively small number of cases of minority roles in the early years is a major, if not unexpected finding and makes it difficult to compare trends in the depiction of character.

4. We do not differentiate between Hispanics in general and Americans of Hispanic (or Latino) background. We have not made the distinction for Asians either.

5. This issue is also discussed in Chapter 5.

6. Our study has been concerned with the presentation of blacks in film. We demonstrate their increasingly favorable treatment in motion pictures. However, despite the growing presence of blacks both behind and in front of the screen, Jesse Jackson led a protest against the Academy Awards in 1996. He argues that black directors, producers, writers, and actors are still underrepresented in Hollywood.

10

Box Office Hits: 1990–1994

Our study is a large and complex one and took a long time to complete. By the time we had written up our content analysis, a number of years had passed. In order to update our study, we took a random sample of top-grossing movies from 1990 to 1994 (twenty-five out of the fifty top-ten movies). This sample of films strongly suggests that the trends of the previous two decades continue. The most prominent themes in the twenty-five box office hits of the first five years of the 1990s in our sample are crime and ultra-violence, continued negative portrayals of the police and military, unfavorable views of the wealthy (particularly wealthy men), supernatural and extraterrestrial phenomena, and more prominent and favorable roles for women and minorities.

Although we worked within the framework of our previous coding scheme, the numbers are too small to permit a statistical analysis. The summaries below can only be regarded as suggestive. We must emphasize again that one film (even a few films) prove nothing. It is the overall trends that count.

Supercops and Psycho-Robbers

A large proportion of the twenty-five movies we analyzed from this period involve police and career criminals. In keeping with our findings about movies produced since the mid-1960s, the police are increasingly depicted as vulnerable and often corrupt. Cops don't always get the bad guys anymore and the formula often involves some kind of conspiracy, with higher officials and politicians creating problems for the patrolman on the beat. We also detect a substantial amount of bad blood within the police department itself. The officers working for internal affairs (offices in police departments that investigate charges of police misbehavior) are a favorite source of conflict and mistrust and leading characters must contend with cops on the make.

In *Silence of the Lambs* (1991), an overwhelming number of police are assigned to guard the diabolical Hannibal Lechter. Nevertheless, he escapes from custody. Lechter brutally murders two police officers in the process and impersonates one of them by removing the officer's face and placing it over his own. He then escapes from an ambulance on the way to the hospital. While the police are not portrayed negatively in the film, they always appear to be one step behind the criminals and at times they become victims themselves. The same can be said about *Dick Tracy* (1990). If not for Tracy's (Warren Beatty) superhuman efforts, the town would be owned and operated by organized crime. In the film *Speed* (1994), the psychopathic bomber is a disabled police officer and only the tireless efforts of the bomb squad maverick Jack Traven (Keanu Reeves) can make the streets of Los Angeles safe again. As Jack's supervisor marvels, "How many lives have you got, man?"

Conforming to the more tarnished image of the police, the leading male character in *Basic Instinct* (1992), officer Nick Curran (Michael Douglas), is a recovering alcoholic and a former cocaine addict. Apparently, he picked up these vices while working as an undercover cop. To make matters worse, he has a history of shooting innocent bystanders in the course of his job. And Nick is sleeping with Beth, the department psychologist. Later in the film we discover that Beth is a murder suspect's former college roommate and bisexual lover. In the closing scenes, the suspect, Catherine (Sharon Stone) succeeds in convincing everyone that Beth is the killer and Nick actually shoots and kills Beth believing that she has just brutally murdered his partner. Nevertheless, as the picture fades an ice pick is revealed beneath the bed in which Catherine and Nick are making love, suggesting that she may be responsible for the crimes. As in *Silence of the Lambs,* the cops in *Basic Instinct* are duped again and another homicidal maniac apparently goes free.

Further contributing to the erosion of the institutional integrity of the police, the emphasis in the new cops and robbers films is on departmental conflict rather than on cooperation or camaraderie. In *Basic Instinct,* there appears to be very little loyalty among fellow officers apart from Nick's friendship with his partner. Officer Nielson at internal affairs sells Nick's confidential personnel file to the woman under investigation for murder, who also happens to write novels about victims of murder. Nick attacks Nielson when he realizes what has happened. In a similar vein, the internal affairs officer in *Another 48 Hours* (1990) is Jack's (Nick Nolte) nemesis. Jack eventually punches him out in the station. Two other officers on the force are bad cops and wind up shooting it out with Jack and Reggie Hammond (Eddie Murphy) in a strip bar. *Lethal Weapon 3* (1992) also pits internal affairs against Riggs's borderline psychotic antics. It also portrays an ex-cop as a ruthless gun-running kingpin.

In *Die Hard II* (1990), off-duty cop John McClane (Bruce Willis) takes on a group of American soldiers gone terrorist. These right-wing fanatics take over an airport to rescue a Latin American dictator and drug kingpin from extradition. Throughout most of the film, the airport police supervisor is portrayed as incompetent and his police force is unprepared for the emergency. The entire SWAT team is easily subdued after walking into an ambush. The special forces team that arrives only makes matters worse for McClane, since the men turn out to be in league with the paramilitary outfit holding the airport hostage.

All of these leading characters, good or bad, inhabit a world in which ordinary cops can no longer survive. Only renegade supercops—undisciplined, unpredictable, and capable of extreme violence—can measure up to the criminals. The criminals are often policemen themselves or former policemen/intelligence agents/military officers and they share all the trade secrets, making it impossible for protagonists to succeed by resorting to anything less than the most extraordinary show of force.

Mad Dogs in the Military

The image of the military continues to decline in the films of the 1990s. For example, *Another 48 Hours* uses the mad-dog Vietnam veteran profile for one of its villains. The three *Lethal Weapon* movies also use Vietnam veteran status to signify a lack of control and a penchant for violence that places these characters outside normal behavioral guidelines. Whether the particular character is positively or negatively portrayed, the military is implicated as a breeding ground for sociopaths. *Hot Shots Part Deux* (1993), although it is by no means anti-military, is still a spoof on jingoistic war movies like *Rambo* and much of the film satirizes the military establishment. The only military personnel portrayed in *Die Hard II* are a group of right-wing terrorists. In *Clear and Present Danger* (1994), ordinary soldiers are victimized by the wrangling of various conspirators within the upper echelons of the executive branch.

Wealth and Power

As in many movies of the preceding two decades, the wealthy businessperson often behaves unethically. In *Sleeping with the Enemy* (1991), psychopathic wealthy investment counselor Martin Burney (Patrick Bergin) stalks his wife (Julia Roberts), who has left him because he beat and psychologically abused her. In *Indecent Proposal* (1993), a billionaire businessman, though not entirely unsympathetic, is portrayed as a person who uses his riches for illicit purposes. Diana (Demi Moore) and David (Woody Harrelson) are a young professional couple who get into financial trouble during a recession. Unable to make payments on a home construction loan, they go to Las Vegas with five thousand dollars and try to win it back. They lose it all on the roulette table. But a billionaire, John Gage (Robert Redford), is attracted to Diana and after the couple has lost their last penny, he asks Diana to sit with him for good luck. He wagers a million dollars on a dice roll and Diana wins the roll for him. Later Gage offers a million dollars to sleep with Diana for one night.

The couple initially reject the offer but Diana, determined to save herself and her husband from financial ruin, eventually accepts the "indecent proposal" and sleeps with Gage. Although she seems to put the incident behind her, David is not able to stomach what has happened. He becomes increasingly suspicious of his wife, the couple ends up on the verge of divorce, and neither wants the money any longer. Diana is portrayed as the stronger of the two and gets on with her life apart from David. She eventually begins to date Gage but by the film's end he realizes that Diana will never love him as she once loved David and he gives up the affair. Diana returns, on their anniversary date, to the place where David proposed to her only to find David there also. The film ends with the two presumably becoming reconciled.

In *Pretty Woman* (1990), Edward Lewis (Richard Gere) is a wealthy bachelor with too many business commitments to maintain a romantic relationship. After his girlfriend leaves him, he takes a ride in his lawyer's Lotus, gets lost in downtown Hollywood, and ends up bringing a hooker back to his hotel room. He is so struck by the prostitute Vivian's (Julia Roberts) personality that he asks her to escort him for the duration of his business trip. It turns out that Edward's business is completely cutthroat. He buys and breaks up corporations that are in financial trouble. At one point in the film he remarks to Vivian, "You and I are such similar creatures Vivian. We both screw people for money." Largely because of his association with the prostitute with whom he falls in love, Edward has a change of heart and decides to go into business with the company that would have been his next victim. Although Edward is portrayed favorably, his character is really only redeemed by his transformation from corporate raider to entrepreneur. His associates and his company's tactics are shown to be entirely unethical. A central message of the film seems to be that getting rich can only be accomplished by one form of prostitution or another. As Vivian points out to her friend, it is just "easy to clean up when you got money."

What these films have in common is the way in which they present wealth as a barrier to healthy human interaction. Money generates conflict rather than mutually beneficial association. Business itself is frequently represented as immoral and tainted by base motives such as greed, revenge, and domination. As female characters assume previously male-dominated roles, their methods tend to coincide with men's because to escape victimization and economic dependence they must fight back. Their strength of character depends on their ability to combat men by whatever means available—for example through sexual manipulation, violence, or simply by gaining financial independence.

Supernatural and Science Fiction Stories

Some of the 1990s movies also exemplify the earlier shift from traditional religious to supernatural themes. Conventional religion is almost entirely absent. Instead, a number of films intertwine ordinary and supernatural events. In the film *Ghost* (1990), Molly (Demi Moore) is haunted by the ghost of her lover Sam (Patrick Swayze), who is trying to protect her. Sam had been murdered by a thug hired by his own friend and co-worker Carl. Carl is laundering drug money at the stockbrokerage firm where the two work. Some traditional religious themes are present, such as the suggestion of heaven and hell in the afterlife. At the same time, Sam is able to remain partially in the material world to protect Molly from

Carl and his henchman. He converses with other ghosts and with a psychic who can hear him talk and he is able to move objects. The *Addams Family* (1991) also mixes normal and paranormal experiences, blurring the line between reality and dream. Among the family members are "Thing," a severed hand with a mind of its own, and "Cousin It," a human-sized hairball. The freakish family inhabits a spooky old house on the edge of an otherwise ordinary town.

In *Terminator II* (1991), time travel achieves a similar juxtaposition of parallel worlds when the Terminator (Arnold Schwarzenegger) returns from the future to save Sarah Connor and her son John from another kind of terminator sent back to kill them. John must be saved because he will become a future leader of the human forces that fight against machines that run amok. The message of the film is fairly clear: The world requires some kind of superhuman intervention to remedy problems that wouldn't have arisen if science and technology had left well enough alone. Those who have the knowledge to advance the cause of science do not always have the control they would like to have over the consequences of their actions. Only by the skin of their teeth do they manage to avoid propelling humanity down the road to disaster.

Gender Wars

Women continue to be portrayed in previously male-dominated roles and they seem ever more likely to be in conflict with men. Sometimes these roles result in less favorable portrayals, but more often these women are heroines whereas the men they are pitted against are the villains. Even if not villains, men are represented as a little out of touch with the times and are reluctantly forced to acknowledge women's contributions to their own objectives.

Basic Instinct takes the new Hollywood vision of gender relations to extremes. The film is a reversal of the typical male stalker suspense film. The victims of the female serial killer are all men. In a somewhat more cooperative relationship in *Lethal Weapon III* (1992), Martin Riggs finds his romantic match in Lorna Cole (Rene Russo), a martial arts expert from internal affairs who achieves superhero status by the end of the film. This is another very favorable and very tough "nontraditional" role for a female cop.

We find another tough female law enforcement officer in *Silence of the Lambs*. The heroine, Clarice Starling (Jodie Foster) endures sexual harassment and multiple abuses by men in the film. The one saving grace of the diabolical genius Hannibal Lechter (Anthony Hopkins) is his respect and admiration for her professional ability. He sends the entire police force on a wild goose chase while at the same time he sends Clarice alone to the house of the serial murderer, Buffalo Bill. After a suspenseful chase through the eerie basement of the murderer's house, she confronts the killer and is forced to kill him.

In *Sleeping with the Enemy,* Laura (Julia Roberts) at first appears to be an utterly submissive battered wife. In the end, she turns out to be quite strong. She escapes from her husband by pretending to have drowned in a boating accident. Laura then assumes a new identity and relocates to another part of the country to be near her mother, who lives in a nursing home. Soon after Laura's escape, Martin (her husband) realizes that his wife is not dead and he begins to search for her. By locating Laura's mother, Martin closes in on his wife with the intention of either taking her back or killing her. The police and the legal system are viewed as entirely inadequate protection against this kind of domestic terrorism. As a result, extreme violence becomes the only solution. Laura makes a conscious decision in the closing scene to murder Martin. She calls the police, while holding Martin at gunpoint, and reports that she has just shot and killed an intruder in her home. She then shoots Martin dead.

Minority Roles

Extending the trend of the previous two decades, greater numbers of blacks appear in 1990s films and they tend to be portrayed as positive role models. In *City Slickers* (1991), a black dentist and his son participate in a cattle drive vacation. In *Sommersby* (1993), the reconstruction era judge who tries Sommersby for murder is a black man. In *Terminator II,* the creator of the new cybernetic technology is a black scientist. When he learns from Sarah and the Terminator that the technology will lead to nuclear war between the superpowers, he helps them destroy his work at the laboratory and dies heroically when a SWAT team storms the building and shoots him. In *The Hunt for Red October* (1990), the crack radar man who figures out how to track the silent-running submarine is black. The admiral in the film is also an African-American.

Conclusion

In summing up our observations about new movies, we stress again that the trends we identify are not without exceptions. *Hunt for Red October* (1990) is a straightforward military story that presents America and the American military positively. *True Lies* (1994) is "Ramboesque" though with a comic twist. In both films, military characters as well as intelligence agents are presented very favorably. *Sleepless in Seattle* (1993) is for the most part a fairly traditional romance. *City Slickers* is a light-hearted comedy with only faint social commentary on gender relations and modern civilization's "materialistic obsessions." *Maverick* (1994) contains just enough bad language and humanization of the Amerindian to distinguish it from earlier films in the Western genre, but nothing else stands out. Films such as these reflect the fact that box office possibilities do play an important role in the decisions producers and directors make.

The Hollywood community is not monolithic. For example, in spite of its soft environmentalist undercurrent, the astoundingly successful *Lion King* (1994) is hardly a controversial, social commentary film.

Nevertheless, although it may be impossible to judge how far the predilections of writers, directors, and producers influence the creation of any particular film, it seems clear that, in the aggregate, movie content reflects more sophisticated and cynical views than people in the audience would independently hold. A look at top-grossing movies of the 1990s suggests, then, that Hollywood's representations of American society continue to be determined as much by its own distinct set of values and beliefs as by broader societal trends, though the trends may, in different ways, be catching up to the moviemakers.

On the one hand, audiences have gradually become more cynical and it is unlikely that a simple return to past representations is even possible. On the other hand, the blockbuster success of summer 1994, *Forrest Gump*, had Hollywood agog last year and commentators are speaking of a revival of respect for traditional values as well as a "religious" revival, both on television and on the large screen (Gordinier, 1994). However, many of the new productions cited by those who foresee such a revival have a new age quality about them. We doubt that any major religious revival is in the offing as of now, though one can never dismiss such possibilities out of hand. Periods of religious renewal have erupted before in American history and there have been returns to some of the values regarding personal behavior associated with the Christian tradition.

11

Hollywood and the Moviemakers

The Larger Context

Our study thus far has been narrowly empirical. Unlike many of the film critics who specialize in cultural studies, we have assumed that cultural representations of social and economic forces are not the only reality; that, in fact, they interact with a variety of other variables, over time, including the changing institutional structure of the film industry.

Although we agree that we can only know a society through its collective representations, we do not take the further step of arguing that the practices underlying such representations are unknowable, in principle. We can probably never fully understand such institutions and practices, but that does not vitiate the epistemological project of trying to describe social reality. Representations of social institutions and practices constitute the culture of a society. As such, they both mirror and affect other aspects of the society and they can serve to disguise some of its realities. In this realization, classical Marxists were far more sophisticated than today's cultural theorists in their examination of social life.

In an attempt to understand the representations produced by films, we studied both the changing structure of the film industry and the personalities and world views of a sample of key moviemakers. To determine and document the representations, we conducted a systematic content analysis of a sample of Hollywood films from a thirty-five year period. Our results were perhaps less interesting and less complex than are anecdotal readings of films as text but they have the advantage of being subject to meaningful public scrutiny.

A final chore remains. Although we have analyzed some of the sources of the new Hollywood orientation, ascribing them partly to the changing nature of the industry, that cannot be the whole story. The American motion picture industry, like other American institutions, must be understood in context, for just as it is the product of a particular technology and its own institutional history (see Chapter 2) it has also been formed by the ideology and economic and social structure of the society in which it was born. Neither the ideology nor personality characteristics of the Hollywood elite spring fully grown from their heads. They are part of a society that has affected them as they have affected it. Even more specifically, they are part of changes in the complex overall system of social communication in the society. All of these variables must be examined, then, if we are to understand the interaction between Hollywood and its environment, even if some of them seem, initially at least, at one remove from our subject.

It is impossible to develop a directly verifiable empirical theory that measures the impact of the larger society on motion pictures and the impact of motion pictures on the larger society. Too many variables interact simultaneously and we lack relevant information. The best we can do is to offer a theoretical statement concerning such actions, a statement that must be judged on the basis of its accord with the facts at our disposal, its congruence with theories for which we can provide evidence, and its parsimony. In the next several pages we offer the outline of such a theory.[1]

The theory draws from standard historical analysis supplemented by the work of Max Weber and Sigmund Freud. It assumes a complex interplay of representations, economic and social forces, historical accident, and personal character. Since the motion picture industry is really no more than ninety years old at most, whereas the history of America spans over three centuries (longer if one considers the country's antecedents), the role of movies in this analysis will be discussed only toward the very end. At that point, too, we shall more fully analyze the ideologies of expressive individualism, alienation, and liberal collectivism that emerged from our empirical analysis of the attitudes of the moviemakers and other elites (see Chapter 3) and place these in a broader context.

In the Beginning

Capitalism and democracy emerged together in Europe. Particular answers as to how and why this happened will inevitably color one's views of European and American society.

Briefly, we more or less accept the sociological perspective of Max Weber and, more recently, of Daniel Bell (1976). Contrary to the beliefs of those who are familiar primarily with *The Protestant Ethic and the Spirit of Capitalism* (1905, 1930), Weber did not argue that Protestantism was responsible for the development of capitalism and the modern world. Not only did he believe cultural factors were but one part of a complex causal nexus, he was also persuaded that Calvinist Protestantism built on the foundations that Christianity had already created. It was the Christian tradition as a whole that led to this development. Further, although Weber linked the rise of capitalism to Christianity, he never denied that it could develop in other countries with rather different cultural and economic factors, countries that may have copied from the West.[2]

The psychological framework that also guides our work relies heavily on a psychodynamic perspective, though certainly not an orthodox one. For example, unlike Freud, we are persuaded that the energy of aggressive as well as of sexual drives can be sublimated. We also believe that changes in society's cultural grid can play as significant a causal role in personality modification as do changes in patterns of early childhood socialization, although such variables always interact. Thus, although the sexual and aggressive drives are constant across cultures, they can be allowed free reign or sublimated in a variety of ways so as to carry on the work of civilization (Rothman and Lichter, 1982; Weinstein and Platt, 1969). This chapter deals with the interaction between the changing cultural, economic, and social structure of America and the modal personality of Americans.[3]

The Rise and Fall of Liberal Capitalism

David Gutmann argues that the essential differences between the traditional and the modern psyche stem from the development of a powerful superego. To primitive man, power lies outside the self, although the boundaries of self and nonself are not clear. One seeks power by following rules set by the gods through the charismatic leader or tightly knit community structures. The problem is that, unless the gods continually speak, their message dims. Social organization of any kind, therefore, requires rigid and continuous community controls. Communities adapt to their environment. They rarely attempt to master it beyond that which is necessary for survival. The stranger and the different are suspect. Forbidden impulses are projected upon those who differ (Gutmann, 1973, 1976).

In essence, the superego of primitive man is largely located outside himself. Though he longs to identify with shamans or gods, he has little sense of a consistent self as an actor who can exercise power over others to serve internal needs.

Modern western man has been different. Although the psychoanalytic literature tends to emphasize the punitive qualities of the superego, Gutmann joins with Schafer in stressing its positive, loving aspects (Schafer, 1960). By providing an inner mechanism of control, the superego permits the individual to develop a stronger sense of self. Primitive man believes that the gods help the one who does their bidding. Modern men and women attempt to overcome obstacles by living up to their inner ideals. The source of power is within, not without. Furthermore, the sublimated energy derived from modern man's internal control of both erotic and aggressive drives fosters the development of the ego. This enables him to examine and to manipulate nature, and to adapt to new circumstances and bring creative energies to bear upon them. It also enables him to overcome fear of the unknown and of other groups as he develops rational models for understanding nature.

In these ways, the development of superego strength and ego strength permits the emergence of the principled, nonauthoritarian, relatively democratic, flexible woman and man. Drawing upon the work of Max Weber and others, we can trace this social development to Christian doctrines and, more particularly, to the Reformation (Bendix, 1973). Weber demonstrates that the unintended consequence of Christian, and more specifically Calvinist doctrines, was to foster the emergence of the modern world in the form of "liberal capitalism," that is in a capitalist economic system associated with individualism and gradual if imperfect democratization. Weber emphasizes the capitalist side of the equation, but the contribution of this cultural complex to democratization is well-documented (Woodhouse, 1951).

The distinctions we have drawn are obviously not absolute. Some internalization occurs in all societies, even the most primitive. It is also clear that every great historical civilization has been accompanied by a heightening of superego development, usually based on the emergence of a new, more universalistic religious system (Coulborn, 1959). Indeed, it is possible that, in some of these civilizations, superego development was comparable to that of the West. As Weber argues, however, cultural developments in the West were unusual. First, the emergence of a prophetic religion gave a peculiar intensity to the superego. Second, the emphasis was on an individual rather than a communal relationship with God. Third, religious-cultural imperatives stressed general universal moral rules. Fourth, God was conceived as standing apart from nature and his workings could be comprehended through reason. Finally, great emphasis was placed upon repressing the passions in the service of worldly asceticism—for example, fulfilling one's obligations through activity in this world.

To be sure, some of these themes were present in other civilizations. Historically and comparatively, though, this was a unique combination. It is undoubtedly true that Confucianism, with its emphasis on the control of the passions, produced a similar end result in China and Japan via a shame culture (George de Vos, 1973). However, Confucian doctrine is essentially conservative and it is not unreasonable to believe that although the Japanese, for example, could use the energy derived from the repression of sexual and aggressive drives in the service of science and industry, Confucian doctrine was such that neither the Japanese nor the Chinese could initiate the creation of what became the modern scientific, industrial, and political world. However, given an appropriate response by elites in Japan, and later in Hong Kong, Singapore, Taiwan, and Korea, these areas could adapt to the requirements of an industrial society fairly easily compared to other Asian, African, or even Latin American nations.[4] In all of these cases, patterns of child rearing and socialization were strongly influenced by the culture even as they influenced it (Levine, 1965; Solomon, 1971; Pye, 1963; Bock, 1988).[5]

Quite clearly, this portrait of modern Western man differs sharply from that of other cultures, to take one example from the work of Herbert Marcuse, who saw the technological rationality fostered by the "Enlightenment" as a major source of "one-dimensionality" (Marcuse, 1955, 1964). We argue that liberal capitalism, whatever its limitations, historically has encouraged rationality, emotional complexity, growth, and the capacity for a democratic polity.[6]

Daniel Bell maintains that liberal capitalism contains the seeds of its own decay in rather different ways than Marx predicted. America can be examined as a paradigmatic case, for it has epitomized the Western version of modernity. An "empty land," settled initially by English Protestants who shaped its culture, it came to represent the ideal type of liberal capitalism for observers as diverse as Tocqueville, Hegel, and Marx (Hartz, 1955; Lipset, 1977).[7]

To be sure, there were myriad other influences, including the frontier and mass immigration of very diverse groups. Nevertheless, American liberalism, with its highly individualistic and relatively egalitarian and "pragmatic" social ideology and reality, lacked the earlier communal European traditions with which European liberals had to struggle.

American liberal individualism emphasized freedom but within a framework that set stringent limits upon its expression. Individuals were free to act and were held responsible for their actions. However, their behavior was mediated by an emphasis upon the restraint of impulse, including sexual impulse, and their energies were concentrated on hard work and the accumulation of material wealth. Contrary to popular folklore, the Puritans were not antisex. The emphasis was upon fidelity in marriage and constancy of emotion in sexual as well as other aspects of behavior.[8] As Edmund Leites points out (1986):

> There were ascetic tendencies in Puritanism, but the Puritans also stressed constancy and self control for a major purpose that was not ascetic. . . . Puritan preachers and theologians urged spouses to maintain a steady and reliable delight in their mates, a pleasure both sensuous and spiritual. They did not call for ascetic denial of impulse but for a fusion of self-denial and worldly desire, for a style of feeling and action that was at once self-controlled and free. (p. 3)

Originally, then, the justification for restraint, the acceptance of discipline and hierarchy, and the accumulation of wealth all rested on religious foundations. These foundations, however, assumed a sense of community that also set boundaries for individualism. Those who were fortunate enough to make wealth had a duty to exhibit "mercy, gentleness, [and] temperance" (Miller and Johnson, 1963:195–196). As late as at the end of the nineteenth century, this creed in somewhat different form played an important role in shaping the American ethos. And, of course, it evolved in tandem with patterns of child rearing (Leites, 1986; Demos, 1986).

Anthony Wallace summarizes some of the elements of the dominant American creed of the time in his perceptive discussion of the development of a small American industrial community.

> It was in Rockdale, and in dozens of other industrial communities like Rockdale, that an American world view developed that pervades the present—or did so until recently—with a sense of superior Christian virtue, a sense of global mission, a sense of responsibility and capability of bringing enlightenment to a dark and superstitious world, for overthrowing ancient and new tyrannies, and for making backward infidels into Christian men of enterprise. (Wallace, 1978:474)

He might have added that religious justification was reenforced by the deference with which businessmen were treated by ordinary folk.

Twentieth-century intellectuals have not been kind to nineteenth-century businessmen. The vast majority of nineteenth-century entrepreneurs were not merely ruthless "robber barons." They did believe in the morality of unrestrained market competition. However, most combined the desire for wealth and power with the desire to create something important for the community.[9] The vigor with which they fought the nascent trade union movement was counterbalanced by the large amount of money donated to charity. Indeed, historically, philanthropic giving has been far more extensive in the United States than in any other country and that, too, has been an integral part of the liberal tradition (Lipset, 1990:142–146).

For example, Robert Dalzell describes the life and work of the "Boston Associates" (Dalzell, 1987). Most of them were driven by a strong religious impulse and combined business with philanthropy and politics. Collectively, they helped build the Massachusetts General Hospital in Boston as well as McLean Hospital in Belmont. They also donated money to many private schools, were responsible for the Bunker Hill monument, and heavily supported the arts as well as the Boston Library. As Dalzell notes, they did so for a variety of reasons. Christian doctrine stated that the rich should share with the poor and they would be rewarded with the promise of eternal life. "Also charity was supposed to provide the donor with an immediate sense of deep inner satisfaction. Always, too, there was the specter of what the community might become without the generosity of the rich" (Dalzell, 1987:157).

Or take the efforts of Samuel and Emily Williston. Starting out in the 1820s as a young couple who could barely make ends meet, they manufactured buttons, which eventually led to great wealth (Cleary, 1991). They furnished vast sums of money to Mount Holyoke and Amherst colleges, various Protestant churches, a library, and lodging houses. They also endowed Williston Seminary, the first high school in Easthampton, Massachusetts.

Samuel had originally intended to enter the clergy. Failing eyesight led him to abandon that career and to turn to business, although he was very much dependent upon Emily. One of their first charitable projects was the building of a new church for Easthampton.

It was more than a bit ironic. The Willistons felt they were on a mission from God, and obligated to further his work by building a church. But although they might finance the construction of one of the grandest buildings in Easthampton, they were still living with Samuel's parents. To them their new wealth was not for personal pleasure but for the glory of God. (Cleary, 1991:9)

Of course this did not stop the Willistons from being rather hard-nosed businesspeople who competed fairly ruthlessly with their rivals or who often fought unions with passion.

Rothman has developed these themes in more detail elsewhere and the examples offered are not unrepresentative. America's past cannot be understood without understanding the thrust of the American liberal idea (Rothman, 1992).

The religious values that underlay American culture began to erode during the late nineteenth century, partly as the result of rationalizing tendencies inherent in liberal capitalism itself (Bell, 1976). Weber makes the same observation in "The Protestant Sects and the Spirit of Capitalism" (Gerth and Mills, 1947).

These associations were especially the typical vehicles of social ascent into the circle of the entrepreneurial middle class. They served to diffuse and to maintain the bourgeois capitalist business ethos among the broad strata of the middle classes (the farmers included). (Gerth and Mills, 1947:308)

It is obvious that in all these points the modern functions of American sects and sect like associations . . . are revealed as straight derivatives, rudiments, and survivals of those conditions that once prevailed in all ascetic sects and conventicles. Today they are decaying. (Gerth and Mills, 1947:319)[10]

As they did decay, religious justifications for the goals and limitations imposed by the culture were replaced by a belief in material progress as an end in itself. Hard work and self-restraint in a liberal capitalist system would lead to secular progress and ever better tomorrows for all. And, because they were contributing to that end, businessmen could still count on the respect of ordinary citizens to persuade them that their work constituted a genuine achievement. In small communities, at least, the other side of the coin was that entrepreneurs were hostage to this respect and it contributed to their desire to at least be seen as treating their business as a calling. Of course many businessmen retained their religious beliefs and others continued to follow patterns of behavior that were, at their source, derived from a Calvinist perspective even though the men no longer considered themselves to be particularly religious.

By the 1940s, Leo Lowenthal could report that in America the "idols of production" were being replaced by the "idols of consumption" (Lowenthal, 1944:507–548). Highly visible and successful writers such as Sinclair Lewis, in *Babbitt*, and F. Scott Fitzgerald, in *The Great Gatsby*, had leveled powerful critiques at the old ideology. One no longer lived to work and if affluence itself were now the goal, then life must eventually come to revolve around consuming things. And, of course, it did, especially after World War II. By the 1960s, consuming things had begun to lose meaning. For the children of the affluent, it no longer provided a framework for a meaningful life and American culture was to undergo yet another shift.

The movement from small-town America to the city and the emergence of the metropolis contributed to a shift in values. In small towns, people had lived face to face. They knew their neighbors and they knew the businessman with whom they dealt. Their opinions and their respect mattered to him. It was their admiration that he sought, and in fact needed, if he were to succeed. There was, if not private, at least public obeisance to a modified Calvinist morality that thus enforced that morality to some extent. Much the same pattern obtained in most of the ethnic enclaves of large cities. The morality that was enforced may have been oppressive, parochial, and exclusionary in many ways but in comparative and historical terms it did sustain communities characterized by an ongoing sense of themselves as such.

As America became a socially and geographically mobile metropolitan society and ethnic enclaves in the cities crumbled under the impact of social change, traditional attitudes and traditional, highly personal community controls also eroded. By the late 1950s, the idols of consumption had been enthroned for large segments of the population. This in turn furthered the transformation of the traditional Calvinist ethos. Many more works appeared that participated in direct attacks on bourgeois, traditional, "square" values and attitudes.

The Beats of the 1950s certainly expressed this rejection of traditional values in novels like Jack Kerouac's *On the Road* (Kerouac, 1976), but so did many others, as the writings of such popular psychologists as Erich Fromm and Abraham Maslow attest. Perhaps one of the best examples is Allen Ginsberg's long poem of 1955, *Howl* (Ginsberg, 1984). Throughout part 2, the poem assails bourgeois America directly. The poem is significant as a direct confrontation with and total rejection of the traditional ethic we have been discussing here. In the end of one section, the "best minds of my generation" have bid farewell to Moloch (an Old Testament idol of the Ammonites and the Phoenicians to whom children were sacrificed) and to the sterile community of greed and violence it represents: "They bade farewell! They jumped off the roof! to solitude! waving! carrying flowers! Down to the river! into the street!" (line 93). The poem is also significant because of its *reception*. After all, Robinson Jeffers had been writing Jeremiads in a similar vein for thirty years, even using a similar diction and prosody.

Jeffers' work, however, never had the kind of impact that Ginsberg's exerted and continues to exert. Clearly, by 1955 and after, many more people were ready to listen. This is hardly to argue that America woke up changed in 1955. After all, since we are looking selectively at works of art from that time, we would do well to remember that a film like Frank Capra's *It's a Wonderful Life* was much more popular than any poem. The film's hero, George Bailey, leads an exemplary kind of secularized Calvinist existence, dedicating himself to the prosperity of his community instead of taking advantage of opportunities to escape, "see the world," and make big money. At the same time, however, we might ask ourselves which work now appears the more dated. Although Capra's film and Ginsberg's poem are both canonized works, the film, however whimsical, codifies values that clearly no longer seem to obtain—and, perhaps, did not obtain at the time the film was made, hence adding more than guardian angels to its essentially nostalgic appeal. In contrast, the poem, in its resurgent attacks on the social order in the name of a disfigured self, seems all the more relevant to the critiques of America that have gained power since it appeared.

The creation of the modern American "self" of course stands in relation to what preceded it in Calvinist and then liberal ideology. Our argument is that by the late 1950s, this ideology of self was so different from the earlier forms that led to it, that many Americans found it fit, in a number of ways, to transmit a radical critique of the dominant culture. In the 1960s, an opportunity to integrate this previously amorphous ideological critique emerged and it is no accident, to use a standard Marxist phrase, that the leading cadres of the New Left came at first primarily from the most "liberated," self-realizing segment of the professional middle classes.

The shift in cultural values was accompanied and encouraged by the growth of a stratum of service personnel, themselves products of economic and social as well as ideological developments in American society. Many of these people were highly educated professionals working either in the public sector or, if in the private sector, in areas associated with the production and transmission of knowledge.

The growth in size of this stratum is indicated in data provided by Daniel Bell. In 1889–90, 382 doctorates were granted in the United States. The total number of such degree recipients as of 1967 was close to 400,000. In 1940, only 5 million Americans had completed four or more years of college. By the mid-1960s, the figure had jumped to some 12 million (Bell, 1973). These are quantum jumps even when allowing for the increase of population.

These "Metro Americans," as Erich Goldman called them, tended to be rather skeptical of traditional values, of the economics of liberal capitalism, and of American foreign policy (Goldman, 1969). They provided the readership for new, sophisticated critical journals, such as the *New York Review of Books*, that probably would not have been successful before the 1960s and, on another level, of such magazines as *Playboy*, whose combination of liberal politics and promotion of sexual "liberation" strongly appealed to college-educated professionals.

Intellectuals, broadly defined, and more specifically those in universities, constituted an important segment of the new stratum. By the mid-1960s, a half million academics were teaching at American universities (Bell, 1973). Moreover, the graduates of these universities were providing audiences for books and essays written by the academics. Most studies indicate that although the academic profession has been somewhat more liberal than the population as a whole since the turn of the century, the gap in ideologies grew markedly in the 1950s and 1960s.

Thus, in 1944, college faculties were only 3 percent more Democratic than the general public; in 1952, they voted 12 percent more Democratic and in 1972, they gave George McGovern 18 percent more votes than did the general public (Rothman, 1978).

Voting statistics tell only part of the story. Academics, especially those in the social sciences, were gradually replacing the vaguely Protestant milieu of elite universities with a more skeptical secular orientation. They tended to be fairly critical of traditional American institutions, emphasizing the inequalities that, they argued, were concealed by national rhetoric and the negative effects of an impersonal capitalist society whose heritage still emphasized authoritarian repressiveness. It was from the academic community that the children of traditional elites as well as those of the newer elites learned of the advantages of a democratic, egalitarian society characterized by the free (and thus healthy) expression of emotion. They also learned that the society itself was responsible for social problems that once had been blamed on individuals and that the society should take the responsibility for solving these problems. The lessons were reinforced by large numbers of books and articles demonstrating these and other propositions. In addition, these academics learned from intellectuals and professionals (including social workers and psychologists) that democratic families and democratic child rearing practices were superior to rigid and authoritarian rule by a patriarchal father (Lasch, 1977, 1978, 1985).

If the universities per se were having an impact upon the ideas and behavior of the middle class, their influence was magnified by the postwar revolution in communications and transportation. Before World War II, patterns of communication were still markedly local and regional. Magazines such as *Time* and *Life* were beginning to create a national community as were radio and the motion picture industry. However, the media and entertainment industry's influence was still limited and the dominant ethos of the community limited the range of issues that they could influence. In the postwar period, a quantum leap occurred. Key elements of change included the widespread availability of automobiles, jet aircraft, and television. The last, especially, meant that what happened in New York and a few other urban centers became the common property of the nation within a relatively short time. In earlier times the bohemianism of New York, Chicago, or Los Angeles had little impact on small towns or even the ethnic enclaves of large cities. But in the 1950s and 1960s, new lifestyles swept across the nation almost overnight. For the first time, America developed a network of national news media. Those who staffed the television networks and the national print media—like *Time* magazine and the *New York Times*—were increasingly college-educated liberal cosmopolitans who gradually came to share the views of liberal intellectuals, at least in part because they lived in New York or Washington themselves (Rothman, 1992a; Lichter, Rothman, and Lichter, 1986). By the late 1950s, those who worked in television and the print media were becoming a powerful force. They provided intellectuals with a larger audience and, thus, helped extend the intellectual community's influence to ever broader segments of the populace

(Lichter, Rothman, and Lichter, 1986; Rothman, 1992a). As the Hollywood studio system fell apart, this new elite was responsible for legitimizing the increasing dominance of a new Hollywood ethos.

The Impact of New York and Hollywood

Television probably played a more important role in these shifts than any other single factor, both because of the nature of television as a medium of communication and because of the values of those elites who controlled the production of news and entertainment.

During the 1960s and 1970s, the influence of television grew exponentially. Limited at one time by large-scale equipment needs, technological change increasingly permitted television to cover the whole world on the fly and to transmit images almost instantaneously from and to all portions of the globe.

As television became more ubiquitous, its credibility grew. No one could deny the power of its portrayals of reality when it was showing events "as they happened." In addition, television now could call upon experts to add to its credibility and, indeed, it created experts by defining them as such on television news and talk shows.

What television had done, of course, was to nationalize and standardize communication to an extent never before achieved in the United States. New York, Los Angeles, and Washington styles and modes now became national styles and modes. And if the *New York Times* was read by the New York and the Washington elites and those who produced the news for the television networks, the issues that it considered important and the approach it took to them would become national currency.

It was expected that cable television, because it dramatically increased the number of broadcast channels available, would produce a return to localism as well as encourage special interest broadcasting. Certainly, the development of satellite and other technologies has encouraged local stations to act independently of the networks to some extent in news broadcasting. Other new technologies, including fiber optics, that permit an expansion of available telephone lines may also encourage decentralization in information processing and distribution. So far, however, national patterns and influences continue to predominate. This is true, in part at least, because cable television has also tended to become concentrated in a few hands. It is also true, one suspects, because the nationalization of television communication has gone too far to be easily reversed.

By the middle 1960s, most Americans owned television sets and adults and children were watching television programs three or more hours a day. Television had become an integral part of American life, a genuine national news and image source. That continues to be true in the 1990s.

Television, Motion Pictures, and the New Sensibility

It is difficult to separate the effects of television as an instrument of communication from the fact that it is a commercial enterprise. But one does not have to accept McLuhan's hyperbole to recognize television's profound effects on American life. By its very nature television adds new dimensions to the communication of information and radically changes the rules of the game. The consequences for certain aspects of American life are clear. Far more than newspapers, radio, or movies, television provides its audience with a sense that what it sees is true and real. The audience sees events taking place in its living room. Stories, documentaries, even drama take on a reality with which other media cannot compete. The written word and even the spoken word remain somewhat abstract to most readers and listeners but moving pictures seen in the privacy of one's home are extremely compelling. Even if one knows that footage may have been spliced together and conceivably presents a somewhat distorted perspective of the events being portrayed (and few are aware of that fact), it is hard to escape the perception that one is viewing reality.

Television has broken down class and regional boundaries to a far greater extent than other media. Books and newspapers are segregated by area and readership. Only the well-educated can read serious books and the style of the *New York Times* only appeals to those with a certain level of education and affluence. Thus, to some extent, newspapers and books encourage the segregation of knowledge. Radio began to break down that segregation. Television goes much further. There are programs that cater to more elite audiences and are watched only by them but insofar as television seeks the lowest common denominator and finds it, Americans as a group are introduced to the same themes in the same way. *Roots* and other "docudramas," as well as the six o'clock news, are watched by millions of Americans of all educational and social backgrounds and they see the same pictures and receive the same information.

The process begins early in childhood. As Meyrowitz (1985) points out, cultures in which knowledge is dependent on the ability to read require substantial preparation before one can penetrate many of the secrets of adult life. Television has broken that barrier. Children can and do watch television programs that tell them about the off-stage behavior of parents and introduce them to themes that they would not have encountered until much later in life in the past. Young children are exposed to the news almost every day along with their parents. Most so-called family programs deal with concerns with which children would not have been familiar even twenty-five years ago and millions of children are still awake at hours when more "mature" television programs are shown.

It is impossible to understand the revolution that took place in American values and attitudes from the 1960s to the 1990s without taking into account the influence of television on the fabric of American life, including its breaking down of old barriers and its weakening of old ties. For the first time, metropolitan America was becoming all of America. In the 1920s, the new therapeutic ethic of self-realization had only permeated a small section of America's metropolitan upper middle class. By the 1970s, as the authors of *Habits of the Heart* (Bellah, Madsen, et al., 1985) point out, it had spread far more widely. Not surprisingly, few realize how rapid the pace of change has been. The events of the 1960s, including the rapid loss of faith in American institutions and the legitimation of life-styles once considered to be deviant, could not have occurred in a pretelevision age. The Reagan administration conceivably slowed change down a little. It clearly did not reverse direction or even stop it.

America has become, as Richard Merelman points out in *Making Something of Ourselves* (1984), a "loose bounded culture." Americans' primordial ties to family, locality, church, and what is considered appropriate behavior have eroded and Americans have lost their sense of place. They are not alone in this, of course. Their experience is increasingly shared by Europeans, the Japanese, and perhaps even Russians. Certainly mass television is not the only factor at work. The revolution is real, however, and the epoch we live in is quite new.[11] Working class parochials may continue to identify with those they know and with whom they work and live but public reality is now such that we also know and develop ersatz intimate and intense relationships with public figures of all kinds, from anchormen to rock performers to politicians.

These changes in popular culture are largely the result of technological and structural factors. However, as Rothman and his colleagues and others have demonstrated elsewhere, the skeptical liberal cosmopolitanism of journalists is, over time and despite their best efforts, reflected in the manner in which they describe the world, with significant consequences for the larger culture.

The same liberal, cosmopolitan values are characteristic of television drama. To be sure, television entertainment does seek the lowest common denominator and stresses sensationalism, including sex and violence in order to sell. However, that factor alone cannot explain the changes that have taken place in the stories told on television.

Television's America once looked like Los Angeles's Orange County writ large— waspish, businesslike, religious, patriotic, and middle-American. Today it better resembles the upper middle class "liberated" world of San Francisco's Marin County—trendy, self-expressive, culturally diverse, and cosmopolitan. Pace neo-Marxist, poststructuralist, and multiculturalist arguments, television leaders, who make up this limited sector of American society, have accelerated the acceptance of a liberal cosmopolitan perspective by other segments of the population.

As with the motion picture elite, with whom they increasingly overlap, an overwhelming segment of television's creative leaders believe that TV entertainment should "play a major role in promoting social reform" (Lichter, Lichter, and Rothman, 1991:17).

Motion pictures and television entertainment have, as we have seen, affected each other from the very beginning of the new medium (see Chapter 3). Mass television undoubtedly encouraged the makers of motion pictures to increase the amount of sex and violence in their products in an attempt to maintain a hold on their audience. In turn, the gradual liberation of Hollywood from old taboos encouraged television producers to take increasing chances in presenting daring material.

Of the two media, television is probably the more influential. However, the impact of the movie theater should not be discounted and as television networks increasingly create their own movies (and show commercial films) relying on those who make and act in films for the big screen, the two media are increasingly intertwined.

The Transformation of the American Civic Culture

In "A Model of Christian Charity," Governor John Winthrop describes the activities of the "city set upon a hill":

> We must delight in each other, make others' conditions our own, rejoice together, mourn together, labor and suffer together, always having before our eyes our community as members of the same body. (Quoted in Bellah et al., 1985:85)

Liberty, success, wealth, and the other virtues of this world, as we have discussed, were part of an explicitly religious metaphorical system for Winthrop and many who came after him. The pursuit of economic well-being always took place within the framework of a set of communal assumptions, such as the call for philanthropic help to the unfortunate, that described the moral obligations of each member of the community.

American Calvinism provided the larger cultural context in which the personal virtues associated with capitalism—such as philanthropy, but also including a number of psychological restraints on social behavior—could flourish. Although transmuted considerably since the days of Winthrop, the traditional American ethos still demands a moral and spiritual life that emphasizes measure and achievement (Weber, 1930; McClosky and Zaller, 1984; Hirschman, 1977). As we pointed out earlier, the remnants of this traditional American cultural ethos have clearly been challenged by what Lionel Trilling calls the adversary culture and what Daniel Bell calls the culture of modernism (Bell, 1976; Trilling, 1965; Shils, 1980:289–335).

In Chapter 3, we discussed the three distinct strands of this new ideology that showed up in our survey research. Why and when did they emerge? In our view, "expressive individualism" became significant among substantial segments of the urban intelligentsia in the 1920s; "collectivist liberalism" drew its power from the great Depression, though its roots extend back to at least the progressive era; and "alienation" from both the culture and the social system developed out of the sociopolitical eruptions of the 1960s. The three trends coalesced in the ideology of the New Left.

Many social theorists, including Bell, Kristol, Gouldner, and Habermas, take the view that the cultural "contradictions" of capitalism itself are the cause of the rise of the adversary culture. In their theories, the cultural sphere is given a certain neo-Hegelian autonomy and closure of its own. Change in the cultural sphere is endogenous to the cultural system. In this view, changes in cultural ideas possess an immanence and autonomy because they develop from an internal logic at work within a cultural tradition. New ideas and forms derive from a kind of dialogue with or rebellion against previous ideas and forms. The disjunction, then, between the culture of the Puritan ethic and the success of capitalism has resulted in the decay of the traditional culture and an erosion of its legitimacy (Bell, 1976).

Further, according to Bell, changes in culture as a whole, particularly the emergence of new life-styles, are made possible not only by changes in social sensibility but also by shifts in social structure. One can see this most readily in American society in the development of new buying habits in a high-consumption economy and in the resultant erosion of the Protestant ethic and the Puritan temper, the two codes that sustained the traditional American bourgeois value system (Bell, 1976).

Affluence then is both the product of traditional American culture and personality as well as the partial source of its transformation. The economy of capitalism produces the affluence, the technology, the corporate structure, and the consumption life-style that undercuts the very system of norms and values that give capitalism its legitimacy. We are living, claims Irving Kristol, on the cultural capital of an earlier period (Kristol, 1978).

In this framework, cultural innovations such as "expressive individualism" emerge to fill the void left by the underlying disjunctions between the Protestant ethic and the economic order. New cultural systems must inevitably arise because the economic order has undercut its own justifications. Precisely because many systems are in the grip of inertia, however, it often takes historical crises of legitimacy to focus attention on new problems and thus to cause cultural change (Nisbet, 1972:1–45). LaPiere, Geertz, and others observe how periods of "non-fit" can go on for years, decades, and even centuries (LaPiere, 1965; Geertz, 1973:142–169; Harootunian, 1970; Metzger, 1977; Nisbet, 1972). A crisis of legitimacy is the condition that draws our attention to the "non-fit."

Individual historical events function as markers of legitimation crises, historical discontinuities, and thus social change. These events are occurrences that suspend, or at least disrupt, the normal. As Nisbet points out in a similar context, "An event is an intrusion" (Nisbet, 1972). In retrospect, the great Depression of the 1930s was such an event. In the wake of the delegitimation of the existing cultural order, it permitted the public emergence of what Robert Bellah calls "expressive individualism" in the humanistic, artistic, and literary realms, and a move toward democratic socialism in the economic sphere (Bellah et al., 1985; Bellah et al., 1991; Bell, 1976; Shils, 1980; Janowitz, 1983).

The era beginning in the 1920s was marked by: 1) the development of a critical mass of highly differentiated intellectuals on the fringe of American society; and, 2) their active opposition to genteel culture and the liberal-bourgeois aesthetic (Shils, 1980; Coser, 1965). Many intellectuals taught a course or two at a university and some would occasionally work for an establishment magazine or major publisher but the fundamental source of their identity lay in the rejection of the dominant society and in their role as independent, "free" critics who could not be co-opted (Bell, 1976; Shils, 1980). It was these groups of intellectuals who established expressive individualism as part of the high culture of the time in New York and Hollywood.

By the 1950s, the battle between expressive individualism and the established order was over, for most practical purposes. Despite the conservative veneer of the decade, expressive individualism had won. The anti-bourgeois aesthetic triumphed within institutions attracted to, and attractive to, intellectuals (for example, the universities, mass media outlets, television, motion pictures, and book publishing).

The new strategic elites, especially members of the various cultural elites, such as leaders of the motion picture industry, are stronger proponents of expressive individualism than are their traditional counterparts, as they make clear in their attitudes toward sexual freedom, homosexuality, adultery and marriage, and a host of other cultural issues.

In the 1920s, there were few government programs protecting workers from the harsh realities of the private economic sector—unemployment, inadequate wages, dangerous and unsanitary working conditions, industrial accidents—and almost no regulations dealing with work in the private factory. Needless to say, there was no assumption that the federal government would intervene in education; civil rights for minorities, women, and the disabled; health and medical care for the poor and elderly; poverty; and so on. "Collectivist liberalism" in its contemporary form demands that the regulatory state create an equality of both opportunity and result in wealth, housing, education, civil rights, health and medical care, culture, and the arts among various groups of Americans.

Thus the new liberalism is, in many ways, an inversion of the old. Traditional liberalism called for economic freedom within a framework of emotional and expressive restraint. The new liberalism discards expressive restraints but adds economic controls.

The crisis of the 1960s integrated both "collectivist liberalism" and expressive individualism into a new pattern. In the view of the New Left, reason and objectivity represented and legitimated power in bourgeois society. Because the social order of bourgeois-liberal society is inherently dehumanizing and repressive, rejecting authority and order also required rejecting reason and objectivity.

If we assume that the ultimate goal is the freedom of the self, we find that the self seeks to be free as authority seeks to oppress; self and authority are in inherent conflict. The affluent society and its technology cannot provide the sum and substance for a good society; the culture of mass society caters to trivial and vulgar satisfactions; and the sciences, technology, and the professions all perpetuate conditions of inequality and evil allocations of power. All emanate from the conditions of the contemporary social order and all mask the true nature of power in bourgeois life.

This underlying discourse would account for the seemingly disjointed convergence of sexual libertarianism with a rejection of science and technology, and a rejection of the professional standards and ethics of such professions as journalism, law, and medicine. It would also account for membership in "libertarian" communes and the birth of a revolutionary counterculture.

The New Left as movement had died by the middle 1970s, but its impact continued to be felt as many of its ideas, in a modified and somewhat sublimated form, became part of the larger culture. These are manifest as modes of both expressive individualism and "liberal collectivism." They include a loss of faith in the efficacy and legitimacy of the political system as well as a loss of faith in the values of Western culture. At best, Western culture is seen as but one of many expressions of the human condition, albeit a failing one. At worst it is seen as sick and morally inferior to alternate perspectives. The poet Amiri Baraka, recently writing about a resurgence of what he refers to as "formalism" in poetry, typifies the second attitude:

> More generally [the McCarthyist Auto Da Fe] marked a qualitative change in American Culture, stripped of its populist democratic idealism, it is more blatantly, principally, an *imperialist* culture! So that even domestic expressions of the political power focus are openly fake, hypocritical, neo-fascist, sexually pathological, racist, male chauvinist, given to horror (its fascist consciousness strengthening—murdering horribly, murdering, murdering murdering) counter-historical, self-congratulatorily reactionary, fostering teenage pornography and fantasy as adult concerns. The establishment aesthetic is openly Tarzanic—ignorant, brutal, drooling, square, banal, insipid, sick. (Baraka, 1986:32)

Of course many of these notions are generally held in a very confused form. Most intellectuals who view alternate cultures as equal or superior to Western culture are not admirers of Islamic fundamentalism. In general, they support other cultures as a mechanism for undermining continued western notions of restraint upon behavior.

Liberal capitalism is in a state of decay. The unconscious restraints that underlie the rationality of action in liberal capitalist societies are eroded by both affluence and rationality itself. Rationality undermines the religious foundations of that restraint, and affluence undermines the need to discipline one's behavior in the marketplace. Thus rational self-interest, restrained by unconscious assumptions about the legitimate parameters of behavior, is replaced by the pursuit of any sensation or experience that gives satisfaction without directly harming others or by the immediate satisfactions of wealth or power.

The metro Americans (large numbers of whom were in the business of creating and disseminating cultural products), whose children formed the leading cadres of the New Left, were the first to adopt these new life-styles that have gradually spread to other segments of the population, especially to other strategic elites (Rothman and Lichter, 1982).

Among other things, the expressive world view transforms marriage and child-bearing from duties and obligations to experiences in self-realization. Children are not disciplined or given much attention, both because parents want to allow them to "realize themselves" and because it is too much trouble and takes too much time (Lasch, 1977, 1978, 1985; Carlson, 1988; Hamburg, 1992). Added to this has been an escalating divorce and illegitimacy rate that left an increasingly large number of children to be raised by one parent, usually the mother (Christensen, ed., 1991; Phillips, 1988).[12]

Traditional elites (businessmen, corporate lawyers, etc.) are being won over by the new ideologies even if, as yet, the pathology is not quite as severe as among the poor. Those who enter business today are less likely to regard it as a calling than were their nineteenth century counterparts. In addition to personality factors, the religious sources of that drive have withered, as has social respect.[13] Large businesses today are often anonymous bureaucratic enterprises whose leaders may inspire envy but rarely the respect that their forbears did. They are managers rather than genuine entrepreneurs. They may become celebrities but they have no personal ties with other members of a viable local community. Further, why should they seek public respect for their work, freely given in the nineteenth and early twentieth centuries, when under the best of circumstances today it probably will not be forthcoming?

John DeLorean is, in some ways, representative of the new breed of businessmen. As David Halberstam (1986) notes:

> DeLorean combined the worst of two cultures. He was the swinger as car man and the car man as swinger. The original entrepreneurs of Detroit had been true Calvinists, men obsessed by their visions, who worked long into the night in their kitchens or garages and sacrificed all their time and money to bring those dreams to life. DeLorean was different, the company founder in an age when narcissism had replaced Calvinism. (623)

DeLorean's criminal drug activity was the logical outcome of the ideology of the age and of the personal qualities that drove him. There is good reason, then, to believe that the patterns of ego control, so laboriously constructed in Europe and the United States, are breaking down even as are conventional superego restraints. The two results are an erosion of the capacity to sublimate both aggressive and erotic drives in the service of the work of civilization and a replacement of bourgeois commitments to achievement and constancy by increased defensive projection, "acting out," and drives for power and control. There is at least some evidence that the number of persons displaying this type of behavior in the United States is on the increase.[14]

In his 1975 book *Hollywood Babylon* (1975), Kenneth Anger points out that many in Hollywood in the 1920s had already embraced the culture of expressive individualism and alienation for themselves. Even then, Hollywood's elite wished to export this culture to the rest of America and to the world to liberate us from the confines of bourgeois sensibility.[15]

They could not do so at the time. The traditional culture was still too strong for them, they were not quite powerful enough in the creative community, and the Hollywood moguls kept them in line, concealing their peccadilloes (widespread drug use and sexual promiscuity) from the public at large. The norms were enforced in part because of the attitudes of the moguls and in part because of the continued power in the United States of religion, religious groups, and such conservative secular organizations as the American Legion. These groups enforced both a political and informal censorship on the product of the Hollywood creative elite. The postindustrial segment of Hollywood's creative elite, having become dominant in the Hollywood community in the past generation, has finally won its battle. The moviemakers certainly did not win by themselves. They were joined by the creative television elite and other groups. The moviemakers played out their role in conjunction with a number of social forces that created an environment receptive to change and changed their world outlook. They were also constrained by their desire to attract audiences. Thus, their role was probably a relatively small one, overall. Hollywood apologists are certainly partly correct in arguing that violence and sex dominate Hollywood because violence and sex sell. However, violence and sex have always potentially sold. Hollywood did not turn to them in the past because of larger social and political restraints that were implicit in the very liberal creed that, paradoxically, ultimately undermined such restraints. [16]

However, the wish of the liberal Hollywood elite has come true for it always supported the newer cultural understandings, certainly in the area of sexual freedom. Thus, the Hollywood elite and the television elite have, over time, contributed in important ways to the emergence of ever larger segments of the television and movie audience that no longer believe in the old verities. A return to even some of these verities is unlikely in the immediate future, despite current talk of a religious revival.[17]

A similar pattern is to be found with respect to violence. There seems to be widespread agreement among students of aggression that violent television and motion pictures increase aggressive behavior in viewers of the violence, though the limitations of social sciences that study human behavior make it hard to demonstrate the assertion with any certainty.[18] As we know, fairy tales have always been quite violent yet there is little evidence that they contributed to crime rates, and, although the Japanese media are as violent as the American media, crime rates in Japan remain very low. Insofar as movies and television entertainment contribute to violence, the key variable may be the nature of the violence presented and its purposes. Bruno Bettleheim's argument may be stated again. In fairy tales, good and evil are sharply delineated and the evildoers are always defeated. (All but the youngest children are not unaware that those involved in the fairy story are make-believe characters.) For both reasons, such violence orders the universe and helps children to control their own violent impulses, and adult fairy tales do the same for the child in every adult.

Violence in American films was very much like that of fairy tales until the recent past. Some of it is like that today. Most of the audience watching *True Lies* (1994), a fairy tale in modern dress, know that no one is really being killed and the distinction between good and evil violence (and the triumph of the good) is quite clear. *Natural Born Killers* (1994) is another matter. As in so many other films today, the line between good and evil is vague. Indeed it is not clear that good exists. The film is also quite graphic.

Films like *Natural Born Killers* reflect the alienation of many in the Hollywood community and such films are, of course, far more sophisticated than fairy tales like *True Lies*. It is not clear that they are conducive to public order in the long run (Phillips and Hensley, 1984).

It remains to be seen to what extent the present Hollywood elite, or perhaps the next generation, will judge whether the brave new world many of them have helped create is an improvement on the old. The life-style of the Hollywood elite, though it has not always recognized it, was only possible because the rest of America cleaved to an earlier understanding. As this understanding crumbles in society at large, the moviemakers may find that decadence is not as lovely a goddess as she initially appears to be. Indeed, many already have reluctantly concluded that her face is tarnished.[19] Unfortunately, no one seems to know how to change course and too many continue to believe that they can enjoy all the benefits of a society in which the free expression of impulse is encouraged without paying any of the costs that the creation of such a culture entails.

NOTES

1. The theory has actually guided Rothman's work over the past twenty years. His studies of the news media, television entertainment, philanthropic giving, and education have all been designed to test the theory and enable him to develop it further. A fuller statement of the theory will be found in *Elites in Conflict: Social Change in America Today* (forthcoming). We should point out that, aside from the efforts of Marxists and some members of the Frankfurt school, little effort has been made to place the motion picture industry in social context.

2. See the now classic summary of Weber's thought in Bendix (1973). For discussions of economic development in Japan from a Weberian perspective, see Bellah (1957) and, more recently, Morishima (1984).

3. This section of the chapter is a much-revised version of Rothman (1992).

4. This issue will be discussed in more detail in Rothman's forthcoming study, *The End of the Experiment: The Decline of Liberal Capitalism in the United States*. However, on the Japanese and Chinese patterns see, among many others, Bellah (1957); Morishima (1984), and Rozman (1991).

5. The argument of this essay will be developed in much greater detail in two forthcoming books, *Elites in Conflict: Social Change in America Today*, and *The End of the Experiment*.

6. Robert Lane agrees that capitalism does encourage such development, although he would argue that it fails in some respects (Lane, 1979, 1981a and b).

7. The current trend is to downplay the role of these men and this ideology in the interest of fostering "multiculturalism." Although we cannot go into detail here, such arguments, in our mind, are not worthy of serious consideration.

8. The same may be said of the Victorians. Whatever the myths and whatever may have been their public behavior, both husbands and wives were expected to reach orgasm during sexual intercourse. The husband believed he had failed in his duty if he did not provide such satisfaction for his wife. See Mason (1993).

9. Indeed, as Rosenberg and Birdzell point out in *How The West Grew Rich* (1986), the success of capitalism required a more substantial commitment to obeying general moral economic rules than did earlier economic systems. Such rules included the honoring of contracts made with strangers.

10. We cannot develop the argument here. However, there is little question but that Catholic migrants to America and, indeed, the American Catholic hierarchy unconsciously adopted significant elements of American Protestant culture.

11. American motion pictures had come to dominate the European market by the 1930s. Since World War II, the impact of American popular culture has become ever greater. It has spread via television, movies, and popular entertainment (rock and rap stars) with, one suspects, significant consequences. Grenier (1986); *New York Times*, January 30, 1994, section 2, pp. 1ff; *American Enterprise* (1992); Siwek (1992).

We are not as persuaded as are some of television's direct contribution to violent crime. We are persuaded, however, that it has been associated quite directly with increased fear of crime. For an essay which blames the decline of America's civic culture almost entirely on television see Putnam (1996) pp. 34–48.

12. The number of children raised by a single parent for at least a segment of their lives has risen to an estimated 15.8 million. Sixty percent of all African-American children are in that position (*New York Times*, June 7, 1991:1ff).

13. Whereas Americans still claim to believe in God and to be religious, there is strong evidence that serious religious involvement is declining (*New York Times* June 6, 1992:28; May 30, 1994:1ff; May 29, 1994:1ff).

14. A 1986 study (*Time*, September 8, 1986:57) of Harvard students found that their stated goals were "money first, followed by power, then making a reputation." As Ted Robert Gurr (1979) points out, violent crime declined in Europe and America in the "bourgeois" nineteenth and twentieth centuries until 1950, when it started to rise again. One must note that these cultural changes have also been associated with a decline of racism and ethnocentrism as well as a number of other changes (such as increased opportunities for women) of which we personally approve. We would like to believe that these changes could have occurred without the accompanying disorientation. However, it is possible that, paradoxically, we can only live in the best of times when they are accompanied by the worst of times. We also recognize that what we have called decay may merely be a prelude to a reorganization of world society that will eventually produce a more stable and humane social order than that of the modern West. Our views, like those of others, are necessarily colored by our own perspectives.

15. In *Eros and Civilization* (1955), Herbert Marcuse argues that artists by their nature are the great spreaders of a certain kind of liberty (erotic) in an overrationalized bourgeois society. There is something to what he says. Artists have almost always had serious reservations about bourgeois society from either the traditional (precapitalist) Right or the Left. In both cases, they reject the development of powerful egos and, indeed, the whole thrust of the enlightenment. They clearly play a more prominent role today than they once did both because of the new technologies and the general breakdown of the contemporary bourgeois sensibility. For a classic discussion of the role of art and artists from a psychoanalytic perspective, see Kris (1952). It should also be stressed that the very weakness of countervailing institutions such as the family today, partly the result of the rise of the new media, increases the influence of the media.

16. It should be stressed that many other very serious problems are facing the United States at this point. The conflicts created by race, immigration, and other issues can clearly not be blamed merely on the changes in American cultural understandings. However, although these new understandings have, to some extent, made us a more inclusive and egalitarian society (which is to the good) we would be prepared to argue that they have also exacerbated the problems we face.

17. As we have noted in this chapter, we doubt the likelihood of a religious and cultural renewal in the short run. However, such renewals have occurred before and cannot be discounted.

18. For a very small selection of the truly massive literature on the subject, see Centerwall (1993); Phillips and Hensley (1984); National Institutes of Mental Health (1982); and Paik and Comstock (1994).

19. As noted in Chapter 1, at least some of the Hollywood elite dislikes as well as fears the pressure of the new interest groups, whose power has increased even as that of more traditional groups has declined.

The Poverty of Film Theory

BY

DAVID J. ROTHMAN

Film Theory, the Formalist Legacy,
and the Idea of the World as Discourse

I also show . . . how he [Proudhon] [is] hunting for a so called "science" by which a formula for the solution of the social question is to be excogitated a priori, instead of deriving science from a critical knowledge of the historical movement.

Karl Marx, *The Poverty of Philosophy*[1]

There are a number of thorny theoretical and practical questions involved in creating an empirical data base from movie content, even if, as we emphasize throughout this book, the data that we have collected are only a tool that must be understood in the context of a particular argument. Even to ask the kinds of questions that we do and to assume to code, reliably, representations of the social order as they appear in movies is to take a theoretical stand that runs against the grain of much current scholarly work. As we think that the claims and purposes of content analysis and empirical study in the social sciences are often misunderstood, we would like to outline our differences with the lion's share of contemporary academic film scholarship, especially the film-theory scholars who make the strongest claims about the political, social, and cultural contexts of cinematic representation.

Of course, it is impossible to review the entirety of contemporary film theory in a single chapter. Our aim is not to provide a history of the field, or even a complete overview of the contemporary scene, and we recognize that there are many strains of development that we will not fully engage here.[2] At the same time, we feel confident asserting that a significant body of contemporary work derives from continental semiotics as articulated by the Swiss linguist Ferdinand de Saussure (1857–1913) and from the formalism and structuralism subsequently developed from his work by the Russian formalists (foremost among them Roman Jakobson), the Prague linguistic circle, Claude Lévi-Strauss, and Roland Barthes, followed by the move to poststructuralism by Jacques Derrida, Paul de Man, Jacques Lacan, and Michel Foucault, along with others in this group who have devoted themselves more closely to film including Jean Mitry, Christian Metz, and Jean-Louis Baudry.

A number of the American scholars of film are followers of these European scholars and theorists and they make increasingly strong claims about how their research includes politics, culture, and society either as the ultimate frame of meaning for theory or in the specifics of interpretation. In particular, as Barbara Klinger points out, much recent film theory descends from the work that Laura Mulvey and Jean-Louis Baudry produced in the 1970s (Klinger, 1988:129–130), which synthesized the post-Saussurian tradition as it applies to film. In what follows, we will look closely at their most influential writings and at a range of other work by James Dudley Andrew, Peter Brunette, David Wills, Vivian Sobchack, Michael Rogin, and Theresa de Lauretis along with earlier, influential work by the theorists and scholars named above and by Walter Benjamin, Andre Bazin, and others. Our aim is to describe the problems that arise when scholars in the continental semiotic tradition attempt to place poststructuralist theories in the service of political and broadly cultural analysis.

In brief, the dominant trend among the poststructuralist scholars who write about film—particularly in America—is to read movies as if they largely define the society that produced them, at least insofar as we can understand the reality of that society. As a result of their theoretical heritage, most film theorists are uninterested in discovering how social institutions work (or change) but focus instead on analyzing the codes of meaning embedded in discourses such as popular film, television, and politics. For them, movies do not so much reflect public life or consciousness as constitute and direct it, like propaganda.

No effort is made, however, to sample films or to develop a systematic content analysis to test the strong political assumptions and conclusions that these writers often make. There is no perceived need to do so because facts are understood as being always already enmeshed in representation. The search for facts that exist outside of representation is a doomed project; the only facts are representations.

The study of representations thus quickly becomes a way of decoding politics, society, and culture. The majority of American film theorists interpret Hollywood films, in congruence with other dominant cultural discourses, as an integral part of an oppressively conservative (or reactionary) ideological hegemony, which they seek to expose and destroy. Many argue that a virtual partnership exists between the government and Hollywood. This partnership is obscure, an unconscious agreement about how to represent social issues and how to create social meaning. Only theory, therefore, can describe and reveal the true machinations of such power.

For example, the representation of gender in movies becomes a sufficient basis to investigate the meaning of gender in society, for gender is always seen as an issue of representation, with little or no biological basis. In this way of thinking, sometimes called social constructionism,[3] any identifiable meaning can be understood only as the result of a sign system, and all systems of discourse, including film and politics, are comparable through structural coincidence. Many theorists, therefore, find no contradiction in treating political, cultural, or social issues as analogous to media (print, fine art, or electronic). Hence Marcie Frank, who wrote one of the essays in a 1991 issue of *PMLA* (the prestigious and influential publication of the Modern Language Association) that included a group of essays on cinema, can abstract the fundamental premise of her article "The Camera and the Speculum: David Cronenberg's *Dead Ringers*" in this way: "Feminist film theory sees the instruments of both gynecology and filmmaking as tools for examining women" (Frank,1991:622).

The immediate objections to Frank's formulation may appear obvious: the distinctions between different phenomenal and social realms have been elided with the metaphor of a "theory" that itself "sees" the technology of medical practice as identical with the apparatus of motion pictures. Frank's reading of the film, although tendentious, is more complex than her own abstract suggests. Still, in her assumptions—particularly in the way she relies on film theory to discuss the status of women in society via the interpretation of movies—Frank draws on the tradition of continental, idealist theorizing under consideration.

The intellectual developments that make statements like Frank's possible, developments in which film scholars turn to a highly charged and abstract rhetoric of politics and culture as the foundation of their analytical work, have a long history. In fact, Frank's and others' palimpsests of art and culture do not derive from sociology at all, although Frank aims to explain society as much as film. Her terms and methods grow out of investigations of the instability of meaning in language (particularly in aesthetic discourses such as literature and narrative film, but in philosophy as well). The concern with the instability of systems of meaning that characterizes poststructuralist thought derives, in turn, from critiques of the continental semiotics, formalism, and structuralism whose early advocates posited such stability as the ground for aesthetic analysis.

To understand the rationale underlying these ideas, we must look at the work of Saussure, although this is not the place for what would have to be a lengthy discussion of the Saussurian concept of the sign, a discussion that has been ably advanced by many other scholars. What interests us more is the way that subsequent thinkers outside the field of linguistics appropriated Saussure's way of talking about language as a complex, integrated *system* of signification in addition to being a collection of isolated facts of utterance. Even a brief discussion will help us to understand how Frank and other film scholars justify their methods.

Saussure held that "langue," or the structure of language, should be studied separately from "parole," or everyday speech. According to Saussure, "langue" is the realm where the structure of language as a sign system exists. "Langue" is the scientific answer to the unsystematic chaos of philology, for it reimagines language as a system instead of just trying to describe its parts as they are manifest in practice, whether present or past. As a principle, "langue" thus separates the study of language from the study of mere speech, and remakes the subject of linguistics into "a self-contained whole" (Saussure, 1959:9). As Saussure puts it, "Language is a well-defined object in the heterogeneous mass of speech facts" (Saussure, 1959:14).

The most significant attribute that all the movements descending from Saussure hold in common is the attempt to adapt the Saussurian concept of the language system to describe things that are more than, or different from, language, including the phenomenal world. This is ironic, because Saussure defined semiology in order to make the study of language a science, separating it from other fields so that language could "be studied in itself" (Saussure, 1959:16). For him "linguistics is only a part of the general science of semiology" (Saussure, 1959:16), but many of his intellectual heirs have taken that to mean that every realm conceivable as a sign system (such as film) operates like language, thus recollapsing the categories.

Many of the connections between Saussure and his various revisionists are explicit and have been fully documented, often by the revisionists themselves and particularly by adherents of deconstruction.[4] Most notably, Jakobson and other formalists sought to discuss literary artifacts as aspects of a closed Saussurian system of signs. But even Jakobson, distantly anticipating the critiques of poststructuralism, realized that this would not do, as the same functions that appear to distinguish great literary art from advertising copy and doggerel, like the use of rhyme, for example, appear in those forms as well. Hence the shift, by the late 1920s, to what came to be called structuralism.

The structuralists identified principles of poetics that could characterize any kind of discourse but were most pronounced in literature. The point was to recognize that the forms of art exist not only in great art works, although they are most prominent there. Yet in this argument, the structuralists paved the way for others to expand formalist, Saussurian approaches to art objects to include, ultimately, any kind of representation, and anything that can be conceptualized as if it were a representation, including film and the society that it represents.

As an example of the structuralist project, consider Roland Barthes' influential *Elements of Semiology* (1968) in which he appropriated Saussurian terminology and methods, seeking to fulfill Saussure's dream of a new science of signs. As Barthes puts it in the opening paragraph of his "Introduction":

> In his *Course in General Linguistics*, first published in 1916, Saussure postulated the existence of a general science of signs, or Semiology, of which linguistics would form only one part. Semiology therefore aims to take in any system of signs, whatever their substance and limits; images, gestures, musical sounds, objects, and the complex associations of all these, which form the content of ritual, convention or public enter-

tainment: these constitute, if not *languages*, at least systems of signification. There is no doubt that the development of mass communications confers particular relevance today upon the vast field of signifying media, just when the success of disciplines such as linguistics, information theory, formal logic and structural anthropology provide semantic analysis with new instruments. There is at present a kind of demand for semiology, stemming not from the fads of a few scholars, but from the very history of the modern world. (Barthes, 1968:9)

The most revealing phrase in the passage is "There is no doubt," because it obscures the questionable premise that the only way to study all the fields Barthes mentions must inevitably be with Saussurian terminology (we concede the importance of studying them but suggest another method). At any rate, Barthes extends the terms and methods of Saussurian signification to hypothetical analyses of "the garment system" (Barthes, 1968:25ff), "the food system" (Barthes, 1968:27ff), "The car system, the furniture system" (Barthes, 1968:28ff), and so on. In the end (and Barthes was one of the first people to work on film in this way), film becomes another subject for Barthes's attempt to make cultural study a science along the lines of the new linguistics. Indeed, Barthes justifies the growing need for semiology in terms of "the development of mass communications."[5]

Consider also the following passage, from Philip Rosen's "Introduction" to *Narrative, Apparatus, Ideology: A Film Theory Reader* (1986). After providing a solid and clear summary of Saussure's linguistics and the ways in which subsequent scholars appropriated his ideas for their own fields, Rosen comments on how film theorists began to do the same:

> To anyone who has studied film history, the impact, both economic and aesthetic, of the American film industry will probably seem undeniable. but [sic] here we are concerned with another question, namely the search for a systematizable object that will permit the semiotician to formulate something in cinema comparable to *langue* in verbal language. The investigation of classical narrative cinema, in the extended sense of that term, has provided such an object. Even if we leave aside the question of whether cinema as such has anything strictly comparable to the linguistic system, it is still possible to argue that cinema *in its historical actuality* has norms so dominant and long-lasting (for a medium less than one hundred years old) that such norms can be treated as the parameters of a system that can hold the methodological place occupied by *langue* in Saussurian linguistics. This classical system is the basis for what we ordinarily take as understandable, and pleasurable, movies. (Rosen, 1986:8; emphasis in original)

This resonates with the passage from Barthes in that both writers (like Metz and others) recognize that there are significant hurdles in transforming the idea of classic cinema (to use Andre Bazin's term) into a structuralist project. Nevertheless, the scholars involved have been quite insistent that what was happening was no less than a revolution in the intellectual discourse on film. Metz, in particular, sought to inaugurate not only a new chapter in the history of film scholarship, but a radically new kind of film discourse.[6]

The key sentence in Rosen's paragraph is the one at its center in which he emphasizes that the point of contact between film theory and the Saussurian model lies in the system of classical cinema as a "historical actuality." Although Rosen is only summarizing the views of others, the best he can do is locate the "systematizable object" of film semiotics in a historical context—the very situation that Saussure was at such pains to point out had interfered with the establishment of semiology to begin with.

This is highly ironic. According to Rosen, the "science" of semiology can only construe its subject in film by resorting to history, not to any abstract sign system that is truly a language or even like a language. His emphasis on analogy is telling, because it bridges a gap in his argument. The fact is that even the most thoughtful attempts to construe cinema as language (or like language) are not satisfied with the language of symbolism (of any school), but work long into a procrustean semiological night. At the end of this labor, however, all that becomes apparent is the poor quality of the fit, which no amount of dialectical hacking can make right. The linguistically derived systematizing of film remains an extended metaphor, not a science, a relatively impoverished way to describe the symbolic world of film.

Consider just a few of the more obvious difficulties in the analogy that supposedly grounds this science in the case of film. There is no possible distinction in film between the written and the spoken, as there is in language. If the film itself is comparable to writing, what is the speech to which it bears relation, and what is the nature of the relation? If such speech is taken to be the acts that are recorded on film, how do we describe their grammar, since they can encompass the entire universe of visible possibilities and even computer generated images?

Further, if we try to conceptualize film as writing without worrying about this fundamental distinction, it inevitably cannot be used for one of the functions of all written language (particularly alphabetic systems): indexing. If cinema is so much like a written language that it can be studied as if it were one, why do we still need writing to index films? Why cannot we use the same language to index the films as we supposedly use in our viewing of them? For that matter, why do we need writing and speaking in order to discuss them at all? These problems seem to us profound and they have not been bridged by the uneasy analogies that film theorists offer between movies and the Saussurian theory of language, however modified. The application of ideas of grammar to film remains an appealing metaphor but the differences with language are more significant than the similarities.

Few theorists have recognized that the contradictions in the treatment of film along post-Saussurian lines may lie in the nature of the abstractions themselves, and they generally respond to the problems they encounter in their theorizing by refining the methods to which they have already committed themselves. In short, scholars influenced by these developments continue to treat phenomena other than language, with certain caveats, *as if they were language*, as if they constitute a system analogous to the Saussurian "langue," that can thus be discussed in terms of signs that break down into signifiers and signifieds. In this tradition, meanings emerge, in all cases, *in the way that a discourse is organized*, not in the facts that it explains (which have become merely another code or construction). For if every field of inquiry, even every subject, constitutes a language, then anything can constitute a "text" for interrogation—hence Barthes' "food system," and so on—including film, for which this approach has truly won the day in academia. The existence or significance of extralinguistic or a priori phenomena *as facts* are not so much disproven as they are rendered irrelevant. As we will see in more detail later in this appendix, this is why poststructuralist discussions of culture and politics tend to be so watery—they grow out of a failed aesthetic critique, whose practitioners are usually poorly informed about the theory, practice, and history of social science.

The way that post-Saussurian aesthetic theorists deduced the necessity of culture, society, and politics to their post-structuralist critique of art occurred in the following way. Eventually, even as Barthes was trying to codify semiology, some critics within structuralism took the next step and argued that structuralist functions were still not enough to explain works of art as somehow different from other kinds of verbal discourse in a "scientific" way. Even if they were only generalized "functions" (present in all kinds of verbal discourse) and not strict formal distinctions, the qualities that differentiated poetry from any other use of language could not be defined in such a way as to separate the goats from the sheep. Hence, the Saussurian system, which had first supposedly explained the distinction between works of verbal art and other kinds of discourse, then became the ground for showing that it was impossible to indicate any such difference in a systematic way. This is the key to poststructuralism.

Among others, Barbara Herrnstein Smith lays out the poststructuralist critique of structuralism in *Contingencies of Value: Alternative Perspectives for Critical Theory* (1988), when she writes that:

> Since there are no functions performed by artworks that may be specified as generically unique and also no way to distinguish the "rewards" provided by art-related experiences or behavior from those provided by innumerable other kinds of experience and behavior, any distinctions drawn between "aesthetic" and "nonaesthetic" (or "extra-aesthetic") value must be regarded as fundamentally problematic. (Smith, 1988:34)

This brings us full circle. Whereas Jakobson, Barthes, and others appropriated Saussurian terms to describe the formal or structural properties of literary and other artworks as manifestations of integral systems, the poststructuralist critique demonstrates the impossibility of this project.

This is crucial. For it is the failure of the science of semiology that has led scholars and theorists of art, inexorably and deductively, to turn to culture and politics to explain the power of aesthetic objects, including film, even as they continue to use structuralist terms. Since works of art cannot be defined in terms of the formal properties that they so ostentatiously exhibit, the definition must lie elsewhere, in social formations that have nothing to do with art per se. As a result, to understand art, most poststructuralists argue that we must study the culture that produced it. In this view, art has no imaginative realm of its own but is utterly determined by political and cultural forces, which are most commonly understood in the American academy today to be race, class, and gender.

The scholars who inherit this tradition remain indifferent (if not hostile) to the idea that society enjoys any kind of empirical existence that can be studied sui generis. They are generally uninterested in empirically collected data that presuppose objective truths—however carefully qualified—about interpretation and representation. If anything, the more rigorous among them are at pains to trace the impossibility of connecting the real and the represented but always emphasize the forms of representation themselves. In other words, these scholars are still primarily concerned with strategies for reading, treating sign systems as discontinuous with any other realm, much like the more radical versions of the aestheticism of which they often appear so critical. Their examination of the world is always an analysis of representations and this is the way they choose to discuss political and social issues. Indeed, many film theorists—particularly in America—now tend to see political, cultural, and social issues (and, in particular, issues of race, gender, and class) primarily in terms of representation.

This is the rationalization for the intensely political rhetoric that has come to permeate literary and film theory, in which semiotic terms do duty for social and cultural analysis. In *Concepts in Film Theory* (1984), James Dudley Andrew characterizes some of the underlying assumptions of recent film theory in this way:

> In the arena of modern film theory, meaning, significance, and value are never thought to be discovered, intuited, or otherwise attained naturally. Everything results from a mechanics of work: the work of ideology, the work of the psyche, and work of a certain language designed to bring psyche and society into coincidence, and the work of technology enabling that language to so operate. (Andrew, 1984:12–15)

There are no "facts" in this analytical model, no correspondences between representations and the real that have not already been construed into a system of representation by discourse. Each time an observation is made, the individual observes something that has already been transformed and encoded; in effect, what is being observed is the code itself. Thus Andrew's "mechanics of work" applies to the real and material world, but primarily not in an economic sense. Production is not only industrial but also semiotic, although still meaningful in terms of power.

Despite his dismissal of naive Marxist critics (Andrew, 1984:125–132), Andrew understands the project of modern film theory as an unmasking of the ideology of film production, which is ultimately a social phenomenon:

> At all levels, then, from the technology of the medium to the basic units (images) and their concatenation in moments of discourse where signification is forced upon a set of conventions, the film complex is seen as a set of multiple, interlocking systems inflected by work. This is its analytic base, and this its materialism. (Andrew, 1984:17)

Fighting our way through the jargon, we can see that this adapts neo-Marxist analytic to a rhetoric of codes or figures, the key link being Saussure's work (as Andrew acknowledges on page 59ff) revised in the work of Jean Mitry, Roland Barthes, Christian Metz, and so on. In its poststructuralist formulation, the social production of the sign (in this case the film) makes sense only in terms of systematic codes and the production of these codes is similar to the economic production of value. Thus, since empiricism is already contaminated by assumptions about what is "natural," the new film theorist must pay attention primarily to codes of representation, not to what is being represented. In this way, the theorist comes to analyze movies as embodiments of culture, society, and politics—although this analysis is still taking place in broadly aesthetic terms, however modified and abstract they may appear.

As an application of the insights Barthes put forward in his essays on film and photography (collected in *Image-Music-Text*, 1977), this is a disturbing reduction. Although Barthes was on the Left (a very different thing in France than in the United States), his inquiry into the apparent paradox that photographs contain messages without systematic codes (see, for example, "The Photographic Message," 1977:16–20) was characterized by a certain intellectual caution and multifariousness. Many other film theorists of the past fifteen to twenty years use a similar rhetoric but make more reductive ideological claims.

Thus, in discussing the work of Stephen Heath, Andrew points out that all films are part of a "complex exchange system which makes up the cinema" (Andrew, 1984:110), producing not only capital but also meaning. Still discussing Heath's work, Andrew argues that:

> genres are specific networks of formulas which deliver a certified product to the waiting customer . . . As a specific production practice in the industry . . . and as a site of spectatorial pleasure. . . . genres equilibrate spectators and that vast technical, signifying and ideological machine of the cinema. (Andrew, 1984:110–111)

For a theorist like Heath, changing representations of social classes (such as we describe in our study) could only be abstracted from the hegemony of "the cinema complex" (Andrew, 1984:12) with difficulty. This is because in his theory, all movies produce meaning in the same way, and all participate equally in the dissemination of a cultural hegemony over viewers in which the viewers also participate. The idea of the genre is so abstract that the messy facts of divergence and change become very difficult to describe.

As this suggests, one result of the poststructuralist emphasis on signs and rhetorical codes is the difficulty of studying the facts of historical change, something necessary for any meaningful description of social life. Historical analysis of change has at least three dimensions in the contemplation of an art form over an extended period of time: change in types of representation; social change; and the complex, evolving relations always at work between the two realms. Of course, all social science taxonomies are systematic, but most are a good deal more pragmatic and less idealist than either neo-Marxist dialectics or post-Saussurian thinking.

The difference is this: social scientists committed to empiricism believe it is possible to describe and measure many kinds of change before being able fully to explain them with a "systematics." The explanatory hypothesis must bear a convincingly inductive relation to the observations and data and should be only a partial, inherently disprovable explanation of messy facts. This is why idealist systems, particularly poststructuralist investigations, run into trouble when dealing with the chaotic facts of social change, because their only realm of observation is within the terms of that which has already been deductively or dialectically defined. But although information in and of itself is meaningless, the project of trying to describe the world without it is absurd.

The poststructuralist critique grounds the social constructionism that has emerged from continental theories of art, in which culture and society are viewed primarily as the product of systems of representation. The most fascinating thing about this, from our perspective, is that poststructuralist theorists and scholars who claim to be interested in politics and society have in no way turned to the social sciences to study society but remain utterly committed to the language of aesthetic critique in the formalist and structuralist traditions. The likes of Weber, C. Wright Mills, and Daniel Bell rarely, if ever, appear in their bibliographies. Their critique of aesthetics and structuralism takes place largely within aesthetics and structuralism and they continue to use the very terms that supposedly failed to define art to begin with.

As we will see more specifically below, this approach tends to collapse all movies into a homogenized discourse of film, whose ultimate meaning is usually described as political in some sense. This work thus enacts an intellectual species of the very hegemony it claims to repudiate. In response to all this, we argue that Hollywood movies create and traffic in symbols but the institution of Hollywood film production itself is emphatically not defined by such symbols. In the largest possible framework, politics, film, and the film industry are different aspects of society, not of discourse, however much they may appear in discourse. In addition to producing images and stories, Hollywood operates both as a powerful business and as a social institution and its movies do not only reflect or constitute politics but also participate in it.

Contemporary Film Theory: Readings

To make our critique more precise, we would like to look briefly at several influential works of film scholarship in the poststructuralist mode, offering some responses as we go along. First we would like to focus on the question of gender theory as it intersects with film, particularly in the work of Laura Mulvey; then examine a recent work, *Screen/Play: Derrida and Film Theory* by Peter Brunette and David Wills (1989); then discuss several influential essays about the "cinematic apparatus" by Jean-Louis Baudry; and finally look at a group of contemporary books and articles that emphasize politics in their readings of film, all by well-known American scholars in the field.

Laura Mulvey and Feminist Film Theory

As those who have followed the development of academic cinema studies are aware, film scholars have been preoccupied with questions of gender representation for some time, especially representations of women.[7] When analyzing gender in the movies, many film scholars rely on a revisionary psychoanalytic rhetoric similar to that which Laura Mulvey employs in her influential and widely anthologized essay of 1975, "Visual Pleasure and Narrative Cinema."[8] In that essay, Mulvey, building on the work of Lacan, Metz, and others, takes for her point of departure the notion that "the paradox of phallocentrism in all its manifestations is that it depends on the image of the castrated woman to give order and meaning to its world" (Mast and Cohen, eds., 1985:803). She makes it clear that she uses this rhetoric in the service of a feminist, explicitly political critique:

> There is an obvious interest in this analysis for feminists, a beauty in its exact rendering of the frustration experienced under the phallocentric order. It gets us nearer to the roots of our oppression, it brings an articulation of the problem closer, it faces us with the ultimate challenge: how to fight the unconscious structured like a language (formed critically at the moment of arrival of language) while still caught within the language of the patriarchy. (Mast and Cohen, eds., 1985:804)

We are less concerned with a contest over the inherent validity of the Lacanian model than with the careful exclusions of Mulvey's rhetoric, when applying that model to the study of cinema.

The most important rhetorical gesture in Mulvey's initial assertion is the definition of a single "center" of representational meaning (however much this center is hypothetically resisted or unmasked by the critic). This definition is reinforced by the totalizing phrase "in all its manifestations" and by the emphasis on an "order and meaning" that purportedly organizes an entire world. The implication is that despite the intensely theoretical nature of the hypothesis, it is absolute and there are no possible caveats or qualifications. The hypothesis excludes the possibility of systematic inquiry that might contradict or qualify the poststructuralist argument or terms: for example, the question of whether "order and meaning," particularly in a psychodynamic context, are necessarily most powerfully created by images; whether art-images and imaginary images can be conflated; if all cinematic experience can be reduced to the dynamics of the Lacanian gaze; or if one can measure Mulvey's hypothesis about reception among actual viewers of real movies.

One key to Mulvey's rhetoric is to realize that, as she admits, she seeks less to understand film than to use Lacanian ideas to challenge "mainstream film and the pleasure it provides" (Mast and Cohen, eds., 1985:815). Thus, whereas she makes strong critical claims about the world, she does so not in the tradition of theorizing mixed with empirical investigation that originally constituted psychoanalysis but more in the tradition of idealist critique (tempered by poststructuralism). To her credit, Mulvey pulls no punches: "The first blow against the monolithic accumulation of traditional film conventions . . . is to free the look of the camera into its materiality in time and space and the look of the audience into dialectics, passionate detachment" (Mast and Cohen, eds., 1985:816).

The argument is that the force of the critique will foreground the repressed or masked "materiality" of cinema, revealing its true conditions. Yet if we are to demonstrate how the movies and the movie industry have changed over time and what their relationships to the larger society may be, instead of seeking to "strike a blow against them," this approach is unlikely to help. For in addition to its uncompromising hostility to "mainstream film," the theory requires the hypothetically static nemesis it appears to resist. It is Mulvey's rhetoric that reduces the multiplicity of film to a hegemonic, undifferentiated datum, "the monolithic accumulation of traditional film conventions," that only her approach can supposedly unmask. But the movies are a multifarious and complex phenomenon whose manifold meanings and pleasures constitute more than a fetishistic scopophilia founded on castration anxiety. *Dr. Strangelove* and *Birth of a Nation* are both about America but the differences are more significant than the hypothetically equivalent psychodynamics of our viewing of them. Indeed, even the categories of difference (time, place, plot line, politics, and so on) would take some time to work out.

Mulvey's readings of films are overdetermined, mere props to advance her thesis that, as she puts it in one of her section headings, "Destruction of Pleasure is a Radical Weapon" (Mast and Cohen, eds., 1985:804). At one point, summarizing part of her own argument, she writes that:

Each [mode of representation of woman in film and conventions surrounding the diegesis] is associated with a look: that of the spectator in direct scopophilic contact with the female form displayed for his enjoyment (connoting male phantasy) and that of the spectator fascinated with the image of his like set in an illusion of natural space, and through him gaining control and possession of the woman within the diegesis. (This tension and the shift from one pole to the other can structure a single text. Thus both in *Only Angels Have Wings* and in *To Have and Have Not*, the film opens with the woman as object of the combined gaze of spectator and all the male protagonists in the film. She is isolated, glamorous, on display, sexualized. But as the narrative progresses she falls in love with the main male protagonist and becomes his property, losing her outward glamorous characteristics, her generalized sexuality, her show-girl connotations; her eroticism is subjected to the male star alone. By means of identification with him, through participation in his power, the spectator can indirectly possess her too.)(Mast and Cohen, eds., 1985:811)

To begin with, we can debate the merits of the interpretations of the two films. For example, does Mulvey's description really do justice to the complexity of the relation between Bogart and Bacall in *To Have and Have Not*, especially when we consider the well-known historical circumstances surrounding the film (that the two were in fact falling in love)? What about the ending, in which Bacall's eroticism, although now associated with Bogart, is still very much on display? Don't the final frames display a generalized sexuality as powerful as any in the film? Is it only possible or are we required by the nature of film watching to view Bacall as a fetishized sex object indistinguishable from so many other forgotten characters? For that matter, in both of these films, don't the women characters play roles significantly different from the thousands of more passive heroines who have appeared in so many movies?

These questions would probably appear to be beside the point to Mulvey, for her aim is not to read films in order to understand them in their own details. Even in her more extended analyses, her goal is always radical political analysis, consciousness as a form of action. The theory is more important than the movies and all readings therefore become part of one reading. Hence, the extraordinary differences between the two films she discusses in this passage are elided in abstraction.

In response to Mulvey's approach, we think that all one needs to do is suggest counterexamples that complicate her categories. What about Mae West's films, for example, something like *My Little Chickadee* (1940)? This film was written primarily by West and she received twice as much as W. C. Fields for her acting and writing ($300,000 to his $150,000). Further, she hardly loses her generalized sexuality in the course of the movie but manipulates Fields throughout, never consummating the marriage into which she enticed him for her own ends. At one point, she humiliates him, for example, by placing a goat in the bed where he thinks she is waiting for him. Her relationships with the other male protagonists are similarly un-Mulveyan. In art and in life, West hardly appears to be merely an "icon, displayed for the gaze and enjoyment of men" (Mast and Cohen, 1985:811). However attractive, she seems extraordinarily self-possessed.

To pick another film, made more than fifty years later, the French *La Femme Nikita* (1991) tells the story of a young woman who is convicted of murdering a policeman during a robbery.[9] She is condemned to life in prison and the state arranges for her to appear to commit suicide so that she can be trained as an assassin, a role for which her athleticism and ruthlessness well qualify her. The deal is that if she agrees to fulfill the missions she may be assigned at any time, she gets to live what appears to be a normal life on the outside. True to its source in the myth of Pygmalion and Galatea (and Shaw's and other modern versions of that story), the young woman is transformed by her training, becoming, in this case, a person who wishes to renounce violence and live an ordinary life. She is also torn between her trainer—an emotionally sadistic operative who nevertheless loves her, although she comes to detest him—and her gentle lover, who only discovers her secret life toward the end of the movie.

In the context of Mulvey's argument, the crux is this: there is no "happy" ending. When Nikita's lover does find out about her past, she simply leaves and the film ends. The emotional punch of the movie comes at the point at which she realizes that she must leave the one man she has ever truly loved (and who has loved her) and confronts the possibility that this is the only tenderness she has ever known and may ever know in her life.

This movie plays a twist on the Pygmalion theme in that the very training that disciplines Nikita's violence enables her to overcome the emotional problems that fostered it to begin with (although the film never explores the particulars of her past). In the context of Mulvey's theory, the larger point is that the resolution, however much it may have to do with representations of love, is so radically different from those in the other films described by Mulvey and by us above, that a single hegemonic theory of how movies represent women or how male viewers see them must exclude more than it can describe. For in the end of this film, Nikita, far from being any man's "property," strikes out on her own and literally leaves the scene. The final tableau shows the two men in her life, her mentor who is interrogating her lover, acknowledging how much they will miss her. Mulvey might argue that in all filmic representations of women,

> the structure of looking in narrative fiction film contains a contradiction in its own premises: the female image as a castration threat constantly endangers the unity of the diegesis and bursts through the world of illusion as an intrusive, static one-dimensional fetish. (Mast and Cohen, eds., 1985: 816)

Yet, without asking such a small anecdotal sample to bear more critical weight than it can sustain, we can ask if Mulvey's theory can account for the variety of stories that the movies present. It would seem that in Mulvey's theory even dialogue between male and female characters is virtually impossible, yet we think that even Mulvey's own examples do not do justice to the medium.

More importantly, simply rebutting our interpretation of these few films would not suffice; we could always come up with others. Mulvey's problem is that her arguments are about the perception of film in general and absolute terms and yet she can only discuss a relatively limited number of works, selected for the purposes of the argument. No number of examples and rebuttals could make the theory stick in the way she would like it to, because it is not really about movies but rather about their cultural role. Yet although she is grounded in poststructuralist ideas and supposedly hostile to the notions of pleasure and pain that undergird aesthetic experience, Mulvey still works like a scholar in the tradition of the fine arts, buttressing large statements about psychology and culture with anecdotal readings and limited examples.

This would be easier to accept if the point were to discuss the works in question, but that is not her goal. In her method, she differs even from Freud, who used examples from literature and the arts to theorize about the facts of real people's lives. In the end, Mulvey is concerned only with representation—a weak basis for such sweeping generalizations about psychology, culture, and politics.

Much of the scholarly work done on gender and film since the late 1970s relies on the work of Metz, Lacan, Foucault, Heath, and others in ways suggested most powerfully by Mulvey. Many scholars argue that all representation of women in film has been the product of a hegemonic patriarchal culture and therefore primarily an engine of oppression and abuse. Considering that, in most of this work, even the act of looking is defined from the beginning as patriarchal (because it fetishizes the female body as a way of dealing with castration anxiety), the meanings of most of the films under discussion are not usually discovered but rather foreclosed.

Most of these writers argue in less abstract terms than Mulvey. Christine Gledhill opens her influential essay "Recent Developments in Feminist Criticism" (1978) with the observation that "a crucial issue of Feminist film criticism is the examination of the fact that 'women as women' are not represented in the cinema, that they do not have a voice, that the female point of view is not heard" (Mast and Cohen, eds., 1985:817). Gledhill cites yet another critic in this context, Sharon Smith, who argues that "Women, in any fully human form, have almost completely been left out of film . . . That is, from its very beginning they were present, but not in characterization any self-respecting person could identify with" (quoted in Mast and Cohen, 1985:817). The language is more accessible but the same kinds of problems arise. Abstraction conquers the complications of fact, just as in Mulvey's analyses. Men in Hollywood and in the film industry in other countries, in the past and the present, have discriminated against women; does that mean that there is a single "female point of view?" Did Mae West have less power to make movies than many of her contemporaries? To pick perhaps the best-known woman filmmaker of all time, who had extensive creative control over her own work, did Leni Riefenstahl express the female point of view in *Triumph of the Will*? The terms of the question make little sense.

Jean-Louis Baudry and the Question of the Apparatus

Jean-Louis Baudry has written two essays on the structure and function of film technology that have had a great influence in this country.[10] The first, published in 1970, "Ideological Effects of the Basic Cinematographic Apparatus" (Rosen, ed., 1986), describes the role of the "optical instruments" that create what we call "movies," aesthetic artifacts that Baudry defines as subjective modes as much as they are created things. The second, "The Apparatus: Metapsychological Approaches to the Impression of Reality in the Cinema," (Rosen, ed., 1986) which appeared in 1975, places the apparatus of film production, including its essential subjectivity, in relation to: 1) the philosophy of perception that descends from Plato's speculations on the nature of reality in the allegory of the cave; and 2) the Freudian theory of dreams.

Both essays insist on the subjective quality of all filmic experience. This subjectivity is built into the way the apparatus, broadly conceived to include the camera, the film, the projector, the screen, and other elements, works on the viewer. Baudry argues that the subjectivity of film is always already part of the apparatus that apparently creates it. As Baudry puts it in the second essay:

> in order to explain the cinema effect, it is necessary to consider it from the viewpoint of the apparatus that it constitutes, apparatus that in its totality includes the subject. (Rosen, ed., 1986:312)

Baudry's conclusion in his 1975 essay is that, although it has an apparent technological form, the true apparatus of the cinema is the unconscious and the metaphysical strategies by which we represent the unconscious to ourselves.

Baudry locates "the ideological mechanism" of film not in the kinds of images or stories that are produced but in the construction of the viewing subject in a particular way. In his theory, all viewers of all films are part of a mechanism that subjugates them by offering them an idealized phantasm that corresponds with a regressive psychological state.[11] As he puts it, near the conclusion of the 1970 essay, it is this regressive psychological mechanism that gives the state its opportunity to exert psychopolitical hegemony over them:

> The ideological mechanism at work in the cinema seems thus to be concentrated in the relationship between the camera and its subject. The question is whether the former will permit the latter to constitute and seize itself in a particular mode of specular reflection. Ultimately, the forms of narrative adopted, the "contents" of the image, are of little importance so long as an identification remains possible. What emerges here (in outline) is the specific function fulfilled by the cinema as support and instrument of ideology. It constitutes the "subject" by the illusory delimitation of a central location—whether this be that of a god or any other substitute. It is an apparatus destined to obtain a precise ideological effect, necessary to the dominant ideology; creating a phantasmatization of the subject, it collaborates with a marked efficacy in the maintenance of idealism. (Rosen, ed., 1986:295)

Baudry seeks to overturn this idealism in favor of a politics based on dialectical materialism, as modified by neo-Marxist theorists.

Baudry sees the entire question of the meaning of movies as one of subjective constructions, like the dreams of psychoanalysis. Hence, despite the analytical quality of his argument, he is profoundly skeptical about empirical research into film content. Indeed, Baudry justifies his investigations, in the earlier essay, in part through a critique of the study of film content, which, he argues, has ignored the apparatus and the way it involves subjectivity (Rosen, ed., 1986:287). But Baudry's argument, whatever its merits as a description of how movies correspond to the regressive state of dreams, does not require the conclusion that we cannot also classify aspects of film content and study them empirically. Such categorical imperatives, after all, are exactly what Freud pursued in *The Interpretation of Dreams*, albeit not statistically. It would be difficult to do the dream work if the contents of the dream were held not to matter. There are different kinds of dreams; there are different kinds of films. The contents are significant and content analysis can help us to understand them as they change over time.

Further, the idea that aesthetic or cultural products of a society can only be understood as meaningful because of the philosophical idealism that maintains ideological hegemony begs its own question. If the semantic dimensions of these objects are fully defined before they are studied, meanings are foreclosed, not analyzed. This is what leads Baudry to dismiss the contents of film as "of little importance," much like Mulvey—a very strange attitude to take toward art. Would anyone make the same arguments for books? Yet books all have a highly complex apparatus of production, a complex phenomenology of transmission, and a mode of production. Does that mean that the differences in the "contents" of *Mein Kampf* and the Old Testament are insignificant? Especially if our aim is to understand the social function of these works?

This homogenization of the idea of content reveals the profound weaknesses of Baudry's argument at exactly the point that he wishes to make his strongest statements about politics. Indeed, Baudry's appeal, like that of Barthes, Derrida, Lacan, Foucault, and others who work in similar ways, lies mostly in his facility at handling systematic abstraction, not messy facts. Consider this passage, again from the earlier essay:

> Contrary to Japanese painting, Western easel painting, presenting as it does a motionless and continuous whole, elaborates a total vision that corresponds to the idealist conception of the fullness and homogeneity of "being," and is, so to speak, representative of this conception. (Rosen, ed., 1986:289)

The crux, of course, lies in the phrase "so to speak," which occludes a powerful metaphor that is immediately transformed into a science of critique:

> In this sense it [western easel painting] contributes in a singularly emphatic way to the ideological function of art, which is to provide the tangible representation of metaphysics. The principle of transcendence that conditions and is conditioned by the perspective construction represented in painting and in the photographic image that copies from it seems to inspire all the idealist paeans to which the cinema has given rise. (Rosen, ed., 1986:289)

This passage, provocative as it may seem, accomplishes the very totalizing Baudry claims to resist. There are many theories of western art. The idea that all of them are the manifestation of one particular strain of philosophizing, expressed in terms of Hegelian idealism, is the necessary reduction of Baudry's own argument. Indeed, much modern art draws on a poetics of "becoming" rather than "being," in a highly self-conscious revision of a wide variety of nineteenth-century ideas.

Baudry's suggestion that all art has one ideological function is similarly reductive. Does Monet's easel painting represent the same "motionless and continuous whole" as, say, David's, or is Carpaccio's use of perspective the same as Picasso's?

Characteristically embedded in Baudry's prose are his own assumptions, which are hardly addressed but compacted and used in a facile way as grounds for argument. Does art have a singular ideological function? Why must perspective be only a function of philosophical idealism? The philosophical relations are far more complex and multifarious than Baudry is willing to grant because of his own agenda. His work is compelling because of the powerful way he constructs his speculative assumptions into a total system—but it is ultimately impoverished as a tool of social analysis, or of symbolic analysis or of arguments about historical change.

The Ongoing Influence of Derrida

Lacan has probably had a greater impact on film studies than Derrida, as evidenced in the work of both Mulvey and Baudry, but Derrida's critique of Saussure and Jakobson has had a tremendous influence in the American versions of poststructuralism. Although he is cited far less in film theory than in literary theory, many of the terms that characterize contemporary film theory can be found in his work.

Peter Brunette and David Wills, in *Screen/play: Derrida and Film Theory* (1989), bring a good deal of this material together and make the lengthiest case to date for involving Derrida's work more explicitly in film theory. They make the poststructuralist focus on aesthetic interpretation abundantly clear when they chide their colleagues for not being sufficiently rigorous in their appropriations of deconstruction for film studies:

> One is often tempted, in speaking of cinema, to refer to the real that it represents. And one usually feels constrained to place that reality within quotation marks, conscious of the mediation that the "real" has inevitably undergone. The strength of Derrida's argument is that the slight qualification that these quotation marks signal is enough to undo the whole coherence of the representational process. Those marks, traces of an other than simple duplication, as any duplication must by definition be, open a spacing that is sufficient to allow a medium as pure as a silent mime imitating nothing with an assignable origin. (Brunette and Wills, 1989:93)

Brunette and Wills emphasize that Derrida is not seeking to deconstruct "reality" but rather the idea that art can have an analogical relation with it, as embodied in theories of mimesis. They do not deny the real, but replace every criterion of realism with a theoretical investigation of realism: "The cinema would be read as that which, by coming between the act of perception and the presence of reality, irrevocably problematizes the relation of perception to reality" (Brunette and Wills, 1989:94).

But this immediately brings us up against an insurmountable epistemological problem: the categories and relations Brunette and Wills see the cinema as problematizing are the very ones that they claim are inaccessible, because they are always already represented. Their analysis relies as heavily on the notion of reality as any that they dispute.

This is not such a debilitating problem if reading is conceived to be an imaginative act carried out upon symbolic structures. The problem, again, is that these scholars believe that their theoretical models enable them to articulate ideas about social or political reality with the same analytical power that they bring to bear on art. As a result, they recast social phenomena in terms of categories that derive entirely from metaphysical investigations of representation along post-Saussurian lines.[12]

The irony is that Brunette and Wills, like many others, want to explain facts at the same time that they sweat mightily to deny fact any theoretical status. Indeed, they devote a good part of their lengthy first chapter to arguing that although many film theorists have avoided explicitly invoking Derrida's work because deconstruction appears too dryly formalist and therefore antipolitical, his work can be used to question the ideologies of institution-building that undergird all meaning, including political meaning. The chapter closes with this sentence, in which they approvingly characterize some recent feminist uses of deconstruction:

> One must be intent on altering power relations . . . but these relations can never be altered if we continue to view the elements within them as hierarchically dependent according to a logocentric model of reasoning, no matter which term of the opposition is privileged. (Brunette and Wills, 1989:32)

We do not have room here to explain what the authors and Derrida mean by terms like "logocentric," but the argument is nevertheless not too difficult to understand. The point is not to pursue politics through opposition, which only reflects the dominant power structure and therefore reinforces it. Rather, deconstruction brings the entire edifice of meaning, including politics, into question and therefore renders it problematic and open to transformation. Therefore, Brunette's and Wills' answer to problems such as the fact that "In film history the inchoate mass of details of nearly a century of filmmaking, including thousands upon thousands of films, are reduced and fitted to the Procrustean bed of historical narrative" (Brunette and Wills, 1989:36) is to show that this project is impossible. Rather, by deconstructing the edifice upon which any kind of reference to a hypothetically extralinguistic reality (such as "film history") is assumed in writing about film, they hope to give their analytic critique a certain disruptive political force.

This is a common claim in deconstructive writing in America, that through the interrogation of the philosophical sources of the idea of meaning, or "presence," in metaphysics, politics will be transformed. As Brunette and Wills put it, "The radicality of deconstruction thus lies not in its irresponsibility but rather in its very pertinent insistence on interrogating the grounding of its own discourse and that of the institution in general" (Brunette and Wills, 1989:25). They are quite right to point out, along with Derrida, that this interrogation is quite different from purposeful irrationalism or nihilism, but it is nevertheless a philosophical critique that aims to affect all thinking, including political thinking.

Needless to say, we think that this is a path that is unlikely to lead to any real understanding of how society and film relate to each other. After all, if both are subsumed into a critique of meaning, how can one distinguish between them? Brunette and Wills, like Derrida, go to tremendous lengths to transform the pesky fact of the world into an abstraction, a function of discourse and representation, an illusion created by the philosophical tradition. The problem, of course, is that there is always something else to which such a discourse is referring that is not itself language. As a result, although they insist on the significance of their work to politics, Brunette and Wills must avoid even trying to describe facts (like the responses of actual viewers to real films) with any depth, because their theoretical models derive utterly from metaphysics and the forms and meanings of representation. As they put it, when discussing the possibility of normative reading—and therefore, implicitly, empirical investigation—into content:

> one must accept that there simply is no normal viewing experience, that material conditions as simple as the number of people in the cinema or the quality of the print will always affect a viewer's perception and thus his or her reading of the film. . . . Once the text is considered in the light of Derrida's radicalized notion of context, there is no way around treating its disseminative possibilities. (Brunette and Wills, 1989:90)

Granting that this sounds convincing in a theoretical sense, we should remember that the "viewing experience" Brunette and Wills describe would probably not affect the empirical scoring of a number of significant aspects of film content, such as which genre(s) the movie participates in, whether characters are villains or heroes, how their class background is represented, what their occupations are, and so on—all categories that we were able to code for hundreds of films. Indeed, the question of whether such perceptions would be significantly affected by the conditions Brunette and Wills describe could be empirically tested through audience research. In this sense we think that Brunette and Wills are a bit hasty in dismissing the usefulness of "reductive empirical discourse" (Brunette and Wills, 1989:68) in its potential to inform theories of film, especially if the question is film's relation to social change and political structures.

In effect, the kinds of perception that Brunette and Wills refer to are so finely calibrated that they belong more to the aconceptual realms of pleasure and pain, in other words, to aesthetics—which the authors claim to have problematized—than to any politically oriented discussion of representation. Their prescription sounds more like a call for extreme subjectivism rather than a critique of aesthetics. Finally, as we have been at pains to point out throughout this appendix, their discussion requires an assumption of the existence of the very phenomena they claim cannot be measured. It is a poor argument for throwing empiricism out of court, when all one need do is acknowledge its reductive, limited quality and then make the data publicly available to other scholars.

Further Political Critique in Film Theory

A 1990 issue of the journal *Representations* included five essays that typify many of the trends we have been discussing, in a forum entitled "Entertaining History: American Cinema and Popular Culture" (*Representations*, 1990:1–123). All of the articles, a number of which are by well-known scholars such as Michael Rogin, Richard Slotkin, and Vivian Sobchack, rely in one way or another on the theoretical groundwork we have been analyzing in this chapter and all take extremely harsh critical stances toward the politics and cultural temper of America, particularly what they often refer to as the hegemonic film discourse of the Reagan period.

Through the 1980s, Reagan's successful Hollywood career appeared in the theorists' work again and again as a significant metaphor, providing grist for arguments about the entwining of politics and movies as discursive praxis. Michael Rogin's essay "'Make My Day!': Spectacle as Amnesia in Imperial Politics" argues that Hollywood and Reaganism became political and cultural conspirators in the Reagan era:

> Covert spectacles, the Reagan Era's main contribution to American imperial representation, display state-supported American heroes in violent, racial combat. Covert spectacles—movies like *Rambo* (which begins, "A covert action is being geared up in the Far East") and political schemes like aid to the Nicaraguan "freedom fighters"— preserve the fiction of a center. (*Representations*, 1990:107)

To decode this passage, it is necessary to remember that in contemporary literary theory the term "center" has become highly derogatory, a symptom of the discredited unity of structuralist thought. If it can be shown that a culture has a "center," it is then open to critique along poststructuralist lines as a hypothetically closed (and therefore theoretically flawed) system of representations. This is in line with the developments we discussed above in which critics attacked the hypothetically stable sign systems of structuralism. For such critics, cultural discourses that appeal to any "center" around which meaning revolves are by definition authoritarian. The only discourse that is not authoritarian takes place on the margins, as an elusive, indeterminate, and therefore subversive play.

Nevertheless, jargon aside, Rogin's stance is fairly clear—he refers to his argument as that of a "Marxist modernist" (*Representations*, 1990:106), and he attacks in one breath Hollywood films such as *Rambo*, Contra aid, and political manipulation of television as coordinated forms of politics. Again, the connections among these media are not overt. Nevertheless, to lift a term from Fredric Jameson, they combine as elements in "the political unconscious" of capitalism.

According to Rogin, this discourse replaces critical thinking with forgetfulness. Entertainment or spectacle is thus the true opiate of the masses. "American imperialist representation" does not oppress workers so much as it excludes marginalized people—third world people, women, blacks, gays, and others—from any possibility of authentic representation, and therefore liberated consciousness, meaningfulness, and power. Notice that what this does is transform political questions into questions of representation, colonizing politics in terms of poststructuralist theory. As Rogin puts it, "Political spectacle in the postmodern empire . . . is itself a form of power and not simply window dressing that diverts attention from the secret substance of American foreign policy" (*Representations,* 1990:100).

Or a page later: "The Reagan spectacle points . . . neither to the insignificance nor to the autonomy of the sign but rather to its role in producing power" (*Representations,* 1990:101). Political power resides in signs. Therefore, according to Rogin, we need only to study media products in order to understand the workings of power.

Rogin does not attempt to justify his choice of films in his sweeping arguments about American politics, except to note that many that he mentions, most importantly *Sudden Impact* (1983) and *Rambo: First Blood, Part II* (1985) were produced during the Reagan era and that the phrase "Make my day," uttered by Dirty Harry in *Sudden Impact,* was used by Reagan (along with millions of other Americans). However, in the course of his argument, Rogin also cites films from other time periods without offering any empirical justification, and there is no way to judge how representative Rogin's films are of what he claims to be discussing. He has selected them because he believes they are cultural icons but the question of their power and influence, as opposed to films like *Stripes, Beverly Hills Cop,* and *Police Academy* (all top-ten box office films from the early 1980s that deal with law enforcement and the military in very different ways than *Sudden Impact* or *Rambo*), is left unexamined. His sample is too small to justify any of his highly tendentious conclusions about politics and his interpretations are highly idiosyncratic.

The ironic thing is that Rogin wants to make statements of fact and statements about systematic audience perception and trends in content. Here is an example of how he goes about this. At one point in his discussion, Rogin is examining the scene in *Sudden Impact* in which Harry Callahan utters the famous line Rogin is analyzing. Quoting at length will give readers some sense of Rogin's broad, tendentious claims and scholarly standards:

> Eastwood made *Sudden Impact* during the Reagan presidency, as the racial and sexual antagonisms of the 1980s put women and blacks into the picture at their own expense. The president who quoted Eastwood's line had made women and blacks his targets, notably through the tax cuts that eviscerated their welfare-state benefits and that he was defending when he said "Make my day!" But my claim here is not only that women and blacks were present in the presidential unconscious but also that

they were absent from the memories of those who had seen the picture. Whenever I spoke on Reagan and the movies after seeing *Sudden Impact*, to student and nonstudent audiences, in my own classes and in public lectures, I asked whether anyone remembered the context of the famous words. Everyone recognized the line, for it has become a cultural cliché. But those who thought they had seen the movie foundered on the scene. Some wrongly placed the words in the episode, between men alone, of the first movie. Others got the movie and general setting right, but forgot key characters. As my sample reached the thousands, only one person remembered either the black man or the woman. That exception was himself a black man; he forgot the woman. Amnesia allows Eastwood and Reagan to have their race and gender conflict and digest it too. The white hero is remembered; the context that produced him is buried so that it can continue to support *Standing Tall* (the title of yet another Reagan-quoted movie) in the world. In the American myth we remember, men alone risk their lives in equal combat. In the one we forget, white men show how tough they are by resubordinating and sacrificing their race and gender others. The white man dares Moamar Qadaffi to blow up a cafe (maybe he did and maybe he didn't) so that he can drop bombs on men, women and children of color. "Go ahead. Make my day!" (*Representations*, 1990:104)

Rogin dips into the language of social science in this passage, talking about a "sample" that runs into the thousands. But are his results on record anywhere? Were they in any way standardized? What exactly was the range of responses? How were the questions asked? None of this is addressed; the social science language is itself window dressing for a purely anecdotal report.

Further, Rogin utterly subordinates the film to a hegemonic notion of film production. According to him, it is not Eastwood who put the characters into place in the film and they are not individuals. Rather, "the racial and sexual antagonisms of the 1980s put women and blacks into the picture at their own expense." How, exactly do racial and sexual antagonisms create movies? Movies are made by people, who have a wide variety of reasons for doing so. Although people have ideas, which are related in complex ways to diverse social phenomena, those social phenomena do not make the movies.

For that matter, Rogin has done a good deal of his own forgetting. Harry Callahan, in *Sudden Impact*, utters the expression "Make my day" while pointing his gun at a young black criminal who is threatening a woman; Rogin therefore argues that the movie is a way for white men in a position of "political helplessness" (*Representations*, 1990:103) to feel powerful, by identifying with one of their own in a racist, sexist context: "By reinscribing race and gender difference and identifying with the rescuer, Clint Eastwood, the film offers viewers imaginary access to power" (*Representations*, 1990:103–104). Rogin omits the fact that Harry uses the same expression at the end of the film when facing down a white rapist/murderer whom he actually kills. The black robber is not killed. Rogin also fails to tell us that all of the villains killed in the film are white males with the exception of one white female and that most are killed by an active white woman seeking revenge for her and her sister's rape. He also fails to mention that the secondary hero of the film is a black police officer, a close friend of Harry's. This black male is killed by the white villains, who are overtly racist. In the end, Harry allows the rapist-killing woman to go free and it is even implied that they are becoming romantically involved. One can therefore just as readily see the film as an apology for abused women who take charge of their lives by killing those who abuse them and as an attack upon white racism. This analysis is at least as plausible as Rogin's.

Rogin is particularly interested in race, conflating it with all other political categories, and seeing it as the crux of his analysis: "Imaginary racial massacres make peoples of color not simply disposable but indispensable as well, for . . . the fantasy of savage violence defines the imperial imagination" (*Representations,* 1990:109). Therefore *Rambo,* like *Sudden Impact,* is essentially an imperialist, racist film. As he says of Stallone's First Blood films, among others, "Entering racially alien ground, he [the covert operator] regresses to primitivism in order to destroy the subversive and appropriate his power" (*Representations,* 1990:107). Rogin ignores the fact that the heroine in the film is Vietnamese and that Rambo's principal antagonists are Russian.

Rogin also argues that the 1954 "cold-war" "anticommunist" motion picture *Them!* exemplifies racist America. In this picture, huge ants threaten mankind as the result of mutations induced by nuclear tests. To Rogin, the film is a metaphorical defense of using nuclear weapons on Japanese "rats" who have been transformed into ants for the purposes of the movie. Given the fact that, at the time, the United States was testing nuclear weapons and that, in the film, the mutation of the ants was the result of nuclear testing, one could far more plausibly argue that the movie was a liberal attempt to discourage the continued testing of nuclear weapons by this country. This interpretation is reinforced by the portentous warning of other possible disasters if testing continues. These warnings are uttered by the scientist hero, who had discovered the original threat, at the conclusion of the film.

This discussion only begins to analyze the rhetorical excess of Rogin's essay. His work has deserved even this much discussion, however, because he enjoys widespread prestige as an analyst of American culture, including motion pictures. Further, the evidence and reasoning upon which he relies are typical of a wide swath of contemporary American scholarship on film and politics. His work is published in the *London Review of Books* and reviewed favorably in the *New York Times,* which speaks volumes about the current state of segments of the American (and English) intellectual community.

Rogin's essay, although the most incendiary of the articles in this issue of *Representations,* only articulates more aggressively many of the attitudes and methods underlying the other contributions. In "Rock and Roll in Representations of the Invasion of Vietnam," David E. James writes:

Socialist culture—or more precisely the Third World and other forms of marginal cultural practices that in the present stand in for socialist culture—can be integrated into it ["a totally mediated environment"], but only as their opposition becomes a charade. Conversely, interruptions of the hegemony—events that cannot be assimilated to its mythologies yet which are of such moment that even if direct address to them can be suppressed their effects cannot—baffle late-capitalist culture. The British miners' strike, AIDS, systemic judicial racism in the United States—these can neither be satisfactorily represented nor concealed. (*Representations,* 1990:79)

Representation in a postmodern capitalist society thus becomes the cause and form of political oppression. But James's argument about the homogenization of dissent has more to do with how poststructuralist theory represents politics than with the facts.

Obviously, most of the scholars we have quoted make no bones about holding strong political views. Many characterize their work as an attempt to subvert, disrupt, and, if possible, destroy patriarchal, imperialist, racist consciousness as it has been expressed in the artifacts of culture. Others have written about how cinema studies, feminism as an aspect of radical politics, and poststructuralist literary theory came together and remain interconnected. In her introduction to four articles on cinema in the May 1991 issue of *PMLA*, the flagship journal of the Modern Language Association (the largest scholarly group in America) Teresa de Lauretis characterizes the early 1970s, when film studies was being formulated in American universities as a distinct scholarly enterprise, in this way:

in the new academic areas of film, women's, African American, and ethnic studies, some form of radical politics, precursor of what is now called the politics of difference, was central and integrated into the curriculum from the start. Hence feminism has been a significant and indeed a formative presence in film studies, then and now. (de Lauretis, 1991:413)

The critical targets of this curriculum are fairly clear. As Vivian Sobchack recently wrote in her essay on the Hollywood historical epic in the *Representations* forum:

The era of the Hollywood historical epic from its beginnings in the early 1900s through its decline in the 1960s can be characterized as informed by those cultural values identified with rational humanism, with bourgeois patriarchy, with colonialism and imperialism, and with entrepreneurial and corporate capitalism. (*Representations,* 1990:41)

Needless to say, Sobchack does not like these "cultural values" much and aims to interrogate them, but she doesn't exactly say what they are, burying this crucial definition in a stack of abstract qualifiers and passive syntax. If anything, her formulation raises more questions than it can answer. What, for example, is a cultural value? Is it an ideal or belief held by an entire culture or by a group within that culture or by individuals within it? Who are the people who hold it? What does it mean to assert that such a value is "characterized as being informed" by an abstraction such as "bourgeois patriarchy?" Is "bourgeois patriarchy" a social institution (like the military, or the Catholic church) that actively propagates "values"? Can all the other values so closely "identified" with it also be simultaneously identified with each other and with all the other values suggested in such a monolithic way in Sobchack's formulation? Can they then be analyzed as a subject of representation? And so on. Far from interrogating or analyzing social phenomena, Sobchack's formulation *relies* on the phenomena, however unexamined and chimerical, for her own oppositional rhetoric.

Politics, Film Theory, and the Ghost of Walter Benjamin

Readers may find the examples we have been discussing in this chapter extraordinary but they are not. The burden of our argument has been to show that these writings that discuss politics, society, and culture stand on an intellectual foundation that characterizes the entire field of film theory, despite the differences among schools within it. From our view, informed and convincing models and sustained discussions of society and social change have not been forthcoming in this work. Although much has been made recently of "cultural studies" and the political or sociological potential of feminist and poststructuralist approaches to art, we find that even in their nonhistorical social analyses, these scholars usually banish fact from the field with a theoretical flourish—which makes it a rough go when you want to talk about reality. The premise seems to be, as Borges once quipped about metaphor in surrealist poetry, that anything can be compared with anything else. In the case of poststructuralist theory this holds, as long as the two things under comparison can be rationalized as parts of a system of representation, figuration, or signs.

Poststructuralism is an impoverished approach when the aims are to discover political import in the aesthetic realm and reveal the social significance of art. The impulse on the part of many theorists seems to be to respond to the entire existential plane as if it were indistinguishable from a fiction. Hence, Sobchack can claim to discover the "values" associated with a wide range of historical and social phenomena—such as "colonialism" and "rational humanism"—by discussing *Ben Hur* and other Hollywood historical movies in poststructuralist rhetoric. However provocative such assertions may be, they trivialize both art and social science. It is not sufficient to argue that all art is already political, if the means for interrogating that politics derive primarily from the study of representation. *Instead of politicizing the study of art, such an approach aestheticizes the study of politics.*

As this formulation suggests, we think that the ghost of Walter Benjamin, particularly his 1936 essay "The Work of Art in the Age of Mechanical Reproduction," lurks behind many recent arguments about the relation of film to politics, although film theorists do not invoke his name as frequently as one might expect. In his well-known essay, Benjamin claimed to be formulating a theory of art that would be "completely useless for the purposes of Fascism" (Benjamin, 1968:218). His aim was to describe how the ruling class under Fascism used mass art, particularly film, to aestheticize politics, in other words to make spectacle and the perception of beauty more important than justice, thereby harnessing the masses to their own subjugation, including mobilization for war.

Insisting on the significance of the apparatus long before Baudry and on the importance of psychoanalysis to film art long before Baudry, Metz, and Mulvey, Benjamin emphasizes how the technology of film had, by the 1930s, already deeply affected the way we see the world:

> Evidently a different nature opens itself to the camera than opens to the naked eye—if only because an unconsciously penetrated space is substituted for a space consciously explored by man. . . . The camera introduces us to unconscious optics as does psychoanalysis to unconscious impulses. (Benjamin, 1968:237–238)

At the same time, this scene of action is utterly fragmented (by editing), which creates the "shock effect" (Benjamin, 1968:238) of film.

Benjamin also argues that mechanical reproducibility destroys an artwork's "aura" as a unique and individually created object. As a result, we discover the social significance of film by realizing its "destructive, cathartic aspect, that is, the liquidation of the traditional value of the cultural heritage" (Benjamin, 1968:221). For film has no "authentic" or "unique" existence aside from its multiple, identical products. Hence no aura is available for ritual and no authenticity of the object is available for the cult of art.

According to Benjamin, this is the point at which those with a particularly aggressive political agenda—which they do not wish to be fully articulated, as it subjugates those to whom it is being presented—can seize upon art to concentrate and control power over the masses. Benjamin is referring, of course, to the Fascists, although they constitute for him only an extreme example of a ruling capitalist class and its lackeys: "the instant the criterion of authenticity ceases to be applicable to artistic production, the total function of art is reversed. Instead of being based on ritual, it begins to be based on another practice—politics" (Benjamin, 1968:224).

Film art thus provides both a shockingly powerful aesthetic experience (of speed, change, and space), a depersonalized object (reproducible art with no aura), and an unheralded mass audience, one that has also become a new political mass. As a result, film is more like architecture than theater (Benjamin, 1968:239), for its technology of representation absorbs and permeates its audience "in a state of distraction" (Benjamin, 1968:240). This effect on the viewer is distinct from the way onlookers perceived art works before the age of mechanical reproduction, when they could only be absorbed by a small, particular group at a unique moment. Film thus gives the masses a sense of ritual and political power, when in fact, under fascism, they remain just as disenfranchised and oppressed as they were before:

> Fascism attempts to organize the newly created proletarian masses without affecting the property structure that the masses strive to eliminate. Fascism sees its salvation in giving these masses not their right, but instead a chance to express themselves. The

masses have a right to change property relations; Fascism seeks to give them an expression while preserving property. (Benjamin, 1968:241)

This form of expression that substitutes for real political action is film, which can easily be used both to shock and pacify the mass audience. Thus, as in much contemporary film theory, pleasure in art is up for interrogation, suspect because it is exactly pleasure in art that may obscure more sinister cultural politics. The notion that political ideology is a social force unto itself in endlessly complex ways, one that may or may not appropriate media to any number of ends, escapes such a theory, which is less concerned with fact than with fighting a battle of resistance.

As Benjamin summed up his own argument, "The logical result of Fascism is the introduction of aesthetics into political life. . . . All efforts to render politics aesthetic culminate in one thing: war" (Benjamin, 1968:241). By this, he meant that the Fascists had learned how to use mechanically reproduced images—particularly movies—to consolidate reactionary political sentiments both by making mass politics a beautiful spectacle (Leni Riefenstahl's films of the Nuremburg rallies and the 1936 Olympics come immediately to mind) and by tricking the masses into thinking that a beautiful spectacle was enough to satisfy their (mostly still unconscious) true political aspirations.

Unmasking and analyzing the way that the technology of movies (and other mechanically reproduced art) allowed this manipulation of art by politics to happen, Benjamin hoped, would unite those who opposed Fascism, in particular the Communists. The unified answer to the Fascist aestheticization of politics, Benjamin argued, would be a consciously politicized art: "This is the situation of politics that Fascism is rendering aesthetic. Communism responds by politicizing art" (Benjamin, 1936:242).

In retrospect, Benjamin's essay is one of the most perceptive discussions of the development of visual media ever written—yet judged as political action, it can only be seen as a tragic failure. Fascism was not defeated by abstruse Communist theories of art, however scientific or materially dialectical their authors claimed them to be. Clausewitz had more to do with it. Indeed, Benjamin does not even address the thorny question of whether or not the aestheticization of politics is inherently fascist or the complicated relations that this aestheticization has with the politicization of art, which he claims is its reverse.

If anything, it would seem that the politicization of art has a pronounced tendency to become the aestheticization of politics, no matter what the professed ideology of the critics may be. Artists who take up political questions have never needed theories to justify their work, for politics is an inherent part of both representation and ethics. It is part of life. Rather it is theorists of art who seek to discuss art *as art* yet insist that all art is determined and fashioned by political concerns, who are most liable to do the opposite of what they claim. For if politics, culture, and society are the subject, but the methodology rigorously derives from aesthetic categories, the methodology will ultimately determine the nature of the thinking. Theorists who claim to analyze culture and politics, but do so with models that derive from aesthetic formalism, do exactly what Benjamin warned us against, treating the real world as if it were merely an aesthetic or discursive structure, which is not the case. Those who rail most loudly against politics as if it were a mode of representation are the most beholden to the very aestheticization that renders their own discussions of history, culture, and politics trivial.

Conclusion and Prospectus

It would be a mistake to underestimate the influence of poststructuralist views on American academic film criticism. Although we do not claim that our survey of the field is exhaustive and we recognize that there are many internecine disagreements that we have not examined, much of the scholarly work that discusses social, political, and cultural issues in American movies is committed to the discourse of poststructuralism along the lines we have described. As a result, neither popular criticism nor the current state of film theory provide much help when we ask the question of how and why representation in the movies has changed over the decades. Journalism has obvious limitations, however helpful it may be in taking the contemporary pulse. And, despite strong claims, much current film scholarship is incapable of responding to the question in a social science context, which would involve a willingness to consider reliable empirical data.

To most academic film critics this would seem unimportant. To our charge that they have politicized the study of motion pictures, they would respond that all motion picture criticism is ideological-political, that our choice of method represents by its very nature a political choice. It does not seem to have occurred to many of them that, as the somewhat chastened literary theorist Stanley Fish recently put it, "There is a great difference between trying to figure out what a poem means and trying to figure out which interpretation of a poem will contribute to the toppling of patriarchy or to the war effort" (Fish, 1993:11). One can label all approaches to the study of motion pictures political if one wishes, but then important distinctions vanish.

Despite the appearance of Saussurian or Althuserrian "science" in their work, film theorists study only philosophical models, not facts that can be measured or can be construed as measurable—although they inevitably assume the existence of precisely these facts for their ultimate frame of meaning. When discussing particular kinds of representation, film theorists, like critics, usually focus on a relatively small number of films and "read" them closely, along the lines of the various modes of literary exegesis, instead of systematically discussing general changes in a wide number of films over time. In this sense, although the theoretical constructions are much more complicated and abstruse in, for example, Metz, Baudry, or Mulvey than in Bazin, the field has not been as radically transformed as the former scholars would have us believe. All the evidence about particular films is still, from a social science perspective, anecdotal. The model for understanding particular films, however much informed by the wide experience of the writer, is still interpretation within a broadly defined aesthetic context.

There is, obviously, nothing wrong with this. It is a powerful tool of critical thinking. What matters, however, are the claims the writer makes for the method. The problem from a sociological perspective is that despite the strong claims of the scholars we have examined here and others not reviewed herein, film theory does not provide a strong basis for testing broad claims about changes in the industry as a whole, let alone in society. Even a discussion of one hundred films, chosen primarily on the basis of the critic's interests, would yield only a very small and unrepresentative sample for study.

Consequently, our study, as noted earlier, relies on a random sample from a universe of nearly 500 top-grossing films over the 45-year period of 1946–1990. The statistics that we rely on as a tool were generated from individual categories that themselves had to be tested until the results met standard statistical criteria for replicability among coders who knew nothing about the aims of the study.[13]

The film theorists we have discussed do not and could not describe the institutional changes we document in our study because their analytic apparatus is still oriented around aesthetic questions, despite claims to the contrary. Notwithstanding hostility to "aesthetic ideology" among theorists in favor of "political" readings, their approach to film is profoundly antiempirical and still relies on highly subjective readings of individual works. Discussions of social and political institutions are therefore often uninformed about factual matters.

Based on our findings about the changes in both the Hollywood elite and the content of the many films we surveyed, we do not think that the differences among major commercial films can be fashioned into an ideology of "sameness" (Andrew, 1984:112). In contrast to the theorists, who set themselves up as critics of the "cinema complex" and are more or less enmeshed in the pleasures of the medium they aim to critique, we take the relatively common sense position that substantive differences among films in the same production system exist, matter quite a bit, and can be systematically and reliably discovered through empirical scoring. Although we are as susceptible to pleasure and pain as the next person, pleasure and its critique are not the criteria of our discussion in this study.

It bears reemphasizing that we are completely uninterested in the aesthetic or subjective impacts (including merit) of specific films except insofar as they can be empirically described through reliable intersubjective coding (the descriptions of individual films that we do undertake correspond to our empirically derived codings). Further, we argue that this body of facts can tell us a good deal about the changing role of elite filmmakers in American society and we are confident that we have succeeded in constructing reliable ways to measure the changes in film content that this leadership group has achieved.

Ultimately, we think that the changes in representation that have occurred in Hollywood movies since World War II are related to changes in American society as a whole and that the developments in Hollywood film content over the past five decades—particularly changes in representations of society—can only be satisfactorily understood through a theory of Hollywood as a social institution within an ever changing larger society that it influences even as it is influenced. Explanations that are too rigidly pragmatic tend to become reductive, explaining social change exclusively in terms of the movements of capital. And film theory, because it focuses on static sign systems, is particularly weak at generating convincing paradigms of historical change. In contrast, our approach helps us to describe why Hollywood movies tell the stories that they do, creating and articulating particular moral structures, in other words, the norms that give legitimacy and authority to social action.

As we have shown, there has been an extraordinary ideological transformation of Hollywood filmmakers, producers, and writers over the last generation and they now constitute a group in the society many of whom adhere to different political and social attitudes than other elite groups and the majority of the public they entertain. This is as important a social transformation as other events that are more often seen as affecting Hollywood movie content, such as American domestic politics or foreign policy. Our studies indicate that the Reagan and Bush years had relatively little effect on movie content. Indeed, as the press has emphasized, the Hollywood elite may now enjoy greater political influence than at any time in the past.[14]

It has been said that social science is measuring. A corollary to this might be that social scientists must try to be aware of the limitations of what they can measure. Accordingly, we have not aimed to quantify changes in movie content against complex changes in society, although we did pay attention to this where possible. Rather, we measured changes in movie content against expressions of ideology on the part of the movie elite and other groups as well, injecting empirical evidence into arguments about the realism or relevance of particular movies and trends in representation. For example, we questioned if changing Hollywood representations of the American military reflect more a change in the consensus of the society as a whole or changes within one segment of it or a complex interactive combination of both factors.

Our goal has been to describe historical developments and contemporary realities in a way that is systematic, yet accounts for the complexity of social phenomena. Therefore, in the balance of this book, we not only analyzed the transformation of the movie industry over several decades and the evolution of Hollywood film content, but sought whenever possible to test our arguments against both an extensive social survey and a systematic content analysis. Such an inductive approach, which requires an a priori acknowledgment of the recalcitrance of social facts to systematic thinking, is far more likely to explain them satisfactorily than any theory that scants their existence.

NOTES

1. Marx wrote *The Poverty of Philosophy* as a critique of Proudhon's tract *The Philosophy of Poverty* (trans., 1972 as *The Philosophy of Misery*). He criticizes Proudhon for building an abstract theory rather than examining the underlying empirical-theoretical reality. In a nutshell, that is our critique of poststructural film theory.

2. For example, Marxist theory was and still is quite popular among academic analysts of the television and motion picture industries. During the 1970s and 1980s, such theorists increasingly turned to the Italian neo-Marxist Gramsci (1891–1937), building on his argument that the cultural hegemony that a particular class creates can exercise independent influence in a society by determining the population's understanding of "reality." Many theorists of this stripe (Clover and Rogin, 1990) now add to this mixture a dose of poststructuralism, including some version of Lacanian psychoanalysis.

In addition, we have largely ignored efforts by some scholars to develop a sociology of contemporary art, whether empirically or through theoretical analysis. Among the more widely cited empirical studies of this genre are Dimaggio's analysis of art managers (1987); Judith Blau's analysis of the distribution of elite and popular culture (1989); and David Halle's analysis of art in the American home (1993). More expressly theoretical work includes Becker (1982), who presents a universal social model of artistic production as a form of labor that involves a wide range of people (in addition to the artists) who make up any given "art world"; and Zolberg (1990), who draws on Becker (among many others) in a review of theories of art and its institutions in which she generally focuses on (and argues for) art and its reception as social constructs.

In contrast to scholars such as Halle, Blau, Becker, and Zolberg, it is not our primary goal to offer new sociological definitions of various kinds of art and audience, and how such entities gain their definition in contemporary society. We are also less concerned with the contemporary conditions of artistic production per se, the impacts of artworks on different audiences, and the redefinition of aesthetic values in a sociological context. While theorists of the social contexts of art ask provocative questions, and we do not necessarily disagree with their various arguments, our work takes its point of departure from the more pragmatic notion that, with the appropriate caveats, the content of narrative aesthetic objects can be measured in a broadly statistical manner, independently of conditions of production, reception, and aesthetic value. Our primary concern is to measure actual content and broad shifts in content over time, in one such art form—Hollywood movies—along with changes in the expressed backgrounds and attitudes within the elite group that produces these films. We think that all the categories in this formulation are relatively straightforward and meaningful. In other words, our goal is not the articulation of a theoretical sociology of art, although obviously our work rests on particular theoretical assumptions and arguments; rather, our work is an actual study of one particular art and the people who make it.

3. The term was coined by Peter Berger and Thomas Luckmann (1966). However, whereas they have always argued that reality is, in part, defined by our images of our relationships to others, they never carried the argument as far as a number of the poststructuralist writers.

4. For discussions see, among others, Victor Erlich's *Russian Formalism*, Fredric Jameson's *The Prison House of Language*, and Jonathan Culler's *Structuralist Poetics* and *On Deconstruction*, all of which emphasize not only Saussure's work but the history of its ap-

propriation by subsequent thinkers. In his "Introduction" to *Narrative, Apparatus, Ideology: A Film Theory Reader*, Rosen provides an overview of how Saussurian ideas developed in the context of film theory. Jacques Derrida is the French philosopher and literary critic who, along with Paul de Man, developed the theory of deconstruction, which is heavily indebted to Saussure, and the subsequent formalist elaboration of Saussure's ideas, particularly in *Of Grammatology*. The French psychoanalyst Jacques Lacan (1901–1981), although considering himself a strict Freudian, stressed the notion that the unconscious should be treated like a language, as Saussure defined the term.

5. Barthes's best known work along these lines are his essays in *Image-Music-Text* (1977).

6. For a similar rhetorical turn in Metz, see his 1973 essay "Current Problems of Film Theory: Mitry's *L'Esthetique et Psychologie du Cinema*, Vol. II," excerpts from which are reprinted in Nichols, ed., *Movies and Methods* (568–578). See also Metz's volume *Language and Cinema* (1974b), which discusses these issue at length. Ultimately Metz is highly aware of the distinctions between language and cinema but still invests his critical method directly in the Saussurian tradition. See especially the "Conclusion," pages 285–288, and the essay "The Cinema: Language or Language System?" in his volume *Film Language* (31–91). Metz's discussion of psychoanalysis and cinema, cast in a poststructuralist light, can be found in *The Imaginary Signifier: Psychoanalysis and the Cinema* (1972:9).

7. There are a number of small, scholarly, feminist journals that focus exclusively on these issues in their numerous articles on film. They include *Genders, Women & Performance*, and *Women's Studies*, among others. Larger cinema studies journals like *Screen* and *Film Quarterly* have also published many essays in this area. One smaller cinema studies journal that often focused on these questions was *Ciné-Tracts*, which was published in Montreal.

8. Mulvey's essay first appeared in *Screen* and is one of the most widely cited essays in subsequent studies of gender and film. It can be found in Mast and Cohen, 803–816.

9. This film was remade in the United States a few years later as *No Way Out*, starring Brigitte Fonda. There are some differences between the two versions, but many scenes are astonishingly similar, down to the camera angles.

10. Both essays are included in Rosen, ed. (1986), from which we take all our citations.

11. This idea owes a good deal to Benjamin's essay "The Work of Art in the Age of Mechanical Reproduction" (1968), discussed at greater length later in this chapter.

12. Discussing similar developments in another field, Alan Liu has argued that the New Historicism (a relevant theoretical development even though its practitioners are more concerned with literary study than with film theory) is deeply indebted to the formalism that constitutes the ground of poststructuralism. Even this movement is therefore still essentially anti-historicist. See Liu's essay "The Power of Formalism: The New Historicism" (1989). Although he reaches different conclusions (arguing for a renewed, more self-critical formalism), Liu's critique of the New Historicism resonates with ours of film theory and its intellectual ground: "it is simply not the case that the New Historicism is essentially different from formalism. It is more true to say that it is an ultimate formalism so 'powerful' that it colonizes the very world as its 'text.' The New Historicism opens the door between text and context in a spirit of seeming equivalence such that the metaphoricity . . . ultimately confuses tenor and vehicle: the context *is* the text and vice versa. . . . But from the perspective of literary studies, we recognize, the result is an imperialism of textual and specifically formal analysis" (Liu, 1989:754–755).

13. The coders were mostly female college students of various ethnic and racial backgrounds. We found no significant differences in scoring patterns based on such backgrounds or in any other variable that we could measure.

14. See *New York Times* reporter Maureen Dowd's front-page article "Washington Is Star Struck As Hollywood Gets Serious" (Dowd, 1993).

APPENDIX B

The Interview Sample

Since the study of the motion picture industry was conducted in the context of an overall examination of leading strategic elites, we have included material from the complete sample.

Sample

Bureaucrats. The sample of high-ranking bureaucrats was drawn from the Office of Personnel Management's *List of Senior Executive Personnel.* Political appointees were excluded. Half the sample was drawn from "activist" agencies, which included: the Civil Rights Division of the Justice Department, the Environmental Protection Agency (EPA), the Department of Housing and Urban Development (HUD), the Federal Trade Commission (FTC), Action, the Consumer Products Safety Commission, Equal Employment Opportunity Commission (EEOC), and Health and Human Services. The other half were from "traditional" agencies: the departments of Commerce, Agriculture, Treasury, Immigration and Naturalization Service (INS), and the Bureau of Prisons. Interviews were conducted in 1982, with a response rate of 85 percent. The final sample size was 200.

The Business Elite. Upper- and middle-management personnel were randomly drawn from the official company lists of four Fortune 500 companies and of one firm selected from the *Fortune* lists of the fifty leading retail outlets, banks, and public utilities, respectively. In exchange for cooperation, we agreed not to publicly disclose the names of the corporations. Interviews were conducted in 1979. The response rate was 96 percent and the final sample size was 242.

Congressional Aides. The random sample of Congressional aides is drawn from key committee and personal staff listed in the *Washington Monitor's 1982 Congressional Yellow Book* and cross-checked with the *Congressional Staff Directory.* The interviews were conducted in 1982, with a response rate of 71 percent. The final sample size was 134.

Federal Judges.   The random sample of federal judges consisted of those on the bench as of February, 1982. Ten judges at the appeal level and ten district judges were randomly selected from each chosen circuit. The first subsample from New York, Chicago, Los Angeles, and Washington, D.C., were interviewed in 1984; the second subsample from Dallas/Ft. Worth, Detroit, St. Louis, San Francisco, Minneapolis/St. Paul, and Raleigh, North Carolina, were interviewed in 1985. The response rate for all samples was 54 percent; the final sample size was 114.

Labor Union Leaders.   The random sample consisted of presidents and secretary-treasurers from national unions and trade associations with a thousand or more members, and presidents, vice presidents, research directors, and business managers of major union and trade association locals, based on the U.S. Department of Labor's *Directory of National Unions and Employee Associations.* The sample was subsequently updated through phone calls. There are two subsamples: one from Washington, D.C., New York, Chicago, and Los Angeles, done in 1984: the second, from Detroit and Minneapolis/St. Paul, completed in 1985. The response rate was 54 percent and the final sample size was 95.

Corporate Lawyers.   The random sample of elite corporate lawyers consists of partners from New York and Washington, D.C. law firms with more than fifty partners based on the *Martindale-Hubbell Law Directory.* Interviews were conducted in 1982. The response rate was 66 percent; the final sample size was 150.

The Media Elite.   The media sample consists of a random sample of journalists and editors from the *New York Times,* the *Washington Post,* the *Wall Street Journal, Time, Newsweek, U.S. News and World Report,* and the news organizations at NBC, ABC, CBS, and PBS. The sampling frame was derived from internal phone directories and the names of individuals listed on mastheads in the case of news magazines. Staff members with responsibility for news coverage were chosen in consultation with knowledgeable people. A computer-generated random sample was chosen from this pool of names. Interviews were conducted in 1979. The response rate was 74 percent; the final sample size was 238.

The Military Elite.   The military elite are a random sample of field grade officers drawn from the Pentagon phone book and from the class roster of the National Defense University (NDU). The Pentagon sample consists of general and flag grade officers; the NDU sample consists of noncivilian students, mostly at the rank of colonel, commander, and above. Interviews were conducted in 1982. The response rate was 77 percent; the final sample size was 152.

The Movie Elite.   The random sample was drawn from a list of writers, producers, and directors of the fifty top-grossing films made between 1965 and 1982, based on *Variety.* Interviews were conducted in 1982. The final sample size is 96; the response rate was 64 percent.

The Public Interest Elite. The random sample was drawn from lists of presidents and members of boards of directors of formal lobbying groups, based on *Public Interest Profiles, Washington Five,* and the *Encyclopedia of Associations;* and lists of attorneys in public interest law firms drawn from *Public Interest Law: Five Years Later and Balancing the Scales of Justice.* Knowledgeable individuals were also consulted. Equal numbers were drawn from lobby groups and public interest law firms and restricted to Washington, D.C. and New York. Interviews were conducted in 1982. The response rate was 84 percent; the final sample size was 158.

The Religious Elite. In order to find the most influential religious leaders, we contacted the leaders of those Christian denominations with one million or more members and the editors of leading religious periodicals, such as *Christian Century* (we used their published list of the most influential religious leaders of 1982) and *Christianity and Crisis.* We asked them to nominate the most influential American religious figures and to include the leading figures from the major Christian denominations, leaders of religiously based social action groups, editors of religious journals, and theologians. These nominees provided the basis of our sample.

Names that appear on multiple lists were included in our preliminary listing, which was sent out for further review by many of the above groups and individuals. Once again, only consensual choices were retained in our final sample. Among our respondents were the heads of Protestant churches and Catholic orders, university and seminary presidents, editors of major religious publications, prominent "television evangelists," and individuals in leadership positions in such organizations as the National Council of Churches, the Moral Majority, the National Conference of Catholic Bishops, the Religious Roundtable, and the National Association of Evangelicals. The interviewing was conducted in 1984 and 1985. The final sample size was 178; the response rate was 77 percent.

The Television Elite. The television sample was based on a reputational sampling frame of an initial list of 350 writers, producers, and executives associated with the development of two or more successful prime-time television series. Interviews were conducted in 1982. The response rate was 60 percent; the final sample size was 104.

The interviewing firms were: Response Analysis Corporation, Princeton, NJ; Metro Research, Washington, D.C.; Depth Research, New York, NY; Carol Davis Research, Los Angeles, CA; Joyner Hutcheson Researchers, Atlanta, GA; Arlene Fine Associates, Chicago, IL; Davideen Swanger, Dallas, TX; High Scope Research, Detroit, MI; Quality Control Services, Minneapolis/St. Paul, MN; Bartlett

Research, San Francisco, CA; and Field Service, Inc., St. Louis, MO. All interviewers were employees of the firms and received special training, orientation seminars, and preliminary practice interviews. Response Analysis supervised the pretesting of the original questionnaire.

Questions Asked of Elite Groups

Questions Asked of Twelve-Group Sample

Number Wording

V142   Less government regulation of business would be good for the country.

V143   The American legal system mainly favors the wealthy.

V144   The American private enterprise system is generally fair to working people.

V145   It is a woman's right to decide whether or not to have an abortion.

V147   It is not the proper role of government to insure that everyone has a job.

V148   Under a fair economic system, people with more ability should earn higher salaries.

V149   Lesbians and homosexuals should not be allowed to teach in public schools.

V151   Our environmental problems are not as serious as people have been led to believe.

V152   The government should work to substantially reduce the income gap between the rich and the poor.

V153   The United States needs a complete restructuring of its basic institutions.

V154   Big corporations should be taken out of private ownership and run in the public interest.

V157   The structure of our society causes most people to feel alienated.

V158   It is wrong for a married person to have sexual relations with someone other than his or her spouse.

V159   It is wrong for adults of the same sex to have sexual relations.

V160   The United States has a moral obligation to prevent the destruction of Israel.

V161   It is sometimes necessary for the CIA to protect U.S. interests by undermining hostile governments.

V163   The main goal of U.S. foreign policy has been to protect U.S. business interests.

Additional Questions Asked of Eight-Group Sample

V166   We should be more forceful in our dealings with the Soviet Union, even if it increases the risk of war.

V167   Special preference in hiring should be given to blacks.

V168   Special preference in hiring should be given to women.

V171   Hard work will always pay off if you have faith in yourself and stick to it.

V175   In general, people are poor because of circumstances beyond their control rather than lack of effort.

V176   In general, blacks don't have the chance for the education it takes to rise out of poverty.

V177   In general, blacks don't have the motivation or willpower to pull themselves out of poverty.

V178   Almost all the gains made by blacks in recent years have come at the expense of whites.

V184   The government ought to make sure everyone has a good standard of living.

V185   It is important for America to have the strongest military force in the world, no matter what it costs.

V186   A woman with young children should not work outside the home, unless it is financially necessary.

V187   The U.S. would be better off if it moved toward socialism.

V188   There is too much concern in the courts for the rights of criminals.

The questions asked of the elite groups are all in Likert scale format. (Strongly agree, agree, disagree, strongly disagree).

The eight groups are: bureaucrats, military, public interest leaders, lawyers, congressional aides, religious leaders, judges, and labor union leaders.

Questions Loading on Each Factor

Factor 1. System Alienation

V143   The American legal system mainly favors the wealthy.

V144   The American private enterprise system is generally fair to working people.

V153   The United States needs a complete restructuring of its basic institutions.

V154   Big corporations should be taken out of private ownership and run in the public interest.

V157   The structure of our society causes most people to feel alienated.

V163   The main goal of U.S. foreign policy has been to protect U.S. business interests.

Factor 2. Expressive Individualism

V145   It is a woman's right to decide whether or not to have an abortion.

V149   Lesbians and homosexuals should not be allowed to teach in public schools.

V158   It is wrong for a married person to have sexual relations with someone other than his or her spouse.

V159   It is wrong for adults of the same sex to have sexual relations.

Factor 3. Collectivist Liberalism

V142   Less government regulation of business would be good for the country.

V147   It is not the proper role of government to insure that everyone has a job.

V151   Our environmental problems are not as serious as people have been led to believe.

V152   The government should work to substantially reduce the income gap between the rich and the poor.

APPENDIX C

The Movie Sample and Content Analysis

The study of motion pictures is part of the Center's ongoing inquiry into the influence of the mass media on American life. It relies on the same basic research method as our studies of journalists in *The Media Elite* (1986) and creators of prime time television in *Watching America* (1991), combining systematic content analysis with attitudinal data. Leading motion picture producers, writers, and directors have been interviewed and information gathered on their beliefs, values, and attitudes. The attitudinal data was first reported in Stanley Rothman and S. Robert Lichter's "What are Moviemakers Made Of?" (Rothman and Lichter, 1984:14–18). David Prindle's more recent survey of Hollywood professionals, reporting very similar findings, appeared in *Social Science Quarterly* (Prindle, 1993). The TATs were administered to the movie professionals in 1982 at the same time the attitudinal surveys were conducted.

This appendix consists of three parts: (1) a description of our film sampling techniques;(2) a description of our content analysis methodology;(3) a list of the films actually coded.

Work on the content analysis of motion pictures began in January, 1988. We defined the population of movies to be studied as the ten top-grossing films for each year beginning with 1946 and ending with 1985, for a total of 400 movies. Listings of the ten top-grossing pictures for the study were obtained from *Variety* magazine, a trade publication of the Hollywood movie industry. The total population actually consists of 394 films. This deviates from the ideal total of 400 movies for two reasons:

1. In 1947, two movies tied for tenth place making a total of eleven movies for that year.
2. Seven movies were listed among the ten top grossers for two different years. Instead of being counted twice, they were counted once for the purpose of determining the total population of films.

The procedures used in preparing the list of films and in drawing the sample were as follows:

1. For each year (1946 through 1985), the movies were listed from one to ten according to the gross income of each. The two movies tied for tenth place in 1947 were listed alphabetically.

2. For the movies appearing on lists in two different years, the highest-ranked listing was retained and the lower ranked listing was eliminated. One movie had the same ranking for both years it was listed. In this case, the listing in the earliest year was retained while the listing in the later year was eliminated.

3. The movie lists were divided into four strata according to decade: 1946–1955, 1956–1965, 1966–1975, and 1976–1985. From each stratum, a simple random sample of 25 movies was drawn. The strata populations, samples, and availability of films are as shownTable C1.

Since this is, in effect, a historical study relying on archival material, we face a problem commonly found in historical research. As we go back in time, it becomes more difficult to obtain the data that we need. This is evident in Table C1, where we indicate the number of films in the populations and samples for each decade that are available on videocassette tapes or through film rentals. We can obtain virtually all of the recent films, whereas the number of available films decreases as we go back in time.

The movies in the sample that were not available were treated as nonresponses in the research design. The proportion of available films increases for each decade to a high of 100 percent in the most recent decade of 1976 to 1985. With these increasingly high rates of availability, we can make meaningful generalizations from the samples to the populations and we can effectively compare films between the decades. Although additional error creeps into our analyses as we go back in time, we still have high enough rates of availability to justify confidence in our findings. Besides the pattern of less availability as we go back in time, the only other systematic pattern observed is the relatively low availability of Walt Disney films.

As of September, 1989, all 89 of the 110 sample movies were coded and the data was entered on the computer, giving us a "response rate" of 81 percent. We subsequently enlarged the original sample in order to facilitate investigation of some

TABLE C.1   Number of Films by Decade, Population, Sample, and Availability

	1946–1955	1956–1965	1966–1975	1976–1990
Population	101	98	100	95
Pop. viewed cassettes	62	69	87	93
Pop. viewed films (rental)	8	2	0	0
Sample	35*	25	25	25
Sample on cassette	16	22	23	25
Sample on film (rental)	3	0	0	0
Total films available	19	22	23	25

*To compensate for the number of unavailable films in the first decade, we randomly selected an additional 10 films from the 1946–1955 sample population—thus, the 35 movies recorded here.

recent trends in top-grossing films. We expanded the sample in three ways: first, we enlarged the original sample size by selecting an additional 10 movies from each decade (15 from the 1946–1955 decade); second, we updated the sample through 1989 by selecting 20 of 40 top-grossing movies from 1986–1989 (at the time we resampled, 1989 was the last year for which we had box office return information); finally, to study a couple of issues in sufficient detail, we needed to draw special subsamples from listings of movies addressing those subjects.

I. The second general sample is also a stratified random sample. It is drawn from the remaining 290 films of the original 400-film sample population or universe. The movies were again broken down by decade. Ten movies were selected (using a random number table) from each of the four decades; however, we oversampled in the 1946–1955 decade again, selecting 15 movies from this period. Thus, the second sample would have ideally rendered 45 new films to be coded but as some of them were unavailable, the actual number of films coded was 37 (82 percent). The total number of movies sampled from 1946–1985 is 126 (31 percent of the 400-movie population).

II. In addition, we decided to bring the sample up to date by including films from 1986 through 1989. From the 40 films comprising the ten top grossers of these four years, we randomly selected (again using random number tables) twenty films or a 50 percent sample. Because the films are so recent, we were able to obtain all of them for coding. Since we have only four additional years, we added these to the 1976–1985 decade (hence the switch from "decade" to "period" when referring to the 1976 to 1990 movies).

III. Finally, as we mentioned above, because we were particularly interested in analyzing some specific movie genres that turned out to be sparsely represented and/or unevenly distributed over time, we carefully sampled additional movies on two special topics: the military, and religion and the supernatural. Additional movies were still drawn from the original population of 400 top-grossing films, however this time random samples were drawn from only those movies pertaining to either the military or religion and the supernatural.

A. In the case of the military subsample, we assembled a list of films with significant military characters from the 200-movie population from 1966 to 1985. Sampling for the military movies was limited to the 1966–1975 and 1976–1985 decades because military movies were adequately represented in the earlier two decades but nearly absent from the two more recent decades. Relying on our general knowledge of the content of the 200 films, upon movie review materials such as *Halliwell's Film Guide* and books discussing war films (Suid, 1978; Ryan and Kellner, 1988), we produced an exhaustive list of top-grossing movies about the military. We randomly selected 7 movies, 3 from 1966–1975 and 4 from 1976–1985 from a list of these films. In order to update the military sample through 1989, we also coded 4 additional military movies, all from the 40-movie population of the years 1986–1989, for a total of 11 movies.

B. Also, the 2 general movie samples yielded only a small number of movies on religion and the supernatural, so we utilized a similar procedure to obtain more films on these topics. A list of relevant top-grossing films, spanning all 40 years of the study, was compiled and we randomly selected an additional 7 films from the list. The 1986–1989 general breakdown of movies in the general stratified random sample over the four decades is shown in Table C.2.

The core of the newly expanded random sample consisted of 89 original movies, 37 additional movies between 1946 and 1985, and 20 additional movies from 1986 to 1990, for a total of 146 movies selected from a list of 440 top-grossing films from 1946 to 1990. In addition, we coded 11 more movies in a targeted sample of military movies. Since these were actually selected prior to the expansion of the general sample, we included them in the lists of movies from which we eventually selected the additional general sample. Five of these military films turned up in our general sample, so only 6 of the 11 actually count toward the grand total of movies coded. Seven additional movies were coded for the study of religion and the supernatural. Thus, the total number of films coded since the original sample of 89 movies was completed is 70, bringing the grand total to 159 films. All additional films selected to augment the military and religion/supernatural studies were excluded from other analyses, since they were not part of the general random sample and might have skewed results.

The study took sufficiently long, so that by the time of its completion we were into the 1990s. To bring the material up to date once more, we chose a random sample of 5 of the 10 top-grossing films from 1990 to 1994. It would have in-

TABLE C.2   First and Second Movie Sample Breakdown

	1946–1955	1956–1965	1966–1975	1976–1990
Original sample	35*	25	25	25
Available movies	19	22	23	25
Second sample	15**	10	10	10
Available movies	11	7	9	10
Total movies available	30	29	32	35
1986–1990 sample				20

*To compensate for the number of unavailable films in the first decade, we randomly selected an additional 10 films from the 1946–1955 sample population—thus the 35 movies recorded here.

**Similarly, we oversampled in the second general sample to compensate for the unavailability of films in this period—thus, the 15 movies recorded here.

volved too much work to incorporate these into our systematic content analysis. Consequently, we produced a more subjective interpretation of these films based on the categories we had developed earlier.

Since the reliability of data collected through the method of content analysis is what gives us confidence in our results, the next major task of the study was the development, testing, and revising of a coding scheme to record the data. The initial set of coding instructions was adapted from materials used by S. Robert Lichter and Linda Lichter in their study of television drama. We developed two separate coding schemes with two different levels of analysis. We designed a character code questionnaire to obtain extensive data on each character with a speaking part in the movies. An important division among these characters resulted from the coder's determination of character rating for each individual in the films. If the character was neutral, only demographic information was recorded. If the character was nonneutral (positive, negative, or mixed—depending on her or his role in the film), additional information on the character's goals and methods and the incidence of victimization and resolution (success, defeat) was recorded. Some 4,000 characters were coded overall. Among these, over 1,000 characters were nonneutral and thus fully profiled. A second coding scheme was designed to investigate the presence or absence of a number of themes or issues in the movies, as well. Here, the movie itself was the unit of analysis.

College students were hired and trained to do both character and thematic movie coding, using a set of adapted instructions. After the coding was completed, a series of meetings was held with the students to obtain their reactions and evaluations of the coding instrument. The coding scheme was modified to improve the intersubjective reliability of coded information. Reliability tests were performed on both the character and the thematic analyses. The reliabilities obtained on the character analyses range from .70 to .80. Obtaining high reliability levels for the thematic analysis proved more difficult because the identification of themes and messages in the movies is more subjective than the character analysis, which is based largely on demographic characteristics of individuals. Nevertheless, after some revision of the coding instructions, we eventually obtained reliabilities in the .50s and .60s. Because of the relatively low reliability here, we use the thematic data with greater caution and as a preliminary tool of analysis in conjunction with the character data.

The character content analysis itself involved a series of demographic and "role-descriptive" variables. Thus, we were able to compile data on gender, race, nationality, age, religion, education levels, economic status, occupation, marital status, and the number of children, if any. We also devised categories to determine the role (star, supporting, or minor character) of characters, the setting of the movie (urban/suburban, small town/rural, or other), the use of alcohol, tobacco, drugs, whether the character committed crimes and what type, and adultery.

Next, each character was coded with a character rating. To quote from the coding instructions "this variable focuses on the most salient aspect of the character's overall portrayal." A positive rating was assigned to each character who was "basically positive or seen as a good person. He/she performs some valuable or admirable activity, usually involving actions meant to benefit others." A negative character rating was assigned when the character was perceived as "basically negative or seen as a bad person. He/she performs some act which invites disapproval from the average person. These acts will almost always demonstrate a lack of good intentions." Mixed ratings were assigned when "the character has good intentions, but despite these, commits some foolish act or behaves in a coarse, rude, or gruff manner without meaning to hurt someone's feelings. The person's intentions or general spirit are portrayed sympathetically, but his/her actions are often ridiculed. This also includes characters who perform both good and bad acts in the movie or who change from good to bad or vice versa." The vast majority of minor characters received neutral character ratings. The coding description for this category states that "the character's functions are usually short or limited. They mostly provide information that moves the plot along. The character is never developed enough to indicate any positive, negative, or mixed functions."

For those characters who received nonneutral ratings, coders were instructed to go on and evaluate the goals and methods they employed, whether they were victimized in the story, and lastly, their resolution in the plot: for example, did they succeed, fail, or was the outcome unclear, based on their goals and methods? The goals or motivations categories were treated as multiple response variables and up to three distinct goals could be coded for each character. The categories that the coders were instructed to choose from were as follows: mental/intellectual impairment; romance/sex; self-interest; protection of other; moral, ethical, or political motives—including commitment to moral or religious standards, patriotism, loyalty; adventure/excitement/knowledge; greed; malevolence/revenge; poverty; altruism/sympathy; other; unexplained/unclear. For methods employed by the characters (again, up to three methods could be coded for each character), coders could choose from the following categories: money; violence; deceit/trickery; personal charm/charisma/rational persuasion; role or position of authority/discipline; legal recourse; embarrassment/ridicule/insults; sex; other—not in criminal justice system; other.

Victimizations could include a wide range of circumstances but to quote from the coding instructions "victimization takes place when the character is by deliberate action, negligence, or circumstance injured, held back, persecuted or in some way disadvantaged by the acts of another." Examples of the categories include: acts by superiors, equals, or subordinates in the workplace; family members; friends or lovers; strangers; the justice system; business abuse; hospitals and doctors; churches/religious leaders; cults/cult leaders; schools/teachers; government action or inaction; other; none. The plot resolution for each nonneutral character was either success—"the character attains his/her main goal, regardless of function;" defeat—"the character fails to attain his/her main goal, regardless of function;" or unresolved/unclear—"there is not enough information to judge whether the character has attained his/her goal."

Our full code book is on file, along with all the materials of this study, for examination by other scholars at the Roper Public Opinion Center. In retrospect, we are convinced we could have captured other themes with a slightly better coding system, but that is hindsight.

Original Alphabetized List of Movies: 1946–1985

1. The Amityville Horror (79)
2. Anatomy of a Murder (59)
3. The Andromeda Strain (71)
4. The Apartment (60)
5. Arthur (81)
6. Auntie Mame (59)
7. The Bells of Saint Mary's (46)
8. Benji (75)
9. Beverly Hills Cop (84)
10. Bob and Carol and Ted and Alice (70)
11. Butch Cassidy and the Sundance Kid (74)
12. Carnal Knowledge (71)
13. Chariots of Fire (82)
14. Cinderella (50)
15. Cocoon (85)
16. The Deer Hunter (79)
17. Deliverance (73)
18. Diamonds Are Forever (72)
19. The Dirty Dozen (67)
20. Doctor Zhivago (66)
21. Dog Day Afternoon (76)
22. The Egg and I (47)
23. The Electric Horseman (80)
24. The Empire Strikes Back (80)
25. The Enforcer (77)
26. The Exorcist (74)
27. Father's Little Dividend (51)
28. From Here to Eternity (53)
29. Funny Lady (75)
30. The Getaway (73)
31. The Godfather (72)
32. The Goodbye Girl (78)
33. Grease (78)
34. The Greatest Show on Earth (52)

35. Guess Who's Coming to Dinner (68)
36. Hans Christian Anderson (53)
37. Hatari (62)
38. High Society (56)
39. Hombre (67)
40. Hooper (78)
41. The Karate Kid (84)
42. The Longest Day (63)
43. Mr. Mom (83)
44. Mr. Roberts (55)
45. Moby Dick (56)
46. The Muppet Movie (79)
47. Murder on the Orient Express (75)
48. The Music Man (62)
49. No Time for Sergeants (58)
50. Notorious (46)
51. The Nun's Story (59)
52. Oliver (69)
53. On the Beach (60)
54. Papillon (74)
55. Pillow Talk (59)
56. The Pink Panther (64)
57. A Place in the Sun (51)
58. Police Academy (84)
59. Porky's (82)
60. Quo Vadis (52)
61. Rambo: First Blood, Part II (85)
62. Rear Window (54)
63. Red River (48)
64. Return of the Jedi (83)
65. Road to Rio (48)
66. The Robe (53)
67. Rocky III (82)
68. Romancing the Stone (84)
69. Sayonara (58)
70. The Shining (80)
71. Singing in the Rain (52)
72. The Snows of Kilimanjaro (52)
73. Some Like it Hot (59)
74. Son of Flubber (63)
75. The Sound of Music (65)
76. Star Wars (77)
77. The Sting (74)

78. Strategic Air Command (55)
79. Superman III (83)
80. The Swiss Family Robinson (61)
81. The Ten Commandments (57)
82. To Sir with Love (67)
83. Tommy (75)
84. The Unsinkable Molly Brown (64)
85. Valley of the Dolls (68)
86. The Vikings (58)
87. White Christmas (54)
88. Who's Afraid of Virginia Woolf (66)
89. The World of Suzie Wong (61)

Alphabetized List of Additional Movies: 1946–1990

1. Barefoot in the Park (67)
2. Beetlejuice (88)
3. Beverly Hills Cop II (87)
4. Big (88)
5. Blazing Saddles (74)
6. Born Yesterday (51)
7. The Caine Mutiny (54)
8. Casino Royale (67)
9. Close Encounters of the Third Kind (77)
10. Cocktail (88)
11. Coming to America (88)
12. A Date with Judy (48)
13. Down and Out in Beverly Hills (86)
14. Dragnet (87)
15. Every Which Way But Loose (79)
16. The Golden Child (86)
17. Goldfinger (65)
18. Good Morning Vietnam (87)
19. Green Dolphin Street (47)
20. Guys and Dolls (56)
21. House of Wax (53)
22. Imitation of Life (59)
23. Indiana Jones and the Last Crusade (89)
24. It's a Mad Mad Mad Mad World (64)
25. Jolson Sings Again (49)
26. Lethal Weapon (87)
27. Little Big Man (71)
28. Look Who's Talking (89)

29. Love Me Tender (57)
30. Lovers and Other Strangers (70)
31. Moonstruck (87)
32. The Naked Gun (88)
33. National Lampoon's Christmas Vacation (89)
34. On Golden Pond (82)
35. The Owl and the Pussycat (71)
36. Platoon (86)
37. Police Academy II (85)
38. Private Benjamin
39. Rain Man (88)
40. Rocky (77)
41. The Russians Are Coming, The Russians Are Coming (66)
42. The Sandpiper (65)
43. Serpico (74)
44. Seven Brides for Seven Brothers (54)
45. Shampoo (75)
46. Shane (53)
47. South Pacific (58)
48. Spellbound (45)
49. Stripes (81)
50. Superman (79)
51. 12 O'Clock High (50)
52. Twins (88)
53. A View to a Kill (85))
54. When Harry Met Sally (89)
55. The Witches of Eastwick (87)
56. Words and Music (49)
57. You Only Live Twice (67)

Sample Population List Updated: 1986–1990

1986

1. Top Gun
2. Crocodile Dundee
3. Platoon
4. The Karate Kid Part II
5. Star Trek IV
6. Back to School
7. The Golden Child
8. Ruthless People
9. Ferris Beuller's Day Off
10. Down and Out in Beverly Hills

1987

1. Three Men and a Baby
2. Beverly Hills Cop II
3. Fatal Attraction
4. Good Morning Vietnam
5. The Untouchables
6. Moonstruck
7. The Witches of Eastwick
8. Predator
9. Dragnet
10. Lethal Weapon

1988

1. Rain Man
2. Who Framed Roger Rabbit?
3. Coming to America
4. Crocodile Dundee II
5. Twins
6. Big
7. Die Hard
8. Cocktail
9. The Naked Gun
10. Beetlejuice

1989

1. Batman
2. Indiana Jones and the Last Crusade
3. Lethal Weapon II
4. Back to the Future II
5. Ghostbusters II
6. Look Who's Talking
7. Parenthood
8. Dead Poet's Society
9. National Lampoon's Christmas Vacation
10. When Harry Met Sally

Twenty-Movie Random Sample: 1986–1990

1986

1. Platoon
2. The Golden Child
3. Down and Out in Beverly Hills

1987

1. Beverly Hills Cop II
2. Good Morning Vietnam
3. Moonstruck
4. The Witches of Eastwick
5. Dragnet
6. Lethal Weapon

1988

1. Rain Man
2. Coming to America
3. Twins
4. Big
5. Cocktail
6. The Naked Gun
7. Beetlejuice

1989

1. Indiana Jones and the Last Crusade
2. Look Who's Talking
3. National Lampoon's Christmas Vacation
4. When Harry Met Sally

Forty-five New Movies for the Forty-Year Sample
1946–1955

Spellbound (45)
Two Years Before the Mast (46) N/A
Welcome Stranger (47) N/A
Green Dolphin Street (47)
The Razor's Edge (46) N/A
A Date with Judy (48)
Jolson Sings Again (49)
Words and Music (49)
12 O'Clock High (50)
Born Yesterday (51)
Shane (53)
House of Wax (53)
The Caine Mutiny (54)
Seven Brides for Seven Brothers (54)
Sea Chase (55) N/A

1956–1965

  Guys and Dolls (56)
  The Pride and the Passion (57) N/A
  Love Me Tender (57)
  Search for Paradise (58) N/A
  South Pacific (58)
  Imitation of Life (59)
  It's a Mad Mad Mad Mad World (64)
  Goldfinger (65)
  The Sandpiper (65)
  The Yellow Rolls Royce (65) N/A

1966–1975

  The Russians Are Coming, The Russians Are Coming (66)
  You Only Live Twice (67)
  Casino Royale (67)
  Barefoot in the Park (67)
  Lovers and Other Strangers (70)
  Little Big Man (71)
  The Owl and the Pussycat (71)
  Trial of Billy Jack (74) N/A
  Serpico (74)
  Shampoo (75)

1976–1985

  Blazing Saddles (74)
  Rocky (77)
  Close Encounters of the Third Kind(77)
  Superman (79)
  Every Which Way but Loose (79)
  Private Benjamin (80)
  Stripes (81)
  On Golden Pond (82)
  Police Academy II (85)
  A View to a Kill (85)

Military Subsample

1966–1990: Eleven Films

1966–1975

  1. *Little Big Man
  2. Catch–22

    3. M*A*S*H
    4. Patton

1976–1985

    1. Wargames
    2. *Private Benjamin
    3. *Close Encounters of the Third Kind

1986–1989

    1. *Platoon
    2. Top Gun
    3. Predator
    4. *Good Morning Vietnam

   *Movies from the military subsample that were also picked up in the second random sampling for the forty-year period.

Religion and Supernatural Subsample

1946–1985: Seven Films

1946–1955

    1. Samson and Delilah

1956–1965

    1. Exodus

1966–1975

    1. A Man for All Seasons
    2. Rosemary's Baby
    3. Jesus Christ Superstar

1976–1985

    1. In Search of Noah's Ark
    2. Poltergeist

Total Number of Movies Coded for Study

Original Sample (1946–1985)	89
Second General Sample (1946–1985)	37
Sample Update (1986–1990)	20
Subtotal of General Sample (1946–1990)	146
Military Subsample: 5 of the 11 were picked up in the second general sample (1946–1990)	$11 - 5 = 6$
Religion Subsample (1946–1985)	7
Grand Total	159

Sample Movies: 1990–1994

Another 48 Hours (1990)
Back to the Future III (1990)
Dick Tracy (1990)
Die Hard II (1990)
Ghost (1990)
Home Alone (1990)
The Hunt for Red October (1990)
Pretty Woman (1990)
Addams Family (1991)
City Slickers (1991)
Home Alone II (1991)
The Silence of the Lambs (1991)
Terminator II (1991)
Basic Instinct (1992)
Lethal Weapon III (1992)
Hot Shots Part Deux (1993)
Indecent Proposal (1993)
Sleeping with the Enemy (1993)
Sleepless in Seattle (1993)
Sommersby (1993)
Clear and Present Danger (1994)
The Lion King (1994)
Maverick (1994)
Speed (1994)
True Lies (1994)

References

Abrams, M. H., *et al.*, eds. *The Norton Anthology of English Literature*, Third Edition, Vol. 1 (New York: W. W. Norton & Company, 1974).

Achembach, Thomas M., and Catherine T. Howell. "Are American Children's Problems Getting Worse? A 13 Year Comparison." *The Journal of the American Academy of Child and Adolescent Psychiatry* 32, 6 (November, 1993), pp. 1145–1163.

Almond, Gabriel, and Sidney Verba. *The Civic Culture: Political Attitudes and Democracy in Five Nations: An Analytic Study* (Boston: Little Brown, 1965).

Alter-Read, Karen, *et al.* "Sexual Abuse of Children: A Review of the Empirical Findings." *Clinical Psychology Review* 6 (1986), pp. 249–266.

American Enterprise, "The Export of American Culture." (May/June, 1992), pp. 117–120.

Andrew, Dudley. *Concepts in Film Theory* (Oxford: Oxford University Press, 1984).

Andrews, Suzzana. "The Great Divide: The Sexes at the Box Office." *New York Times* (May 23, 1993), pp. C 15ff.

Anger, Kenneth. *Hollywood Babylon* (San Francisco: Straight Arrow Books, 1975).

Armstrong, Scott. "Tinseltown marks best year ever in tickets sold." *The Christian Science Monitor* (January 6, 1994), p. 4.

Arnold, Edwin, and Eugene Miller. *The Films and Career of Robert Aldrich* (Knoxville: University of Tennessee Press, 1986).

Atkinson, John, ed. *Motives in Fantasy, Action and Society* (New York: Van Nostrand, 1958).

Ayckbourn, Alan. *How the Other Half Loves: A Play in Two Acts* (New York: S. French, 1971).

Balio, Tino, ed. *The American Film Industry* (Madison: University of Wisconsin Press, 1985).

Balio, Tino. *United Artists: The Company that Changed the Film Industry* (Madison: University of Wisconsin Press, 1987).

Baraka, Amiri. "The Poetry of Urgent Necessity." *Poetry East* 20, 21 (Fall, 1986), p. 32.

Barthes, Roland. *Elements of Semiology*, trans. Annette Lavers and Colin Smith. (New York: Noonday Press, Farrar, Straus and Giroux, 1968).

Barthes, Roland. *Image-Music-Text*, trans. Stephen Heath. (New York: Hill and Wang, 1977).

Basinger, Jeanine. *A Woman's View: How Hollywood Spoke to Women, 1930–1960* (New York: Alfred A. Knopf, 1993).

Bates, James. "Video sales, rentals top 17 billion in 92." *Los Angeles Times* (January 9, 1993), p. D1.

Baumgold, Julie. "Killer Women." *New York* (July 29, 1991), pp. 24–29.

Becker, Howard. *Art Worlds* (Berkeley: University of California Press, 1982).

Belden, T. G., and M. R. Belden. *The Lengthening Shadow: The Life of Thomas J. Watson* (Boston: Little Brown, 1962).

Bell, Daniel. *The Coming of Post Industrial Society* (New York: Basic Books, 1973).

Bell, Daniel. *The Cultural Contradictions of Capitalism* (New York: Basic Books, 1976).

Bellah, Robert. *Tokugawa Religion* (Glencoe, Ill.: Free Press, 1957).

Bellah, Robert N., Richard Madsen, William M. Sullivan, Ann Swidler, and Steven M. Tipton. *Habits of the Heart* (Berkeley: University of California Press, 1985).

Bellah, Robert N., et al. *The Good Society* (New York: Knopf, 1991).

Bendix, Rinehard. *Max Weber: An Intellectual Portrait* (New York: Basic Books, 1973).

Benjamin, Walter. *Illuminations*, ed., with an introduction, by Hannah Arendt, trans. Harry Zohn (New York: Schocken Books, 1968).

Bennett, William J. *The Index of Leading Cultural Indicators* (Washington: Heritage Foundation, 1993).

Berger, Peter, and Thomas Luckmann. *The Social Construction of Reality: A Treatise in the Sociology of Knowledge* (Garden City: Doubleday, 1966).

Bergman, Andrew. *We're In the Money: Depression America and Its Films* (New York: New York University Press, 1971).

Bettelheim, Bruno. *The Uses of Enchantment: The Meaning and Importance of Fairy Tales* (New York: Alfred A. Knopf, 1976).

Bird, Kai. *The Chairman: John J. McCloy and the Making of the American Establishment* (New York: Simon and Schuster, 1992).

Blau, Judith. *The Shape of Culture: A Study of Contemporary Social Patterns in the United States* (Cambridge: Cambridge University Press, 1989).

Bock, Philip K. *Rethinking Psychological Anthropology* (New York: W. H. Freeman, 1988).

Bongartz, Roy. "The Chocolate Camelot." *American Heritage* 23, 4 (June, 1973), pp. 4–11, 91–99.

Breskin, David. "Steven Spielberg: The Rolling Stone Interview." *Rolling Stone* 459 (October 24, 1985), pp. 22–24, 70–80.

Brownstein, Ronald. *The Power and the Glitter: The Hollywood-Washington Connection* (New York: Pantheon Books, 1990).

Brunette, Peter, and David Wills. *Screen/play: Derrida and Film Theory* (Princeton: Princeton University Press, 1989).

Bryant, J., and D. Zillman, eds. *Media Effects: Advances in Theory and Research* (Hilsdale, NJ: Lawrence Earlbaum, 1994).

Buckley, Gail L. "When a Kiss Is Not Just a Kiss." *New York Times* (March 31, 1991), 2nd section, pp. 1ff.

Burnett, Ron, ed. *Explorations in Film Theory: Selected Essays from Ciné-Tracts* (Bloomington: Indiana University Press, 1991).

Carlson, Allan C. *Family Questions* (Rutgers: Transaction Books, 1988).

Carroll, Noel. "Back to Basics." *Wilson Quarterly* 10 (Summer, 1986), pp. 58–69.

Centerwall, Brandon S. "Television and Violent Crime." *The Public Interest* 111 (Spring, 1993), pp. 56–71

Chatman, Seymour, ed. *Approaches to Poetics: English Institute Essays, 1972* (New York: Columbia University Press, 1973).

Christensen, Bryce. ed. *When Families Fail: The Social Costs* (Lanham, MD: University Press of America, 1991).

Christensen, Terry. *Reel Politics: American Political Movies from Birth of a Nation to Platoon* (New York: Basil Blackwell, 1987).

Citron, Alan. "Blockbusters lose box office grip." *Los Angeles Times* (June 19, 1991), p. D1.

Cleary, Margot. "The Williston Story." *Hampshire Life* (February 22, 1991), pp. 8–10, 26.

Clover, Carol J., and Michael Rogin, eds. Special Forum: "Entertaining History: American Cinema and Popular Culture." *Representations* 29 (1990), pp. 1–123.

Cohn, Lawrence. "The Box Officer." *Premier* 7, 11 (August, 1994), p. 41.

Comstock, George A. *Television in America* (Beverly Hills: Sage Publications, 1980).

Copperweld Corporation v. Independence Tube Corporation. 1045.CT.2731 (1984).

Coser, Lewis A. *Men of Ideas: A Sociologist's View* (New York: Free Press, 1965).

Coulborn, Rushton. *The Origin of Civilized Societies* (Princeton: Princeton University Press, 1959).

Crane, Diane. *The Production of Culture: Media and the Urban Arts* (Newbury Park, Calif.: Sage Publications, 1992).

Culler, Jonathan D. *Structuralist Poetics; Structuralism, Linguistics and the Study of Literature* (Ithaca: Cornell University Press, 1975).

Culler, Jonathan. *On Deconstruction: Theory and Criticism after Structuralism* (Ithaca: Cornell University Press, 1982).

Dahl, Robert. *Who Governs?: Democracy and Power in an American City* (New Haven: Yale University Press, 1961).

Dahl, Robert A. *After the Revolution? Authority in a Good Society* (New Haven: Yale University Press, 1970).

Dahl, Robert A. *Dilemmas of Pluralist Democracy: Autonomy versus Control* (New Haven: Yale University Press, 1982).

Dahl, Robert A. *Democracy and Its Critics* (New Haven: Yale University Press, 1989).

Dahl, Robert A., and G. William Domhoff. *Who Really Rules? New Haven and Community Power Reexamined* (New Brunswick, N.J.: Transaction Books, 1977).

Daly, Martin, and Margo Wilson. "Evolutionary Social Psychology and Family Homicide." *Science* 242, 4878 (October 28, 1988), pp. 519–524.

Daly, Martin, and Margot Wilson. "Parent-Offspring Conflict and Violence in Evolutionary Perspective." In Nancy J. Bell, ed., *Sociobiology and the Social Sciences* (Lubbock, Tex: Texas Tech University Press, 1989), pp. 25–43.

Daly, Martin, and Margot Wilson. "Cinderella Revisited." *Ethology and Sociobiology* 15, 1 (January, 1994), p. 58.

Dalzell, Robert F., Jr. *Enterprising Elite: The Boston Associates and their World* (Cambridge: Harvard University Press, 1987).

Davis, James Allan, and Tom Smith. *General Social Surveys, 1972–1990,* Principal investigator, James A. Davis; Director and Co-principal investigator, Tom W. Smith. NORC, ed. (Chicago: National Opinion Research Center, producer, 1989; Storrs, Conn: Roper Center for Public Opinion Research, University of Connecticut, distributor).

de Lauretis, Teresa. "Introduction: On the Cinema Topic." *PMLA: Publications of the Modern Language Association of America* 106, 3 (1991), pp. 412–428.

de Man, Paul. *The Resistance to Theory,* foreword by Wlad Godzich (Minneapolis: University of Minnesota Press, 1986).

Demos, John. *Past, Present, and Personal: The Family and the Lifecourse in American History* (New York: Oxford University Press, 1986).

Derrida, Jacques. *Margins of Philosophy,* trans. and additional notes Alan Bass (Chicago: University of Chicago Press, 1982).

Derrida, Jacques. *Of Grammatology,* trans. Gayatri Chakravorty Spivak (Baltimore: Johns Hopkins University Press, 1976).

de Saussure, Ferdinand. *Course in General Linguistics*, trans. Charles Baskin, ed. Charles Bally and Albert Secheheaye with Albert Riedlinger (New York: McGraw-Hill, 1959).

de Vos, George. *Socialization for Achievement: Essays on the Cultural Psychology of the Japanese* (Berkeley: University of California Press, 1973).

Dewey, John. *Individualism Old and New* (New York: Minton, Balch, 1930).

Dimaggio, Paul. *Managers of the Arts* (Washington, D.C.: Seven Locks Press, 1987).

Domhoff, G. William. *Who Rules America?* (Englewood Cliffs, NJ: Prentice-Hall, 1967).

Domhoff, G. William. *Who Rules America Now? A View for the '80s* (Chicago: Guild Books, 1983).

Domhoff, G. William. *The Power Elite and the State: How Policy Is Made in America* (New York: Aldine De Gruyter, 1990).

Dowd, Maureen. "Washington Is Star Struck As Hollywood Gets Serious." *New York Times* (May 9, 1993), pp. A 1ff.

Dreiser, Theodore. *An American Tragedy* (New York: Modern Library, 1956).

Dye, Thomas R. *Who's Running America: The Reagan Years*, Third Edition (Englewood Cliffs, NJ: Prentice-Hall, 1983).

Eco, Umberto. *A Theory of Semiotics* (Bloomington: Indiana University Press, 1976).

Economist, "The Batmogul and the Abyss." (August 26, 1989a), p. 73.

Economist, "The Entertainment Industry: Raising the Stakes." (December 23, 1989b), pp. 3–18.

Economist, "Home Truths for Hollywood." (July 30, 1983), pp. 72–73.

Emery, Robert E. "Children and Divorce: Transition or Trauma?" *The Public Perspective* (March/April, 1991), pp. 23–25.

Erlich, Victor. *Russian Formalism: History-Doctrine*, third edition (New Haven: Yale University Press, 1981).

Facey, Paul. *The Legion of Decency: A Sociological Analysis of the Emergence and Development of a Pressure Group* (New York: Arno Press, 1974).

Faludi, Susan. *Backlash: The Undeclared War Against Women* (New York: Crown, 1991).

Farber, Stephen. *The Movie Rating Game* (Washington, D.C.: Public Affairs Press, 1972).

Farber, Stephen. "George Lucas: The Stinky Kid Hits the Big Time." *Film Quarterly* 27 (Spring, 1974), pp. 2–9.

Faulkner, Robert, and Andy Anderson. "Short Term Projects and Emergent Careers: Evidence from Hollywood." *American Journal of Sociology* 72 (January, 1987), pp. 879–909.

Featherstone, Darin R., *et al.* "Differences in School Behavior and Achievement Between Children from Intact, Reconstituted and Single Parent Families." *Adolescence* 27 (1992), pp. 1–11.

Feldman, Stanley. "Economic Individualism and American Public Opinion." *American Politics Quarterly* 11 (January, 1983), pp. 3–29.

Fish, Stanley. "Why Literary Criticism Is like Virtue." *London Review of Books* 10 (June, 1993), pp. 11–16.

Fitzgerald, F. Scott. *The Great Gatsby*, Vol. 1 of *The Bodley Head Scott Fitzgerald* (London: Bodley Head, 1963).

Frank, Marcie. "The Camera and the Speculum: David Cronenberg's *Dead Ringers*." *PMLA: Publications of the Modern Language Association of America* 106, 3 (1991), pp. 459–470.

Friedan, Betty. *The Feminist Mystique*, 20th anniversary edition (New York: Norton, 1983).

Fuchs, Victor R., and Diane M. Reklis. "Economic Perspectives and Policy Options." *Science* 255 (1992), pp. 41–56.

Gabler, Neal. *An Empire of Their Own: How the Jews Invented Hollywood* (New York, Crown Publishers, 1988).

Galerstein, Carolyn. *Working Women on the Hollywood Screen: A Filmography* (New York: Garland, 1989).

Gallagher, John. *Film Directors on Directing* (New York: Greenwood Press, 1989).

Gans, Herbert J. "Hollywood Entertainment: Commerce or Ideology?" [Brief reply to Prindle and Endersby's "Hollywood Liberalism."] *Social Science Quarterly* 74, 1 (1993), pp. 150–153.

Geertz, Clifford. "Ideology as a Cultural System," in Clifford Geertz, *The Interpretation of Cultures* (New York: Basic Books, 1973).

Gerth, Hans, and C. Wright Mills, eds. *From Max Weber: Essays in Sociology* (London: Kegan Paul, Trench, Trubner and Co., 1947).

Ginsberg, Allen. *Collected Poems, 1947–1980* (New York: Harper and Row, 1984).

Gitlin, Todd. *Popular Culture and High Culture* (New York: Basic Books, 1974).

Gitlin, Todd. *Inside Prime Time* (New York: Pantheon, 1983).

Gledhill, Christine. "Recent Developments in Feminist Criticism," in Gerald Mast and Marshall Cohen, eds. *Film Theory and Criticism: Introductory Readings* (New York: Oxford University Press, 1985), pp. 817–845.

Goldman, Eric F. *The Tragedy of Lyndon Johnson* (New York: Alfred A. Knopf, 1969).

Gomery, Douglas. *The Hollywood Studio System* (London: MacMillan, 1986a).

Gomery, Douglas. "Hollywood's Business." *Wilson Quarterly* 10 (Summer, 1986b), pp. 43–57.

Gordinier, Jeff. "On a Ka-Ching and a Prayer. . . ," *Entertainment* (October 7, 1994), pp. 34–40.

Graber, Doris. "Political Communication: Scope, Progress, Promise," in Ada W. Finifter, ed. *The State of the Discipline II* (Washington: American Political Science Association, 1993), pp. 305–344.

Grenier, Richard. "Around the World in American Ways." *Public Opinion* 9, 1 (February/ March, 1986), pp. 3ff.

Grenier, Richard. *Capturing the Culture: Film, Art and Politics.* (Washington: Ethics and Public Policy Center, 1991).

Grenier, Richard. "Hurrah for Hollywood." (London) *Times Literary Supplement* (July 23, 1993), p. 10.

Gurr, Ted Robert. "On the History of Violent Crime in Europe and America," in H. D. Graham and T. R. Gurr, eds. *Violence in America: Historical and Comparative Perspectives,* revised edition (Beverly Hills, Calif.: Sage Publications, 1979).

Gutmann, D. "The Subjective Politics of Power: The Dilemma of Post-superego man." *Social Research* (Winter, 1973), pp. 570–616.

Gutmann, D. "A Cross-Cultural View of Adult Life in the Extended Family," in K. Riegel and J. Meacham, eds. *The Developing Individual in a Changing World* (Chicago: Aldine, 1976), pp. 364–373.

Halberstam, David. *The Reckoning* (New York: Morrow, 1986).

Halle, David. *Inside Culture: Art and Class in the American Home* (Chicago: University of Chicago Press, 1993).

Hamburg, David. *Today's Children: Creating a Future for a Generation in Crisis* (New York: Random House, 1992).

Harootunian, H.D. *Towards Restoration: The Growth of Political Consciousness in Tokugawa Japan* (Berkeley: University of California, 1970).

Harries, Karsten. "Metaphor and Transcendence," in Sheldon Sacks, ed. *On Metaphor* (Chicago: University of Chicago Press, 1979), pp. 71–88.

Hartz, Louis. *The Liberal Tradition in America* (New York: Harcourt Brace, 1955).

Haskell, Molly. *From Reverence to Rape: The Treatment of Women in the Movies,* second edition (Chicago: University of Chicago Press, 1987).

Heckman, James J. "Is Job Training Oversold?" *The Public Interest* 115 (Spring, 1994), pp. 91–115.

Hirschman, Albert O. *The Passions and the Interests: Political Arguments for Capitalism Before Its Triumph* (Princeton: Princeton University Press, 1977).

Hurley, Neil. *The Reel Revolution: A Film Primer on Revolution* (Maryknoll, N.Y.: Orbis Books, 1978).

Isaacson, Walter, and Evan Thomas. *The Wise Men* (New York: Simon and Schuster, 1986).

Jackson, Robert Louis, and Stephen Rudy. *Russian Formalism: A Retrospective Glance. A Festschrift in Honor of Victor Erlich* (New Haven: Yale Center for International and Area Studies, 1985), p. l65.

Jacobs, Diane. *Hollywood Renaissance* (Cranbury, N.J.: Tantivy Press, 1977).

Jakobson, Roman. *Language in Literature*, eds. Krystyna Pomorska and Stephen Rudy (Cambridge: Belknap Press of Harvard University Press, 1987).

James, David. "Rock and Roll in Representations of the Invasion of Vietnam." Special Forum, "Entertaining History: American Cinema and Popular Culture." *Representations* 29 (Winter, 1990), pp. 78–98.

Jameson, Fredric. *The Ideologies of Theory: Essays 1971–1986*, 2 vols. (Minneapolis: University of Minnesota Press, 1988).

Jameson, Fredric. *The Prison-House of Language: A Critical Account of Structuralism and Russian Formalism* (Princeton: Princeton University Press, 1972).

Janowitz, Morris. *The Reconstruction of Patriotism* (Chicago: University of Chicago Press, 1983).

Jeffers, Robinson. *The Selected Poetry of Robinson Jeffers* (New York: Random House, 1935).

Jowett, Garth, and James Linton. *Movies as Mass Communication* (Beverly Hills, Calif.: Sage Publications, 1980).

Kant, Immanuel. *The Critique of Pure Reason,* trans. F. Max Müller (Garden City: Doubleday, 1966).

Kearney, Jill. "Francis Ford Coppola Simply Wants to Create a New Art Form." *Mother Jones* 13 (September, 1988), pp. 19–24.

Keller, Suzanne. *Beyond the Ruling Class* (New York: Random House, 1963).

Kellstedt, Lyman A., *et al.* "Religious Traditions and Religious Commitments in the USA." Paper prepared for the 22nd International Conference for the Sociology of Religion, Budapest, Hungary, July 19–23, 1993.

Kerouac, Jack. *On the Road* (New York: Penguin, 1976).

Keyser, Les, and Barbara Keyser. *Hollywood and the Catholic Church: The Image of Roman Catholicism in American Movies* (Chicago: Loyola University Press, 1984).

Kilday, Gregg. "Two or Three Things We Know About the Eighties, Eighties, Eighties." *Film Comment* (November/December, 1989), pp. 60–66.

Klinger, Barbara. "In Retrospect: Film Studies Today." *Yale Journal of Criticism* 2, 1 (1988), pp. 129–151.

Kris, Ernst. *Psychoanalytic Explorations in Art* (New York: International Universities Press, 1952).

Kristol, Irving. *Two Cheers for Capitalism* (New York: Basic Books, 1978).

Kroll, Jack. "Altman's New Stage." *Newsweek* (October 26, 1981), p. 72.

Lacayo, Richard. "Law and Disorder." *Time* (April 1, 1991), pp. 18–21.

Lacey, Robert. *Ford: The Man and the Machine* (Boston: Little Brown, 1986).

Ladd, Everett Carll, *et al.* "Participating Citizens in the Individualist Society." *The Public Perspective* 5, 3 (March/April, 1994), pp. 13–18.

Lane, Robert E. "The Dialectics of Freedom in a Market Society." Department of Political Science, University of Illinois at Urbana, 1979.

Lane, Robert E. "Personal Freedom in a Market Society." *Society* 18 (March-April, 1981a), pp. 63–76.

Lane, Robert E. "Markets and Politics: The Human Product." *British Journal of Political Science* II (1981b), pp. 1–16.

LaPiere, Richard T. *Social Change* (New York: McGraw Hill, 1965).

Lasch, Christopher. *Haven in a Heartless World* (New York: McGraw-Hill, 1977).

Lasch, Christopher. *The Culture of Narcissism* (New York: W. W. Norton, 1978).

Lasch, Christopher. *The Minimal Self* (New York: W. W. Norton, 1985).

Lasswell, Harold. *Politics: Who Gets What, When, How* (New York: P. Smith, 1950).

Lasswell, Harold. *The World Revolution of Our Time: A Framework for Basic Policy Research* (Stanford: Stanford University Press, 1951).

Lasswell, Harold, and Daniel Lerner. *The Comparative Study of Elites* (Stanford: Stanford University Press, 1952).

Lasswell, Harold D., *et al. Propaganda and Communication in World History: A Pluralizing World in Formation*, Vol. 3 (Honolulu: University Press of Hawaii, 1980).

Lauretis, Teresa de. See "de Lauretis."

Lazere, D., ed. *American Media and Mass Culture* (Berkeley: University of California Press, 1987).

Leff, Leonard, and Jerold Simmons. *The Dame in the Kimono: Hollywood, Censorship, and the Production Code from the 1920s to the 1960s* (London: Weidenfeld and Nicolson, 1990).

Leims, Thomas. "Sensationsjournalismus, Sex und Gewalt in japanischen Fernsehen- Japanologische Anmerkungen zu einem aktuellen Thema." *Communications* 18 (1993), pp. 355–379.

Leites, Edmund. *The Puritan Conscience and Modern Sexuality* (New Haven: Yale University Press, 1986).

Lerner, Robert, Althea K. Nagai, and Stanley Rothman. "Marginality and Liberalism Among Jewish Elites." *Public Opinion Quarterly* 53 (Fall, 1989), pp. 330–352.

Lerner, Robert, Althea K. Nagai, and Stanley Rothman. "Elite Dissensus and Its Origins." *Journal of Political and Military Sociology* 18 (Summer, 1990), pp. 25–39.

Lerner, Robert, Althea Nagai, and Stanley Rothman. *Molding the Good Citizen: The Politics of High School History Texts* (Westport, CT: Greenwood/Praeger, 1995).

Lerner, Robert, Althea Nagai, and Stanley Rothman. *American Elites* (New Haven: Yale University Press, 1996).

Levine, Donald N. *Wax and Gold* (Chicago: University of Chicago Press, 1965).

Li, Jiang Hong, and Roger A. Wojtkiewicz. "A New Look at the Effects of Family Structure on Status Attainment." *Social Science Quarterly* 73 (1992), pp. 581–595.

Lichter, S. Robert, Stanley Rothman, and Linda S. Lichter. *The Media Elite: America's New Powerbrokers* (Bethesda, Md.: Adler and Adler, 1986).

Lichter, S. Robert, Linda Lichter, and Stanley Rothman. *Watching America: What TV Tells Us About Our Lives* (New York: Prentice Hall, 1991).

Lichter, S. Robert, Linda Lichter, and Stanley Rothman. *Prime Time* (Washington: Regnery, 1994).

Lifton, Robert J. *Protean Man* (New York: Basic Books, 1994).

Lipset, Seymour Martin. *The First New Nation* (New York: Basic Books, 1967).

Lipset, Seymour Martin. "Why No Socialism in the United States?" in S. Bialer and S. Sluzer, eds., *Sources of Contemporary Radicalism* (Boulder: Westview Press, 1977).

Lipset, Seymour Martin. *Continental Divide* (New York: Routledge, 1990).

Litwak, Mark. *Reel Power: The Struggle for Influence and Success in the New Hollywood* (New York: William Morrow, 1986).

Liu, Alan. "The Power of Formalism: The New Historicism." *English Literary History* 56 (1989), pp. 721–771.

Los Angeles Times, "Independent Films Cash in Abroad." (January 22, 1993), p. D2.

Lowenthal, Leo. "Biographies in Popular Magazines," in P. F. Lazarsfeld and F. Stanton, eds. *Radio Research: 1942–1943* (New York: Duell, Sloan and Pearce, 1944).

Luker, Kristin. *Abortion and the Politics of Motherhood* (Berkeley: University of California Press, 1984).

MacCann, Richard. *Hollywood in Transition* (Boston: Houghton Mifflin, 1962).

Madsen, Axel. *The New Hollywood: American Movies in the '70s* (New York: Thomas Crowell, 1975).

Marcuse, Herbert. *Eros and Civilization* (Boston: Beacon Press, 1955).

Marcuse, Herbert. *One-Dimensional Man: Studies in the Ideology of Advanced Industrial Society* (Boston: Beacon Press, 1964).

Margolin, Leslie. "Child Abuse by Mothers' Boyfriends: Why the Overrepresentation?" *Child Abuse and Neglect* 16 (1992), pp. 541–552.

Marradi, Alberto. "Factor Analysis as an Aid in the Formation and Refinement of Empirically Useful Concepts," in David J. Jackson and Edgar F. Borgatta, *Factor Analysis and Measurement in Sociological Research: A Multi-Dimensional Approach* (Beverly Hills, Calif.: Sage, 1981), pp. 11–49.

Marx, Karl. *The Poverty of Philosophy* (Moscow: Foreign Languages Publishing House, 1956).

Maslin, Janet. "Give Him a Puppy. And Get the Lady a Gun." *New York Times* (July 21, 1991), section 2, pp. 1ff.

Maslin, Janet. "Is NC–17 an X in a Clean Raincoat?" *New York Times* (October 21, 1990), pp. 1, 25.

Mason, Michael. *The Making of Victorian Sexuality* (New York: Oxford University Press, 1993).

Mast, Gerald, ed. *The Movies in Our Midst: Documents in the Cultural History of Film in America* (Chicago: University of Chicago Press, 1982).

Mast, Gerald, and Marshall Cohen, eds. *Film Theory and Criticism: Introductory Readings*, third edition (New York: Oxford University Press, 1985).

Mathews, Jay. "Maverick Movie Producers Turn Financier for Backing." *Washington Post* (April 17, 1994), p. H4.

McAdams, Dan. *Intimacy and the Life Story* (New York: Guilford Press, 1988).

McAdams, Dan. *The Need to be Close* (New York: Doubleday, 1989).

McBride, Joseph. *Filmmakers on Filmmaking* (Boston: Houghton Mifflin, 1983).

McClelland, David. *The Achieving Society* (New York: Free Press, 1961).

McClelland, David. *Power: The Inner Experience* (New York: John Wiley and Sons, 1975).

McClosky, Herbert, and John Zaller. *The American Ethos: Public Attitudes Toward Capitalism and Democracy* (Cambridge: Harvard University Press, 1984).

McGauhey, Peggy J., and Barbara Starfield. "Child Health and the Social Environment of White and Black Children." *Social Science and Medicine* 36 (1993), pp. 867–874.

McGilligan, Pat. "Point Man: Oliver Stone Interviewed by Pat McGilligan." *Film Comment* 23 (February, 1987), pp. 11–20, 60.

McGuire, William J. "Possible Excuses for Claiming Mass Media Effects Despite the Weak Evidence." In Rothman, ed., *Mass Media in Liberal Democratic Societies* (New York: Paragon House (1992), pp. 121–146.

Medved, Michael. "Hollywood vs. Religion." *Imprimis* 18, 12 (December, 1989).

Medved, Michael. *Hollywood vs. America: Popular Culture and the War on Traditional Values* (New York: Harper Collins, 1992).

Medved, Michael. "Hollywood's Dirty Little Secrets." *Crisis* (March, 1993), pp. 18–22.

Merelman, Richard. *Making Something of Ourselves* (Berkeley: University of California Press, 1984).

Metz, Christian. *Film Language: A Semiotics of the Cinema*, trans. Michael Taylor (New York: Oxford University Press, 1974a).

Metz, Christian. *Language and Cinema*, trans. Donn Jean Umiker-Sebeok (The Hague: Mouton, 1974b).

Metz, Christian. *The Imaginary Signifier: Psychoanalysis and the Cinema*, trans. Celia Britton, Annwyl Williams, Ben Brewster, and Alfred Guzzetti (Bloomington: Indiana University Press, 1982).

Metzger, Thomas A. *Escape from Predicament* (New York: Columbia University Press, 1977).

Meyerowitz, Joanne. "The Mystique That Wasn't: A Reassessment of Postwar Mass Culture, 1946–1958," *Journal of American History* (March, 1993), pp. 1455–1482.

Meyrowitz, Joshua. *No Sense of Place: The Impact of Electronic Media on Social Behavior* (New York: Oxford University Press, 1985).

Milavsky, J. Ronald, *et al. Television and Aggression: Results of a Panel Study* (New York: Academic Press, 1983).

Miller, Mark Crispin, ed. *Seeing Through Movies* (New York: Pantheon Books, 1990).

Miller, Perry, and Thomas H. Johnson. *The Puritans*, Revised Edition (New York: Harper and Row, 1963).

Mills, C. Wright. *The Power Elite* (New York: Oxford University Press, 1956).

Mills, Nicolaus. "Reaganizing Hollywood." *Dissent* 31 (Spring, 1984), pp. 230–232.

Morishima, Michio. *Why has Japan Succeeded: Western Technology and the Japanese Ethos* (New York: Cambridge University Press, 1984).

Monaco, James. *American Film Now: The People, the Power, the Money, the Movies* (New York: Oxford University Press, 1979).

Monaco, Paul. *Ribbons in Time: Movies and Society Since 1945* (Bloomington: Indiana University Press, 1987).

Morley, David. *The Nationwide Audience: Structure and Decoding* (London: British Film Institute, 1980).

Morrow, Lance. "Rough Justice." *Time* (April 1, 1991), pp. 16–17.

Mosley, Leonard. *Zanuck: The Rise and Fall of Hollywood's Last Tycoon* (Boston: Little, Brown, 1984).

Mosca, Gaetano. *The Ruling Class* (New York: McGraw-Hill, 1939).

Mott, Donald, and Cheryl Saunders. *Steven Spielberg* (Boston: Twayne, 1986).

Mulvey, Laura. *Visual and Other Pleasures* (Bloomington: Indiana University Press, 1989).

Murray, Charles, and R. J. Herrnstein. "What's Really Behind the SAT-Score Decline?" *The Public Interest* 106 (Winter, 1992), pp. 32–56.

Murray, Charles, and R. J. Herrnstein. "The Coming White Underclass." *Wall Street Journal* (October 29, 1993), pp. A14.

Nagai, Althea, Robert Lerner, and Stanley Rothman. *Giving for Social Change* (Westport, Conn.: Greenwood/Praeger, 1994).

National Institutes of Mental Health. *Television and Behavior: Ten Years of Scientific Progress and Implications for the Eighties*, Vols. 1 and 2 (Washington: GPO, 1982).

Newcomb, Horace, and Robert S. Alley. *The Producer's Medium* (New York: Oxford University Press, 1983).

New York Times (May 30, 1994), 1ff.

New York Times (May 29, 1994), 1ff.

New York Times (May 9, 1993), 1, 22.

New York Times (January 30, 1994), section 2, 1ff.

New York Times (June 6, 1992), 28.

New York Times (May 31, 1992), section 9, 1ff.

New York Times (June 7, 1991), 1 ff.

Nichols, Bill, ed. *Movies and Methods* (Berkeley: University of California Press, 1976).

Nichols, Peter. "Big May Be Beautiful in Most Stores, But Small Films Put Out By Small Companies Do Have a Niche." *New York Times* (September 24, 1992), pp. B4, C17.

Nisbet, Robert. "Introduction: The Problem of Social Change," in Robert Nisbet, ed., *Social Change* (New York: Harper and Row, 1972).

Norman, Barry. *The Story of Hollywood* (New York: NAL Penguin, 1987).

O'Brien, Tom. *The Screening of America: Movies and Values from* Rocky *to* Rain Man (New York: Continuum, 1990).

O'Connell, Brian, ed. *America's Voluntary Spirit* (New York: The Foundation Center, 1983).

Paik, HeaJung, and George Comstock. "The Effects of Television Violence on Anti-Social Behavior: A Meta-Analysis," *Communication Research* 21 (1994), pp. 516–546.

Pareto, Vilfredo. *Sociological Writings* (New York: Praeger, 1966).

Parker, Jonathan. "Politics and Television Entertainment: Issue Content in Prime-Time Television Drama." Prepared for Delivery at the 1994 Annual Meeting of the American Political Science Association.

Phillips, David, and John E. Hensley. "When Violence Is Rewarded or Punished: The Impact of Mass Media Stories on Homicide." *Journal of Communication,* Vol 34, 3 (Summer, 1984), pp. 101–116.

Phillips, Gene. *Major Film Directors of the American and British Cinema* (Bethlehem, Pa.: Lehigh University Press, 1990).

Phillips, Roderick. *Putting Asunder: A History of Divorce in Western Society* (New York: Cambridge University Press, 1988).

Playboy, "Playboy Interview: Martin Scorsese." (April, 1991), pp. 57–161.

PMLA: Publications of the Modern Language Association of America, Special topic: "Cinema." 106, 3 (May, 1991), pp. 412–470.

Pogel, Nancy. *Woody Allen* (Boston: Twayne , 1987).

Poloakow, Valerie. *Lives on the Edge: Single Mothers and Their Children in the Other America* (Chicago: University of Chicago Press, 1993).

Postman, Neil. *Amusing Ourselves to Death: Public Discourse in the Age of Show Business* (New York: Viking, 1985).

Powers, Stephen P., David J. Rothman, and Stanley Rothman. "Hollywood Views the Military." *Society* 28, 1 (1990), pp. 79–84.

Powers, Stephen P., David J. Rothman, and Stanley Rothman. "Hollywood Movies, Society and Political Criticism." *The World and I*, April 1991a, pp. 563–581.

Powers, Stephen P., David J. Rothman, and Stanley Rothman. "Hollywood's Class Act." *Society* 29, 2 (1991b), pp. 57–64.

Powers, Stephen P., David J. Rothman, and Stanley Rothman. "The Transformation of the Hollywood Elite: A History," in Stanley Rothman, ed., *The Mass Media in Liberal Democratic Societies* (New York: Paragon House, 1992).

Powers, Stephen, David J. Rothman, and Stanley Rothman. "The Transformation of Gender Roles in Hollywood Movies: 1946–1990." *Political Communication* 10, 3 (Fall, 1993): pp. 259–283.

Prindle, David. *The Politics of Glamour: Ideology and Democracy in the Screen Actors Guild* (Madison: University of Wisconsin Press, 1988).

Prindle, David. *Risky Business: The Political Economy of Hollywood* (Boulder: Westview Press, 1993).

Prindle, David, and James W. Endersby. "Hollywood Liberalism." *Social Science Quarterly* 74, 1 (March, 1993), pp. 137–156.

Proudhon, P. J. *System of Economical Contradictions or The Philosophy of Misery* (New York: Arno Press, 1972).

Putnam, Robert D. "The Strange Disappearance of Civic America," *The American Prospect* 24 (Winter 1996), pp. 34–48.

Pye, Lucian W., ed. *Communications and Political Development* (Princeton: Princeton University Press, 1963).

Pye, Michael, and Lynda Myles. *The Movie Brats: How the Film Generation Took Over Hollywood* (New York: Holt, Rinehart and Winston, 1979).

Quart, Leonard, and Albert Auster. *American Film and Society Since 1945* (New York: Praeger Publishers, 1984).

Rebhorn, Marlette. *Screening America: Using Hollywood Films To Teach History* (New York: Lang, 1988).

Representations: Entertaining History: American Cinema and Popular Culture 29 (Winter 1990).

Ressner, Jeffrey. "The Burning Truth." *Rolling Stone* (November 17, 1988), pp. 45–48.

Rockwell, John. "The New Colossus: American Culture as Power Export." *New York Times* (January 30, 1994), Arts and Leisure section, p. 1, 30.

Rogin, Michael. "'Make My Day!': Spectacle as Amnesia in Imperial Politics." *Representations* 29 (Winter, 1990), pp. 99–123.

Rosen, Philip, ed. *Narrative, Apparatus, Ideology: A Film Theory Reader* (New York: Columbia University Press, 1986).

Rosenberg, Nathan, and L. E. Birdzell, Jr. *How the West Grew Rich: The Economic Transformation of the Industrial World* (New York: Basic Books, 1986).

Rossi, Alice. "Parenthood in Transition," in Jane B. Lancaster, Jeanne Altman, Alice Rossi, and Lonnie R. Sherrod, eds., *Parenting Across the Lifespan* (New York: Aldine, 1987).

Rosten, Leo. *Hollywood: The Movie Colony, the Movie Makers* (New York: Harcourt, Brace, 1941).

Rothman, Stanley. "Intellectuals and the New Left: A Reassessment." *The Journal of Psychohistory* 5 (Spring, 1978), pp. 552–566.

Rothman, Stanley, ed. *The Mass Media in Liberal Democratic Societies* (New York: Paragon House, 1992a).

Rothman, Stanley. "Liberalism and the Decay of the American Political Economy." *Journal of Socio-Economics* 21, 4 (1992b), pp. 277–301.

Rothman, Stanley. *The End of the Experiment: The Decline of Liberal Capitalism in the United States* (forthcoming).

Rothman, Stanley, and S. Robert Lichter. *Roots of Radicalism: Jews, Christians, and the New Left* (New York: Oxford University Press, 1982).

Rothman, Stanley, and S. Robert Lichter. "Personality, Ideology and World View: A Comparison of Media and Business Elites." *British Journal of Political Science* 15, 1 (1984a), pp. 29–49.

Rothman, Stanley, and S. Robert Lichter. "What Are Movie-makers Made Of?" *Public Opinion* (December/January 1984b), pp. 14–18.

Rothman, Stanley, and S. Robert Lichter. "Elite Ideology and Risk Perception in Nuclear Energy Policy." *American Political Science Review* 81, 2 (June, 1987), pp. 383–404.

Rothman, Stanley, S. Robert Lichter, and Linda Lichter. *Elites in Conflict: Social Change in America Today* (Westport, Conn.: Greenwood/Praeger, forthcoming).

Rowland, Willard D. *The Politics of TV Violence* (Beverly Hills, Calif.: Sage Publications, 1983).

Rozman, Gilbert, ed. *The East Asian Region: Confucian Heritage and its Modern Adaptation* (Princeton: Princeton University Press, 1991).

Ryan, Michael, and Douglas Kellner. *Camera Politica: The Politics and Ideology of Contemporary Hollywood Film* (Bloomington: Indiana University Press, 1988).

Sacks, Sheldon, ed. *On Metaphor* (Chicago: University of Chicago Press, 1979).

Sajak, Pat. "We've Got a Little Secret (or Two)." *National Review* (November 21, 1994), pp. 71–72.

Sameroff, Arnold, *et al.* "Stability of Intelligence from Pre-School to Adolescence: The Influence of Social and Family Factors." *Child Development* 64 (1993), pp. 80–97.

Saussure, Ferdinand de. See "de Saussure".

Schafer, Roy. "The Loving and Beloved Superego," in Ruth S. Eisler *et al.*, eds., *The Psychoanalytic Study of the Child* XV (New York: International Universities Press, 1960).

Schatz, Thomas. *The Genius of the System: Hollywood Filmmaking in the Studio Era* (New York: Pantheon Books, 1988).

Schickel, Richard. "The Crisis in Movie Narrative." *Gannet Center Journal* (Summer, 1989), pp. 1–8.

Sebeok, Thomas A., ed. *Style in Language* (New York: Technology Press of Massachusetts Institute of Technology and John Wiley & Sons, 1960).

Shales, Tom. "Woody: The First Fifty Years." *Esquire* 107 (April, 1987), pp. 88–95.

Sharkey, Betsy. "Knocking on Hollywood's Door." *American Film* 14, 9 (July/August, 1989), pp. 22–27, 52–54.

Shaw, Bernard. *Pygmalion: A Romance in Five Acts* (Baltimore: Penguin Books, 1951).

Shils, Edward. "Learning and Liberalism," in Edward Shils, ed., *The Calling of Sociology and Other Essays on the Pursuit of Learning* (Chicago: University of Chicago Press, 1980), pp. 289–355.

Short, Thomas. "A New Racism on Campus?" *Commentary* 86, 2 (August, 1988), pp. 46–50.

Sidorsky, David. "Moral Pluralism and Philanthropy," in Ellen Frankel Paul, Fred D. Miller, Jr., Jeffrey Paul, and John Ahrens, eds., *Beneficence, Philanthropy, and the Public Good* (Oxford and New York: Basil Blackwell, 1987), pp. 93–112.

Sight and Sound, "Altman Talking." 50 (Summer, 1981), pp. 184–187.

Simon, John G. "Foundations and Public Controversy: An Affirmative View," in Fritz F. Heinmann, ed., *The Future of Foundations* (Englewood Cliffs, N.J.: Prentice-Hall, 1973), pp. 43–57.

Singal, Daniel J. "The Other Crisis in American Education." *Atlantic Monthly* (November 1991), pp. 59–74.

Singer, Isaac. "The Talk of the Town." *New Yorker* (November 17, 1975), pp. 39–40.

Sinyard, Neil. *The Films of Richard Lester* (London: Croom Helm, 1985).

Sitkoff, Harvard. "The New Deal and Race Relations," in Harvard Sitkoff, ed., *Fifty Years Later: The New Deal Evaluated* (Philadelphia: Temple University Press, 1985), pp. 93–112.

Siwek, Stephen E. "The Dimensions of the Export of American Mass Culture." Conference paper, American Enterprise Institute, "The New Global Popular Culture," March 10, 1992.

Smilgis, Martha. "Hollywood Goes to Heaven." *Time*, June 3, 1991, pp. 70–71.

Smith, Barbara Herrnstein. *Contingencies of Value: Alternative Perspectives for Critical Theory* (Cambridge: Harvard University Press, 1988).

Smith, Dian. *American Filmmakers Today* (New York: Simon and Schuster, 1983).

Smith, James Allen. *The Idea Brokers: Think Tanks and the Rise of the New Policy Elite* (New York: Free Press, 1991).

Smith, T. V. "The New Deal as a Cultural Phenomenon." In F.S.C. Northrop, ed., *Ideological Differences and World Order* (New Haven: Yale University Press, 1949), pp. 208–228.

Sobchack, Vivian. "'Surge and Splendor': A Phenomenology of the Hollywood Historical Epic." *Representations* 29 (1990), pp. 24–49.

Solomon, Richard H. *Mao's Revolution and the Chinese Political Culture* (Berkeley: University of California Press, 1971).

Stanmeyer, William A. "National Committee for Responsive Philanthropy." *Institution Analysis* 8 (August, 1978), pp. 1–17.

Statistical Abstracts of the United States, 1992, 112th Edition (Washington: Government Printing Office, 1992).

Stein, Ben. *The View from Sunset Boulevard* (New York: Basic Books, 1979).

Stewart, Abigail, ed. *Motivation and Society: a Volume in Honor of David C. McClelland* (San Francisco: Jossey-Bass, 1982).

Stolber, Andrea, and Paul R. Amato. "Single Parent Households and Children's Behavior." *Sociological Quarterly* 34 (1993), pp. 269–282.

Suid, Lawrence. *Guts and Glory: Great American War Movies* (Reading, Mass.: Addison-Wesley Publishing Co., 1978).

Sundquist, James L. *Politics and Policy: The Eisenhower, Kennedy, and Johnson Years* (Washington: Brookings Institution, 1968).

Sutton, Francis X. "Introduction," in Dwight Macdonald, *The Ford Foundation: The Men and the Millions* (New Brunswick, N.J.: Transaction, 1989), pp. vii-xxi.

Tavris, Carol. "Beware the Incest Survivor Machine." *New York Times Book Review* (January 3, 1993), pp. 1ff.

Taylor, John. *Strangers in Paradise: The Hollywood Emigres, 1933–1950* (New York: Holt, Rinehart and Winston, 1983).

Theobald, Robin. "Patrimonialism." *World Politics* 34 (December, 1982), pp. 548–559.

Time, September 8, 1986, p. 57.

Trattner, Walter I. *From Poor Law to Welfare State*, second edition (New York: Free Press, 1979).

Traube, Elizabeth G. *Dreaming Identities: Class, Gender, and Generation in 1980s Hollywood Movies* (Boulder: Westview Press, 1992).

Trilling, Lionel. *Beyond Culture* (New York: Viking Press, 1965).

Trolander, Judith Ann. *Professionalism and Social Change: From the Settlement House Movement to Neighborhood Centers 1896 to the Present* (New York: Columbia University Press, 1987).

United States v. Paramount Pictures. 68S.CT.915 (1946).

Useem, Michael. "Corporate Philanthropy," in Walter W. Powell, ed. *The Nonprofit Sector: A Research Handbook* (New Haven: Yale University Press, 1987), pp. 340–359.

U.S. News and World Report, "A Conversation with Francis Coppola." (April 5, 1982), p. 68.

Verba, Sidney, and Gary R. Orren. *Equality in America: The View from the Top* (Cambridge: Harvard University Press, 1985).

Vos, George de. See "de Vos."

Walker, Beverly. "The Disappearing Director." *Film Comment* (January/February, 1989), pp. 28–31.

Wallace, A.F.C. *Rockdale* (New York: Alfred A. Knopf, 1978).

Wall Street Journal, "Hollywood Official Gives Gloomy Picture for Studios." (February 6, 1991), p. B6.

Walton, Ann D., and F. Emerson Andrews, eds. *The Foundation Directory, Edition 1* (New York: Russell Sage, 1960).

Watson, Frank Dekker. *The Charity Organization Movement in the United States* (New York: Macmillan, 1922).

Watters, Jim. "The New Hollywood Hotshots." *Life Magazine* (April, 1979), pp. 34–44.

Weaver, Warren. *U.S. Philanthropic Foundations: Their History, Structure, Management, and Record* (New York: Harper and Row, 1967).

Weber, Max. *The Protestant Ethic and the Spirit of Capitalism*, trans. Talcott Parsons (New York: Scribner's, 1930, originally published 1905).

Weber, Max. "The Protestant Sects and the Spirit of Capitalism," in Hans Gerth and C. Wright Mills, eds., *From Max Weber: Essays in Sociology* (London: Kegan Paul, Trench, Trubner, 1947).

Weinraub, Bernard. "Hollywood Grants Team to Create Major Movie Studio: Katzenberg to Join with Spielberg and Geffen." *New York Times*, October 13, 1994, p. A1.

Weinraub, Bernard. "Women Criticizing Women's Film Roles." *New York Times* (June 2, 1993), pp. c 25ff.

Weinstein, F., and Gerald Platt. *The Wish To Be Free* (Berkeley: University of California Press, 1969).

Whitehead, Barbara Dafoe. "Dan Quayle Was Right." *Atlantic Monthly* (April, 1993), pp. 47ff.

Wilson, James Q., and Richard J. Herrnstein. *Crime and Human Nature* (New York: Simon and Schuster, 1985).

Wilson, William Julius. "Poverty, Joblessness and Family Structure in the Inner City." A paper delivered at Chicago Urban Poverty and Family Life Conference, October, 1991.

Winter, David. *The Power Motive* (New York: Free Press, 1973).

Winter, David, and Abigail Stewart. "The Power Motive," in Harvey London and John Exner, eds., *Dimensions of Personality* (New York: John Wiley and Sons, 1978), pp. 391–447.

Wohlfert, Lee. "Robert Altman's New Play: Directing Six Women!" *Harper's Bazaar* (February, 1982), pp. 136–137, 165.

Wood, Michael. *America in the Movies: or "Santa Maria, It Had Slipped My Mind"* (New York: Basic Books, 1975).

Woodhouse, A.S.P., ed. *Puritanism and Liberty* (Chicago: University of Chicago Press, 1951).

Wright, Will. *Six Guns and Society* (Berkeley: University of California Press, 1975).

Yang, Ni, and Daniel Linz. "Movie Ratings and the Content of Adult Videos: The Sex-Violence Ratio." *Journal of Communications* 40 (Spring, 1990), pp. 28–41.

Zeldow, Peter B., *et al.* "Intimacy, Power and Psychological Well Being in Medical Students." *Journal of Nervous and Mental Disease* 176, 3 (March, 1988), pp. 182–187.

Zolberg, Vera. *Constructing a Sociology of the Arts* (New York: Cambridge University Press, 1990).

SUPREME COURT CASES CITED

Burstyn v. Wilson 343 U.S. 495 (1951).
United States v. Paramount Pictures Inc. 334 U.S. 131 (1948).

About the Book and Authors

American motion pictures still dominate the world market with an impact that is difficult to measure. Their role in American culture has been a powerful one since the 1930s and is a hallmark of our culture today. Though much has been written about the film industry, there has been very little systematic attention paid to the ideology of its creative elite. How does the outlook of that elite impact the portrayals of America that appear on the screen? How do their views interact with the demands of the market and the structure of the industry to determine the product that is seen by mass audiences?

Hollywood's America is a marvelously rich and careful discussion of these questions. It combines a meticulous systematic content analysis of fifty years of top-grossing films with a history of the changing structure of the industry. To that mixture it adds an in-depth survey of Hollywood's creative elite, comparing them to other leadership groups. The result is a balanced discussion of unique breadth and depth on a subject of national importance.

Placing the film industry in the context of American society as a whole, the authors point out that Hollywood's creative leadership impacts the larger society even as it is influenced by that society. The creators of films cannot remove themselves too far from the values of the audiences that they serve. However, the fact that films are made by a relatively small number of people, who, as the authors demonstrate, tend to share a common outlook, means that, over time, motion pictures have had an undeniable impact on the beliefs, lifestyles, and action of Americans.

This study contributes to the debate over the role and influence of those who create and distribute the products of mass culture in the United States.

The book also contains a devastating critique of the poststructuralist theories that currently dominate academic film criticism, demonstrating how they fail in their attempt to explain the political significance of motion pictures.

Stephen Powers is a research associate at the Center for the Study of Social Change and Political Change at Smith College. **David J. Rothman** holds a Ph.D. in English with a concentration on Poetics from New York University. He teaches English at Western State College of Colorado, in Gunnison, and lives with his family in nearby Crested Butte. **Stanley Rothman**, coauthor of *American Elites* (1996) among numerous books, is director of the Center for the Study of Social and Political Change and is Mary Huggins Gamble Professor of Government Emeritus at Smith College.

Index

Abortion, 56–57, 61, 64, 169
Academic community, 13(n17), 78(n3), 203, 204, 209–210
Addams Family, The, 192
Aldrich, Robert, 47
Alice Doesn't Live Here Anymore, 48
Alien, 123, 137
Alienation, 208, 212
Allen, Woody, 45, 49
Altman, Robert, 28, 30, 45, 47–48
American Tragedy, An, 141
Amerindians portrayed in film, 176–178, 180, 181(table)
Amityville Horror, The, 132
Andrew, James Dudley, 218, 224, 225
Andromeda Strain, 183
Another 48 Hours, 189, 190
Anti-establishment, 104
  attitude of filmmakers, 28, 33–34, 46–52, 67, 77
  themes in film, 30, 33–34, 47, 86, 91, 93, 97, 111–112
  See also Hollywood elite, as anti-authoritarian
Antigenre film, 33, 34
Anti-hero, 27
Antitrust violations
  Burstyn v. Wilson (1952), 20–21
  Copperweld Corp. v. Independence Tube Corp. (1984), 34
  and Music Corporation of America, 22
  Sherman Antitrust Act, 20, 34
  United States v. Paramount Pictures, Inc. (1948), 16, 17, 19–20, 21
Apartment, The, 142, 159, 162

Apocalypse Now, 28, 48
Arthur, 142–143, 151
Asians portrayed in film, 175–178, 180, 181(table), 183, 184
  assimilation of, 183, 184
  and crime, 180, 181(table)
Audience, 10, 36
  Afro-American, 172
  attendance, 37, 45, 104, 127, 154
  middle-class, 29, 46
  tastes, 4, 101
  youth, 25, 29, 44, 46, 47, 76, 104, 121, 127
Auntie Mame, 141, 156

Banks. *See* Movies, financing of
Barthes, Roland, 218, 220–221, 223, 225, 233
Basic Instinct, 189, 192
Baudry, Jean-Louis, 218, 231–234
  "The Apparatus: Metapsychological Approaches to the Impression of Reality in the Cinema" 231–232
  "Ideological Effects of the Basic Cinematographic Apparatus" 231–232, 233
Beetlejuice, 122, 135
Bell, Daniel, xv, 67, 77, 78(n2), 196, 199, 208, 209
Bellah, Robert N., 56, 206, 209
Bells of St. Mary's, The, 124
Benjamin, Walter, 218, 242–245
Bettelheim, Bruno, 119(n1), 137, 213
Beverly Hills Cop, 114, 115, 144, 150, 172, 185, 238

Big, 165
Big Eight, 14, 15, 16
    defined, 37(n2)
Black directors, 172, 187(n1)
Blacklisting in Hollywood, 17–18
Black Robe, 120
Blacks portrayed in film, 172–187, 193,
    238, 239, 240
    assimilation of, 182–184
    character ratings, 177, 178, 180, 182
    and crime, 173, 180–182
    and violence, 179, 180
Blade Runner, 8
Blazing Saddles, 27, 28, 113, 185
Bob and Carol and Ted and Alice, 162
Born on the Fourth of July, 49, 99
Brando, Marlon, 27
Brooks, Mel, 28, 45
Brunette, Peter, 218, 234–236
Burstyn v. Wilson (1952), 20–21
Business leaders, 212
    background characteristics of, 53
        (table), 54–55
    personality traits, 68–73
    robber barons, 200, 201
    sample groups defined, 251.
    See also Businesspeople portrayed in
        film
Businesspeople portrayed in film, 164,
    165, 169
    negative depictions of, 142, 143, 144,
        145, 150, 190, 191
Butch Cassidy and the Sundance Kid, 27,
    112
By the Dawn's Early Light, 99

Calvinism, 55, 198, 201, 202, 203, 208. *See*
    also Protestantism; Protestant ethic;
    Puritans
Capitalism, 57, 197, 208, 209, 211
    rise of, 196–197
Capra, Frank, 44, 140, 202, 203
Carnal Knowledge, 162
Catch 22, 92
Catholic Church. *See* Legion of Decency
Censorship, 20–21, 23, 36, 44, 76

and the studio era, 17–19. *See also*
    Production Code
Chaplin, Charlie, 16
Character rating
    coding procedure, 261–262
Cineplexes, 28–29
City Slickers, 193
Civil rights movement, 46, 186
Class boundaries, 138, 139, 140, 141,
    150–151, 206
Class representation in film
    class defined, 144
    lower-class, 141, 148, 150
    middle-class, 141, 150
    motivation and behavior patterns,
        147–151
    upper-class, 139–152, 190, 191
Clear and Present Danger, 190
Clinton administration, 23
Close Encounters of the Third Kind, 94, 96,
    122–123, 135
Cocoon, 123
Collectivist liberalism, 55(table), 56, 210,
    210, 211
Color Purple, The, 50
Coming to America, 172, 184
Communications/transportation
    revolution, 204, 205
Communism, 17, 99
Community controls, 197, 199, 202, 208
Conan the Barbarian, 51
Conglomerates, 34–35
Content analysis of motion pictures
    coding procedure, 13(n15)
    gender roles, 154–159, 160–169, 170
    law enforcement personnel, 107–109,
        111
    methodology, 5–10, 12(n12), 257,
        261–263
    military imagery, 82–97
    minority characters, 175–182, 184–185
    religious themes, 127–130
    social and economic class, 144–150
Continental semiotics
    de Saussure, Ferdinand, 218, 219–221,
        225, 234

*Copperweld Corp. v. Independence Tube
    Corp.* (1984), 34
Coppola, Francis Ford, 28, 30, 45, 47, 48,
    49
Costner, Kevin, 186
Crime, 101, 104, 106, 107
    of characters, 104–119, 142, 144, 188,
        189, 190
Cultural elites. *See* Elite leadership;
        Hollywood elite, compared to other
        elite groups
Culture of consumption, 201, 202, 203,
    205, 209
Curtiz, Michael, 25

Dances with Wolves, 186
Date with Judy, A, 174
Deconstructionist theory, 220, 234, 235,
    236, 249(n4) *See also* Derrida,
    Jacques; Poststructuralism
Deer Hunter, The, 91, 92, 93
Deliverance, 113
DeMille, Cecil B., 120
Depression era, 16, 210, 211
Derrida, Jacques, 218, 227, 233, 234–237,
    249(n4)
de Saussure, Ferdinand, 218–221, 225, 234
Diamonds Are Forever, 143, 150
Dick Tracy, 189
Die Hard II, 189, 190
Dietrich, Marlene, 154
Dirty Dozen, The, 47, 91
Dirty Harry films, 30, 33, 51, 103, 111, 112
Distribution and release patterns, 29
Dog Day Afternoon, 103, 111, 112, 114, 185

Eastwood, Clint, 27, 110, 240, 241
Easy Rider, 44
Economics, 211
    effects on movie industry, 4, 11(n9), 29
    funding for films, 15–16, 37(n3)
    profits, 76
    See also Captitalism; Liberal capitalism
Egg and I, The, 155, 174
Electric Horseman, The, 27, 143, 151, 161
Elite leadership, 52, 210, 212

    conflict among, 2
    sample groups defined, 251–254
    theories about, 1–2. *See also* Hollywood
        elite
Enforcer, The, 111, 166
Environmental movement, 50, 61
E.T., 50, 77
European influence on movies, 24–26, 36
Evil, 121–122, 123, 131–137
Exorcist, The, 121, 132
Expressive individualism, 57, 208, 209,
    210, 211
    defined, 56
    and hollywood elite, 55(table), 61, 64,
        170, 212

Fairbanks, Douglas, Jr., 16
Faludi, Susan, 8, 153, 171(n7)
Family structure, 212
Fascism and art, 242, 243, 244
Fatal Attraction, 8
Father's Little Dividend, 109, 155
Feminism, 46, 48
Feminist film theory, 227–231
Field of Dreams, 121
Film
    impact of, 9, 10
    sampling techniques in study, 257–260
    and social and political change, 1, 2, 5,
        26, 41–42, 46, 50–51, 66, 77, 104,
        110, 116, 194, 195, 247
Film critics, 8, 13(n17), 78(n3)
Film theorists. *See* Continental semiotics;
        Formalism and structuralism;
        Poststructuralism
Film theory, 217–250
    feminist, 227–231
    political critique, 235, 237–242
    on politics and art, 242–245
    and social and political change, 246,
        247. *See also* Continental semiotics;
        Formalism and structuralism;
        Poststructuralism
First Amendment rights, 20, 36
Fonda, Jane, 27
Ford, John, 25

Formalism and structuralism
  Barthes, Roland, 218, 220–221, 223,
    225, 233
  Jakobson, Roman, 218, 219, 220, 223,
    234
Forrest Gump, 194
Fox, William, 14
Frank, Marcie, 219
Freedom of expression. *See* First
    amendement rights; Rating system
    for movies, new
Free-lancing by Hollywood artists, 16, 19,
    22–23
Freeman, Morgan, 172
French New Wave cinema. *See* European
    influence on movies
Freudian theory. *See* Psychodynamic
    perspective
Friday the 13th, 122
From Here to Eternity, 86–87, 159

Gans, Herbert, 4, 11(n7)
Garbo, Greta, 154
Gauntlet, The, 112
Geertz, Clifford, 11(n5)
Gender roles. *See* Men portrayed in film;
    Women portrayed in film
Gender theory
  and film, 227–231
Ghost, 121, 191
Ghostbusters, 122
Ginsberg, Allen, 202, 203
Gledhill, Christine, 231
Godfather, The, 28, 142, 150
Godfather movies, 48, 77
Golden Child, The, 122, 134–135
Goodbye Girl, The, 162, 170
Good Morning Vietnam, 95–96, 186
Greatest Show on Earth, The, 108
Great Gatsby, The, 138–139
Guess Who's Coming to Dinner, 183
Gulf War, 98
Guys and Dolls, 110

Hand That Rocks the Cradle, The, 8
Hartz, Louis, 55

Hatari, 174
Heat, 119(n3)
Heath, Stephen, 227
Hepburn, Katherine, 154
High Noon, 8
High Society, 140, 141, 150, 155
Hispanics portrayed in film, 176, 177, 178,
    180, 181(table)
Historical analysis
  of relationship between film and
    society, 196–205
Hitchcock, Alfred, 25
Hoffman, Dustin, 27
Holiday, 140, 143
Hollywood elite
  activism of, 50
  and alienation, 36–37, 44, 57, 64, 102,
    173
  as anti-authoritarian, 5, 46, 46–52, 47,
    48, 49, 50, 51, 77, 97, 173,
  attitude toward sex/marriage, 61,
    63(table), 64, 169, 210
  autonomy of, 35, 44–45
  background characteristics of, 53(table),
    54–55
  on capitalism, 48
  compared to other elite groups, 52–55,
    57–67, 210, 247
  composition of, 45
  dominance of, 30, 31
  on economic and social systems, 61,
    151
  and feminism, 48, 169
  homogenity of views, 49–50
  and liberalism, 3, 34, 50, 51, 52,
    66–67, 76, 77, 145, 151, 169, 170,
    171, 186
  patriotism of, 51
  perceptions of other elites, 64, 66
  and personality traits, 67–73
  political views, 53(table), 54, 55
  on race, 50, 173
  religious views, 120, 121, 123–124
  sample group defined, 252–253

as shapers of public opinion, 1, 2–3, 4, 41, 41–42, 152, 212–213, 214. *See also* Alienation; Anti-establishment, attitude of filmmakers; Collectivist liberalism; Expressive individualism; Film, and social and political change
Hombre, 27, 143
Homosexuality and moviemakers' attitudes, 61
Hooper, 143
Hot Shots Part Deux, 190
House of Wax, 109
House Un-American Activities Committee (HUAC), 17–18
HUAC. *See* House Un-American Activities Committee
Hughes, Howard, 21
Hunt for Red October, The, 193
Huston, John, 25

Imitation of Life, 174
Indecent Proposal, 190
Independent filmmakers, 28, 29, 30, 37, 195. *See also* Independent production
Independent production, 15, 16, 27, 76 rise of, 21–23, 24, 36, 37
Individualism, 198, 199, 200, 203, 210
Intellectuals. *See* Academic community
Invasion of the Body Snatchers, 8
It's a Wonderful Life, 140, 202

Jakobson, Roman, 218, 219, 220, 223, 234
Jaws, 29
Jews and movie elite, 14, 79(n13)
JFK, 49
Journalists. *See* News media, journalists

Karate Kid, The, 183
King, Rodney, 103
Kubrick, Stanley, 45, 123, 134

Lacan, Jacques, 218, 227, 228, 231, 233, 249(n4)

Laemmle, Carl, 14
La Femme Nikita, 229–231
Language, 219, 220, 221, 222, 223, 224
Lasch, Christopher, 78,
Lasswell, Harold, xv, 2
Last Temptation of Christ, The, 120
Law enforcement personnel in film character rating, 107–109, 114, 117 as inept/corrupt, 101, 103, 111, 113, 114–115, 142, 188, 189, 190 as mavericks, 101, 103, 110, 111, 118, 190 moral influence, 107–110 public support for, 103 *See also* Violence
Lee, Spike, 172
Legion of Decency, 18–19, 38(n6), 124
Lester, Richard, 49
Lethal Weapon, 114, 116, 184
Lethal Weapon 3, 189, 192
Lethal Weapon films, 103, 190
Liberal capitalism, 197–205, 211
Liberalism. *See* Hollywood elite, and liberalism; Liberal capitalism
Lifton, Robert, 78
Lion King, 193
Lion's Gate Films, 28
Lipset, Seymour Martin, 55
Little Big Man, 27, 92, 186
Longest Day, The, 87
Look Who's Talking, 165
Love Me Tender, 155
Lucas, George, 28, 30, 45, 50
Lucasfilm Limited, 28

MacLaine, Shirley, 27
McQueen, Steve, 27
Magnum Force, 111
Man For All Seasons, A, 126
Marcuse, Herbert, 199, 216(n16)
Marxist/Neo-Marxist theory, 199, 225, 226, 232, 237, 248(n2)
*M*A*S*H*, 28, 47, 92
Maslin, Janet, 38(n9), 153, 171(n1)
Maverick, 193
Mayer, Louis, 14, 139

MCA. *See* Music Corporation of America
Media
    influence of, 205–208
    theorists, 40–41.
    See also Film, and social and political
        change; Television
Medved, Michael, 11(n8), 121, 123
Men portrayed in film
    in business, 164, 165
    character ratings, 163, 164, 165, 168
    methods and goals, 155, 167, 170
    and romance/marriage, 155, 156, 160,
        162
    and violence, 167
Methodology
    of film study, 5–9, 257–263
Metz, Christian 218, 221, 225, 227
Meyrowitz, Joshua, 78(n2)
Middle-class professionals, 203, 204
Midnight Cowboy, 27
Military imagery in film, 47, 48, 190
    achieving goals, 82, 86, 87, 88, 89–91,
        96
    attitude toward authority, 85–89, 91, 93
    character ratings, 82, 83–87, 88, 89–92,
        94–95
    and patriotism, 81, 84, 87, 88(table),
        91–92, 93–94
    thematic analysis, 83–84. *See also*
        Vietnam War, depicted in film
Military leaders
    as affected by Hollywood, 102
    background characteristics of, 53(table),
        54–55
    sample group defined, 252
Milius, John, 51
Mills, C. Wright, 2
Minorities portrayed in film, 172, 182, 193
    Amerindians, 175(table), 176–178, 180,
        181(table)
    Asians, 175–178, 180, 181(table), 183,
        184
    assimilation, 182–184
    blacks, 172–187, 193, 238, 239, 240

character ratings, 176–178, 180, 181,
        186, 193
    and class, 174
    and crime, 180–182, 186–187
    during the studio era, 173–175
    in law enforcement and military
        occupations, 184–186, 187
    methods and goals, 178–180
    percent of characters represented,
        175–176
    and racial conflict, 182, 185, 186, 187,
        239–240
    stereotypes, 173, 174–175
Miracle Case, 20–21
Mister Roberts, 87
Mitry, Jean, 218, 225
Monty Python's Life of Brian, 120
Moonstruck, 165
Morris, William, 76
Movie content
    and attitudes of filmmakers, 26–30
    and dissent, 197
    as influenced by the 1960s, 26
    and liberalism, 45
Mr. Mom, 143, 150, 161
Mulvey, Laura, 218, 227–231, 233
Music Corporation of America (MCA),
        22, 76
Music Man, The, 155, 160
My Little Chickadee, 229

Naked Gun, The, 103, 115
National Crime Survey, 105(table), 106
National Recovery Act, 16
Natural Born Killers, 119(n1), 216
New Left, 205, 210, 212, 213
Newman, Paul, 27
News media, 206, 207, 208
    journalists, 53(table), 54, 55(table)
New Wave in America, 24–27, 30, 33, 34,
        75–78
New York, 15, 79(n5), 205, 210
Nightmare on Elm Street, 122
Nun's Story, The, 126, 174

Oh God, 120

Only Angels Have Wings, 228
On the Beach, 87

Pacino, Al, 27
Patriotism, 57
Patton, 91–92
Personality and culture, 42
Personality traits of elites
  alienation, 78
  authoritariansim, 72–73
  narcissism, 72, 78, 197
  need for achievement, 67–69,
    70(table)
  need for and fear of power, 67–73, 77
Philadelphia Story, The, 140
Pillow Talk, 158, 159, 160
Place in the Sun, A, 110, 140, 141, 159, 162
Platoon, 49, 95–96, 97, 186
Polanski, Roman, 121
Police. *See* Law enforcement personnel in
  film
Police Academy, 103, 114, 166, 185, 238
Police Academy II, 115, 166
Political critique in film theory, 235,
    237–242
Poltergeist, 134
Postman, Neil, 40–41
Poststructuralists
  Andrew, James Dudley, 218, 224, 225
  Baudry, Jean-Louis, 218, 231–234
  Brunette, Peter, 218, 234–236
  de Lauretis, Theresa, 218, 241
  de Man, Paul, 218
  Derrida, Jacques, 218, 227, 233,
    234–237, 249(n4)
  Foucault, Michel, 218, 233
  Frank, Marcie, 219
  Gledhill, Christine, 231
  Herrnstein Smith, Barbara, 223
  Lacan, Jacques, 218, 227, 229, 231, 233,
    249(n4)
  Metz, Christian, 218, 221, 225, 227
  Mitry, Jean, 218, 225
  Mulvey, Laura, 218, 227–231, 233
  Rogin, Michael, 218, 237–240
  Rosen, Philip, 221, 222

  Slotkin, Richard, 237
  Sobchack, Vivian, 218, 237, 241, 242
  Wills, David, 218, 234–236
Postwar era, 19, 21, 29, 139, 204
Predator, 91, 92, 96
Pretty Woman, 191
Private Benjamin, 94
Production Code, 18–19, 21, 22, 38(n5),
    104, 106, 124, 154. *See also* Self-
    censorship
Production costs, 31
Protestant ethic, 55–56, 209
Protestantism, 196–199, 200, 201, 202
Psychodynamic perspective, 196, 197, 198,
    233
  ego, 197, 198, 212
  sublimation of drives, 212
  superego, 197, 198, 212
Public interest elites, 53(table), 54,
    55(table), 253
Public opinion, 46, 52, 61, 66, 74(table),
    75(table), 76, 81, 97
Puritans, 199, 209

Quo Vadis, 125

Rambo: First Blood Part II, 33, 46, 77, 81,
    84, 91–93, 98, 111, 166, 238, 240
Rambo films, 33, 95, 97, 190
Rating system for movies
  new, 19, 22–23, 24, 110, 159
Reagan, Ronald, 39(15n), 139. *See also*
    Reagan era
Reagan era, 33, 46, 81, 151, 207, 237, 238,
    239
Red Dawn, 51
Redford, Robert, 50
Redgrave, Vanessa, 27
Religion in film, 194
  and aliens, 135
  character ratings, 127–130, 136
  during the studio era, 124–127
  and evil, 121–122, 123, 131–137
  and horror, 131–133
  influence of Production Code, 124
  and satire, 122, 133–134

and the supernatural, 122, 131,
    134–135, 191–192
    See also Hollywood elite, religious views
Religious elite
    sample groups defined, 253
Return of the Pink Panther, 110
Road to Rio, 109, 177
Robe, The, 125
Rocky III, 183
Rogin, Michael, 218, 237–240
Romancing the Stone, 143
Rosemary's Baby, 121, 131
Rosen, Philip, 221, 222
Rosten, Leo, 14, 17, 43
Russell, 45
Russell, Rosalind, 154, 156

Samson and Delilah, 125
Sandpiper, The, 126, 129
Saussarian model. *See* de Saussure,
    Ferdinand
Sayonara, 89–90, 175
Schlesinger, John, 27
Science fiction movies, 122, 123
Scorsese, Martin, 30, 45, 48
Screen/Play: Derrida and Film Theory, 227,
    234–237
Secular orientation of elites, 120, 121,
    123–124, 136–137. *See also*
    Hollywood elite, religious views
Self-censorship, 22, 23, 24, 30, 35–36, 159.
    See also Production Code
Selznick, Lewis, 14
Semiology, 40, 218, 219, 220, 221, 222,
    223, 224. *See also* de Saussure,
    Ferdinand
Separate spheres
    of men and women, 154
Serpico, 103, 111, 112
Seven Brides for Seven Brothers, 155
Sexual activity outside of marriage,
    158–159, 160
Sexual and aggressive drives, 197, 199
Sexuality, 159, 160, 162, 163, 168–169, 171,
    207, 213, 229
Shadowlands, 120

Shenandoah, 27
Sherman Antitrust Act, 20, 34
Shining, The, 134
Silence of the Lambs, 188, 189, 192
Singleton, John, 172
Sleeping with the Enemy, 190, 192
Sleepless in Seattle, 193
Snows of Kilimanjaro, The, 174
Sobchack, Vivian, 218, 237, 241, 242
Social and political change. *See* Film, and
    social and political change
Some Like It Hot, 109, 141
Sommersby, 193
Speed, 189
Spielberg, Steven, 28, 30, 37, 45, 50–51
Star Wars films, 28, 29, 33, 34, 50, 122,
    123, 135, 161, 166
Stone, Oliver, 32, 45, 49, 99, 119(n1), 186
Strategic Air Command, 87, 98
Streisand, Barbra, 27
Stripes, 166, 238
Structuralism. *See* Formalism and
    structuralism
Studio moguls, 14, 16, 18, 21, 46, 127,
    139–140, 213
Studio system, 14–19, 25, 104, 107, 18,
    124, 151
    censorship, 17–19
    decline of, 17, 20, 21, 22, 30, 33, 44, 205
    distribution networks/organization,
        14–15
    financing, 15, 16
    labor unrest, 16–17
    and politics, 43–44, 45
    post–World War II, 19–21
    and star system, 16, 27
Sublimation of drives, 197, 199
Sudden Impact, 238, 239, 240
Superman: The Movie, 49
Superman II, 49
Superman III, 49, 144, 150
System alienation, 55(table), 60(table), 64,
    65(table)
    defined, 57

Talent agencies, 22–23

power of, 30–31
TAT. *See* Thematic Apperception Test
Taxi Driver, 48
Television
  and demise of studio system, 19
  influence of, 205–208, 213
  and liberalism, 52, 207
  and movie attendance, 21, 44
  revolution, 21
  See also News media; Television elite,
    sample group defined
Television elite
  sample group defined, 253–254
Ten Commandments, The, 125
Terminator II, 153, 192, 193
Thelma and Louise, 153
Them!, 240
Thematic Apperception Test(TAT)
  and business leaders, 68–73
  and hollywood elites, 67–73
Time-Warner, 34
To Have and Have Not, 228, 229
Tommy, 122, 133
Top Gun, 81, 91, 92, 96–97
To Sir with Love, 183
Trilling, Lionel, 208
True Grit, 27
True Lies, 119(n1), 193, 214
2001: A Space Odyssey, 123

Unionization of Hollywood labor, 16
United Artists, 16, 21–22. *See also* Big
  Eight
United States v. Paramount Pictures, Inc.
  (1948) 16, 17, 19, 20, 21
Unsinkable Molly Brown, The, 141, 142,
  150, 158

Values and attitudes
  of American public, 206, 207. *See also*
    Public opinion
Victimization
  of characters, 105–107, 111, 114, 115,
    117
  coding procedure, 262–263
  defined, 105

Video revolution, 30, 32, 35, 36
Vietnam War, 26, 36, 46, 47, 98
  depicted in film, 92–93, 95–97, 98, 99,
    111, 116
Violence, 24, 213, 214
  and black characters, 172, 179–180, 186,
    187
  and class, 142, 148–149, 150, 152
  and law enforcement, 101–119
  in military films, 86, 89, 93–96, 98, 190
  and patriotism, 87–88
  and television, 23, 207, 213
  urban, 101, 111, 173
  and white characters 180, 186, 187
  and women, 164, 167, 168, 170
V.I. Warshawski, 153

Wagner Act, 16
Wall Street, 49
Wargames, 94
Warner brothers, 14, 139
Watching America, 172, 173
Watergate, 26, 36, 46
Wayne, John, 102
Weber, Max, 55, 196, 198, 201
Welles, Orson, 25
West, Mae, 154, 229
Westerns, 12(n13), 27, 103, 113, 119(n2),
  124
When Harry Met Sally, 163
Who's Afraid of Virginia Woolf?, 162
Wilder, Billy, 142
Wills, David, 218, 234–236
Witches of Eastwick, The, 122, 133, 164
Women portrayed in film, 153, 227–231,
  239
  and big business, 164, 165, 169
  character ratings, 163, 164, 165, 166,
    168, 169
  independence of, 153, 154, 161,
    192–193
  and marriage, 155, 156, 157, 158
  motivation and goals, 155, 160, 166,
    168, 170

in nontraditional occupations, 157, 158, 159, 161, 162, 163, 164, 166, 167, 168, 169, 170
percent of characters represented, 154, 169
and romance, 155, 157, 158, 159, 160, 161, 162, 170
in traditional occupations, 156, 157(table), 158, 159, 161, 162, 166, 167

and violence, 164, 167, 168
Women's movement. *See* Feminism
World of Suzie Wong, The, 141

Zanuck, Darryl, 79(n5)
Zinneman, Fred, 126
Zoetrope Studios, 28
Zukor, Adolph, 14, 139